Smarter Stock Picking

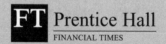

Smarter Stock Picking

Using strategies from the professionals to improve your returns

David Stevenson

Financial Times
Prentice Hall
is an imprint of

Harlow, England • London • New York • Boston • San Francisco • Toronto • Sydney • Singapore • Hong Kong
Tokyo • Seoul • Taipei • New Delhi • Cape Town • Madrid • Mexico City • Amsterdam • Munich • Paris • Milan

PEARSON EDUCATION LIMITED

Edinburgh Gate
Harlow CM20 2JE
Tel: +44 (0)1279 623623
Fax: +44 (0)1279 431059
Website: www.pearsoned.co.uk

First published in Great Britain in 2011

ISBN: 978-0-273-72781-1

British Library Cataloguing-in-Publication Data
A catalogue record for this book is available from the British Library

Library of Congress Cataloging-in-Publication Data
Stevenson, David.
  Smarter stock picking : using strategies from the professionals to improve your returns /
  David Stevenson.
    p. cm.
  Includes index.
  ISBN 978-0-273-72781-1 (pbk.)
  1. Investment analysis. 2. Stocks. 3. Portfolio management. I. Title.
  HG4529.S74 2010
  332.63'222--dc22
                          2010028205

10 9 8 7 6 5 4 3 2 1
14 13 12 11 10

Typeset in 9/13 Stone Serif by 30
Printed and bound in Great Britain by Ashford Colour Press, Gosport

To Vanessa, Zac and Rebecca & my Mum!

Thanks to Andrew Lapthorne and his team at SG Cross Asset Research

Contents

About the author

David Stevenson is the Adventurous Investor columnist for the *Financial Times* and writer/columnist for the *Investors Chronicle*. He also writes a weekly contrarian column for *Investment Week* and used to write for *Citywire*.

In a former life David was an investigative producer for BBC TV and was also one of the founders of The Rocket Science Group, a successful corporate communications consultancy. In his spare time David writes books on investment and he is also a magistrate for his sins.

Publisher's acknowledgements

We are grateful to the following for permission to reproduce copyright material:

Figures

Figure 1.1 from *Credit Suisse Global Investment Returns Yearbook 2010*, February 2010, Credit Suisse (Wilmot, J. 2010) Fig. 3, p.23, reprinted with permission from the author; Figure 1.2 from Elroy Dimson, Paul Marsh and Mike Staunton, *Credit Suisse Global Investment Returns Sourcebook 2010*, Credit Suisse Research Institute, 2010, reproduced with permission from the authors; Figure 1.3 from Marketing actions can modulate neural representations of experienced utility, *The Proceedings of the National Academy of Sciences*, 10 March (Plassmann, H., O'Doherty, Shiv and Rangel 2008), Copyright 2008 National Academy of Sciences, USA; Figures 1.4, 1.5 from www.aaii.com, The American Association of Individual Investors; Figures 2.1, 2.2, 4.7, 6.4, 7.1, 7.2, 7.3, 7.4, 7.6, 7.13, 7.16, 11.4, 11.5, 11.6, 11.7, 11.8, 11.9, 11.10, 11.11, 11.13, 11.20, 11.21, A1.1, from ShareScope, www.sharescope.co.uk; Figure 2.3 from Moneychimp.com; Figures 2.3, 10.1, 10.2, 10.3, 11.1, 11.2, 11.3, 11.12, 11.14, 11.15, 11.16, 11.17, 11.18, 11.19, 11.22, 11.23, 11.24, 11.25, 11.28, 11.29, 11.30, 11.31, 11.32, 11.33, 11.34, 11.35, 11.36, 11.37, 11.38, 11.39 Microsoft screenshot frames reprinted with permission from Microsoft Corporation; Figure 2.4 from Momentum Strategies, *Journal of Finance*, Vol. 51, No. 5 pp. 1681–1713 (Lakonishok, J., Chan, L. K. C. and Jegadeesh, N. 1996), Copyright © 1996 American Finance Association, reproduced with permission of Blackwell Publishing Ltd; Figure 2.6 from *The Cashflow Solution: Equity Income Portfolios*, Liontrust, www.liontrust.co.uk; Figure 3.1 from http://www.dfaus.com/, Dimensional Fund Advisors Ltd; Figure 3.2 from *Common Sense on Mutual Funds: Fully Updated 10th Anniversary Edition*, Wiley (Bogle, J. C. and Swensen, D. F. 2009) Fig. 10.3, Copyright © 2010 by John C. Bogle. Reproduced with permission of John Wiley & Sons, Inc; Figure 3.4 from *Value Investing*, John Wiley & Sons (Montier, J. 2009), with permission from John Wiley & Sons Ltd; Figure 4.1

from *Barclays Equity Gilt Study*, with permission from Barclays Capital; Figure 4.10 from *S&P Europe 350 Dividend Aristocrats Analytical Contacts*, Standards and Poors (Soe, A.M.) December 2008, Copyright © 2010 by Standard & Poor's Financial Services LLC. All rights reserved. S&P® and STANDARD & POOR'S® are registered trademarks of Standard & Poor's Financial Services LLC; Figure 6.1 from A Great Company Can be a Great Investment, *Financial Analysts Journal*, Vol. 62, No. 4, pp. 8–93 (Anderson, J. and Smith, G. 2006), Copyright 2006, CFA Institute. Reproduced and republished from *Financial Analysts Journal* with permission from CFA Institute. All rights reserved; Figure 7.5 from ASOS 02/01/02 to 22/12/09 + volumes, Investor Ease for Windows, Investor Ease (UK) Ltd; Figures 7.7, 7.8 from *ABN AMRO/LBS Global Investment Returns Yearbook 2008*, ABN AMRO (Dimson, E., Marsh, P., Staunton, M. 2008), with permission from ABN AMRO Bank NV; Figures 7.9, 7.10 from Elroy Dimson and Paul Marsh, *The RBS Hoare Govett Smaller Companies Index 2010*, Royal Bank of Scotland, 2010, with permission from the authors; Figures 10.1, 10.2, 10.3 from ShareMaestro, © ShareMaestro Limited www.sharemaestro.co.uk; Figures 11.1, 11.2, 11.3, 11.12, 11.14, 11.15, 11.16, 11.17, 11.18, 11.19, 11.22, 11.23, 11.24, 11.25 from ShareScope Plus – One Share, www.sharescope.co.uk; Figure 11.26 from Company REFS: Refs Online, http://www.companyrefs.com/refsonline/edit_tables.asp?id=6587, Capital Ideas Financial Publishing Ltd; Figure 11.27 from REFS page for Group NBT, www.companyrefs.com © 2010 HS Financial Planning, Capital Ideas Financial Publishing Ltd; Figures 11.28, 11.29, 11.30, 11.31, 11.32, 11.33, 11.34, 11.35, 11.36, 11.37, 11.38, 11.39 from http://www.investorease.com, Investor Ease (UK) Ltd; Figure A1.4 from Smithers & Co. Ltd; www.smithers.co.uk/q&FAQs; Figure A1.7 from http://finance.yahoo.com/, Copyright 2009 Yahoo! Inc, reproduced with permission.

Tables

Table 2.1 adapted from *Scottish and Southern Energy 2009 Annual Report*, Scottish and Southern Energy PLC; Tables 2.2, 2.3 from *Scottish and Southern Energy 2009 Annual Report*, Scottish and Southern Energy PLC; Table 2.4 from ShareScope – Aero Inventory PLC, www.sharescope.co.uk; Tables 4.2, 4.3 from *S&P Global Strategies Report*, September 2009, Copyright © 2010 by Standard & Poor's Financial Services LLC. All rights reserved. S&P® and STANDARD & POOR'S® are registered trademarks of Standard & Poor's Financial Services LLC; Tables 4.4, 4.5 from *S&P Europe 350 Dividend Aris-*

tocrats, Standards and Poors (Soe, A.M.) October 2008, Copyright © 2010 by Standard & Poor's Financial Services LLC. All rights reserved. S&P® and STANDARD & POOR'S® are registered trademarks of Standard & Poor's Financial Services LLC; Table 4.9 from Rob Davies, The Munro Fund, http://www.themunrofund.com/; Table 5.1 from data on the indices and ETN funds, with permission from John W. Gambla, Nuveen HydePark; Table 7.4 from Investor Ease, Investor Ease (UK) Ltd; Table 7.6 from CompanyREFS Guide, Hemington Scott, 2008, Capital Ideas Financial Publishing Ltd; Tables A1.1, A1.3, A1.7 from Smithers & Co. Ltd; Tables A1.2, A1.8 from Crestmont Research, www.crestmontresearch.com; Table A1.5 from John Maudlin, www.frontlinethoughts.com.

Text

Extracts on page 52, pages 52–53 from *Analyst Recommendations, Mutual Fund Herding, and Overreaction in Stock Prices* (Brown, N.C., Wei, K.D., Wermers, R.) Draft: December 2007, with permission from Russell Wermers; Extract on pages 57–58 from *The Cashflow Solution: Equity Income Portfolios*, Liontrust, www.liontrust.co.uk; Epigraph on page 60 from *The New Palgrave Dictionary of Economics*, 2nd ed., Palgrave Macmillan (Blume, L. and Durlauf, S., eds 2008) Efficient Markets Hypothesis by Andrew J. Lo, reproduced with permission of Palgrave Macmillan; Extract on pages 63–64 adapted from *The Little Book of Commonsense Investing: The Only Way to Guarantee Your Fair Share of Stock Market Returns*, John Wiley & Sons, Inc. (Bogle, J.C. 2007), Copyright © 2007 by John C. Bogle. Reproduced with permission of John Wiley & Sons, Inc; Interview on pages 95–98 from Professors Elroy Dimson and Paul Marsh, London Business School, interviewed at London Business School on 5 May 2009; Box on page 114 from *S&P Europe 350 Dividend Aristocrats*, Standards and Poors (Soe, A.M.) October 2008, Copyright © 2010 by Standard & Poor's Financial Services LLC. All rights reserved. S&P® and STANDARD & POOR'S® are registered trademarks of Standard & Poor's Financial Services LLC; Extracts on page 145, pages 145–46 from http://www.nuveen.com/HydePark/Products.aspx, with permission from John W. Gambla, Nuveen HydePark; Interview on pages 176–180 from James Montier; Extracts on page 184, page 185, page 186 from A Great Company Can be a Great Investment, *Financial Analysts Journal*, Vol. 62, No. 4, pp. 8–93 (Anderson, J. and Smith, G. 2006), Copyright 2006, CFA Institute. Reproduced and republished from *Financial Analysts Journal* with permission from CFA Institute. All rights reserved;

Extracts on page 187, page 188, from *Analyst Recommendations, Mutual Fund Herding, and Overreaction in Stock Prices* (Brown, N.C., Wei, K.D., Wermers, R.) December 2009, available at www.ssrn.com/abstract=1092744, with permission from Russell Wermers; Box on pages 205–207 from *The Essays of Warren Buffett: Lessons for Corporate America*, The Cunningham Group (Buffett, W. A., edited by Lawrence A. Cunningham 2009), the material is copyrighted and used with permission of the author; Epigraph on page 234 from Wayne A. Thorp, CFA; Extracts on page 261, page 471, page 474, page 475 from http://www.companyrefs.com/Guide/guideindex.htm, Capital Ideas Financial Publishing Ltd; Interviews on page 272, pages 398–405, page 428 from Rob Arnott, reproduced with permission; Interview on pages 419–421 adapted from an interview with Graham Secker, with permission from the author; Interview on pages 438–446 from Andrew Lapthorne, Global Quantitative Strategist, Research, Société Générale.

The Financial Times

Figures 11.40, 11.41, 11.42, 11.43, 11.44, 11.45, 11.46 from http://markets.ft.com, The Financial Times Ltd; Table on page 43 from 'Flight of Fancy', *Investors Chronicle* (Bearbull), www.investorschronicle.co.uk, The Financial Times Ltd.

In some instances we have been unable to trace the owners of copyright material, and we would appreciate any information that would enable us to do so.

Stock picking strategies: the context

Introduction

We know too much, and are convinced of too little. T.S. Eliot

Shares for the long term

Shares have been a great investment for those investors willing to stick with them over the very long term. In virtually every study of extremely long term data on returns from the global stock markets, shares – analysts also use the terms stocks or equities interchangeably – have trounced both bonds and cash.

In the US, Professor Jeremy Siegel has mined this rich seam of data but probably the most definitive source is a group of British academics based at the London Business School – Professor Elroy Dimson, Professor Paul Marsh and Dr Mike Staunton. In a series of papers and books (namely the seminal *Triumph of the Optimists*) they've delved back into market data all the way back to 1900 and looked at comparative returns – with fairly unequivocal conclusions.

Their most recent publication – the *Credit Suisse Global Investment Returns Sourcebook 2010* – sums it up thus:

Over the last 109 years, the real value of equities, with income reinvested, grew by a factor of 224 as compared to 4.5 for bonds and 3.1 for bills. Figure 2 shows that, since 1900, equities beat bonds by 3.6% and bills by 4.0% per year. Figure 3 shows that the long-term real return on UK equities was an annualized 5.1% as compared to bonds and bills, which gave a real return of 1.4% and 1.1% respectively.[1]

---

[1] Dimson, E., Marsh, P. and Staunton, M. (2010) *Credit Suisse Global Investment Returns Sourcebook 2010*, Credit Suisse Research Institute.

Figure 1.1 that shows US equity returns is fairly typical of this kind of long-itudinal data analysis. Because it's based on American data it's able to show data going back to the middle of the 19th century and the message is clear: shares have largely moved upwards with a long-term trend return of just above 6% per annum. Other long-term studies for the US market have put the mean and median return slightly higher at just above 7%, but the message is unambiguous: shares are a great long-term investment idea for those willing to take some risk. That last word – risk – is hugely important because you'll notice from Figure 1.1 that the line isn't smooth. Quite the contrary in fact because in key decades like the 1930s for instance the line looks rather jagged – no prizes for guessing what produced the sharp falls in 1931 and 1936!

These 'jagged returns' remind us that shares are risky but on balance they've been worth that risk compared to supposedly safer assets like bonds and cash. In fact in the UK the return from shares has been worth about 4% extra on average since 1900, as shown in Figure 1.2 (overleaf). This graph shows the annualised risk premium received for investing in equities versus Treasury Bills and bonds. Add 4% per annum up over 100 hundred or more years, factor in the magic of compounding, and hey presto, shares have been the wunderkind of the investment universe!

Which shares for the long term?

These huge exercises in data mining are of course fraught with danger and difficulty. What is generally true over long periods of time, for instance, isn't always true during smaller periods. A great many analysts like US fund manager Rob Arnott of Research Associates have been pointing out that over the 20 years between 1989 and 2009 shares have been a lousy investment compared to bonds. Perhaps the most stunning example of this revisionism is contained within a wonderful study entitled *A New Historical Database for the NYSE 1815 to 1925*.[2] This rather dry sounding historical paper digs out data from as far back as 1815 and looks at returns up to 1925. The authors report that the capital appreciation over this period was a rather less exciting 1.24% per annum, a good 5% below most estimates for long-term equity growth. The message from the revisionists? Equities

[2] Geotzmann, W., Peng, L. and Ibbotson, R. (2000) 'A new historical database for the NYSE 1815 to 1925: Performance and predicitability', Yale ICF Working Paper No. ICF-00-13, available at http://ssm.com/abstract=236692.

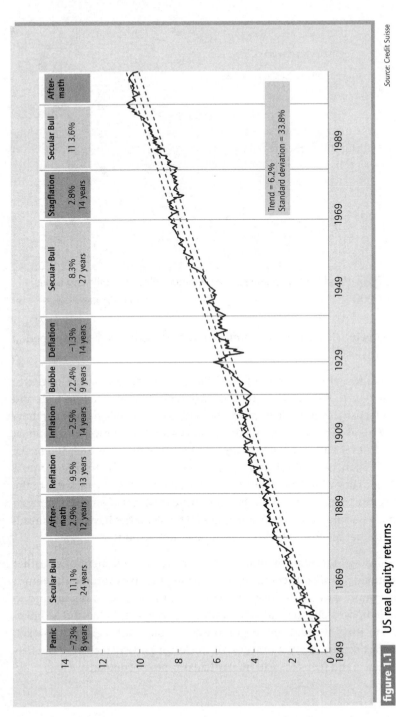

figure 1.1 US real equity returns

Source: Credit Suisse

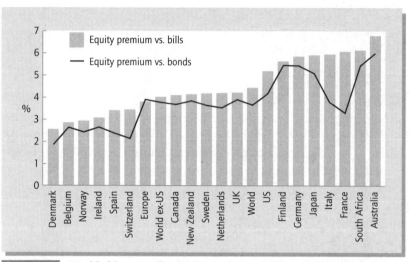

figure 1.2 Worldwide annualised risk premiums relative to bills and bonds, 1900–2009

Source: Credit Suisse Global Investment Returns Sourcebook 2010

have largely been a great investment but that's not true for every period under analysis.

There is also a more insurmountable difficulty – how to access this long-term average return. Precisely because this huge mountain of data is as wide and comprehensive as possible you face the not inconsiderable problem of 'buying the trend'. The vast majority of investors – both private and institutional – would never have been able to buy all the contents of the S&P 500 or the FTSE All Share or the FTSE 100 or whatever share index is tracked for their portfolio. They would have been forced to wait until the very back end of the 20th century before they could buy the entire contents of an index through an index tracking fund, i.e. in a period in which equities have been a dreadful performer relative to bonds, according to Rob Arnott!

The Dimson, Marsh and Staunton study for Credit Suisse mentioned earlier does provide a valuable clue as to how you might have captured this return using a more focused strategy, but you would have had to dig around to stumble upon a chapter called 'Investment Style: Size, Value and Momentum'.[3] In this the academics begin to filter through the 'aggregate market' – in effect screen the vast universe of stocks for particular themes or characteristics – and focus instead on particular types of company.

[3] See note 1.

Three specific categories are identified – small cap stocks, cheap value shares and shares whose price is performing strongly relative to the wider market (otherwise known as momentum stocks). Looking first at small cap stocks, the authors discover that in the UK between 1955 and 2008 (the period under analysis is much shorter than the main study because the data just isn't there before 1955) really small companies measured by their market capitalisation would have produced an annual return of 17.7%, small caps (slightly bigger) 14.8% and the benchmark index, namely the whole UK market 12.4%. Dimson *et al.* also frame this return in the following terms: £1 invested in the UK 'equity market at the start of 1955 with dividends re-invested would have grown to £540 by the end of 2008 ... the same investment in [a small cap index] would have generated £1666 over three times as much ... micro-caps would have yielded £6587'.[4]

Sadly our earlier accessibility problem – how you capture the broad trend – isn't helped by this twist in the research findings. There are literally hundreds and thousands of small and micro-small caps in the UK market making any move to track that return impossible (there is in fact no UK small cap index tracking fund that buys all those stocks). But the next category of superior returns is a more useful one for private investors, namely what are called cheap or value stocks – a term we'll explore in much greater detail in this book. In essence these are companies whose share price is good value or cheap relative to a key measure like the company's total assets, i.e. you might be able to buy a share that costs you £1 but is backed by £2 of assets! Alternatively, you might have picked a bunch of shares that paid out a big dividend cheque relative to the share price – giving you a big yield as a percentage – and then focused on the biggest companies as measured by their market capitalisation. Again the results are startling: high yielding stocks amongst the top 100 companies between 1900 and 2008 would have given you an average annual return of 10.8% compared to 9.2% for the market and 7.7% for low yielding stocks.

The data on what are called momentum stocks – those shares performing relatively strongly over a fixed period of time, like six months, relative to the wider market – also produced some stellar results! In fact Dimson *et al.* conclude that the best tactic in our 21st century markets might be to simply and methodically buy the top performing shares every month, then wait a short while and sell them, moving on to the next bundle of momentum stocks!

---

[4] See note 1.

We've quoted extensively from the Dimson *et al.* LBS research on long-term data for one very simple reason – even if you could 'buy the market' this analysis suggests that it might actually be better to focus in on a more realistic sub-set of shares with easy to define characteristics. In short you might be better off 'screening' through or filtering the stock market using a particular strategy or set of ideas rather than rashly ringing up your broker and shouting 'Buy the market!'

How this book will help you

This book is designed to help you on that journey – ideally your aim is to buy shares because you think they're on balance a potentially good idea but you don't want to buy every share. You want to be discriminating, even intelligent – possibly even smart – about your choice of shares and you want to deploy one or maybe a host of strategies to help with your stock picking.

That journey could well be a hugely profitable one as there's a substantial body of evidence that suggests that intelligent, smart share analysis can produce market beating returns for those willing to be thorough, careful and diligent but it's not without its risks. By and large, as we'll discover in a later chapter on the big theoretical debate about efficient markets, most investors who pick shares (also called stock pickers) fail.

The diligent academics have discovered that in reality most stock pickers are not thorough in their selection of shares: they are not that smart when it comes to success in stock selection, and they over-estimate their own judgement and ability. This large group of ordinary stock pickers – private and institutional – are more likely to buy a share based on a tip they see in the paper or copy their friends than be unemotional and thorough in their stock selection process.

Most academics conclude that as a result of these 'vices' the struggle to beat the market is pointless because markets by and large get the pricing of shares just about right, i.e. the markets are efficient. This book is not about to tell you that all the analysis surveyed in Chapter 3 on the theory behind investing is entirely wrong – far from it as it reveals a number of important themes and ideas that smart stock pickers need to adhere to. As is so often the way with financial matters American investor and sage of Omaha Warren Buffett has summed it up nicely. Observing the academics who've built complex models of beautifully efficient markets he noted dryly of these experts that: 'Observing correctly that the market was frequently efficient, they went on to conclude incorrectly that it was always efficient.'[5] As we'll see later not every investor or strategy is doomed to failure simply because the market largely gets the pricing of shares just about right. The odds against you making a decent profit over long periods of time from careful strategic stock selection are not massive but they're relatively high if you think it through first and then stick with the strategy!

The ever-expanding equity universe

Our quick tour through long-term returns data should hopefully galvanise you to make a difference, to deploy strategies that can better those long-term returns and exploit the wide range of anomalies such as value or momentum that have been proven in the past to deliver superior returns compared to the supposedly efficient markets. With this in mind a number of important ideas should be clear, ideas that will be examined again and again throughout this book.

The first idea is that although equities are potentially a very good idea over the long term they can be risky and they can even be risky for relatively long periods of time. The next key concept is that you can cut down on that risk and increase your returns by selecting certain types of shares or screening the market but you have to be fairly specific in the way that you screen. Lastly you'll probably need some specific measures that will help you filter through or screen the market and hopefully, if properly applied, these will cut risk and increase returns. In the next chapter on measures used we'll start to look at these accounting based tools in more detail.

To understand how you might apply this relatively simple series of ideas, let's look at the universe of UK stocks or shares. There are an inordinate number of websites and software packages and publications (including the FT of course!) that let you screen through the market. As reference we'll use an offline software package discussed in a later chapter called ShareScope. If you go to Chapter 11 you'll see how to use this software package with screenshots and an easy to follow methodology.

---

[5] Buffett, W. (2000) 'In Defence of Fundamental Analysis: securities, arbitrage and the efficient market theory', *Quarterly Journal of Austrian Economics*, Vol. 3, No. 1.

Launching the ShareScope software you'll quickly be able to grasp that it can 'screen' the market by filtering through the universe of stocks that comprises just under 2000 listed London Stock Exchange shares – 1909 to be exact. This huge range of companies starts with tiny Voller Energy, worth just under £100,000, and finishes with giant global banking group HSBC which is worth a staggering £122 billion at the time of writing in late 2009! Unless you are a major investment bank there is no sensible way that you could buy any vehicle or fund that purchases all 1909 shares. Even an FTSE All Share tracker index fund won't buy all those shares as the index deliberately excludes really small companies in the long tail.

Drawing on the ideas we've already noted above, you decide that you only want to select companies that pay a decent dividend expressed as a yield. As this is being written, the average yield on the market is around 3.5% so you decide you only want stocks that pay twice this level, namely 7%: that is companies that in the current period have paid £7 in dividends for every £100 worth of shares. Simply applying this screen to the market immediately cuts our 1909 down to 89 stocks – eliminating over 1800 stocks with one simple measure. We also decide that we only want to focus this dividend filter or screen on the biggest companies as measured by the market capitalisation. Using ShareScope's screening tool if we set this level at £100m our list falls to just 29 companies; if we set it to £1bn it crashes to just 10; while a filter set at £5bn reveals just three companies, namely Lloyds, Aviva and Man Group. Immediately the eagle eyed amongst you will point out that although Lloyds paid out a big dividend cheque in 2008/9 (the year this analysis uses) that payment was stopped after the financial meltdown as the UK government was forced to step in and save the banks. So, if we had tried this strategy a few years back, would it have been successful? If you had screened through the market and only selected companies with a yield of 7% in December 2005, you'd have lost an average of 22% in cumulative terms by holding a basket of 22 shares – a loss substantially above that of the wider market which lost 4% over the same time span!

This incredibly simple screen and the quick spin through short-term results immediately demonstrate a number of crucial points. The first is that a screen can indeed very quickly provide an investor with real focus in their efforts to pick certain types of share – computer-based screens are powerful and quick. But dangers are immediately apparent. The first is that the screen is only as powerful as the data fed into it, which is why we concentrate in this book on a small number of reputable data providers and their software. Feed in rubbish and guess what you'll get out at the other end!

Any numbers based strategy, such as our example, is also only as good as the measures and definitions used to screen. In our example, we looked at historic data for 2009 but that isn't dynamic enough. In the case of Lloyds our use of historic data (backward looking data) failed to spot the sudden disappearance of the dividend in 2009, an error easily remedied if we had added a measure that looked at estimated future dividend yield based on analysts' forecasts.

Another immediate danger becomes apparent when we compare our results for this tiny screen with our early discussion of the Dimson *et al.* research. We saw in that huge longitudinal study that dividend strategy produced stellar results yet by the first decade of the next century the results were very poor. The obvious point is that 'things change' – observable phenomena change and evolve as markets evolve and adapt. And the success of evolving strategies also tends to vary with time 'in the market', actually applying the strategy. Our high yield strategy wasn't successful over the past few years but it might well be a huge success over much longer periods of time as the power of those dividends kicked in. The simple message here is that the time span matters.

However, there's another dimension to the Dimson *et al.* study[6] that's very relevant. The authors used long time series data where the dividend was then reinvested back into the shares. We'll encounter the power of dividend reinvestment in Chapter 4 on dividend based strategies but suffice it to say that it is truly powerful and contributes to the vast majority of long-term returns. In our simple test of the screen we only used price return data – these returns weren't based on factoring back in the dividend as a secondary return over and above the change in the share price. If we had factored back in that dividend return – reinvested – the loss would have fallen dramatically to less than 10%.

The last point to make is that no one strategy or measure is ever likely to be enough on its own for investors. Most investors will need to constantly check and research their ideas and strategies and consider using a number of different strategies, maybe in parallel, as volatile markets evolve and adapt. If applied properly this form of evidence based investing, as it's called by some analysts like James Montier of fund management group GMO, can produce some strong results and absolutely beat the market on a regular basis.

---

[6] See note 1.

Investors need to be open minded enough to examine the evidence and try out different strategies and ideas – value investors worried by the relative short-term failure of our high yield strategy might for instance decide to test out the idea of investing in cheap or value stocks as defined by their asset backing. Who wouldn't be attracted to the idea of buying a share that costs you £1 but is backed by more than £1 of assets. It's an idea which we'll encounter much later in this book and originates with the work of legendary investor and financial thinker Ben Graham who operated in the US markets in the last century. He liked the idea of a substantial margin of safety between the share price and its asset backing and he started to de-velop a range of screens or filters that could find these shares.

To see this thinking in action let's return to our example and switch back to the screening system at ShareScope. We will use the tool to look for companies that four years ago (December 2005) had a share price that was below the total value of all the net assets (tangible) expressed on a per share basis: i.e. for each £1 paid for a share you got more than £1 of underlying tangible assets. This strategy, filter or screen would have produced 98 shares and over the succeeding four years would have returned a total of just over 4.5%, which is much greater than the market, which lost 4% – a superior return of 8.5% for a simple share price to book value strategy.

So, this screen would have produced some decent results but our earlier challenges and concern remain. This strategy worked over these four years but we need to look at the evidence over much longer periods of time to see if it backs up using this approach over the very long term. In this book we'll constantly remind investors of the danger of data mining – constantly coming up with numbers based analysis that shows an amazing result over short periods of time. Four years is almost statistically irrelevant for most academic economists – they'd want to see a strategy tested to destruction over 100 years, as in the Dimson *et al.* study.[7] They would also be warning that numbers can be interrogated in any way to reveal any truth if a smart person tries hard enough – the quantitative analysis must be linked to co-herent and rational theories that have been tested and analysed.

The behavioural challenges

There's no doubt that our rigorous academics are right to constantly chal-lenge simple numbers based strategies but what should become immedi-

---

[7] See note 1.

ately apparent is that investors who use these quantitative measures to help guide their process of selecting shares are already a very different beast compared to most market participants. Our strategies based investor may read the newspapers and be influenced by new ideas but at the core of their philosophy is a simple idea – people can make up stories but numbers usually don't lie! It may be tempting to look at a newspaper's list of its chosen hot stocks but it's probably better to be more thorough and careful and analyse the numbers first.

Using analysis to focus in on the numbers also forces investors to abjure some of the annoying behavioural traits we're all vulnerable to. Cross-referencing your ideas with the hard facts – that evidence based investing approach we mentioned earlier – forces you to confront practices such as narrative anchoring where investors talk themselves into a big story anchored not in the facts but their – and others' – opinions! It's also likely to force investors to trade less: investors have a grave tendency to destroy long-term investment plans by trading on a whim. The quantitative influenced approach we'll articulate in this book – using strategies and screens – usually forces investors to accept some set of rules that govern whether a share stays in or drops out of the shortlist or portfolio!

This more systematic approach will probably also help overcome some other terrible biases that afflict investors. Strategist James Montier has mined the reach seam of behavioural finance for the past few decades. For a while he was based at French investment bank SocGen but then moved into fund management in 2009 at GMO. In the box below we've repeated a short and pithy summary of his investing behaviourally-infused and value based world view, summed up in the *Tao of Investing* – while in Chapter 5 on value investing we also interview him on the future of value based strategies. James is also constantly warning investors about their dangerous enthusiasm for all things shiny, new, sexy and horribly expensive. When applied to shares this has disastrous results – that vice of narrative anchoring we mentioned reinforces a tendency to ignore the sensible and cheap, opting instead to buy the expensive. In a report for SG, Montier quotes research from Plassmann *et al.* on a wonderful experiment in wine tasting.

They [the academics] gave subjects five wines to taste, and asked them to rate each of the wines. All the wines were Cabernet Sauvignons. In fact, there were only really three different wines used in the experiment. Two wines were presented twice. In the first version of the experiment subjects were told the price of each wine. For example wine 2 was presented once as $90, and once as $10. [Figure 1.3] below shows the *scores the subjects awarded the wines based on a scale of 1 (didn't like at all) to 6 (really loved it).*

When faced with wine 2 in the guise of a $10 bottle the average rating was around 2.4. However when told the same bottle was a $90 bottle the average rating jumped to 4. In fact, the bottle retailed at $90! A similar finding is true of wine 1. So effectively price tends to an increase in perceived taste ratings of between 50–60%![8]

James concludes this analysis by noting:

When told the wine was cheap (i.e. $5) people really marked the wine down, and when told a wine cost $90 they massively increased its ratings! Is it possible that something similar happens when people think about investing? It certainly seems plausible that investors might think that an expensive stock is a better option than a cheap stock as its expense might signal quality... Are stocks just another item that people dislike when they are on sale?[9]

The answer (unsurprisingly) to Montier's last question is yes, of course, most investors are moth-like and tempted by the shiny and new in an unsystematic way. Investors constantly jettison a focus on hard numbers and instead pile into new fads and dangerous trends motivated by big narrative themes which excite or impress them. The approach discussed in this book

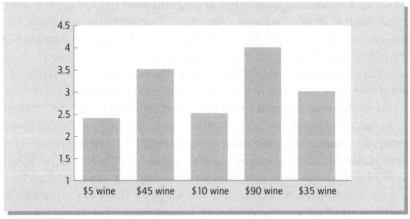

figure 1.3   Average rating of the wine (1 = didn't like, 6 = really loved) with price information
Source: Plassman et al. (2008)

[8] Montier, J. (2009) *Value Investing: Tools and Techniques for Intelligent Investment*, John Wiley & Sons.
[9] Ibid.

forces the investor to start from a very different place – maybe buying the 'cheaper better value' share is a better way to spend your hard earned investment money, based on past evidence, so why not focus your search on quantifying how to find those 'cheap' shares.

Two American academics recently summed up the logic of using strategies when discussing the work of an organisation (the AAII who we'll encounter next) that makes constant use of strategies and stock screens. Frederick P. Schadler and Brett D. Cotton note that:

Taking the emotions out of the decision-making process is also part of the challenge investors must confront. If buy and sell decisions are based entirely on a rigid and easy to follow set of quantitative rules then the emotions become less important. Under the 'rules' approach behaviour plays a role only to the extent that some belief factors will be present when the initial rules are established and in the ongoing attempt to stick to the rules through all phases of the market. The question is whether or not rules that beat the market can be identified.[10]

The tao of investing: the ten tenets of James Montier's investment creed

In this introductory chapter we've quoted from the work of investment strategist James Montier, with particular reference to his fairly unique blend of behavioural investing insights and his faith in buying cheap shares. James has, helpfully, also provided investors with his own ten-point plan for future success, pithily summed in his *Tao of Investing!* James kicks off his strategy by reminding investors of Sir John Templeton's famous injunction: 'For all long-term investors, there is only one objective – maximum total returns after taxes.' For Montier this means that: 'Nothing else matters. The question becomes, how should we invest to deliver this objective?' James then goes on to summarise his ten Tao infused principles:

Tenet I – Value, value, value. Value investing is the only safety first approach I have come across. By putting the margin of safety at the heart of the process, the value approach minimises the risk of overpaying for the hope of growth.

Tenet II – Be contrarian. Sir John Templeton observed that. It is impossible to produce superior performance unless you do something different from the majority.

Tenet III – Be patient. Patience is integral to a value approach on many levels, from waiting for the fat pitch, to dealing with the value manager's curse of being too early.

▶

---

[10] Schadler, F.P. and Cotton, B.D 'Are the AAII stock screens a useful tool for investors?' (2008) *Financial Services Review*, 17, pp. 185–201.

> *Tenet IV – Be unconstrained. While pigeon-holing and labelling are fashionable, I am far from convinced that they aid investment. Surely I should be free to exploit value opportunities wherever they may occur.*
>
> *Tenet V – Don't forecast. We have to find a better way of investing than relying upon our seriously flawed ability to soothsay*
>
> *Tenet VI – Cycles matter. As Howard Marks puts it, we can't predict but we can prepare. An awareness of the economic, credit and sentiment cycles can help with investment.*
>
> *Tenet VII – History matters. The four most dangerous words in investing are 'this time it's different'. A knowledge of history and context can help avoid repeating the blunders of the past.*
>
> *Tenet VIII – Be sceptical. One of my heroes said, 'Blind faith in anything will get you killed. Learning to question what you are told and developing critical thinking skills are vital to long-term success and survival.'*
>
> *Tenet IX – Be top-down and bottom-up. One of the key lessons from the last year is that both top-down and bottom-up viewpoints matter. Neither has a monopoly on insight.*
>
> *Tenet X – Treat your clients as you would treat yourself. Surely the ultimate test of any investment is: would I be willing to invest with my own money?*
>
> Source: James Montier's 'Tao of Investing', 24 February 2009, in *Mind Matters*.

Use strategies implemented through screens

Hopefully everything we've said so far makes sense to a diligent and prudent investor – equities can be a great investment but some equities are a better investment than others. In addition, those more successful equities (based on past analysis of data to be sure) can be selected by careful analysis of the fundamental numbers that help define a company and the simplest way of managing this process is to use a computer based screening system that scans in an instant through the universe of available shares. But the reader will also be aware that although this form of investing is thorough it is, in itself, no guarantee of success. Good strategies are built upon both hard evidence in the numbers but also well thought through arguments and debate.

Hopefully by now you'll begin to see the logic of using evidence based strategies which eschew the dangers of behavioural 'mis-investing', focusing instead on how the hard numbers contained within a balance sheet or a cashflow statement influence an analysis of a company. But this logic does pose one crucial question, namely 'Will it pay off for you as an investor?' Logic and rationality may be appealing but as legendary investor Sir John Templeton reminds us the only true test of any idea is whether it makes a profit, or at the very least delivers a return in excess of the wider market.

In our concluding chapter we'll look at a range of screens and ideas that can deliver great results and (to date) have been very successful. Crucially we'll show you the results that go some way to proving this claim that a small number of strategies do work. But without giving away that cliff hanging ending it's worth looking at some other studies into strategies based stock screening.

The first and perhaps most important piece of evidence is from a truly fabulous organisation called the AAII or American Association of Individual Investors, based in Chicago (www.aaii.org). The author of this book is a (remote, UK based) member of this not for profit organisation and any sensible, thoughtful British investor would be strongly recommended to buy an annual subscription if only because of the AAII's thorough and comprehensive analysis of more than 60 individual stock screens.

Pride of place in that analysis of the AAII's stock screens – built on clearly explained strategies applied to US shares – are the two graphs below which I've taken from its website. This shows the results of two particular screens the AAII used from inception in 1998 through to the end of 2008. Figure 1.4 shows the success of its strategy that builds on the work of New York investor Martin Zweig, who we'll encounter in Chapter 6, on what's called

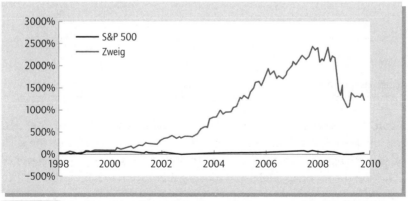

figure 1.4   Returns from the AAII Zweig strategy compared to the S&P 500

Source: www.aaii.com

GARP investing or 'growth at a reasonable price'. Zweig is perhaps the most articulate and certainly one of the most successful of a small group of investors who thinks that the name of the game in investing is to find reasonably priced shares in companies that are growing fast where the stock market is getting excited about future prospects. There are all sorts of fancy titles for this style of investing (including that acronym GARP) but regardless of its title Figure 1.4 suggests that returns from the AAII Zweig strategy for most of the past ten years has been astonishing.

But the AAII is a huge fan of evidence based investing and accepts that other ideas and strategies work for different investors: Thus its 60 plus list of different strategies and screens. Another astonishingly successful screen it runs centres on the work of an accounting professor who also happens, like the AAII, to be based in Chicago. His name is Joseph Piotroski and later in this book we'll encounter his academic analysis and its subsequent application to equity markets. Again as you can see from Table 1.1 the results have been astonishing.

table 1.1 Percentage results from AAII screens (1998–2008)

Screen	Year to date (Dec 2009)	Total period from 1998
Ben Graham Enterprising	26	196
Piotroski	47	755
Price to free cash flow	114	624
Weiss Blue Chip Dividend Yield	19	161
Buffettology	19	319
Zweig	−21	1205
Foolish small Cap 8	10	199
CANSLIM	102	2840
Return on equity (RoE)	27.4	276

Figure 1.5 shows Piotroski's performance compared to the S&P 500 and the low price to book universe. And these two strategies are just the start of an onslaught of screens and ideas that cater for virtually any school of investing theory imaginable, and most of them seem to have worked since

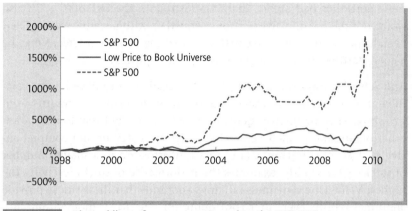

figure 1.5　Piotroski's performance compared to the S&P 500

Source: www.aaii.com

1998. In fact, a cursory check of the home pages for stock screens reveals that of the 43 main strategies defined just three have under-performed the market since 1998.

Cynical types might already be starting to ask questions – what about longer time frames and do these summarised results really tell you the whole story? Luckily the AAII's research has been tested. In a paper for the Financial Services Review, Frederick P. Schadler and Brett D. Cotton dig deep into the data and test out the AAII's ambitious claim that 91% of its screens beat the market, a claim which they suggest has some 'support' based on their finding that: 'Of the 54 screens with full data 50 earned higher gross returns than the S&P 500 index. These results translate to a 92.59% out-performance rate versus the S&P 500.'[11] They then rigorously tested those 54 different screens used by the AAII over eight years and found that if you ignore transaction costs '75.9%... of the AAII portfolios significantly beat the S&P 500'. Once transaction costs were fully included those percentages 'fall to 31.5... when transactions costs are considered. We note that investors can lower their transaction costs by simply avoiding the strategies that require investors to hold large numbers of stocks. Considering this, we conduct our analysis using only strategies with below median average holdings. Here we find that even after transactions costs are considered, 48.1% of the portfolios significantly beat the S&P 500... In addition, all of

[11] Ibid.

these portfolios had higher Sharpe ratios than... the S&P 500.'[12] It's also worth noting that only five portfolios ended up with negative values! Their overall conclusion – 'we agree with AAII that many of their screens may be a good starting point in the portfolio selection process'.

And Schadler and Cotton aren't the only academics to have looked carefully at attempts to use strategies and screens to better the returns from investing. They themselves quote one study from Choi that looked at another organisation called Value Line which uses screens and comprehensive analysis of company data to focus investors on to a smaller number of stocks. Choi's study 'examines the performance of stocks receiving the highest Value Line timeliness rankings and finds that these stocks provide abnormal returns even after controlling for size, BTM, momentum, and earnings surprises'.[13]

One of Wall Street's most brilliant commentators and fund managers has also looked in detail at how you can attempt to beat the market average by using strategies and screens in an intelligent and relatively easy way – and then subjected this to rigorous academic analysis. In the 1990s James O'Shaughnessy produced his results in the hugely successful book *What Works on Wall Street*.[14] In this best seller republished in 2005 he applied a number of straightforward screens to a massive database of US shares (called Compustat) over the period between 1954 and 1994. These screens varied and included most of the fundamentals based measures we'll use in this book but they were all replicable and easy to understand. The results were startling.

A screen that hunted down stocks where the share price was very low compared to the 'book value' (a measure of the assets in a company) demonstrated annual compound returns of 14.4% compared to just 7.5% for firms where the share price was many times the book value. It also showed

---

[12] The academics summarise the AAII investment process thus. AAII performs its screens at the end of each month and then hypothetically purchases an equally weighted portfolio of all stocks that pass the screen. The purchase price of the stocks is the closing price on the last trading day of the month. AAII then assumes that the stocks are sold on the last trading day of the following month. The return is calculated based on the change in price during the month. No dividend payments are included in the return calculation. The process is repeated each month.

[13] Choi, J.J. (2000) 'The Value Line Enigma: The Sum of Known Parts?', *Journal of FInance and Quantitative Analysis*, 35, pp. 485–498.

[14] O'Shaughnessy, J. (2005) *What Works on Wall Street*, McGraw-Hill Professional.

that a screen based around another popular measure – the share price relative to the sales generated by the firm – produced annual compound returns of 15.6% where the price to sales ratio was low, compared to just 4.2% for firms where the PSR was high. O'Shaughnessy went on to list more than a dozen different screens where the shares identified produced above average returns.

There are many other academic studies that focus on individual strategies which we'll encounter later in this book which back up the general conclusion that stock strategies and screens, well thought through and diligently applied, can indeed produce excellent results. Perhaps the best evidence of this simple assertion is the hedge fund community and the large investment banks – these august and lavish institutions are jam packed full of individuals called quants. These quantative experts are usually mathematically or scientifically trained and use number-based systems to constantly buy and sell the market based on a strategy. Their 'black boxes' are just immensely more complicated versions of the ideas detailed in this book, transmuted into clever algorithmic programs which manage portfolios of shares. In London, New York and Paris countless tens of thousands of very clever people sweat away in opulent, numbers driven, 21st century white collar workshops running money using the same principles you'll encounter in this book – and they do this because much of the time they make above average profits for their masters (and themselves!). It doesn't work all the time but quant based investing, and especially those strategies built around value and momentum investing deliver the goods enough of the time to warrant hard-nosed bank executives who invest in strategies to hire some of the best quant brains in the business.

This huge cottage industry is far from being perfect and all too frequently behaves like a pack of lemmings in financially distressed markets, but it self-evidently produces the goods! In our concluding chapter we'll interview one of the most articulate of these quantitative experts – Andrew Lapthorne from French bank SocGen – as he talks about how to link back the exhaustive 'torturing' of the numbers so beloved of quants to common-sense ideas that have stood the test of time.

Choice... and caveats!

So, in this book you'll hopefully encounter a huge range of research-based studies that demonstrate that a great many individual strategies have produced some startling results – all backed up by careful reasoning and detailed analysis of the statistics. The rest of the chapters in this part run through a range of ideas, theories and studies ranging from classic value investing based on the work of legends like Ben Graham (Chapter 5) through to insanely popular momentum-based strategies that spot fast growing small caps where the market is constantly upping its estimate of future growth.

The important point about this huge range of strategies is that you have a choice and you too can test out the screens and strategies and see if they work for you! The stock screening detailed in this book is immensely liberating and democratising as it allows ordinary investors with the correct tools of the trade – all detailed in the part on putting it into practice – to run the kind of analysis that until just a decade ago was exclusively the preserve of those wealthy, hard working quants!

As you read through these chapters you'll begin to realise that there are in fact a small number of fairly spiky, opinionated, even argumentative schools of belief within the investment world that maintain that theirs is the only way forward – that the world according to a guru like Ben Graham or Warren Buffett is the only way forward and that everyone else is barking up the wrong tree. In our concluding chapter we hope to show that the opposite is true, that in fact a combination of measures is useful and that investors might want to think about using different strategies and screens in different market conditions or combine some key measures in one master screen.

And the caveats? Before we plunge into the next chapter it's important to repeat a series of earlier observations on the risks and challenges for a smart investor who wants to use different strategies and screens.

■ Rubbish in, rubbish out – your data sources matter! You need to use authoritative sets of numbers that correspond to the real truth. Also you need to understand the way in which the numbers and measures are framed!

■ Beware data mining – any number of professional quants have been guilty of torturing the numbers to prove their argument but all too frequently the periods of time used have been very narrow. Two to four years is next to useless, five to ten years of some use, 10 to 20 moderately powerful but the best results come from data sets of between 40 and 100 years.

▮ It's all past data! – every strategy in this book uses data from the past although many strategies do use forward looking data based on forecasts (the subject of the next caveat). This data is useful and powerful but the inevitable warning ensues, namely that what's true of the past might not be true of the future. In fact there's a growing body of evidence that suggests that as soon as a trend or phenomena is noted by analysts it's rapidly capitalised upon by investors and the advantage vanishes over time. Remember that the numbers are no substitute for a clearly thought through set of ideas which have been debated and related back to the evidence.

▮ Forecast data is frequently false! – many of the strategies used in this book do make use of forward looking data based on estimates of future profits, sales and dividends. This can be useful and if the data is for relatively short-term periods, i.e. the next 12 months, it tends to be fairly accurate. But most forecast data of more than 12 months is patently absurd – how can anyone sensibly predict what will happen with a trading business two or even three years out – and should be avoided at all costs. And even short-term data forecasts are liable to be blown off course by a failure to predict what impact a business cycle will have on the underlying business. For example, most analysts were still predicting earnings growth in the first half of 2008 until the collapse of November 2009 destroyed the underlying assumptions.

A shortlist of measures and theories

Based on the earlier discussion you'll now see that this book is broken down into three main parts plus two appendices.

After this introduction we'll look at the basics. In our next chapter on the measures used we'll look at two companies (SSE and Aero Inventory) examining their company statements and introducing the reader to a range of basic measures. There are a great number of other books – some from the FT series – which focus exclusively on interpreting company data so if you have read these and are confident you understand the terms we'd recommend skipping to Chapter 3, where we rehearse some of the academic debates about using these measures. Some readers may find this chapter's detailed discussion of the academic theories that produced the efficient markets hypothesis rather beside the point in a book on stock picking. This cynicism is foolish – it's important that readers understand why stock markets are difficult places to make money and why many, if not most, investors are better off investing in index tracking funds which specifically avoid any form of strategy or stock picking. In a much later chapter we return to this theme by looking at a middle ground where investors accept that markets are largely efficient and thus choose to track an index, but in an intelligent fashion using the fundamental measures we'll encounter in Chapter 2. In this fundamental indexing revolution, measures like the relationship of the share price to its asset backing, its dividend, and its cashflow are explored and built into an index which is then methodically tracked by a fund such as an exchange traded fund. But to understand why these measures are so powerful, the investor first must understand how to read those complex and weighty documents issued by companies – they must be able to prise out of the profit and loss and cashflow statement key figures and measures and understand just how important the balance sheet really is to any investor.

Part 2 consists of five chapters under the umbrella title of 'Putting it into practice' while Part 3 puts everything discussed together into an action plan.

2

The measures

Sales are vanity, profits are sanity, cash is reality. Old adage

The fundamentals of company life

In this chapter you will be introduced to the basic measures and numbers which you'll need so that you can understand some of the strategies and screens used later in this book. As mentioned in the introductory chapter, there are already a great many books that are solely focused on understanding company balance sheets and P&Ls (profit and loss statements), and this chapter is not intended to be the definitive source of knowledge. Rather investors should buy a copy of Terry Smith's brilliant and caustic examination of the shady world of company reporting and accounting, *Accounting for Growth*.[1] This bestseller absolutely takes the lid off the dodgy practices used by company managers (and their auditors) as they try to manipulate the numbers to flatter the share price, a game which far too many analysts are complicit in! The smart investor – having read this acerbic masterpiece – will then completely understand why the much ignored Notes section at the back of any report and accounts is so hugely important and why it needs to be scrutinised in the greatest detail.

This chapter has a different purpose from that of Terry Smith's book – it's simply meant to take the novice investor through the statements of two

[1] Smith, T. (1996) *Accounting for Growth: Stripping the camouflage from company accounts*, Century Business.

real companies (although one is now in administration), identify some of the key statistics and then relate them back to key measures. But we have taken on board Terry Smith's – and others' – observations and will be focusing to a limited degree on the crucial Notes section at the back of any accounts, plus one key measure that towers above all, the cashflow statement and how it can be interpreted. On this latter theme – the importance of cash freely available to its shareholders after other commitments – we'll explore the work of one British fund management group, namely Liontrust, and how they've built a compelling analysis of cashflows into their fund selection system.

In this chapter we're going to focus on two companies – Scottish and Southern Energy or SSE and Aero Inventory. The author of this book owns shares in SSE – and has done for some time – but that's not the reason why we've chosen to focus on this giant utility. SSE is exactly the kind of share that many private investors will have in their portfolios, probably for all the right reasons. It's big, heavily regulated and thus possibly lower risk, is doing a half decent job of growing its core business and above all pays out a chunky and well supported dividend that is growing year on year. It even boasts a large and exciting renewable energy business which is guaranteed to excite the green investing brigade. As big boring blue chips go, it's absolutely not without its critics who maintain that it has too much debt, has expanded too fast into risky areas like wind turbines, and that it is constantly vulnerable to volatile energy prices and sudden changes of tactics by the regulators. But the key point here is that it's popular with private investors because of its 'progressive' dividend policy, is highly respected and is highly likely to find its way into the portfolio of investors who use strategies and screens.

Aero Inventory is a very different creature indeed – or should we say was! At the end of 2009 this once sexy growth stock collapsed into administration as the banks pulled the plug on its huge mountain of debt. The cause of its collapse is clear in hindsight to any investor who uses a careful examination of fundamental measures, measures which we'll explore in this chapter. Like SSE it was running up huge debts but unlike SSE didn't have the cashflow coming in at the operating level to keep going. We make no comment on whether Aero Inventory was badly run – although the evidence suggests it may have been – or was up to anything remotely shady and untoward. In this chapter we've instead decided to focus on Aero Inventory because its fundamental measures were dreadful in some key respects while SSE is patently still in business and, on paper at least, is thriving.

Scottish and Southern Energy – SSE

The focus of this chapter is simple – the hard numbers as represented in companies' various interims and annuals. This reductionist way of looking at a vast and successful company like SSE is probably offensive to many investors who suggest you 'get to know' a business first. Maybe that is the case for many investors who start with emotion and then work backwards, but the approach of this book is to start with the investment case and then see if the company is attractive to the investor!

The wider context is valuable – this is one of the UK's last independent multi-utilities with a strong franchise in renewable energy – but we'd suggest that the more important questions are whether it's profitable, what is the intrinsic value of the business and whether its shares are likely to rise in price? Only after answering these questions is it sensible to then broaden out and examine the business franchise itself.

We're going to start our numbers based analysis by looking at the most widely scrutinised statement or document from a big company, namely the P&L – the profit and loss statement. Table 2.1 (overleaf) summarises the 2009 annual statement. As you can see, like many large companies it's made complicated by the fact that there's a row of columns for the overall listed group, SSE, and the underlying trading company known as Scottish and Southern Energy. This distinction is fairly common with large companies mainly because the overall group structure holds actual trading businesses, off balance sheet entities that may have some impact, plus various joint ventures and associated companies. For our purposes the consolidated group columns are the most relevant although anyone wanting to look at the actual trading performance might want to focus additionally on the company columns.

The next complicating set of columns refers to before exceptional and exceptional items. In the good old days exceptional items were precisely that, the occasional exception, but now exceptional items are constant and need to be addressed by the company auditors – as do remeasurements, another slightly odd accounting term.

table 2.1   Summary of the 2009 annual statement

		Group			Company		
		Before exceptional items and certain re-measurements	Exceptional items and certain re-measurements (note 5)	Total	Before exceptional items and certain re-measurements	Exceptional items and certain re-measurements (note 5)	Total
	Note	£m	£m	£m	£m	£m	£m
Revenue	3	25,424.20	–	25,424.2	15,256.30	–	15,256.3
Cost of sales		−23,552.70	−1,291.70	−24,844	−13,509.80	−187.8	−13,697
Gross profit		1,871.50	−1,291.70	579.8	1,746.50	−187.8	1,558
Operating costs	4	−576.5		–	−576.5	−605.7	−605.7
Operating profit before jointly controlled entities and associates		1,295.00	−1,189.00	106	1,140.90	−132.8	1,008
Jointly controlled entities and associates:							
Share of operating profit		246.4	–	246.4	242.6	–	242.6
Share of interest		−128.2	–	−128.2	−127.6	–	−127.6
Share of movement on derivatives		–	3.8	3.8	–	4.2	4.2
Share of tax		−39.3	−1.1	−40.4	−41.9	31.2	−10.7
Share of profit on jointly controlled entities and associates	13	78.9	2.7	81.6	73.1	35.4	108.5
Operating profit	3	1,373.9	−1,186.3	187.6	1,214.0	−97.4	1,116.6
Finance income	7	209.7	–	209.7	202.6	–	202.6
Finance costs	7	−369.8	25.8	−344	−233.9	−1.5	235.4
Profit before taxation		1,213.80	−1,160.50	53.3	1,182.70	−98.9	1,083.80
Taxation	8	−300.6	359.6	59	−306.8	96.2	−210.6
Profit for the year		913.2	−800.9	112.3	875.9	−2.7	873.2
Attributable to: Equity holders of the parent		913.2	−800.9	112.3	875.6	−2.7	872.9
Minority interest		–	–	–	0.3	–	0.3
Basic earnings per share (pence)	10			12.7p			101.1p
Diluted earnings per share (pence)	10			12.8p			101.0p
Adjusted earnings per share (pence)	10			108.0p			105.6p
Dividends paid in the year (£m)	9			£551.9m			£502.8m

Source: Adapted from *Scottish and Southern Energy 2009 Annual Report*, SSE plc.

Opinion is divided on whether to use the pre-exceptional statistics which should refer to the core, organic business or the post-exceptional statistics which are useful for focusing on actual cash in flows and increases or decreases in debt. This distinction is incorporated into the term normalised profits (with the exceptional smoothed out or removed) and FRS3 profits where they are factored back in. There is no right or wrong answer to this although most investors prefer to focus on the normalised profits and accept that some adjustment needs to be made! One data provider called Company REFs (www.companyrefs.com) makes an explicit point of focusing on normalised figures based on a rolling 12-month view of profits including profits plus an analysis of the underlying trading performance of the company.

Regardless of which view you take the big top line number is the least open to manipulation – turnover or sales – which in this period was £25.4bn for the SSE group. This produced a gross profit after cost of sales of £1.87bn after which group central operating costs were subtracted, share of profits in joint ventures added back in (less their share of interest on loans plus tax and derivatives) to give an operating profit of £1.37bn.

The auditors then added back in any income from its investments such as cash and took away the group's interest costs on its loans to give us the all important profit before tax (or PBT) of £1.2bn. Out of this pre-tax profit SSE had to pay corporation tax plus the dividends to shareholders.

These top line figures aren't the main numbers reported to the City institutions though – established auditing practise suggests using the post-exceptional numbers because although they may be exceptional they still make a meaningful difference to the bottom line and to cashflows. On this basis the final profit before tax was a measly £53m. From this very small number the management then divided up that profit by the shares issued to come to an earnings per share (EPS) figure of 12.7p although they've helpfully factored back in an adjusted earnings per share which comes to 108p (this was done after 'excluding the charge for deferred tax, net finance income relating to pensions, items disclosed as exceptional'). This adjusted EPS is probably on balance the crucial figure for most analysts and is the basis for working out the price to earnings multiple which is simply the share price – around 1100p as this is written – divided by those earnings of 108p, giving a PE ratio of about 10.

| table 2.2 | The balance sheet |

		Consolidated		Company	
		2009	2008 restated	2009	2008 restated
	Notes	£m	£m	£m	£m
Assets					
Property, plant and equipment	12	7,232.20	6,334.30		
Intangible assets:					
Goodwill	11	724	659		
Other intangible assets	11	253	256.9		
Investments in associates and jointly controlled entities	13	918.7	917.8	456.9	516.9
Investments in subsidiaries	14			2,154.20	2,137.80
Other investments	13	18.3	6		
Trade and other receivables	17			2,066.90	1,772.70
Retirement benefit assets	27		85.8		85.8
Deferred tax assets	23	100.1	43.1	32.7	
Derivative financial assets	29	29	449.2	318.9	
Non-current assets		9,695.50	8,621.80	4,710.70	4,513.20
Intangible assets	11	213.9	138.9		
Inventories	16	366.7	251.2		
Trade and other receivables	17	5,659.60	3,400.30	3,465.70	2,429.20
Cash and cash equivalents	18	295.9	255.3	135.1	104.2
Derivative financial assets	29	1,537.70	1,106.50	178.1	1.1
Current assets		**8,073.80**	**5,152.20**	**3,778.90**	**2,534.50**
Total assets		**17,769.30**	**13,774.00**	**8,489.60**	**7,047.70**
Liabilities					
Loans and other borrowings	22	1,060.10	1,847.60	916.4	1,696.30
Trade and other payables	19	4,364.90	3,399.90	2,635.50	3,580.20
Current tax liabilities	20	254.6	220.8		9
Provisions	24	13.8	9.5		
Derivative financial liabilities	29	2,451.00	1,229.40	130.8	
Current liabilities		**8,144.40**	**6,707.20**	**3,682.70**	**5,285.50**

| | Notes | Consolidated | | Company | |
		2009	2008 restated	2009	2008 restated
		£m	£m	£m	£m
Loans and other borrowings	22	4,336.10	2,073.60	2,868.50	612.6
Deferred tax liabilities	23	594.7	967.3		9.6
Trade and other payables	19	426	490.1		
Provisions	24	60.2	107.3		
Retirement benefit obligations	27	273.5	134.9		
Derivative financial liabilities	29	959.5	313.3		
Non-current liabilities		6,650.00	4,086.50	2,868.50	622.2
Total liabilities		14,794.40	10,793.70	6,551.20	5,907.70
Net assets		**2,974.90**	**2,980.30**	**1,938.40**	**1,140.00**
Equity:					
Share capital	25	460.2	435.1	460.2	435.1
Share premium	26	835.3	315.7	835.3	315.7
Capital redemption reserve	26	22	22	22	22
Equity reserve	26	0.8	3.9	0.8	3.9
Hedge reserve	26	19.6	2.3	43.3	7.1
Translation reserve	26		146.6		25.4
Retained earnings	26	1,492.70	2,175.60	576.8	356.2
Total equity attributable to equity holders of the parent		**2,977.20**	**2,980.00**	**1,938.40**	**1,140.00**
Minority interest	26	−2.3	0.3		
Total equity		**2,974.90**	**2,980.30**	**1,938.40**	**1,140.00**

Source: Adapted from *Scottish and Southern Energy 2009 Annual Report*, SSE plc.

As you'd expect, the balance sheet (see Table 2.2) is typically very long as well and very detailed with all sorts of clever accounting statements and terms but in reality there are some simple principles. At the top of the table are all the assets – we'll focus on the consolidated group columns. These assets are then broken down into non-current assets like fixed assets which could include buildings and equipment (remember that equipment such as wind turbines are written off in value over time through something called depreciation, which is tax deductible) and current assets which includes the obvious cash on the balance sheet plus stock and trade debtors to whom SSE owes money.

Most investors will be focused on three numbers here – the movement in cash held, the amount of tangible assets after stripping away intangible stuff like brand names and clever R&D, and the movement in trade debtors. Most investors like an increasing cash balance at the bank, while they tend to be very suspicious of any sudden increase in trade debtors and a massive increase in stock or inventory (though both can be explained by normal business practice). Lastly the intangible assets are also valuable – think of the value of the Coca-Cola brand – although they tend to be discounted by many. These investors think that brands are fine but are difficult to sell in a firesale as opposed to buildings, and to a lesser degree equipment, which can always be sold off quickly if needs must!

The bottom part of the balance sheet consists of the liabilities which are, as you'd expect for such a large and complicated company, big and chunky. There are three parts to this. The first two are the current liabilities – trade creditors or the overdraft for instance – and the non-current liabilities which include long-term corporate bonds and debts.

Taken together these add to the total liabilities which are subtracted from the total assets to give net assets which are in reality a debt or liability owed to the shareholders who make sure that SSE stays in business through their investments, i.e the company owes the residual value of the business to those shareholders via equity invested. That net asset value is often expressed on a per share basis – total net assets divided by total number of shares – and is often referred to as the book value, although you may see a variation where all the intangible assets and liabilities are stripped away giving a tangible net asset value or book value.

table 2.3   The cashflow statement

Cash flows from operating
activities

	Consolidated		Company	
	2009	2008	2009	2008
	£m	£m	£m	£m
Profit for the year after tax	112.3	873.2	852	550.6
Taxation	−59	210.6	−40.8	−2.4
Movement on financing and operating derivatives	1,265.90	167.1	−37.5	1.6
Exchange loss in relation to foreign investment	−	22.2	−	−
Finance costs	369.8	233.9	447	251.2
Finance income	−209.7	−202.6	−256.9	−191.7
Share of jointly controlled entities and associates	−81.6	−108.5	−	−
Income from investment in subsidiaries	−	−	−970.7	−609.3
Pension service charges less contributions paid	−49.3	−44.4	−14.5	−13.4
Depreciation and impairment of assets	315.9	267.8	−	−
Amortisation and impairment of intangible assets	14.4	32.5	−	−
Impairment of inventories	8.2	−	−	−
Release of provisions	−47.5	−	−	−
Deferred income released	−16.7	−15.1	−	−
(Increase) in inventories	−127.7	−25.9	−	−
(Increase) in receivables	−2,048.30	−571.5	−1,508.90	−779
Increase/(decrease) in payables	958	725.5	−538	990.1
Increase/(decrease) in provisions	4.7	−6.4	−	−
Charge in respect of employee share awards (before tax)	14.3	10.8	−	−
Profit on disposal of property, plant and equipment	−2	−65.3	−	−
Profit on disposal of 50% of Greater Gabbard Offshore Winds	−102.7		−	

▶

	Consolidated		Company	
	2009	2008	2009	2008
	£m	£m	£m	£m
Profit on disposal of fixed asset investment	−2.2		−	−2.2
Loss on disposal of replaced assets	0.3	0.4		−
Cash generated from operations	**317.1**	**1,504.30**	**−2,070.50**	**197.7**
Dividends received from jointly controlled entities	39.8	35.1	−	−
Dividends paid to minority investment holders	−2.6	−	−	−
Dividends received from subsidiaries	−	−	970.7	979.3
Finance income	74.4	61.2	192.2	124.9
Finance costs	−219.2	−108.6	−348.2	−201.3
Income taxes paid	−255.5	−283.6	−255.3	−289.3
Payment for consortium relief	−0.4	−7.6	−0.4	−7.6
Net cash from operating activities	**−46.4**	**1,200.80**	**−1,511.50**	**803.7**
Cash flows from investing activities				
Purchase of property, plant and equipment	−1,172.20	−798.8	−	−
Purchase of other intangible assets	−37.5	−16.9	−	−
Deferred income received	24.8	8.9	−	−
Proceeds from sale of property, plant and equipment	3.8	100.6	−	−
Proceeds from disposal of 50% of Greater Gabbard Offshore Winds	308.5	−	−	−
Purchase of 50% of Greater Gabbard Offshore Winds	−40	−	−	−
Proceeds from sale of fixed asset investment	2.4	−	2.4	−
Loans to jointly controlled entities	−262	−50.1	−	−
Purchase of Airtricity (note 15)	−2.1	−1,302.20	−2.1	−1,302.20
Purchase of businesses and subsidiaries (note 15)	−26.3	−65.7	−	
Cash acquired in purchases	0.1	597.3	−	−
Investment in jointly controlled entities and associates	−44.7	−	−	−

	Consolidated		Company	
	2009	**2008**	**2009**	**2008**
	£m	£m	£m	£m
Investment in Marchwood Power (note 15)	−19.7	−	−	−
Loans and equity repaid by jointly controlled entities	79.7	10.8	60	−
Increase in other investments	−12.5	−14.5	−	−
Net cash from investing activities	**−1,197.70**	**−1,530.60**	**60.3**	**−1,302.20**
Cash flows from financing activities				
Proceeds from issue of share capital	479.6	2.2	479.6	2.2
Repurchase of ordinary share capital for cancellation		−237		−237
Dividends paid to company's equity holders	−551.9	−502.8	−551.9	−502.8
Employee share awards share purchase	−15.8	−12.4	−15.8	−12.4
New borrowings	*3,203.10*	*2,275.10*	*3,266.50*	*1,696.40*
Borrowings acquired in purchases		−543		
Repayment of borrowings	−1,835.30	−466.6	−1,696.30	−349.5
Net cash from financing activities	**1,279.70**	**515.5**	**1,482.10**	**596.9**
Net increase in cash and cash equivalents	*35.6*	*185.7*	*30.9*	*98.4*
Cash and cash equivalents at the start of year (note 18)	*243.1*	*48.4*	*104.2*	*5.8*
Net increase in cash and cash equivalents	*35.6*	*185.7*	*30.9*	*98.4*
Effect of foreign exchange rate changes	*14.9*	*9*	*−*	*−*
Cash and cash equivalents at the end of year (note 18)	*293.6*	*243.1*	*135.1*	*104.2*

Source: Adapted from *Scottish and Southern Energy 2009 Annual Report,* SSE plc.

The cashflow statement is the final part of the holy trinity of key statements (see Table 2.3) and for some investors the most important – sadly it's also usually the longest! It sums up the movements of cash in and out of the business and is regarded as a great deal more reliable by many investors than earnings which can be easily manipulated.

There's a whole load of 'taking away and adding back in' lines that come after the first part, which is the profit after tax has been paid. Crucially, finance or loan-based costs plus derivatives are taken off, depreciation is added back on, and the net movement of debtors and creditors allowed for – this all goes to a final figure for the first section which is called **Cash generated from operations**. From this number dividends and taxes are subtracted again to give the all important **Net cash from operating activities** – this is the money left over from the business after all operating costs and dividends have been paid out and thus is the sum available to grow the business in the future. In general a negative figure is not regarded as a good sign whereas a big positive amount that has been growing over time is regarded as potentially excellent news by many investors.

After this the cash flow statement then descends into detail about investing activities – money raised via loans and equity issuance (rights issues) plus money coming back in through business and asset sales. Two final summaries are scrutinised by analysts – the first is called the *Net increase in cash and cash equivalents* which simply tells you the increase, or decrease in the cash held at the bank, which in this case is positive (good news). The last summary is called *Cash and cash equivalents at the end of year* which should hopefully be greater than the earlier line which reads *Cash and cash equivalents at the start of year*, i.e the amount of cash in the bank has increased after all the to-ing and fro-ing on the cashflow summary.

The notes

It's absolutely not the purpose of this chapter to dig into the ins and outs of how these figures are arrived at – Terry Smith's book mentioned earlier is by far the best way of understanding this very grey world inhabited by finance directors and auditors. But the smart investor cannot avoid a cursory examination of the notes at the end of the report and accounts. In the case of SSE these extend to 33 different note sections ranging from accounting policy through to detail on the debts owed and the company's treatment of foreign exchange.

These are absolutely crucial sections to many investment analysts and contain detailed information on the following:

■ The pension plan liabilities which with companies like SSE are usually large and growing – investors might ask whether this burden is sustainable and what is likely to happen over the future to this debt? Remember that the regulators of these pension schemes are very much of the view that dividends paid to shareholders from profits run second to the prior claim of pensioners.

■ The exposure to foreign currency hedging risks and other derivatives used in the trading business, which in SSE's case include carbon credits (the section called Risks from use of financial instruments is always a popular and detailed section).

■ The debt structure – how much of it is expiring shortly (within a year or two) and what's the long-term costs of all that debt.

■ How management works out the intangible costs and how it amortises the cost of big acquisitions over time, i.e. how it writes down the value.

Putting it all together

Most analysts and investors spend a lot of their time focusing on two broad themes based on this range of statements – they look at the trends (heading hopefully in the right way) and the basic underlying value (basically positive, we hope!). In the next example of Aero Inventory we'll see what happens when neither of these goes quite to plan – the trend in many key respects is heading in the wrong way and the company increasingly has no real underlying or intrinsic value.

In Figure 2.1 (overleaf) we've used a screen grab from a program we mentioned in the previous chapter called ShareScope – it sums up all the key metrics from our previous example of SSE all on one key page. Don't worry too much about the detail of this graphic at this point because in a later chapter we'll look at how you interpret this page, but a number of key trends observations have emerged in our discussion of SSE.

■ The dividend has steadily been increasing.

■ The sales or turnover has also been steadily increasing over time.

■ Profits have been very volatile with 2009 a difficult year.

■ Cashflow has also been volatile but apart from 2009 basically positive.

■ SSE has been progressively increasing its expenditure on new capital equipment and spent 136p per share on new equipment in 2009. Eventually that should pay off as that new capacity – power stations and wind turbines – produces profits from a heavily regulated business.

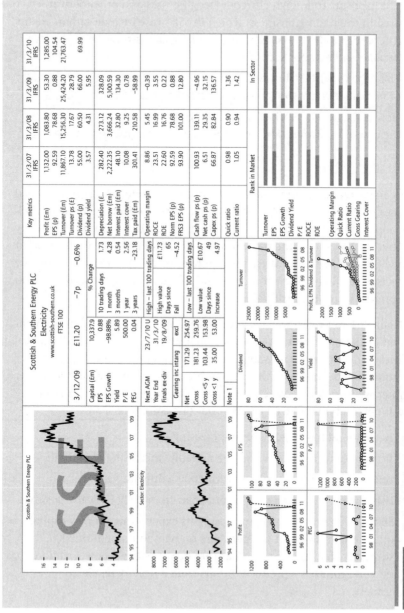

figure 2.1   All the key metrics for SSE from ShareScope

Aero Inventory

With our next company, airlines parts supplier Aero Inventory PLC, we're not going to inflict on the reader the torture of the three-part trinity of the P&L, balance sheet and the cashflow statement. Instead in Table 2.4 and Figure 2.2 (overleaf) we present some top-line numbers over time taken from the ShareScope summary. The point of this exercise is not to explain again what the key measures tell us but to identify the *trends* at Aero Inventory, trends that resulted in it being pushed into administration late in 2009.

table 2.4 Some top line numbers

	The good figures			
	Profit (£m)	EPS (p)	Turnover (£m)	Dividend (p)
2005	7.16	23.05	43	7.33
2006	9.89	21.86	63	9.97
2007	22.72	32.43	123	14.95
2008	36.72	51.06	221	17.94
2009	50.83	71.23	356	25
	The worrying figures			
	Depreciation (£m)	Interest cover	Interest paid (£m)	ROCE %
2005	0.37	7.34	0.71	12.14
2006	0.39	5.41	1.63	8.98
2007	1.39	6.92	3.64	16.71
2008	6.06	4.99	10.15	14.73
2009				
	The bad figures			
	Net borrowings (£m)	Cash flow	Capexps	Quick ratio
2005	25.72	−95	1.79	0.31
2006	−36	−75	3.17	1.93
2007	55.1	−133	42.71	0.44
2008	196	−250	29.95	0.63
2009				

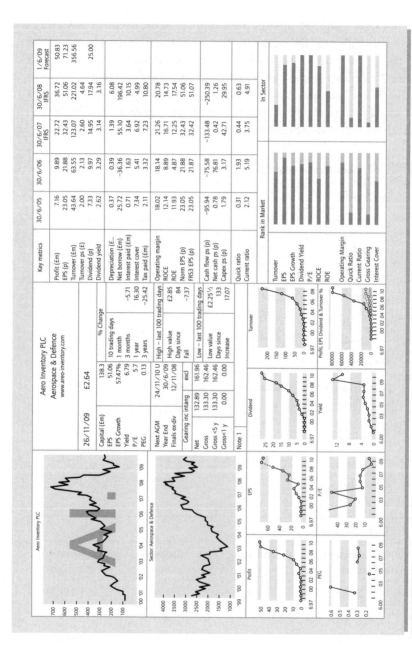

figure 2.2 All the key metrics for Aero Inventory PLC from ShareScope

In Table 2.4 you can see that there are some good numbers – numbers that clearly impressed the City. Turnover has been constantly rising and the company was paying out more and more in the way of dividends. But there are some worrying figures to factor in as well:

- depreciation costs were spiralling upwards as more money was spent on equipment (which is not a problem if the cashflow is there to pay)
- the interest paid out on loans was shooting up (again manageable if the cash was coming in), and
- a key measure of efficiency (defined below in the Technicals section) called the return on capital employed (or ROCE) was heading downwards.

This last measure looks at the cash profits versus the capital invested in the business and looks at the return in terms of a percentage – generally investors like the figure to be above 10% and increasing over time.

Crucially there are also some very worrying numbers from the reports and accounts. Loan debts were shooting up (thus the increase in the interest bill) and actual cash flowing into the business was negative. That last number was getting worse every year as the management spent ever more money on new capital equipment that clearly wasn't pulling in the cash profits to pay for the debts. Lastly a key measure beloved of private equity analysts – called the current ratio, and defined below – was absolutely heading in the wrong direction. This measure, also called the acid test, is basically an indicator of a company's financial strength (or weakness) and is calculated by taking current assets less inventories, divided by current liabilities – a substantial decline is usually regarded as bad news. It's worth noting that in the case of SSE, although it too is spending a fortune on new capital equipment and is also increasing its debts, its quick ratio has actually been increasing.

Eventually of course the bad and the not quite so bad numbers pertaining to Aero Inventory had an impact – the cash was running out, the banks were getting restive and when it hit a technical breach of the loan covenants, the show ended and the once high flying growth stock lapsed into administration. Subsequent commentary[2] from newspapers and magazines such as the *Investors Chronicle* revealed the true inside story. The IC reported that: 'Several former employees, who have spoken to the *Investors Chronicle*

---

[2] Hofmann, J. (2009) 'Why Aero Inventory crash-landed', 20 November, www. investorchronicle.co.uk.

on condition of anonimity, blamed the state of the company's inventory management system, known as Parts Central, and management failings, for the company's demise. "The stock valuations the system was churning out were rarely correct," said one insider. "In the end, we were told to sell at whatever price the computer said; for example, $200 parts could be sold for only $1."[3]

But it's left to the IC's columnist Bearbull to sum up 'the learning points', namely:

- 'Beware of companies that are growing fast
- Beware of companies that have a gargantuan appetite for capital and most of all
- Beware of companies that cannot turn accounting profits into cash profits.'[4]

Bearbull suggests that Aero Inventory was 'using up huge amounts of capital' noting that capital committed grew from £40m to £344m: 'in other words it took £1.50 of extra capital to generate every additional £1 of revenue.' In his opinion this aircraft parts wholesaler was: 'Basically an enormous inventory factoring exercise where it took someone's else's stock, the capital commitment and the risk.' Now to be fair to the management this could be a great business idea if it generated real cash from profits to pay for the loans and the stock – but as we've seen from the numbers above this was never quite the case. Remember that profits do not necessarily equal cash! Even those tangible fixed assets may not even be worth much now that the business is in administration. One website called Investors Champion estimated at the time that investors might be lucky to get 40p in the pound after the firesale of parts and assets.[5]

---

[3] Ibid.

[4] Bearbull (2009) 'Flight of Fancy', 18 November, www.investorschronicle.co.uk/Columnists/BearBull.

[5] 'Small Cap Share Comment', 17 November 2009, www.investorschampion.com.

Year to end June (£m)	2004	2005	2006	2007	2008
Revenues	21	44	64	128	221
Stocks	36	67	104	216	347
Operating profit	2	8	12	31	47
Operating cashflow	−20	−19	−19	962	−102
New loans	0	1	0	57	151
New equity	15	5	88	1	0
Shareholders funds	31	39	135	149	149

Source: Bearbull (2009) 'Flight of Fancy', 18 November, *Investors Chronicle*, www.investorschronicle.co.uk

Next steps – pulling together the numbers in a financial model

Our quick canter through the immensely complex world of company accounting at SSE and Aero Inventory should hopefully have alerted investors to the key measures used by analysts and strategists who constantly monitor shares and develop new strategies for stock selection. Many take these key measures and then integrate them into some basic models that can be used to estimate whether a company is reasonable value compared to its current market cap.

These financial models, and particularly something called the discounted cashflow model (or DCF) are widely used by investors as a vital part of their screening process. Here's perhaps the most famous and certainly one of the most successful fund managers of our time, Neil Woodford of Invesco Perpetual, talking about why he is a big fan of tobacco shares.

Asked why he liked BAT by Patrick Collinson of the *Guardian*, Woodford replied: 'It is a simple equation … It yields just a shade less than 5%, at a time when the company is buying back 2% of its equity every year and growing its dividend by 9–10% a year. On a dividend discount model (DDM), that puts BAT in the mid-teens, which is terrific for a company that is in a low-risk and predictable business.'[6]

---

[6] *The Guardian*, 15 November 2006.

The numbers may have changed slightly at BAT but the underlying point is clear. One of Britain's most successful investors makes extensive use of financial modelling – in this case the dividend discount model – and it seems to work judging by his fund's huge long-term success. But Neil Woodford is far from being the only avid fan of modelling. In the US Merrill Lynch uses a similar model as the core component of its hugely successful Alpha Surprise Model and nearly every one of the most successful Absolute Returns funds in the UK uses a variant of the DCF model to establish what constitutes a reasonable price for a share.

What's hugely compelling about models like DCF in the UK is that we have a stockmarket jammed pack full of relatively large, stable, mature companies churning out regular flows of cash, with share prices that are not hugely expensive – companies like SSE. In sum:

- we have a market full of reasonably dependable companies with cashflows and dividend yields that can be sensibly forecast, and
- we have a market full of boring, cheap, reliable stocks like SSE (and BAT) – the perfect candidates for financial models like DCF and DDM.

Intrinsic value

Lurking behind all these models is a very simple but hugely controversial idea – that a share has some kind of intrinsic value that is different from the actual share price and is hopefully more than the market price. Without wanting to sound philosophical you could say that there's a distinction between something called value and a completely different thing called the current market-based share price. In this world of models, that market share price might absolutely not equate to the underlying value of the business assets less any liabilities, especially over the next few years as the business grows.

A bit more flesh was put on the bones of this idea by one of the great pioneers of investment analysis, John Burr Williams. Way back in 1938 he declared that there were four basic factors needed to appraise the intrinsic value of an operating enterprise and thus its shares, with two of them macro-economic based and two company-specific factors. The macro-economic factors were general price level inflation and the real interest rate while the company-specific factors are the estimated future net cash distributions to the shareholders (dividends) and the discount rate or rates applied to those cash receipts, i.e a margin of safety that pays you back for the risk of holding a volatile share.

Legendary investor Ben Graham (mentor to gurus like Warren Buffett) took these ideas further – we'll encounter him in a later chapter on value investing. He, like Williams, believed that despite wild speculative variations, shares do have a fundamental economic value that is relatively stable and can be easily measured by use of the term intrinsic value. Put simply, investors should only buy shares when their market price is significantly below that of the calculated 'intrinsic value'. Graham actually specified what he meant by intrinsic value in the following equation.

$$\text{Value} = \text{Current (normal) earnings} \times (8.5 + \text{twice the expected annual growth rate})$$

where the growth rate should be that expected over the next seven to ten years.

The DCF model

Financial analysts have come a long way since Graham's early modelling and their preferred model these days is something called the DCF or discounted cash flow model. Look in the textbooks for a definition of this model and you'll get something like this: 'a method of estimating an investment's current value based on the discounting of projected future revenues and costs'.[7] In layman's terms, it's what someone is willing to pay today in order to receive the anticipated cash flow in future years. The end product is usually called the intrinsic value or true value of a stock, which is the value all rational investors should pay for the stock.

There is of course a fairly hideously complex equation that goes with this model – more on that later – but the ideas that stand behind the model are easy to grasp and are found by answering the following questions:

▪ If you commit your cash to a particular share, what cash can you expect to get out of it in return? What is your reward for risk taking?

▪ What are the estimated net cash flows attributable to this share?

▪ What is the present value of these net cash flows, discounted at an appropriate rate of interest? This is the intrinsic economic value of the equity investment.

---

[7] http://financial-dictionary.thefreedictionary.com

■ What is the margin of safety, in pounds and pence and percentage terms? Is the intrinsic value per share greater than the market price by such an amount to justify the long-term risk of holding the shares?

So, with these principles in place, it's worth doubling back and looking at that complex equation:

$$DCF = \frac{CF_1}{(1 + r)^1} + \frac{CF_2}{(1 + r)^2} + ... + \frac{CF_n}{(1 + r)^n}$$

where CF = cash flow and r = discount rate (WACC).

Luckily there are plenty of websites around that do away with the need for you to perform complex number crunching – our favourite is the incredibly simple and easy to use models available on on the MoneyChimp website (www.moneychimp.com).

Figure 2.3 shows how the analysis can work, using our previous example of SSE. Our first task is to find out SSE's normalised or core underlying cash earnings – we're going to use that adjusted EPS figure we discussed above of 108p.

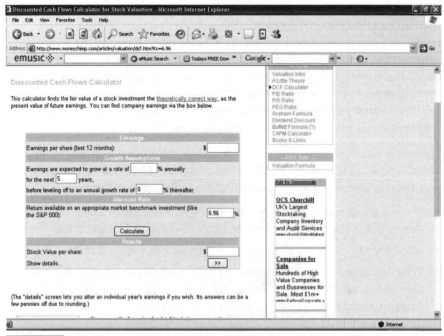

figure 2.3   **How an analysis works – using SSE**   *Source*: www.moneychimp.com

The DCF model at Moneychimp

Our next stop is to visit Moneychimp and its discount model – here you'll see a fairly standard series of simple boxes.[8] These are:

- Earnings per share – use whatever earnings or cash earnings figure you're happy with. We'll use the 108p figure.

- Growth assumptions – here you'll be asked to stick your finger in the air and estimate the growth in earnings per share over two distinct periods. The first is the medium term – usually the next five years – and then the long term into infinity. You can get some idea of medium-term growth rates by looking at analysts' estimates for earnings in the next few years. In SSE's case it's increasingly clear that it'll struggle, medium term, to grow at more than 5% per annum.

- The last box asks us to specify a discount rate. At Moneychimp this is the 'Return available on an appropriate market benchmark investment (like the S&P 500)' – currently it's set at a default of 11% per annum.

Our final step is simply to hit the Calculate box and hey presto, we're given a value for SSE's shares. If we use 108p of adjusted earnings per share SSE's shares look reasonable value. The DCF model at Moneychimp suggests they're worth just under 1400p a share, well above the current price of 1100p a share. But even if we assume no EPS growth at all in the long term the model suggests SSE is still worth just under £10 – 10% below the current share price with zero growth for the next decade, on average. This example shows the great strength of this model – it puts hard numbers on what the shares may be worth assuming the company keeps churning out cash. But the most profound revelation of DCF analysis is that it shows you that changes in long-term growth rates have the greatest impact on share values.

Dividend discount model

Another variation on the same theme is the DDM – it's an even simpler idea and relates back to the stream of dividends paid out by the company. Its central idea is that any share is ultimately worth no more than what it will provide investors in current and future dividends. As with the DCF model,

---

[8] http://www.moneychimp.com/articles/valuation/dcf.htm

one can get enormously complicated and look at the equation that's used in this model, namely:

$$\text{Value of stock} = DPS(1)/Ks - g$$

where DPS(1) = dividends expected to be received in one year; Ks = the required rate of return for the investment; g = growth rate in dividends.

The required rate of return can be estimated using the following formula:

$$\text{Risk-free rate} + (\text{market risk premium} \times \text{beta})$$

The reality is that the dividend discount model uses the same maths as the DCF model except that you're substituting dividends for cash earnings.

Back to that SSE example again, courtesy of the DDM model at Money-chimp. This time we're using the dividend figure instead of earnings – 66p a year in 2009 and a highly likely 70p in 2010. The other big change is that the growth assumptions are now for the dividend. SSE has gone on the record as saying that it will progressively increase its dividend payout and most analysts are expecting 5% increases year on year for the next few years. Beyond that it's anyone's guess – as with the DCF model we could be very conservative and estimate the dividend growth rate at just 3% after the next five years. Input these into ourMoneyChimp model and SSE's shares suddenly look expensive – the DDM model suggests the intrinsic value is just 850p vs 1100p on just 3% growth per annum. If we increased that estimate to 5% the model suggests a more acceptable 1155p a share. This analysis suggests that SSE is under an awful lot of pressure to keep increasing that dividend over the next 5–10 years.

Caveats galore

The reaction of most private investors to all this projecting into indefinite futures is probably one of simple disbelief – how on earth can a financial model based on 'assumptions' ever tell you anything about the supposed 'value' of a share? Behavioural economists go even further in their rubbishing of financial modelling by declaring that the intrinsic 'value' of a share is a waste of time because the price of a share is simply an expression of what the market is willing to pay and that there is no 'ideal' value to any share except what the market is willing to pay.

The deadliest criticism of these models though is that they're highly mechanical and although hugely powerful as one tool amongst many, they're also susceptible to the 'rubbish in, rubbish out' risk we mentioned in the introductory first chapter. The core risk here is that models like DCF assume that meaningful valuations depend on the user's ability to make solid cash flow projections. Small changes in the input values can result in large changes in the value of a company – a difference of just 1% per annum in one key measure can turn SSE, for instance, from hugely over-priced to hugely under-priced and vice versa.

There's also a much bigger, long-term problem. While forecasting cash flows more than a few years into the future is difficult, generating results into eternity (which is a necessary input) is near impossible. By guessing at what a decade of cash flow is worth today, most analysts limit their outlook to ten years but analysts are still tempted to model into infinity. Perhaps the most notorious case is that of a Credit Suisse First Boston analyst who ran a DCF model on Eurotunnel through to 2085, a full 80 years into the future!

The bottom line with these models is that they shouldn't be used solely as the basis for your decision on whether to buy a share or not. DCF and DDM valuations need to be constantly re-run and retested and should only be used as a crucial yardstick for potential value.

Websites

Aswath Damodaran, an Associate Professor of Finance at New York University's Stern School of Business has rather cornered the market in all things to do with DCF models. His website is a treasure trove of useful models, academic papers and a great little spreadsheet that purports to show that the real, intrinsic value of Google shares is just $110 – hundreds of dollars below the current price! You'll find more DCF models than you can ever use at http://pages.stern.nyu.edu/~adamodar/New_Home_Page/spreadsh.htm#valinputs

The *Financial Times* also has its own online model – via the Lex columns at http://news.ft.com/lex/calculator/cashflowmodel and http://news.ft.com/lex/calculator/dividenddiscount

Moneychimp's models are much easier to use though and they're at http://www.moneychimp.com

Market data is also important

So far in this chapter we've focused pretty much exclusively upon what are called fundamental measures and data contained within company statements and accounts. But this is only part of a much wider picture – there are some other equally crucial measures ascribed to a company by the wider market community of analysts and investors.

The most obvious 'external' measure – not under the control of the company managers and their auditors – is its share price. As we've already seen in our discussion on financial models, the share price is a one-dimensional number that doesn't necessarily imply the true 'value' inherent in a share. There are many economists – professional and academic – who strongly disagree with this contention and argue that the share price is *the only number* that matters and that all talk of underlying value is pointless. For this latter group of analysts the market price is all that you need because the market is largely efficient at processing news and company data and turning that into aggregate value via the share price. We'll encounter this group in the next chapter when we look at the theoretical debates swirling around the efficient markets hypothesis.

Regardless of whether you think that a company has an intrinsic value based on assets that is different from its current share price, the value ascribed to the shares must have some (sometimes tenuous) link back to the underlying value of the company. It's also worth remembering that the market share price is a great relative indicator: is the share price going up or down relative to its wider peers?

Many investors focus on what are called technical measures and one of the most widely used technical measures is *relative strength* (or RS). This measures the 'relative' weakness or strength of the share price over a specified time frame – anything between one month and one year. In the US relative strength is defined as the movement of a stock price over the past year as compared to a market index (like the S&P 500). A value below 1.0 means the stock shows relative weakness in price movement (it's underperformed the market) while a value above 1.0 means the stock shows relative strength over the period. For most growth investors a high figure for RS, especially over one year, is a very positive sign. It shows that the market is beginning to appreciate the virtues of the share.

In equation form this measure of relative strength is as follows:

Relative strength = (current stock price/year-ago stock price)/
(current S&P 500)/(year-ago S&P 500)

In the UK this measure of relative strength is usually expressed as a percentage figure. This percentage can be expressed either positively – above 0% – which means positive relative strength compared to the wider market, or negatively, which indicates that the share price has under-performed the wider market. Just to confuse things you'll also see this UK style RS figure expressed on a one-month, three-month, six-month and one-year basis.

On its own a negative RS percentage, say in one month, isn't necessarily that bad but a prolonged period (stretching into years) of RS is definitely viewed as a bad sign by nearly everyone except contrarian investors who, as the title suggests, think completely the opposite to the mainstream!

You might also see another technical term used called the *beta* which is a measure of a share's volatility relative to a chosen benchmark. The beta of the benchmark such as the FTSE 100 is always 1.00, so a stock with a beta of 1.00 has experienced up and down movements in price of roughly the same magnitude as its benchmark. A beta of say 1.75 indicates that for every 1% increase in the benchmark in the past, the individual share will have increased 1.75 times. Generally speaking, the higher the beta, the more risky the investment.

Lastly another technical term that is widely used is called *correlation* which measures how two assets move together. If two assets – the FTSE 100 for instance and SSE shares – move completely in sync with each that correlation is 1. If they move in completely opposite directions that correlation switches to –1. This means the two assets tend to simultaneously move in opposite directions. A correlation of 0 indicates that there is no relationship at all between the price movements of two assets.

Forecast data

The current share price data is also weaved back into a company narrative via another important group of people – stockmarket analysts working for the big banks and brokers. These highly experienced professionals crunch all the company data, look at the share price and the wider business sector and then start issuing projections or forecasts based on the company's own estimates and the analysts' forecasts. A great many astute market commentators take these forward-looking prognostications with a massive pinch of salt but over a 6–12 month forward period these analysts' estimates do make a real difference, even if they don't always hit the mark!

The two key forward-looking estimates penned by analysts consist of the forward earnings per share estimates – the forward EPS – and the estimated future dividend payout – the forward dividend. The estimate of future EPS in the coming year is crucial to working out another popular measure namely the forward price to earnings ratio which is simply the estimate for the coming year's EPS divided into the current share price. You might also see a variant on this theme called the PEG.

There's a considerable body of academic evidence to suggest that what really matters is less the actual figure for EPS projected by the analysts but *the pace of increase or decrease from previous estimates*, i.e. are analysts upping their estimates or lowering them over time.

Perhaps the most compelling study in this area comes from three US academics in a paper entitled 'Analyst Recommendations, Mutual Fund Herding, and Overreaction in Stock Prices'.[9] The research looked at the crowd-like behaviour of analysts and the market reactions to the earnings estimates of analysts – with startling results!

In the conclusion to the paper the researchers documented:

The tendency of mutual fund managers to follow analyst recommendation revisions when they trade stocks, and the impact of these analyst revision-motivated mutual fund 'herds' on stock prices. We find evidence that mutual fund herding impacts stock prices to a much greater degree during our sample period (1994 to 2003) than during prior-studied periods. Most importantly, we find that mutual fund herds form most prominently following a consensus revision in analyst recommendations. Positive consensus recommendation revisions result, most frequently, in a herd of funds buying a stock, while negative revisions result, most frequently, in a herd of funds selling.[10]

It's also worth noting the authors' slightly more caustic concluding observation:

Our most interesting result is that mutual funds appear to overreact when they follow analyst revisions – upgraded stocks heavily bought by herds tend to underperform their size, book-to-market, and momentum cohorts during the following year, while downgraded stocks heavily sold outperform their cohorts. The reversals remain robust

---

[9] Brown, N.C., Wei, K.D. and Wemmers, R. (2009) 'Analyst Recommendations, Mutual Fund Herding, and Overreaction in Stock Prices', 21 July, http://ssm.com
[10] Ibid.

when we examine fund herding on analyst earnings forecast revisions or fund herding driven by extreme money flows. These findings suggest that funds initially overreact to analyst recommendation revisions. Further evidence indicates that funds subsequently reverse their trades to correct their overreaction, but that other market participants also participate in contrarian trades that help to correct the overreaction.[11]

This change in earnings consensus – the dynamic change in time of the average of analysts' estimates – is hugely important in powering what's called 'improving sentiment', but even this phenomenon is over-shadowed by an even more powerful force – the earnings surprise. This peculiar event occurs when a company beats the estimates for profits set by the army of external (supposedly independent) analysts. Study after study has shown that companies that spring an earnings surprise see their shares consistently drift upwards – this idea sits at the core of screens discussed later in this book based around the work of American investor Martin Zweig and the CAN SLIM methodology. Analysts at SocGen have also looked at the earnings surprise phenomena and proclaimed it as a major driving force in the share price. In a bank research paper from 2006 its analysts pointed to L. Chan's article in the December 1996 edition of the *Journal of Finance*. This research demonstrated that:

Stocks with positive earnings momentum have regularly outperformed the American market since 1977. The same article suggests that this outperformance is the product of an under-reaction by analysts to earnings surprises. Here again, this is supported by empirical evidence on the analysts' estimates revisions. [Figure 2.4] shows that analysts continue to downgrade their estimates for six months following a negative earnings surprise whilst positive surprises produce only very slight upgrades.... As a result of the market's under-reaction to earnings surprises, stocks which have provided positive surprises will continue to outperform over a short-term period (between three to six months). Even though most of the adjustment has been made, there is still some outperformance left over the following 6 months (about 20% of the total outperformance).[12]

The SG analysts go on to note that:

We have also made a similar study of European stocks, using IBES consensus figures [Figure 2.5]. Our findings show the same pattern as for the American market, with an even greater degree of under-reaction. Thus earnings surprise strategies should be even more efficient in Europe than in the USA… other criteria can be used to

---

[11] Ibid.

[12] SocGenWISE (2006) 'Detailed Methodology: What's WISE?', *Quantitative Research*, January, www.sgcib.com

measure earnings surprises, such as the relative performance of the stock around the latest earnings announcement, or the earnings revisions made by the consensus in the recent past. **The literature on the US market also shows that earnings momentum and price momentum are closely linked, since the stocks that have surprised positively in recent months have logically been those which have performed the best [emphasis added].**[13]

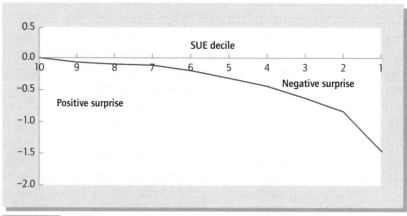

figure 2.4 **Under-reaction by US analysts (1982–1991)** *Source:* Lakonishok, Y. *et al.* (1996).

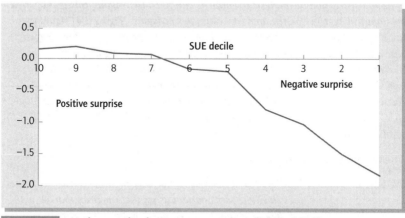

figure 2.5 **Under-reaction by European analysts (1988–1998)**

Source: SocGenWISE (2006).

---

[13] Ibid.

Focusing back on cashflow

For many value investors – an articulate and, until very recently, successful group of investors who we'll encounter in a later chapter – there is really one key measure that investors need to focus on, namely cashflow. A large number of investors base their entire strategy on some aspect of cashflow – in fact we'll look at one fund manager called Liontrust who make a virtue of their methodology based around finding companies churning out cash.

But it's not just value-based professional fund investors who choose to focus in on the cashflow, i.e the actual cash profits made by a business. The accountants used by these firms also use the measure in some of their publicity campaigns – one example is the Hidden Gems survey from Robson Rhodes, now part of Grant Thornton after a big merger. This aims to identify the hidden stars of the UK stockmarket and it does this by focusing in on cash flow. Looked at another way, this shortlist is also a way of spotting the best value companies on the stockmarket. Over the past six years, the Top 50 Hidden Gems have outperformed the FTSE All Share market by 6.7% while in each and every survey (there have been six) the Top 50 companies have consistently outperformed the market. The shortlisted shares also have great short-term defensive value. According to Grant Thornton: 'looking at the [recent] stock market falls the FTSE All Share fell by 8.8%, the "qualifying" group of 245 companies by 8.1% but The Top 50 fell by only 5.8%'.[14]

What's Grant Thornton's analysis based on?

■ The main screen is based on all the companies within the FTSE All Share Index excluding financials.

■ Next Grant Thornton base their assessment on up to seven years' historic and forecast performance of companies showing good cash flow growth.

■ This is then compared to a 'price to cash flow per share' ratio which is derived by dividing the share price by the average for forecast cash flow per share.

■ The resultant figure, produced by dividing the cash flow per share growth by the price to cash flow per share ratio, is characterised as the Hidden Gems Index number (see Table 2.5 overleaf).

---

[14] www.grant-thornton.co.uk/publications/hidden_gems_index.aspx

Interestingly, over time the composition of the Top 50 has subtly changed – reflecting the growing value bias of the UK's top companies. According to Grant Thornton the index currently shows: 'a greater balance between "large caps" – as defined as those within the FTSE 100 and FTSE 250 – and the remainder of the market. On an average price to cash flow per share rating, the 2007/8 Top 50 shows a multiple of 7.4 × (12.7 × for the whole market) compared with 11.1 × in 2006 and 8.9 × in 2005.'[15]

Overall the leading cash generative sector within the Top 50 this year (six companies) proved to be support services followed by oil and gas and software and computer services (five companies each). The survey also identifies that Britain's (currently) beleaguered builders may represent good value: 'While this may appear counter intuitive, as share prices in this area have collapsed ahead of an expected housing slowdown, it is generally accepted that these companies tend to generate more cash into a downturn, as land is sold and costs reduced, than through more buoyant periods when house builders are typically highly acquisitive. According to commentators, there is unlikely to be a better test of this theory than the expected market in 2008.'[16]

table 2.5   The Top Hidden Gems from 2008

HGI rank	Company	Sector	Market Cap	HGI
1	Creston	Media marketing	33	40.9
2	Clarkson	Shipping and industrial services	165	20.5
3	Northgate	Industrial transportation	487	19.3
4	Hunting	Oil services	850	14.2
5	Expro	Oil services	1002	12.7
6	Charter	Industrial engineering	1108	12.1
7	Partygaming	Online betting	1090	12
8	Abbot Group	Oil services	884	10.5

Source: Grant Thornton, www.grant-thornton.co.uk

---

[15] Ibid.
[16] Ibid.

Measuring cashflow is also at the heart of the stock picking approach used by fund managers Gary West and James Inglis-Jones at the Liontrust First Income Fund. According to the managers this fund's objectives are:

- to return more than the stock market over a five-year period
- to yield more than index-linked gilts
- to provide an income stream that will grow faster than inflation over a five-year period

How do the managers go about finding these companies? Liontrust's philosophy is not to trust those analysts' estimates fixated on models and future earnings growth – 'People often deal with information emotionally and irrationally, making their forecasts unreliable'[17] according to West and Inglis Jones, but to focus instead on the cash. Their process is to focus 'on the profit forecasts made by company managers'. This idea is built into the following structure:

1   *Strong company cash flows (after investment spending) are a good indicator of strong growth in future reported profits.*

2   *Conversely, weak cash flows often predict a collapse in reported profits. We buy companies generating strong cash flows and sell those with weak cash flows.*

3   *Focusing on the cash flows of companies with high dividend yields enables us to identify companies that can surprise investors with their profits, without ourselves falling into the trap of trying to forecast to achieve this aim.*

4   *We create a list of high yielding companies with strong cash flows which we believe are likely to beat investors' low profit expectations. We then use our own judgement to select the best investments for portfolios.*

5   *The aim is to buy high yielding companies with good cash flows which are likely to beat investors' low profit expectations. To help us achieve this, two cash flow measures are used: cash flow relative to operating assets and cash flow relative to enterprise value. Companies that score well on this measure (high cash flows relative to their market value) are priced cheaply because investors have low expectations for profits growth. High relative cash flows on this measure suggest that company managers have set cautious forecasts that can be realistically beaten.*

---

[17] http://www.liontrust.co.uk/pdf/The%20Cashflow%20Solution%20-%20Equity%20Income%20portfolios%20(precis).pdf

6 *We use cash flow analysis to find high yielding companies that will surprise investors positively. Taking all stocks in the UK with a market capitalisation of more than £250 million, we compare companies' dividend yields with reference to the yields available on long-dated and index-linked gilts. These comparisons help us decide whether investors' profit expectations for a company are either very low, average or high. We look for:*

▪ *Stocks with yields at least 2% higher than long-dated gilts*

▪ *Stocks with yields at least 2% higher than long-dated index-linked gilts*

▪ *Stocks with yields higher than long dated index-linked gilts.*[18]

Put these ideas into one strategy and you can begin to understand the manager's central claim – in a paper explaining their methodology they note: 'by combining our cash flow ratios we generate a list of stocks cheaper than the market (as measured by cash flow yield) with cash returns on operating assets which are better than the market'.[19]

Figure 2.6 shows the Liontrust portfolio results versus the market.

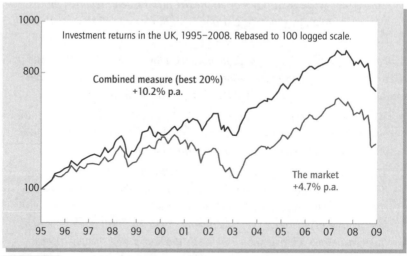

figure 2.6 Combined cashflow measure and market return for Liontrust versus the market

---

[18] Ibid.
[19] Ibid.

Fundamental measures – the good, fair and worrying!

At the very end of this book you'll find an appendix with the key measures explained in much greater detail – we look at everything from the obvious measures such as the PE ratio through to detailed analysis such as current ratio. Most investors tend to focus on the headline numbers built around the earnings per share and dividend per share numbers – worked through into a price to earnings ratio and dividend yield respectively – but we'd suggest that many other measures are equally useful. In Table 2.6 we've broken out some of the key measures that we'll encounter in this book as we discuss various strategies – alongside some basic yardsticks of what constitutes fair value… or not! Bear in mind that these measures change hugely over time and our yardsticks are just that, rough guides to what's good or indifferent.

table 2.6　Some key measures

Measure	Almost too good to be true	Excellent value	Good value	Average over a long period of time	Poor value	Worrying and requires investigation
PE ratio	Under 5	5–10	10–15	15	20 or more	40 or more
PEG	Under 0.3	0.3–1	1–1.5	1.5	2 or more	No PEG
Dividend yield	More than 10%	5–8%	5%	3–5%	2% or less	Under 1%
Dividend cover	Not relevant	5 or more	2 or more	Between 1.5 and 1	Under 1	Under 0.5
ROCE	Above 100%	Above 50%	20–50%	10–20%	5%	Under 5%
PTBV	Under 0.25	0.25–1	1–2	2–5	5–10	10 or more
PSR	Under 0.1	0.1 to 1	1–3	3–5	Above 10	Above 50
RS	Above 100%	50–100%	10–50%	Between −10% and +10%	Under −10%	Under −50%
EPS growth per annum	100% or more	Above 30%	Above 20%	Between 5 and 10%	Under 5%	Under 0%

3

The theory: efficient and not so efficient markets

There is an old joke, widely told among economists, about an economist strolling down the street with a companion when they come upon a $100 bill lying on the ground. As the companion reaches down to pick it up, the economist says 'Don't bother – if it were a real $100 bill, someone would have already picked it up'. Andrew Lo[1]

The headwinds

Back in the autumn of 2006 a small group of ordinary people gathered together in a room at the less glamorous northern edge of the City of London near Shoreditch.

The reason for this gathering was simple – they'd been invited to form a focus group for a major stockbroker who wanted to understand why and how people invest in equities. The brokers had a clear interest in encouraging activity of course – obviously stockbrokers make money from buying and selling – but they also wanted to understand the process of analysis and reflection that led up to trading activity

Thankfully the discussion took on a more philosophical bent – the 12 men and women discussed their attitudes towards the investing process and what they hoped to get out of investing in shares. From the swirl of mediated discussion four very strong and well articulated views started to emerge.

---

[1] In Blume, L. and Darlauf, S. (2007) *The New Palgrave: A Dictionary of Economics*, Palgrave Macmillan.

The first two views were perhaps the most surprising – the first could be summarised in the statement that equities were actually a good idea over the very long term but only as a runner up to houses. That houses were and remain a popular investment – not just a place to live – is perhaps not surprising but this group seemed to be equally well aware of the potential for shares to deliver substantial returns over the long term.

The second view was perhaps the most surprising. As one woman suggested: 'investing is really risky. I am not sure I fancy my chances working out what works against all those City slickers. I'd rather keep it simple and "buy the market".' This last phrase – buy the market – genuinely astounded this author but the researchers working for the stockbroker assured us that they'd heard the term used before. Investors understood the risks, knew that they were up against the big boys – the institutions – and didn't fancy their chances and so wanted to buy anything that gave them access to that big, long-term growth trend in shares. If that meant buying something that tracked the constituents of say the FTSE 100, so be it!

A few heads nodded at the woman's statement but a young man at the opposite end of the room immediately jumped into the debate with a rival view, namely that you could beat the markets and find those elusive 'ten-baggers' – stocks that would shoot up by more than ten fold! This fearless soul completely disagreed with the earlier view that simply shadowing the market was a good idea. To him the extra risk of tracking down shooting stars was absolutely worth the bother!

The last articulated view was equally illuminating. An older member of the focus group said he'd bought a diversified FTSE 100 unit trust but he liked now to concentrate his efforts on the individual shares of big blue chips – massive companies with conservative reputations – that paid a generous dividend, companies rather like SSE from the previous chapter. For him the dividend and stability was all that mattered!

This huge range of well articulated views perfectly summed up the outlines of a vibrant debate amongst both investment professionals and academics. On one side of the debate sit those who maintain that the odds are stacked against the private investor and that trying to outwit the greatest minds of the markets is pointless and not necessarily because those great minds get it right all the time! In fact, as we'll see there's plenty of evidence to suggest that those well paid professional stock pickers are actually, collectively, fairly dreadful at the job. The real insight from our 'buy the market' investor was that you could expend a lot of effort trying to beat the market but it was simpler, all things considered, just to work out what the market likes and then buy that using an index tracking fund.

Our tenbagger and dividend fiend took a different view – they believed that by careful examination of market statistics investors could do better by focusing on certain measures or characteristics. Academics have a slightly annoying term for these characteristics – anomalies. As we'll discover in this chapter, by and large most economists think our 'buy the market' woman is right and that tactics to pick particular stocks with certain characteristics is just a deviation from the overall trend and thus an anomaly at best and pointless at worst.

In essence these academics maintain that markets are incredibly efficient and that precisely because they are so huge and so liquid it's incredibly difficult to beat the trend. Eventually all shares revert in some sense to the mean: all phenomena eventually conform to the average. Some academics even maintain that over long periods of time share price behaviour is essentially random and thus trying to second guess the share price is totally pointless!

It's important to understand this prevailing orthodoxy because the truth of the matter is that the academics are largely right. As we'll discover in this chapter (in our discussion on professional fund managers), most highly paid professionals don't beat the market. By and large most stock pickers who try to buck the market get it wrong and fail – this is the headwind against which most smart stock picking investors have to contend with. As we'll see, markets are largely, or mostly, efficient.

But simply declaring that markets are mostly efficient doesn't mean that they're *always* efficient. This chapter explores the work of a fairly wide range of critics of the orthodoxy amongst academics who suggest that markets do frequently get the share price wrong and that careful use of certain strategies can produce above average returns, i.e. that those anomalies that focus on certain characteristics can persist and can be productive over extended periods of time. This academic justification for many of the strategies explored later in this book needs though to be put in context. As we'll see in the last section of this chapter, strategies to beat the market need to be carefully applied and you need to be aware of some wider behavioural risks that can destroy returns.

The oracle

In 2007, legendary US investment commentator and fund manager John Bogle published a classic text called *The Little Book of Commonsense Investing: The Only Way to Guarantee Your Fair Share of Stock Market Returns*. This is essential reading for any investor and a superb introduction to the thoughts of Saint Jack, as he's sometimes called by his army of admirers (those admirers are also nicknamed Bogle Heads).

With the possible exception of perhaps Warren Buffett, no-one else in the USA has done more to break down the myths – and lies – surrounding the process of investing. Bogle has dedicated his life to two simple ideas: making investing simple to understand and lowering costs for the investor. In his view, the financial services industry has deliberately built a vast global empire out of selling myths and outright lies to gullible investors and then charging them an extortionate amount of money for the consequent puny returns. To counter this 'evil' John Bogle has adopted two strategies – the first and perhaps most important is to build a mutual investment company (Vanguard) that boasts low costs and simple products hard wired into its very DNA. Vanguard is now one of the biggest mutual funds companies in the USA, in part because it has developed simple, cheap products that are rightly popular. John Bogle has also focused his attention on taking the sometimes complex research conclusions of academics and then translating them into easy to understand and pithy observations, thus his *Little Book*.

In *Little Book* John Bogle rips apart the investment industry with a series of simple principles, summarised below.[2]

1   Beware of market forecasts, even by experts – 'Strategists aren't always wrong. But they have been consistent, betting year after year that the market will rise, usually by about 10%. Thus, they got it about right in 2004, 2006 and 2007, but also totally missed the market declines in 2000, 2001 and 2002, and vastly underestimated the resurgence in 2003. Ignore the forecasts of inevitably bullish strategists. Bearish strategists on Wall Street's payroll don't survive for long.'

2   Never under-rate the importance of asset allocation – 'Investing is not about owning only common stocks. Nor are historical stock returns a

---

[2] Reproduced in http://online.wsj.com/article/SB123137479520962869.html, 'Six Lessons for Investors: be diversified and don't assume past performance will continue', by John C. Bogle.

sound guide to future returns. Virtually all investors should keep some "dry powder" in their portfolios in the form of high-grade short- and intermediate-term bonds. Consider not only the probabilities of future returns on stocks, but the consequences if you are wrong.'

3   Mutual funds with superior performance records often falter – 'Chasing past performance is all too often a loser's game. Managers of funds seeking market-beating returns should make it clear to investors that they must be prepared to trail the market – perhaps substantially – in at least one year of every three.'

4   Owning the market remains the strategy of choice – 'As a group, investors are by definition indexers. (That is, they own the entire market.) So indexing wins, not because markets are efficient (sometimes they are, sometimes they are not), but because its all-in annual costs amount to as little as 0.1% to 0.2%. In sum, active management strategies as a group lose because they are expensive. Passive indexing strategies win because they are cheap.'

5   Look before you leap into alternative asset classes – 'Always keep in mind: when the investment grass looks greener on the other side of the fence, look twice before you leap.'

6   Beware of financial innovation – 'Why? Because most of it is designed to enrich the innovators, not investors. Just think of the multiple layers of fees to the salespersons, servicers, banks, underwriters and brokers selling mortgage-backed debt obligations. Our financial system is driven by a giant marketing machine in which the interests of sellers directly conflict with the interests of buyers. The sellers, having (as ever) the information advantage, nearly always win.'

We'll return to some of these themes a little later in this chapter, but perhaps the most incendiary section in his book is where Bogle takes on the work of another legendary American investor, a certain Ben Graham (subject of Chapter 5 on value investing).

Bogle, is like Warren Buffett a great admirer of this legendary Wall Street investor and author of *The Intelligent Investor* (2003) but Bogle's journey has taken him a long way from Graham's early analysis. Where Graham argued for careful stock selection, Bogle disagrees and suggests simply buying the market; when Graham argues for a contrarian strategy, Bogle points to the evidence that markets are efficient by and large.

But Bogle goes further – he maintains that in fact Graham would have taken the same journey if he were still alive today! To prove his point Bogle quotes Graham himself: 'I am no longer an advocate of elaborate techniques of security analysis in order to find superior value opportunities. This was a rewarding activity, say, 40 years ago, but the situation has changed a great deal since then.' Bogle reckons that Graham would probably have agreed with his own view of modern investing: 'In the long run ... the various styles of investing [such as Graham's value investing] ... have a powerful tendency to revert to the stock market mean... Betting on styles is indeed a "strange game" (and ultimately a loser's game)... So how about staying out of the game, and simply relying on an index fund? Yes!' Bogle goes on to declare that 'nothing that has happened in the last decade... persuades me to change a single one of those six rules of intelligent investing'. Those six rules are as follows: 'Invest you *must*. Time is your friend. Impulse is your enemy. Basic arithmetic works. Stick to simplicity. Stay the course.'

Bogle is deploying powerful arguments in his books and his various well-publicised polemics. The first is that costs really matter and that they destroy long-term returns, and secondly that active stock picking based on accepted strategies like value investing (as developed by Ben Graham) contributes extra costs and helps to reduce those long-term returns. In Bogle's view the best solution is to ignore stock picking and buy an index tracking fund, preferably one from Vanguard! (It's worth noting that Vanguard does actually run funds that involve stock picking, very successfully in many cases, but even these are offered to clients at very low cost.)

The decline and fall of the active fund manager

Bogle believes that the best evidence against any form of stock picking or attempting to beat the market using strategies, sits with the record of professional fund managers – if highly paid fund managers can't beat the market systematically what hope is there for private investors? According to Bogle the academic evidence is over-whelming – most fund managers fail. And in this Bogle is resting his argument on a mountain of studies and research reports.

In fact academic economists have been scrutinising the performance of active fund managers for decades now with the first crucial paper produced by Michael Jensen dating back to 1968.[3]

[3] Jensen, M. (1968) 'The performance of Mutual Funds in the Period 1945–1964', *Journal of Finance*, Vol. 23, May.

Although some controversy still rumbles on, the majority of studies now conclude that actively managed funds, on average, under-perform their passively managed counterparts. Study after study has revealed a huge discrepancy between actively and passively (i.e. index tracking) managed funds. This huge weight of evidence was nicely summed up by Rex Sinquefield, boss of Dimensional fund management, an index tracking investment firm. 'Researchers uncovered considerable evidence that past prices were of little benefit in forecasting future prices in ways that would earn excess profits; that fundamental data was too quickly reflected in prices to allow such data to be used for beat-the-market purposes; and, most importantly for us, that professional money managers could simply not outperform markets in any meaningful sense.'

Sinquefield's words summarise well some of the key observations from the research world: that the past isn't much use in forecasting the future, that by and large prices set by the market are sensible and 'efficient', and that it's devilishly difficult for money managers to use that past data to find 'bargains' and make any extra return. If he'd have made reference to Michael Jensen's paper he might also have noted when managers do out perform the market, they largely do so by taking on extra risk.

Sinquefield's analysis is based on a long list of academic studies that suggest that hiring a fund manager with a clever stock selection strategy is not always the right thing to do. Some of these studies are detailed below:

- Gruber in 1996[4] for example found that over the period 1985–1994 the average mutual fund under-performed the passive market index by about 65 basis points per year.

- Carhart in 1997[5] confirmed that net returns are negatively correlated with expense levels, i.e. that the more actively managed a fund, the higher the expenses and the lower the returns. Carhart additionally discovered that the more actively a mutual fund manager trades, the lower the fund's net return to investors. The University of Chicago professor also studied all the mutual funds that existed anytime between 1961 and 1993, and found that on average, actively managed funds under-performed their index by 1.80% per year.

---

[4] Gruber, M.J. (1996) 'Another puzzle: the growth in actively managed mutual funds', *Journal of Finance*, Vol. 51, pp. 783–810.

[5] Carhart, M.M. (1997) 'On persistence in mutual fund performance', *Journal of Finance*, Vol. 52, Issue 1, pp. 52, 57–82.

▨ In yet another study of equity mutual funds, Elton *et al.*[6] examined all funds that existed over the period 1965–84 – a total of 143 funds in all. These funds were then compared to a set of index funds – big stocks, small stocks and fixed income – that most closely corresponded to the actual investment choices made by the mutual funds. The result: on average those actively managed funds under-performed the index funds by a whopping 159 basis points a year. Not a single fund generated positive performance that was statistically significant.

▨ It's also worth noting the first major study of bond market performance, by Blake *et al.*[7] in which they examined 361 bond funds starting in 1977, comparing various active bond fund management strategies with a simple 'buy the index' idea. The authors found that active funds, on average, under-performed the index tracking strategies by 85 basis points a year.

Carhart at Chicago returned to the fray with what's regarded as the definitive study[8] which studied a total of 1892 funds that existed any time between 1961 and 1993. After adjusting for the common factors in returns, an equal-weighted portfolio of the funds under-performed by 1.8% per year. This research has even found support in journalistic circles – an article in the *Wall Street Journal* reported that the average mutual fund under-performed its risk-adjusted benchmark by 140 basis points (1.4%) a year.[9]

For many years research focused on the work of American academics but in the 1990s British economists started examining the subject. One of the first was Dr Jonathan Fletcher in what was a fairly seminal paper called 'An Examination of UK Unit Trust Performance within the Arbitrage Pricing Theory Framework'.[10]

Dr Fletcher's paper looked at a sample of 101 British unit trusts within something called the arbitrage pricing theory framework and then looked at performance data. His conclusion was that: 'there appears to be little

---

[6] Elton, E., Gruber, M., Das, S. and Hlavka, M. (1993) *Efficiency with costly information: a reinterpretation of evidence from managed portfolios*, Society for Financial Studies.

[7] Elton, E., Gruber, M. and Blake, C. (1995) 'Fundamental Economic Variables, Expected Returns, and Bond Fund Performance', *Journal of Finance*, 50.

[8] See note 5.

[9] Jonathan Clements (1999) 'Stock Funds Just Don't Measure Up', The *Wall Street Journal*, 5 October.

[10] Fletcher, J. (1997) 'An Examination of UK Unit Trust Performance within the Arbitrage Pricing Theory Framework', *Review of Quantative Finance and Accounting*.

relationship between performance and the investment objective, size and expenses of the trusts. Also portfolio strategies using past trust performance to rank the trusts fail to generate significant abnormal returns relative to two different benchmark portfolios'.[11]

The bottom line – active fund management didn't seem to work

More research at the start of the 21st century continued to examine statistics: Elton *et al.* for instance published a paper in 1993 that looked at the efficiency of mutual fund performance over the period 1965–84. Their conclusion: 'we find that mutual funds do not earn returns that justify their information acquisition costs'.[12]

Another much more recent paper by Cuthbertson *et al.* looked at another key aspect of active fund management – whether active fund managers consistently out perform or do they eventually revert to mean, while still charging their relatively higher fees? Their conclusion is that: 'only around 2% of all funds truly outperform their benchmarks... For different investment styles, this pattern of very few genuine winner funds is repeated for all companies, small companies and equity income funds... the majority (around 75–85%) of UK mutual funds neither underperform nor outperform their benchmarks'.[13]

Don't trust the manager

The message from this long list of studies (and there are many, many more) seems to be clear: the 'beat-the-market' effort of professional fund managers achieves the exact opposite, namely it increases risk, increases cost and reduces returns. In almost any leading developed world asset class, the only consistently superior performer is the market itself.

As one analyst summed it up: 'Almost no one would wager millions of dollars on the flip of a coin, no matter how fair the flip. Similarly, it does not make sense to wager large sums of money on an active manager, whose performance is erratic at best, when an index fund closely tracks the per-

---

[11] Ibid.

[12] Elton, E.J. *et al.* (1993) 'Efficiency with Costly Information: A Reinterpretation of Evidence from 'Managed Portfolios', *Review of Financial Studies*.

[13] Cuthbertson, L., Nitzsche, D. and O'Sullivan, N. (2008) 'False Discoveries: Winners and Losers in Mutual Fund Performance', *European Financial Management*.

formance target. For any year, the return for an equity fund can only be predicted to be within the S&P 500 return ±7.5%, approximately equal to the standard deviation of S&P 500 returns. Even though drift is random, the volatility of active manager drift is almost half as large as the volatility of the stock market.[14]

It's also worth noting one last set of observations – that even the best active fund managers aren't consistent, i.e. they have good years but also lots of bad years which can destroy your wealth. American fund management group Vanguard, for example, looked to see if excellent past performance was predictive of great, or even above-average, future performance. Their research[15] showed that even if one's strategy was to buy the top 20 equity funds from the prior year, there is almost no chance they will be in the top 20 again, and about a 40% chance that they'll be worse than the average fund in the subsequent year.

Shares are random...

This huge weight of academic research – and Bogle's incessant popularising of its conclusions – confronts smart stock pickers with a huge issue. If most professional fund managers fail most of the time, what does this tell us about modern stockmarkets? The answer according to both the academics and Bogle is that markets are largely efficient and that second guessing them using specific strategies is a mug's game. And underlying this efficiency is an even more powerful observation: that share prices are largely random. The first attempt to sketch an outline of what became known as the random walk of share prices came from a French mathematician Louis Bachelier who penned a dissertation called 'The Theory of Speculation' in 1900.[16]

Bachelier deserves a book all by himself – he's one of those classic mathematicians whose work was initially rejected by the mainstream but was eventually revealed to be decades ahead of his time. His view is summed up in one key observation, namely that 'There is no useful information contained in historical price movements of securities'. However, his more pungent observation that 'The mathematical expectation of the speculator

---

[14] Booth, D. (2001) 'Index and Enhanced Index Funds', www.dfaus.com
[15] https://institutional.vanguard.com/VGApp/iip/site/institutional/researchandcomm
[16] Bachelier, L. (2006) *Louis Bachelier's Theory of Speculation: The Origins of Modern Finance*, Princeton University Press.

is zero' is possibly more relevant to modern investors endlessly chasing elusive profits from hot tips. Just in case the lay reader was in any doubt as to Bachelier's view of speculators, the opening paragraph of his 1900 dissertation nails its colours firmly to the mast stating that 'past, present and even discounted future events are reflected in market price, but often show no apparent relation to price changes'.[17]

In these simple words Bachelier had outlined the foundation stone of much of modern investment economics – in his view share prices change unpredictably based on the result of unexpected information appearing in the market. Many observers have taken this simple idea and suggested that his theory requires that share price changes move randomly for no rational reason. Bachelier, by contrast, maintained that it's not the changes in share prices that are random, but the news that influences that pricing that is random. In essence, news is unpredictable – that is its definition after all, it's new(s) – and so investors behave rationally by reacting to this unpredictable news. The unpredictable prompts the eminently predictable!

Bachelier's work lay largely dormant and unnoticed for many decades until the work of another theoretician came to prominence, that of Maurice Kendall, one of those wonderfully talented statisticians that Britain seems to excel at producing. A genuine polymath – much of his most influential work derives from his spell as head of the World Fertility Survey – Kendall turned his attentions in 1953 to the long-term distribution of returns from shares as well as the price of cotton and wheat, across 19 different indices or markets. Elroy Dimson and Massoud Mussavian in their review of the rise of the efficient markets hypothesis – see below – note that Kendall and his team of researchers were by now using relatively advanced computer processing technology to study long series of price returns. Kendall's assumption was that this new technology could 'analyse an economic time series by extracting from it a long-term movement, or trend, for separate study and then scrutinising the residual portion for short-term oscillatory movements and random fluctuations'.[18] According to Dimson and Mussavian when 'Kendall examined 22 UK stock and commodity price series, however, the results surprised him. Looking at what statisticians call serial correlations – repeated analysis of the relationships between a series of outcomes – Kendall concluded that "this series looks like a wandering one,

---

[17] Ibid.

[18] Dimson, E. and Mussavian, M. (1988) 'A brief history of market efficiency' *European Financial Management*, Vol. 4, No. 1, March, pp. 91–193.

almost as if once a week the Demon of Chance drew a random number from a symmetrical population of fixed dispersion and added it to the current price to determine the next week's price... *The data behave almost like wandering series".'*[19]

In 1959 an American astrophysicist M.F. Maury Osborne drew upon Kendall's observations and outlined a hypothesis that share prices follow a geometric Brownian motion. (It's also worth noting that Osborne worked in detail on the study of risk and extremely unlikely events and was the first to identify what later became known as fat tail risks or events, i.e. big financial crashes that were supposed to be very unlikely but in reality prove to be depressingly common and frequent.) This formed the basis of the random walk theory.

One key insight from the random walk theory had made its mark: notably that because price movements will not follow any pattern or trend, you can't use past price movements to predict future price movements. This analysis suggests that you shouldn't bother to try and second guess the market because you'll fail as randomness and reversion to mean will be your undoing! The logic of the random walk idea also suggests that if the flow of information is 'unimpeded', i.e. that news channels do their job unhindered, and information is immediately reflected in stock prices, then tomorrow's price change will reflect only tomorrow's news and will be independent of the price changes today.

In 1973 in his seminal book *A Random Walk Down Wall Street* (revised edn, 2008, W.W. Norton & Co) Barton Malkiel famously summed up the idea that 'experts' cannot add any value to this random walk by suggesting that 'a blindfolded chimpanzee throwing darts at the *Wall Street Journal* could select a portfolio that would do as well as the experts'. From these building blocks – suggesting that returns from shares are fundamentally random – all that was needed was a causal theory to explain the motives behind participants in this random market – enter the efficient markets hypothesis.

Many of the first building blocks of this unifying theory came via a diehard fan of Bachelier's work, noted US economist Paul Samuelson. In his 1965 paper, Samuelson began with the observation that 'in competitive markets there is a buyer for every seller. If one could be sure that a price would rise, it would have already risen'.[20] According to Dimson and Mussavian's re-

[19] Ibid.

[20] Samuelson, P. (1965) 'Proof that Properly Anticipated Prices Fluctuate Randomly', *Industrial Management Review*, Vol. 6, No. 2, Spring.

counting, Samuelson asserted that 'arguments like this are used to deduce that competitive prices must display price changes... that perform a random walk with no predictable bias'.[21] Samuelson explains that 'we would expect people in the market place, in pursuit of avid and intelligent self-interest, to take account of those elements of future events that in a probability sense may be discerned to be casting their shadows before them'.[22]

Samuelson's work started to lay out the conceptual building blocks of this new hypothesis of efficient markets. Although the maths that sits behind this theory is as elegant as it is sometimes impenetrable to the untrained eye, the efficient markets hypothesis is not, in truth, a complicated concept to understand. At the core of the theory sits one key assertion – that an 'efficient market is one that quickly adjusts prices to reflect all available public information about the future prospects of an investment', a familiar idea from the random walk thesis. When it comes to setting a price for a stock or a bond potential buyers and sellers use the best information available to them. Add up all these individual approximations and estimations and you have the market price of a stock which is equivalent to the market's estimation of the 'fair' price.

Although no one academic completely developed the elegant framework that sits behind the efficient markets hypothesis (EMH) one economist – a certain Eugene Fama – stands head and shoulders above the rest.

In his relatively short work he outlines the key attributes of the EMH including the idea that 'the primary role of the capital market is allocation of the economy's capital stock'.[23]

In addition:

■ The market requires accurate signals to correctly allocate scarce resources, or as Burton Malkiel puts it in a later paper, 'when information arises, the news spreads very quickly and is incorporated into the prices of securities without delay. Thus, neither technical

---

[21] Ibid.

[22] Ibid.

[23] Fama, E. 'Efficient capital markets: a review of theory and empirical work'. (1970) *The Journal of Finance*, Vol. 25, No. 2, Papers and Proceedings of the Twenty-Eighth Annual Meeting of the American Finance Association New York, N.Y., 28–30 December, 1969, pp. 383–417. http://links.jstor.org/sici?sici=0022-1082%28197005%2925%3A2%3C383%3AECMARO%3E2.0.CO%3B2-V.

analysis, which is the study of past stock prices in an attempt to predict future prices, nor even fundamental analysis, which is the analysis of financial information such as company earnings, asset values, etc., to help investors select "undervalued" stocks, would enable an investor to achieve returns greater than those that could be obtained by holding a randomly selected portfolio of individual stocks with comparable risk'.[24]

- The outcome of this allocative framework is a market in which prices always fully reflect the available information, i.e. an efficient market.

- An 'efficient' market is thus defined as a market where there are large numbers of rational, profit-maximisers, actively competing with each other and trying to predict the future market values of individual securities, and where important current information is almost freely available to all participants.

- In an efficient market at any point in time the actual price of a security will be a good estimate of its intrinsic value.

- If a market is efficient, no information or analysis can be expected to result in out-performance of an appropriate index or benchmark.

Proof for this framework is now the subject of academic orthodoxy but the early pioneers focused on two specific examples. The first was called 'event studies' – in essence how the market reacted to specific news-based events in the subsequent pricing of shares. Dimson and Mussavian in their review of this new orthodoxy reveal Fama and his team's conclusion that 'the market appears to anticipate the information, and most of the price adjustment is complete before the event is revealed to the market. When news is released, the remaining price adjustment takes place rapidly and accurately'.[25] A study by Fama *et al.* in particular, demonstrates that prices reflect not only direct estimates of prospective performance by the sample companies, but also information that requires more subtle interpretation.'[26]

These studies nailed the first leg of the efficient markets hypothesis – what later became known as the weak efficient market. Fama and his colleagues now moved on to a tougher nut – the question of whether or not insiders

---

[24] Malkiel, B. (2003) 'The Efficient Market Hypothesis and its critics', *Journal of Economic Perspectives.*

[25] See note 18.

[26] Fama, E., Fisher, L., Jensen, M. and Roll, R. (1969) 'The Adjustment of Stock Prices to New Information', *International Economic Review*, 10, pp. 1–21.

trading on their exclusive knowledge (their inside track) would be able to make extra returns. If Fama could prove that even this failed to produce extra profits consistently over time, then he could prove what became known as a strong form of efficient markets. This particular proof was not to come from Fama though. Researchers around the world had been studying the returns of fund managers whose job it was to capture this inside track and make a quick buck with their funds. Dimson and Mussavian reported on the key research from Michael Jensen in 1968 which analysed 115 fund managers' performance over the period 1955–64: 'On a risk-adjusted basis, he [Jensen] finds that any advantage that the portfolio managers might have is consumed by fees and expenses... Even if investment management fees and loads are added back to performance measures, and returns are measured gross of management expenses (i.e. assuming research and other expenses were obtained free), Jensen concludes that 'on average the funds apparently were not quite successful enough in their trading activities to recoup even their brokerage expenses.'[27]

With this research Fama had found his proof for not only a weak form of market efficiency but a strong one. A number of different forms of efficient markets were thus presented to a sceptical world:

- ▨ A **'Weak'** efficient market claims that all past market prices and data are fully reflected in securities prices. The bottom line – don't bother trying to use clever systems to predict price movements as they'll fail!

- ▨ A **'semistrong'** market argues that all publicly available information is fully reflected in the share price. This attacks the arguments of value investors by suggesting that fundamental analysis is misguided, i.e. that a share has an intrinsic value based on, say, its assets' securities prices.

- ▨ The **'strong'** form asserts that all information is fully reflected in a share's price. In other words, even insider information is of no use.

In essence, Fama's concept of the EMH suggests that because stockmarkets are vibrant, hugely liquid spaces, flooded with tens of thousands of intelligent, well-paid, and well-educated investors seeking to make a return on the market by looking for a system or trying to find cheap shares, information becomes dispersed ever more quickly and efficiently and the pricing that results becomes ever more accurate and thus efficient.

---

[27] Jensen, M. (1968) 'The Performance of Mutual Funds in the Period 1945–1964', *Journal of Finance*, 23, pp. 389–416.

The critics

Many varied lines of attack against the efficient markets hypothesis have emerged over the past few decades, some emanating from within the EMH school, others from outside schools based around classic value investing or behavioural economics influenced by modern cognitive pyschology. Some economists, mathematicians and market practitioners do not believe that man-made markets are inherently efficient, especially when there are good reasons for that inefficiency, including the slow diffusion of information, the undue power of some market participants (e.g. financial institutions) and the existence of apparently sophisticated professional investors.

One of the earliest attacks on the EMH looked at the way that markets react to *surprising news* – this is perhaps the most visible flaw in the EMH called *under-reaction to new information* by its researchers. For example, news events such as surprise interest rate changes from central banks are not instantaneously taken account of in stock prices, but rather cause sustained movement of prices over periods ranging from hours to months. Work by Lo and MacKinlay[28] for instance finds that this phenomenon is clearly observable, leading them to reject the random walk thesis. Even Malkiel himself – a great defender of the EMH in public debates – accepts that 'there does seem to be some momentum in short-run stock prices'.[29] Malkiel also points to research from Lo *et al.*[30] who also find, through the use of sophisticated statistical techniques that can recognise patterns, that some of the stock-price signals used by 'technical analysts' such as 'head and shoulders' formations and 'double bottoms', may actually have some modest predictive power, i.e. that they can predict prices in the short term.

You don't have to use technical analysis to understand the overall outline of this 'inefficient' phenomena – investors see a share price rising and are drawn into the market in a kind of 'bandwagon effect'. Robert Shiller in 2000 also describes the late 1990s stock market boom (or should we say bubble) as the result of psychological contagion leading to irrational exu-

---

[28] Lo, A.W. and MacKinlay, A.C. (1999) *A Non-Random Walk Down Wall Street*, Princeton University Press.
[29] Cited in Malkiel, B.G. (2003) *The Efficient Market Hypothesis and Its Critics*, Princeton University CEPS Working Paper No. 91, April.
[30] Lo, A.W., Mamaysky, H. and Wang, J. (2000) 'Foundations of Technical Analysis: Computational Algorithms, Statistical Inference, and Empirical Implementation', NBER Working Paper No. W7613, available at http://ssrn.com/abstract=228099

berance.[31] Behavioralist economists like James Montier at GMO offer their own explanation for this short-run momentum – a tendency for investors to under-react to new information and distinguish statistical significance from economic significance. EMH enthusiasts certainly seem to accept that this phenomena can exist but Eugene Fama found that under-reaction to information is about as common as over-reaction, and that 'post-event continuation of abnormal returns is as frequent as post-event reversals',[32] i.e. the inefficiency can work both ways and that it's not a workable trading strategy.

Another take on the behavioural oddities of investors comes courtesy of those who observe a discrepancy between EMH and actual, real markets at their most extreme, where irrational behaviour becomes the norm, i.e. as a bubble starts to burst. Towards the end of a crash, markets go into free fall as participants extricate themselves from positions regardless of the unusually good value that their positions represent. Perhaps the most biting attack comes via something called the Grossman-Stiglitz paradox – if markets really are that efficient and everyone knows, no-one will bother to beat the market and the market will begin to wither. One of the 2001 Nobel laureates in economics, Joseph Stiglitz, in collaboration with Sanford Grossman, claimed that the very idea of efficient markets is inherently paradoxical – if a market was 'informationally efficient' (i.e. all relevant information is reflected in market prices) then no single agent would have sufficient incentive to acquire the information on which prices are based. Markets may as well be run by computers in the background, banishing all human experts to day jobs serving hamburgers at McDonald's!

These discrepancies and theoretical attacks are dwarfed though by a more thorough criticism of supposedly efficient markets which suggests that *repeated patterns* do in fact occur in markets that are clearly not efficient and that this ever-present reality presents investors with numerous opportunities to make a profit. The simplest way of understanding this is to look at the small number of investors who have out performed the market over long periods of time, in a way which it is statistically unreasonable to attribute to good luck, including investment sages such as Warren Buffett, Peter Lynch, Bill Miller and Anthony Bolton, until recently the head of the

---

[31] Schiller, R.J. (2000) *Irrational Exuberance*, Princeton University Press, Princeton.
[32] Quoted in Malkiel, B.G. (2008) *A Random Walk Down Wall Street*, W.W. Norton & Co.

star fund at Fidelity. These investors' strategies are to a large extent based on identifying markets where prices do not accurately reflect the available information, in direct contradiction to the EMH which explicitly implies that no such opportunities exist.

Warren Buffett in particular has on several occasions stated that the EMH is not correct, maintaining that 'I'd be a bum on the street with a tin cup if the markets were always efficient' and that 'the professors who taught Efficient Market Theory said that someone throwing darts at the stock tables could select stock portfolio having prospects just as good as one selected by the brightest, most hard-working securities analyst. Observing correctly that the market was frequently efficient, they went on to conclude incorrectly that it was always efficient.'[33]

And Buffett's forthright views are shared by a surprisingly large number of analytically based observers. The British Chartered Financial Analysts association (the CFA is the pre-eminent financial analysts association) recently asked members whether they trusted in 'market efficiency'. According to the *Financial Times*[34] the CFA discovered that more than two-thirds of respondents no longer believed market prices reflect all available information. More startling, 77% of the group 'strongly' or 'very strongly' disagreed that investors behaved 'rationally' – in apparent defiance of the 'wisdom of crowds' idea that has driven investment theory.

Some rigorous academic evidence for these dissenting views comes from a big Vanguard study on the importance of asset allocation and diversification in fund management. The report mainly supports classic efficient market theories yet it did cite that 'a small percentage – 7% – of actively managed balanced funds have been able to consistently outperform their policy benchmarks'.[35] A grand total of 7% may not sound much but in a very diverse and well populated market full of thousands of fund managers, that's actually an awful lot of successful fund managers with a great long-term track record.

---

[33] Quoted in Arora, V., and Das, S. (2007) 'Day of the Week Effects in NSE Stock Returns: An Empirical Study', 14 October, available at http://ssrn.com.abstract=1113332
[34] 'EMH – The Dead Parrot of Finance', posted by Neil Hume on 18 June 2009. FT Alphaville – http://ftalphaville.ft.com/blog/2009/06/18/57881/emh-the-dead-parrot-of-finance/
[35] 'Sources of Portfolio Performance – the enduring importance of asset allocation', https://institutional.vanguard.com

Another academic study, this time by Cohen, Polk and Silli,[36] also looked at the success of fund managers who displayed a strong conviction-based approach to stock picking. These academics examined the 'best ideas' of American fund managers between 1991 and 2005. The researchers defined 'best ideas' as those with the biggest difference between their portfolio holdings and those of the benchmark index. By looking at the best 25% of these best ideas managers – those with the most conviction – the researchers discovered that the average return was more than 19% p.a. against a market return of 12% p.a. Either these fund managers are practising some mysterious form of market magic or the EMH has some pretty big, Emmental-sized holes in it!

More risk, greater returns

How do these star managers produce their super-sized returns? Many mainstream investment economists maintain that these star fund managers simply capitalise on a series of anomalies, or factors as they're sometimes called, which contribute extra risk, and extra rewards, for those sophisticated enough to know where to look. This nuanced view accepts that you can make extra returns but only by taking on more risk and that this extra risk is only found in certain places within the efficient market.

One of these additional forms of factor risk has been called the size risk by economists – this simply suggests that smaller companies grow faster than bigger companies and thus produce greater returns. Therefore any strategy that focuses on small caps or even tiny micro-caps (sub £10 million in market cap) will produce exceptional returns over certain periods of time. Even Burton Malkiel in his study[37] of the critiques of EMH points to data since 1926, that suggests that small-company stocks in the United States have produced rates of return over 1 percentage point larger than the returns from large stocks.

Eugene Fama and Kenneth French[38] have also broken with some of their peers and backed this concept. They examined data from 1963 to 1990 and

---

[36] Cohen, R.B., Polk, C.K. and Silli, B. (2010) 'Best Ideas', 15 March, available at http://ssrn.com/abstract=1364827

[37] Malkiel, B.G. (2005) 'Reflections on the Efficient Markets Hypothesis: 30 Years Later', *Financial Review*, Vol. 40, No. 1.

[38] Fama, E. and French, K.R. (1992) 'The Cross-Section of Expected Stock Returns', *Journal of Finance*, 47(2), pp. 427–65.

divided all shares into deciles according to their size as measured by total capitalisation. The results, according to the two professors, showed a clear tendency for the deciles made up of portfolios of smaller stocks to generate higher average monthly returns than deciles made up of larger stocks. It's worth quickly noting one key caveat made by Malkiel, an erstwhile supporter of Fama and French's work except when it comes to the scale effect – he notes that 'from the mid-1980s through the decade of the 1990s, there has been no gain from holding smaller stocks. Thus, a researcher who examined the ten-year performance of today's small companies would be measuring the performance of those companies that survived – not the ones that failed'.[39]

Another extra form of risk is sometimes called distress risk, although it's also known as the value premium. This is the risk of owning companies that the market perceives as being in some form of financial trouble. While none of us would choose to invest in a single company in potential big trouble – that distress could be defined as a poor balance sheet or falling earnings or even loss – indices of 'value' stocks have historically offered very high returns precisely because most investors follow the crowd and target what are called growth companies, i.e. companies growing fast and that sport expensive share prices relative to their profits. From this simple observation – noted time and time again by analysts for over 50 years – has emerged a whole new branch of the efficient markets school. This schism even has its own moniker – the fundamentalists – and a belief system that suggests that key measures of value (using key balance sheet and profit measures) are crucial to explaining why some shares do better than others.

The value effect

The hard work digging into the numbers that 'prove' the value premium comes from French and Fama. In 1997 for instance Kenneth French looked at data on the entire universe of US stocks for the period 1964–96. He found that small cap stocks that were also good 'value' produced returns of 20.88% compared to 'poor value' (growth) small caps which gave just 13.9%. Likewise, also for larger companies that were good 'value', they returned 15.8% compared to 11.7% for non-value peers. French and Fama's bottom line: take on extra risk and invest in both the size premium and the value effect and you can earn an additional 4–7% per year.

---

[39] See note 37.

Figure 3.1 presents an even more fascinating paradox – it establishes an inverse relationship between profitability and average share returns. What's the bottom line here? Value stocks and small cap stocks that are less profitable than faster growing equivalent stocks produce greater share price returns. In effect this analysis suggests that efficient markets don't behave in quite the way economists first imagined.

As fundamental indexing fund management firm Dimensional puts it: 'Everything we have learned about expected returns in the equity markets can be summarized in three dimensions. The first is that stocks are riskier than bonds and have greater expected returns. Relative performance among stocks is largely driven by the two other dimensions: small/large and value/growth. Many economists believe small cap and value stocks outperform because the market rationally discounts their prices to reflect underlying risk. The lower prices give investors greater upside as compensation for bearing this risk' (http://www.dfaus.com/philosophy/dimensions/).

Another variant on this idea of the value premium is to look at what some called cheapo stocks, otherwise known as bombed out shares – shares that

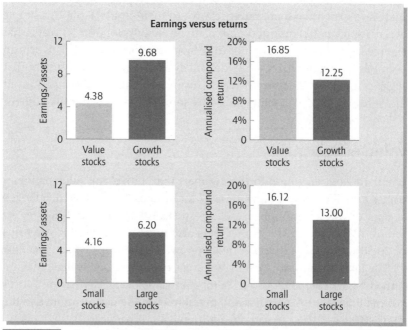

figure 3.1   Company size and financial strength (Annual data: 1964–2000)

Source: http://www.dfaus.com

have crashed in price. A strong school of contrarian thinking suggests that buying these unpopular stocks can produce huge long-term out perfor-mance for those willing to be patient, mainly because markets over-react in their punishment of certain shares and eventually the market is forced to admit the error of its ways by marking up prices. DeBondt and Thaler for example, argue that investors are subject to waves of optimism and pessi-mism which cause prices to crash below their fundamental value (the value of assets for instance) – give the market a few years and these prices revert to mean and reward the brave contrarian. Looking at very long-term hori-zons they found that 'stocks which have underperformed the most over a three- to five-year period average the highest market-adjusted returns over the subsequent period, and *vice versa*'.[40]

Dividend payouts also feature prominently in the arguments of value in-vestors who attack the efficient markets hypothesis on a number of fronts. Academics like Jeremy Siegel at Wharton Business School and James Mon-tier argue that buying high yielding stocks cheaply makes analytical sense. Montier has produced evidence that close to 80% of medium-term returns from holding shares can be attributed to the actual dividend payout and the market's expectation of future higher dividend payouts.

But Fluck *et al.* discovered in their analysis that investors 'who simply pur-chase a portfolio of individual stocks with the highest dividend yields in the market will not earn a particularly high rate of return'[41] – simply buy-ing the highest yielders doesn't always produce abnormal returns.

Yet another camp of fundaments-based investors look specifically to shares with low price-earnings multiples – that is where the stream of profits, ex-pressed as earnings, is at a low multiple to the share price. In many studies these low P/E shares appear to provide higher rates of return than those shares with high P/E ratios, i.e. where the share price is many more times greater than the low level of earnings. A number of academic papers have looked at this particular market inefficiency and their results tend to con-firm the view of the behaviouralist inclined economists who think that

---

[40] DeBondt, W. and Thaler, R. (1995) 'Financial Decision-Making in Markets and Firms: A Behavioral Perspective', in *Handbooks in Operations Research and Management Science: Finance*, edited by R.A. Jarrow, V. Maksimovic and W.T. Ziemba, Elsevier, pp. 385–410.

[41] Fluck, Z., Malkiel, B. and Quandt, R. (1993) 'The Predictability of Stock Returns and the Efficient Markets Hypothesis', Department of Economics, Princeton.

investors tend to be over-confident of their ability to project high earnings growth and thus overpay for 'growth' stocks. Similar results have been shown for price/cashflow multiples, where cashflow is defined as earnings plus depreciation and amortisation.

This constant hum of research and debate has given shape to a whole new way of building indices – fundamentally weighted index funds which are mapped out in greater detail in Chapter 12 by Rob Davies and in conversation with Rob Arnott. Fama, now advisor to fund management firm Dimensional says, 'I agree that stock picking is gambling... I don't agree that the only legitimate indexing approach is holding the market portfolio.'[42] Fama clearly articulates a view that simply 'buying the market' is itself buying a rather arbitrary portfolio of stocks. 'It gives a heavy weighting to financially healthy stocks and a light weighting to distressed stocks' reckons Fama. 'Don't get me wrong: it's hard to fault a market index approach. But if there's more than one type of risk driving returns, it's possible for investors to use a wider range of strategies to gain greater expected returns – all within the bounds of indexing'.[43]

The efficient markets purists' counterattack

I am convinced that Benjamin Graham (1965) was correct in suggesting that while the stock market in the short run may be a voting mechanism, in the long run it is a weighing mechanism. True value will win out in the end. And before the fact, there is no way in which investors can reliably exploit any anomalies or patterns that might exist. I am skeptical that any of the 'predictable patterns' that have been documented in the literature were ever sufficiently robust so as to have created profitable investment opportunities and after they have been discovered and publicized, they will certainly not allow investors to earn excess returns.[44]

Academics supportive of the efficient markets hypothesis in its purer forms don't dispute the weight of evidence that suggests some kind of value premium exists, especially if it's combined with the size risk. But as Burton Malkiel puts it, 'these findings do not necessarily imply inefficiency. They

---

[42] *The New Indexing*, by Eugene Fama Jr. July 2000, online at http://www.dfaus.com/library/articles/new_indexing/

[43] Ibid.

[44] Malkiel, B.F. (2003) *The Efficient Market Hypothesis and Its Critics*, Princeton University CEPS Working Paper No. 91, April.

may simply indicate failure of the capital asset pricing model to capture all the dimensions of risk'.[45]

They also wonder aloud whether this observed past phenomena is that relevant to current markets – according to Malkiel, Fama and French's own data suggests 'the period from the early 1960s through 1990 may have been a unique period in which value stocks rather consistently produced higher rates of return.'[46] In other words, what worked in the past may not be relevant to current markets... and even if it does still exist, it's nigh on impossible to capture through any sensible investment policy.

Fluck *et al.*[47] for instance recognised that the price reversal strategy noted above does seem to exist. They simulated a strategy of buying stocks over a 13-year period during the 1980s and early 1990s that had particularly poor returns over the past three to five years. According to Malkiel, his team found that 'stocks with very low returns over the past three to five years had higher returns in the next period, and that stocks with very high returns over the past three to five years had lower returns in the next period.'[48] Crucially though they also found that 'returns in the next period were similar for both groups, so they could not confirm that a contrarian approach would yield higher-than-average returns. There was a statistically strong pattern of return reversal, but not one that implied inefficiency in the market that would enable investors to make excess returns'[49], i.e. the phenomenon of means reversion might work but it would be very difficult to run it as a trading strategy.

This cynicism about the ability of investors to actually capture these inefficiencies received some support from a study by Schwert[50] who pointed out that the investment firm of Dimensional Fund Advisors actually began a mutual fund that selected value stocks quantitatively according to criteria based on the work of Fama and French. The abnormal return of such

[45] Ibid.

[46] Ibid.

[47] Fluck, Z., Malkiel, B. and Quandt, R. (1997) 'The Predictability of Stock Returns: A Cross-Sectional Simulation.' *Review of Economics and Statistics*, Vol. 79, Issue 2, pp. 176–83.

[48] Ibid.

[49] Ibid.

[50] Schwert, G.W. (2001) *Anomalies and Market Efficiency*, Simon School of Business Working Paper No. FR 02-13. University of Rochester – Simon School; National Bureau of Economic Research (NBER).

a portfolio (adjusting for beta, the capital asset pricing model measure of risk) was a negative 0.2 per cent per month over the 1993–98 period according to Schwert. The implied conclusion here was that if a smart firm like Dimensional – stuffed full of award winning academics who believed index tracking – couldn't produce the goods from some form of systematic use of anomalies then no-one could!

G. William Schwert from the University of Rochester and NBER – an American research institute – suggests one reason for Dimensional's failure. Schwert in a paper entitled 'Anomalies and market efficiency'[51] suggests that the observation of certain anomalies inevitably results in their eventual disappearance as market professionals try to capitalise on the trend. Schwert questions 'whether profit opportunities existed in the past, but have since been arbitraged away, or whether the anomalies were simply statistical aberrations that attracted the attention of academics and practitioners'.[52]

This almost philosophical notion that once a regular pattern has been observed it ceases to exist by the very act of recognition and cognition is beautifully summed up in the following example from Burton Malkiel:

Suppose there is a truly dependable and exploitable January effect, that the stock market – especially stocks of small companies – will generate extraordinary returns during the first five days of January. What will investors do? They will buy on the last day of December, and sell on January 5. But then investors find that the market rallied on the last day of December and so they will need to begin to buy on the next-to-last day of December; and because there is so much 'profit taking' on January 5, investors will have to sell on January 4 to take advantage of this effect. Thus, to beat the gun, investors will have to be buying earlier and earlier in December and selling earlier and earlier in January so that eventually the pattern will self-destruct.[53]

Schwert in his paper on anomalies and market efficiency takes this observation one step further and questions whether this act of recognition has now destroyed any advantages a value-based strategy – or one based on momentum for that matter – might have produced. In his paper he concludes as follows:

---

[51] Schwert, G.W. (2003) 'Abnormalities and Market Efficiency' in the *Handbook of the Economic of Finance*, edited by G.M. Constantinides, M. Harris and R. Stulz, Elsevier Science B.V.

[52] Ibid.

[53] See note 44.

In particular, the size effect and the value effect seem to have disappeared after the papers that highlighted them were published. At about the same time, practitioners began investment vehicles that implemented the strategies implied by the academic papers. The... dividend yield effect also seem to have lost their predictive power after the papers that made them famous were published... the evidence that stock market returns are predictable using variables such as dividend yields or inflation is much weaker in the periods after the papers that documented these findings were published. All of these findings raise the possibility that anomalies are more apparent than real.[54]

The redoubtable John Bogle – founder of Vanguard – has a simple explanation for the decline of the anomaly as a force powering investment. He suggests that over long periods of time the power of reversion to mean – that everything eventually conforms to the big average – is overwhelming.

In one of his books from the 1990s[55] Bogle looks at the various anomalies and how they've been used by fund managers in the US. In particular he's looked at the returns from two groups of fund managers – those that invest in growth stocks (fast growing companies measured by profits growth where the share price is moving forward) and those that try and spot value opportunities. He's examined over 60 years of returns and he suggests that reversion to mean (or RTM) is both powerful and profound.

In the early years, growth funds controlled the game and were clearly the winners from 1937 through 1968. At the end of that long era, an investment in value stocks was worth just 62 percent of an equivalent initial investment in growth stocks. Value stocks then enjoyed a huge resurgence through 1976, redressing almost precisely the entire earlier deficit. (This recent history – covering only 8 of the entire 60 years – has created the value stock mystique.) Then, growth stocks outperformed through 1980, and value stocks have pretty much dominated through 1997.When all of these cyclical fluctuations for the full six decades were linked, the terminal investment in value stocks was equal to about nine-tenths of the investment in growth stocks. For the full 60-year period, the compound total returns were: growth, 11.7 percent; value, 11.5 percent – a tiny difference. I'd call that match a standoff – and another tribute to RTM.[56]

Figure 3.2 (overleaf) shows graphically Bogel's 60 years of analysis.

---

[54] See note 51.

[55] Bogle, J. (2009) *Common Sense on Mutual Funds: Fully Updated 10th Anniversary Edition*, John Wiley & Sons.

[56] Ibid.

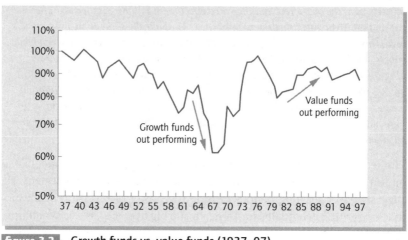

figure 3.2 Growth funds vs. value funds (1937–97)

Source: Bogle and Swensen (2009), Figure 10.3

Making profits from the anomalies

All this fierce academic debate – and charged polemic – from both sides of the efficient markets debate obscures a potentially more profound issue. Maybe these anomalies are real and do persist but how do you actually go about capturing them systematically and profitably?

An exchange at a symposium about a decade ago between Robert Shiller, an economist who is sympathetic to the argument that stock prices are partially predictable but sceptical about market efficiency, and Richard Roll, an academic financial economist who also is a portfolio manager, beautifully demonstrates this difficulty. After Shiller stressed the importance of inefficiencies in the pricing of stocks, Roll responded as follows:

I have personally tried to invest money, my client's money and my own, in every single anomaly and predictive device that academics have dreamed up... I have attempted to exploit the so-called year-end anomalies and a whole variety of strategies supposedly documented by academic research. And I have yet to make a nickel on any of these supposed market inefficiencies... a true market inefficiency ought to be an exploitable opportunity. If there's nothing investors can exploit in a systematic way, time in and time out, then it's very hard to say that information is not being properly incorporated into stock prices.[57]

---

[57] Quoted in Malkiel, B. – see note 44.

Investors are not perfect rational creatures and they don't have 24/7 access to every bit of information available to the market. Efficient market theorists have, to be fair, never argued that all actors in a market are rational but the evidence from most behavioural economists is damning in the extreme. The evidence suggests that investors are in fact frequently irrational, that they fail to pursue careful articulated strategies and that above all they react too quickly to news and rumour.

William Schwert in his paper points to research from some Californian economists that suggests that over-trading is one of the most dangerous behavioural vices:

Odean (1999) examined data from 10 000 individual accounts randomly selected from a large national discount brokerage firm for the period 1987–1993. This sample covers over 160 000 trades. Because the data source is a discount brokerage firm, recommendations from a retail broker are presumably not the source of information used by investors to make trading decisions. Odean found that traders lower their returns through trading, even ignoring transactions costs, because the stocks they sell earn higher subsequent returns than the stocks they purchase. Barber and Odean (2000, 2001) used different data from the same discount brokerage firm and found that active trading accounts earn lower risk-adjusted net returns than less-active accounts. They have also found that men trade more actively than women and thus earn lower risk-adjusted net returns and that the stocks that individual investors buy subsequently under-perform the stocks that they sell.[58]

The lesson: over-trading matters hugely because of cost.

Every time an investor trades there is a charge and that charge is likely to cut into total long-term returns. In a paper called 'The Cost of Active Investing', the economist Kenneth French compares the fees, expenses and trading costs paid on actively managed funds and then compares them to an estimate of what would be paid if everyone invested in a vehicle that could track the benchmark index:

Averaging over 1980 to 2006 I find investors spend 0.67% of the aggregate value of the market each year searching for superior returns. Society's capitalized cost of price discovery is at least 10% of the current market cap. Under reasonable assumptions, the typical investor would increase his average annual return by 67 basis points over the 1980 to 2006 period if he switched to a passive market portfolio... This estimate is conservative.[59]

---

[58] See note 51.

[59] French, K. 'The Cost of Active Investing' (2008), available at http://ssrn.com/abstract=1105775

French also examines over-trading via turnover measures – his hypothesis is that active fund managers trade too often and as trading costs money these expenses sap returns. According to French, 'market turnover is above 110% in the 1920s. It reaches a high of 143% in 1928, then plunges with the market to 52% in 1932. By 1938 it is below 20%. In light of recent experience, it is perhaps surprising that annual turnover remains close to or below 20% from 1938 to 1975. Turnover rises fairly steadily over the next three decades, however, from 20% in 1975 and 59% in 1990, to an impressive 173% in 2006 and 215% in 2007.'[60]

The job of translating all this wealth of academic analysis into the delirious long-term effects of over-trading on returns has fallen to a familiar name, John Bogle. Perhaps his most powerful attack came at the 60th Anniversary Conference of the *Financial Analysts Journal* in February 2005 at Pasadena, California. His message to the gathered audience of US academics was that costs matter. He developed his own thesis to describe it: the cost matters hypothesis. Echoing some of French's work Bogle discovered that during 2004:

- revenues of investment bankers and brokers came to an estimated $22bn
- direct mutual fund costs came to about $7bn
- pension management fees to $1bn
- annuity commissions to some $1bn
- hedge fund fees to about $2bn
- fees paid to personal financial advisors, maybe another $bn

The grand total was approximately $35bn and this was all directly deducted from the returns that the financial markets generated for investors 'before those croupiers' costs were deducted'. He also estimated that in 1985 these costs were a 'mere' $5bn.

Bogle's analysis – and that of Kenneth French – suggests that constantly chasing new strategies and anomalies results in the systematic long destruction of wealth via extra costs. In his view most investors are better off buying a fund – preferably an index tracking fund – and then sticking with it through thick and thin, i.e. becoming a buy and hold investor!

Perhaps the best summary of why our bias towards over-trading and chasing anomalies comes in this passage from Jack Tryenor:

---

[60] Ibid.

I believe in a third view of market efficiency, which holds that the securities market will not always be either quick or accurate in processing new information. On the other hand, it is not easy to transform the resulting opportunities to trade profitably against the market consensus into superior portfolio performance. Unless the active investor understands what really goes on in the trading game, he can easily convert even superior research information into the kind of performance that will drive his clients to the poorhouse... why aren't more active investors consistently successful? The answer lies in the cost of trading.[61]

A middle way – markets are efficiently inefficient

All of this (sometimes impassioned) academic debate and polemic isn't necessarily very practical – what are ordinary investors actually supposed to do and believe in? The building blocks of some kind of middle ground come from a more detailed look at the behavioural antics of investors. In the previous section we noted the tendency of investors to over-trade – constantly incurring costs – based on short-term information, news and gossip. This ever-present reality – the engine of short-term price momentum-driven markets, divorced from many economic fundamentals – has been seized on by some market strategists like James Montier who put behavioural thinking at the core of their approach.

Montier resolutely maintains that markets are in fact efficiently inefficient – they are predictably inefficient – in part because of their bias towards chasing short-term momentum, i.e. they usually price in inaccurate views of longer-term fundamentals or simply price on the basis of the next six months of newsflow.

This view is summed up in a sector handbook report for investment bank SG (former employers of Montier) which observed in 2009 that:

Investors are trading based on what will work over the coming months, rather than what will drive the best returns over time, and where a company's fundamental value is understated. Below [Figure 3.3], is one of James favourite charts (recently extended and updated by SG's Ida Troussieux), indicating that the average holding period for a stock on the NYSE has fallen to 0.7 years (or less than nine months!). This confirms that most investors (even those claiming to be long-term oriented) are often just speculating on expected newsflow, or anticipating momentum. Essentially, most investors are just looking for what will work over the next 6–9 months (if not less).[62]

---

[61] Tryenor, J. (1981) 'What does it take to win the trading game?', *Financial Analysts Journal*, 37(1), pp. 55–60.

[62] Montier, J. (2009) *The SG Global Sector Handbook: Waves, bubbles, leaders, laggards and innovators*, SG.

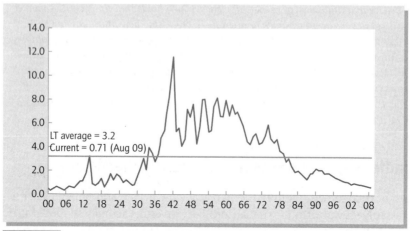

figure 3.3 Average holding period for a stock on the NYSE (years)

This short-termist scramble for what's hot is not only dangerous – it produces bubbles followed by terrible financial collapses – but also terrifically predictable according to Montier (and quite possibly very profitable to the disciplined momentum investor!).

The first stock exchange was founded in 1602' observes Montier. 'The first equity bubble occurred just 118 years later – the South Sea bubble. Since then we have encountered bubbles with an alarming regularity. My friends at GMO define a bubble as a (real) price movement that is at least two standard deviations from trend. Now a two standard deviation event should occur roughly every 44 years. Yet since 1925, GMO have found a staggering 30 plus bubbles. That is equivalent to slightly more than one every three years![63]

For Montier this very predictability is itself the best evidence that markets over-react, first by chasing what's hot, and then by punishing all stocks in the subsequent market collapse: 'To my mind the clear existence and ex ante diagnosis of bubbles represent by far and away the most compelling evidence of the gross inefficiency of markets.'[64]

For many (Montier included) this analysis suggests the following essential truth – that if investors can correctly predict that they'll make money chasing momentum on the way up and then withdraw from the market when prices shoot way over fundamentals, they can also make money by buying

---

[63] Quoted in Montier, J. (2009) *Value Investing*, John Wiley & Sons.
[64] Ibid.

when shares are cheap, in part because those shares have been punished by investors looking to flee the financial burst!

Montier then comes to the nub of the debate – that actually the vast majority of market participants, i.e. the institutions, are not actually doing anything very much different from 'buying the market'. He maintains that this supposedly 'huge' professional army of supposed stock pickers trying to beat the market is in fact a mirage – most institutions are blindly following the ups and downs of the short-termist market and not adding extra skills from stock selection. Montier cites research by one academic that shows that 'the aggregate institutional portfolio barely deviates from the market weights. So institutions aren't even really trying to tilt their portfolios towards the factors we know generate outperformance over the long term'.[65]

Montier quotes the academic's conclusions:

Quite simply, institutions overall seem to do little more than hold the market portfolio... Their aggregate portfolio almost perfectly mimics the value-weighted index, with a market beta of 1.01... [see Figure 3.4] Institutions overall take essentially no bet on any of the most important stock characteristics known to predict returns, like book-to-market, momentum, or accruals. The implication is that to the extent that institutions deviate from the market portfolio, they seem to bet primarily on idiosyncratic returns – bets that aren't particularly successful. Another implication is that institutions, in aggregate, don't exploit anomalies in the way they should.[66]

Montier concludes by observing that: 'The poor overall performance of mutual fund managers in the past is not due to a lack of stock-picking ability, but rather to institutional factors that encourage them to over-diversify'[67] – and chase the index! Montier finishes by reminding us of Sir John Templeton's observation that: 'It is impossible to produce a superior performance unless you do something different from the majority.'[68]

Like many value-based strategists Montier argues that the various anomalies noted earlier in this chapter – value stocks, small cap out performance and the momentum effect – are not produced by some magical internal force that no-one quite understands. These anomalies are tangible and are produced by real behavioural and institutional biases, i.e. institutions

---

[65] Ibid.

[66] Ibid.

[67] Ibid.

[68] Ibid.

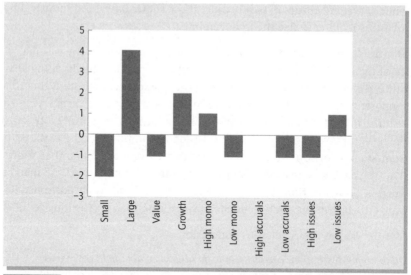

figure 3.4 Institutional investors vs US market (weight differences)

Source: Montier, J. (2009) *Value Investing: Tools and Techniques for Intelligent Investment*, John Wiley & Sons.

ignore large parts of the market allowing inefficiencies over information and trading flows to become in effect systematic and institutionalised. It is precisely because most large players chase the same hot stocks that so many other shares are ignored and thus pricing collapses, sometimes for no discernable good reason.

It's worth staying with Montier's analysis and to look beyond his own bias towards contrarianism, i.e. buying out of favour stocks. The logical conclusion of his analysis of bubbles is that a nimble investor willing to read the markets should also be able to make money simply by chasing those momentum effects we've already observed. Montier's former employers at SocGen (SG) explain in their 2009 Global Cross Sector Handbook how investors can systematically capture this 'anomaly', which all too frequently turns into a bubble lasting many years:

Once they [the investor] identify these long-term waves (and potential bubbles), simply position themselves in these hot sectors... and then hold these funds until the theme has ended. Investors may also choose to ignore entirely the cold sectors (i.e. those cold sectors not participating in the theme-driven wave). As waves usually last between five and ten years (sometimes culminating in a bubble that lasts one to two years), an investor can afford to wait and see which waves develop during the next cycle before investing. In a five to seven year economic cycle, if an investor misses the first year of the wave, but then properly positions himself (being long in hot sectors and avoiding cold sectors altogether), that investor will benefit from four to six years of outperformance, including capturing the bubble performance.[69]

This disquieting thought for a contrarian – that going with the herd can be rewarding some of the time – is conceded even by Montier. In our later chapter on value investing we feature an interview with James where he concedes the power of momentum investing: 'I don't find that comfortable although the evidence is very clear – momentum strategies do work. I find them intellectually rather unsatisfying, which is a terribly snobbish thing to say. I hate buying simply because anybody else is buying – it's never struck me as a terribly good rationale!'

A middle way – some commonsense assumptions

So, who are we to believe in this deeply charged debate? A strong case can be made for boiling down all this wealth of data and academic debate into the following simple common sense statements.

It's difficult to beat the market

You don't have to believe that all financial markets are completely 'perfect' to believe that *most* investors fail to beat the market most of the time.

Stockmarkets are mostly efficient but not always

Even within supposedly perfect markets there are imperfections – Buffett's observation is surely the important one, namely that while markets are mostly efficient that's a long way from saying they're always perfect, all the time. Even the most ardent fans of perfect markets now accept that certain types of share – with certain risk profiles – can out perform the main market, much if not most of the time. This doesn't mean that this inefficiency and these market imperfections are either easy to capture via some kind of index or fund, or that in the future these imperfections will not correct themselves. Inefficiencies have a tendency to change over time and mutate, and a rigid adherence to a fixed set of criteria in, say, a black box – an analytical computer-based system – full of variables, might be a risky tactic if the markets do adapt and evolve.

---

[69] See note 62.

It is possible to construct strategies that can deliver above average returns... some of the time

There is some evidence that investors have in the past 'beaten the market', even supposedly efficient ones, but it's largely through carefully researched strategies implemented over long periods of time, although those extra returns are probably at the expense of higher potential risk.

If you are going to try and beat the market, do it systematically and don't over-trade

Learn the lesson from research on investors' behaviour and don't be tempted to over-trade, and try and reduce your costs – costs absolutely destroy long-term returns. Be focused, systematic and keep costs to the minimum!

Focus your strategies on known and well-researched anomalies

There is a substantial body of evidence that suggests that focusing your strategies on value stocks, on shares that are cheap, on momentum stocks and on small caps could deliver returns above those of an index tracking market portfolio. Look at the evidence and try and work out what has worked in the past

Understand that anomalies or inefficiencies can change over time and stop working for many years

The anomalies encountered in this chapter that can be used by strategies are not immutable. There is some debate as to whether ideas such as value investing fade over time because of reversion to mean or whether the simple act of observation by professionals encourages market participants to arbitrage away any pricing inefficiency. Anomalies capable of being captured by strategies can wax and wane – be prepared to be flexible and use a variety of different strategies depending on the state of the markets.

Dividends matter

In the next chapter we'll discover how virtually every major analysis of long-term returns from shares suggests that dividends – and their re-investment – are the *essential* component of long-term returns and that investors might even be better off focusing their attention on companies with well supported dividend pay outs.

Professors Elroy Dimson and Paul Marsh of the London Business School

Back in the first half of 2009 the author caught up with the UK's pre-eminent stock market historians and academic analysts, Professor Elroy Dimson and Professor Paul Marsh at their office in the London Business School, near Marylebone. The interview – reprinted in summary below – ranged widely , taking in their view of equities as a suitable long-term investment through to the latest research on momentum.

Interviewer: Are you still confident that equities are a more rewarding investment class, even given their volatility and their risk over the long term? Do you stick to your view articulated in your seminal book on long-term market data *Triumph of the Optimists* that shares are a great long-term investment ?

Paul: Yes, we do. They are more rewarding in an expectational sense. In other words, you are going to expect to get a higher return from equities. Probably in our view something like three to three and a half per cent per annum more, but the reason you're going to get that is because of risk. There's a risk premium because people don't like the volatility of equities. Equities are priced at a discount and because of that you expect a higher reward from equities. But that higher reward is not guaranteed and so the notion that equities are good for the long run is fine in so far as it goes, but there is no period over which you are safe. Equities are not a safe investment. By definition they wouldn't give a higher reward unless they were risky.

Elroy: Equities are not a home for money that you will need in five years' or ten years' time. It's the home for money you may want in five or ten years' time, but where you can tolerate the risk that the money may simply not be there when you want it.

Interviewer: But there have been many eras, many decades, including the last one, where equities have been a terrible investment. That matters hugely to individual private investors with discrete 20 to 30 year investing cycles, doesn't it?

Paul: Absolutely, the last decade has been absolutely dreadful for equities. But over the last 20 years they've been OK-ish, over the last 25 years they've been quite good; and you're right, you can pick the wrong period. In fact, in the US, bonds have done just about as well as equities over the last 40 years. But that's partly because bonds have done incredibly well. In absolute terms, equities have not done badly over the last 40 years, it's just that bonds have been the place to be over that interval. And that's what risk is about, you just get hit periodically by extreme performance.

Elroy: If you had a very long time horizon and no defined liabilities then you might be willing to exchange much of your wealth, for the chance of becoming even wealthier in the future through holding equities. So if you were to think of a well-endowed university or college, perhaps with a 100-year horizon, what you're doing is trading off the possibility that you may simply not have most of today's wealth if things go badly. But in exchange you've got the chance of becoming very much better off than other universities. So when you've got a very long time horizon, and no liabilities that's fine. But if, on the other hand, you need to spend some of your savings every year , then you do have some liabilities, and you're just like ordinary investors and a pension fund, and the stock market will be risky for you.

Interviewer: Some investors like Rob Arnott – a fundamentals based investor and analyst – suggest that what really matters is not the time scale but at what price you buy shares. If they're cheap, you'll make money!

Elroy: I think that if you buy into an asset that looks cheap, it will have higher expected returns, but with greater risk.

Interviewer: So should we time our investments in equities only to start when the markets are cheap – use a kind of strategic timing system that says UK shares are cheap overall, I'm going to buy lots of them?

Elroy: You're describing a very simple trading system. You look at prices in relation to fundamental values, and you buy when securities look cheap. That's what most investment managers say they do. They try to buy when prices are low, relative to earnings or relative to dividends or relative to book values! So this is a trading system that everybody knows about, and it should be easy to implement. And yet when we have a look at the record of professional fund managers, their average performance is inferior to simply buying the index and holding it.

Paul: The sad thing about market timing, whether it's just straight market timing or whether it's based on valuation ratios... is that everybody's trying to do it, and that there are a lot of smart people out there. And the evidence sadly suggests that people's market timing abilities are not very great, just as their stock selection abilities are not very great. There are some exceptions to that, but it's difficult. It's really tough out there because it's a very competitive world in the fund management business and so, based on the evidence, I think it's much harder to do these things than to talk about doing it. Whether people label themselves as value, or deep value or growth or momentum or whatever they do, they're all trying to do the same thing, which is to beat the market. And one way or another, they are trying to buy things that are going to go up and sell things that are going to go down. And so, whatever they care to label themselves, whatever strategy they tend to follow, they're all trying to beat the market.

Interviewer: You mentioned value investing. Isn't there a large amount of evidence to suggest that there are various anomalies out there – the small cap effect, value and momentum – that can reward investors who use them through a strategy ? Maybe markets really aren't that efficient after all!

Paul: I think that the issue about market efficiency is that it gets held up as being markets are always right. And that's not what market efficiency says. Market efficiency basically says that markets do the best job they can with the information they've got at the time, and the test of it really is what rule you can actually follow that will beat the market. Efficient market theory really still stands – active managers as a group still struggle to beat the average.

Interviewer: But what about those anomalies, those risk factors – whatever you want to call them? Are they still relevant ? Does value investing still work? Aren't they proof the market is inefficient?

Paul: It does depend on whether they're inefficiencies or whether they are risk related. So that's the first issue one has to address . The small cap premium, which has diminished somewhat since first discovered, could be simply a reward for illiquidity or for certain types of related risk. The value effect – these kinds of low-priced stocks could be higher risk securities. So it may not be that these are pockets of inefficiency; it may be that they're systematic differences in risk.

Elroy: If we trace this historically, when the first evidence appeared on the outperformance of small caps, for instance, this was seen as an anomaly. And then as individuals dug further and reflected more and built their models, it didn't look that way any more. It looked as though there is a factor that influences returns that is shared by small caps. The same could be said for value. We've now reached the contemporary puzzle of momentum. Momentum is perhaps at the stage that the small cap anomaly was at in the 1980s. It would be surprising if, after all costs, there was a recipe for superior performance that could be adopted successfully by a large proportion of investors. We need a theory. There are a number of scholars who have been developing theories as to why there might be momentum patterns in stock prices. But I think it's fair to say we don't yet have a very satisfactory theoretical explanation.

Interviewer: But momentum exists doesn't it – there are patterns of momentum in stock prices?

Paul: There definitely have been, but with a lot of these strategies one gets to the interface between behavioural and risk based explanations. If you take value stocks for example, and you look at a portfolio of traditional value stocks, a lot of these look like losers. They are value stocks because their prices have fallen. When you look at those kinds of stocks, it takes a lot of courage to buy them and sometimes when you buy them they get much worse. The value effect does not by any means work consistently all the time. It is very variable. And so for a fund manager going out on a limb to buy value stocks, this can be a very risky position for them, and a risky one for the ultimate beneficiaries of the portfolio . It's the same with momentum. Momentum has worked extraordinarily well over the long run. Over a hundred and eight years in the UK the momentum returns are extremely strong, but despite that, you can have periods like the start of 2009 when momentum really hits you.

Elroy: If there are irregularities in stock market behaviour which provide profit opportunities, those best placed to take advantage of them are larger investors. Because those large investors can always organise themselves as though they were a consolidated collection of small investors, they can always have the benefits that are open to small investors, as an alternative to operating as a mega investor!

Interviewer: Isn't there another force at work here – that these anomalies change over time or even vanish when noticed! By the time we've all noticed they've been acted upon by market professionals its all too late and the anomaly has gone!

Paul: I think in some cases that's absolutely right. Most anomalies self-destruct. The reason that they get identified is because people spot the phenomenon informally and then they do some academic research that documents it formally; and sure enough, what they knew was there, was there. And of course it was just a chance event and then when you look in the future it isn't there, it's disappeared. That's not actually true for the three that you've talked about – small caps, value and momentum. The three you've talked about do seem to have persistence. The one that probably has the lowest persistence is the size effect, but it seems to have some persistence. The value effect seems to be quite robust, and the momentum effect seems to be quite robust. But that is over very long horizons, and in the short run you can get very badly caught out.

Dividends: back to the source

A cow for her milk, A hen for her eggs, And a stock by heck, For her dividends. John Burr Williams[1]

That 'dividends matter' is a refrain we'll constantly encounter in this chapter, as study after study shows how important the humble dividend cheque really is! A legion of studies tells us that dividends account for anything between one third and 96% of total returns from equities over virtually any long period of time under analysis, be it 30 or even 130 years. The constant dividend cheque can add up to stellar returns over the very long term. Rob Arnott, a leading stockmarket analyst, has even quantified this potentially huge return: 'If *no dividends were spent*' Arnott suggests, 'If no taxes were taken out, and if market returns were earned without fees or expenses, $100 in 1802 would have grown to $766 million by the end of 2000, then cratered all the way down to $459 million by the end of 2002.'[2]

Crucially, as we'll discover later in this chapter, there is also some evidence that weighting your portfolio of shares towards particular types of high yielding stocks can not only provide you with a generous income but also give you a bundle of shares which have historically out performed the key benchmark indices, i.e. that proactively tilting your stock selection strategy towards high yielding shares increases total returns.

---

[1] Quoted in 'The theory of investment value' (2002) in *Triumph of the Optimists* by Dimson, E. Marsh, P. and Staunton, M., Princeton University Press.

[2] Arnott, R.D. (2003) 'Editor's Corner: Dividends and the Three Dwarfs', *Financial Analysts' Journal*, Vol. 59, No. 2, pp. 4 and 6.

Rock solid dividends

Earnings may well garner all the media headlines but that popularity comes with a massive downside – earnings are volatile. In the middle of 2009 for instance various studies by leading investment banks pointed to a precipitous collapse in global stock market earnings of 14% in just one month! More and more analysts now reckon that earnings estimates are in fact so random – and so liable to sudden downwards revision – that investors should ignore them altogether. One simple example should suffice. If we look again at the calendar year 2009, analysts' estimates for global developed markets suggested that they might be valued at anything between eight or 13 times estimates for earnings in 2009, i.e. they could be cheap or they could be expensive depending on how optimistic you are!

The one key measure that many analysts fall back on is dividends. These twice yearly payments are the nearest thing to a sure bet in equity investing and many companies in the US and the UK have spent the past decade or so building up a rock solid reputation for paying out dividends year in, year out! But this once numerous army of large cap, blue chip, progressive dividend payers (they progressively increase their dividend payout) has been dwindling over the past few brutal years. Industrial giant GKN was one such progressive hero, constantly increasing its dividend payout until the dark days of 2009 when it announced that it would stop its payment altogether!

Here's Sir Kevin Smith, GKN's chief executive, on the announcement: 'We haven't withheld a dividend for 29 years and we have a progressive dividend policy, so it's a very big decision for us. But under the circumstances it's better to preserve cash. Our automotive revenues have fallen by about 40 per cent since the middle of last year.'[3] In 2009 GKN's shares crashed by nearly 70% and following that announcement they fell another 2.5%. But GKN is far from being alone in its decision to abandon the ranks of progressive dividend heros – only a few days before its decision, Anglo American, the mining giant, confirmed that it too would be stopping its dividend while in the US one of the most notorious dividend heros, General Electric, announced that it too would cut its dividend for the first time in decades.

This huge uncertainty means that the ever smaller number of perceived 'safe' progressive heros – the companies that have continued to increase their dividends since the dark days of 2009 – will more and more become

---

[3] GKN Annual Report 2009.

the subject of intense scrutiny and interest. There'll be more and more questions asked about the ability of a company to afford the payout but if the market perceives that the payout is indeed safe that company is also likely to attract the interest of the huge number of fund managers involved globally in the search for quality, income generating stocks. Already key players such as Newton Fund Management has warned that a flight into these 'safe' progressive dividend payers might sharply bid up share prices for the lucky few.

Newton has based its prediction on the still ample number of equity income funds headed by managers such as Neil Woodford at Invesco Perpetual and James Henderson at Lowlands Investment Trust, star managers who base their preference for well backed dividend payers on a mountain of solid academic evidence. Dividends make a huge difference to long-term returns. In fact, much long-term analysis suggests that upwards of 90% of total returns come from dividends in one shape or another.

The academic evidence for why dividends matter

The academic literature – backed by a mountain of analysis from City strategists such as Andrew Lapthorne at French bank Société Générale (SG) – suggests that dividends benefit investors over the long term in a number of different ways.

The first and perhaps most obvious is the actual regular dividend payment as a contributor to what's called total shareholder returns but the magic of dividends doesn't stop there. Evidence suggests that a strategy of buying the right kind of dividend payers (progressive dividend payers with a decent balance sheet) will actually deliver better returns in and of itself, i.e. the market itself tends to prioritise the attractions of certain dividend payers and awards their shares a premium rating. The reason for this market preference is obvious in retrospect – dividends are easy to calculate and involve simple, hard numbers made in regular payments. But, as we've already noted above, dividends also tend to be much more stable over time compared to earnings – annual earnings growth has historically been 2.5 times more volatile than dividend growth according to SG – while the discipline of making the regular dividend payout encourages a more focused management, determined to conserve the financial resources of the firm. As Lapthorne at SG reminds us, 'the retention of a too high proportion of earnings can encourage unnecessary mergers and acquisition (and often wasteful) investment in the pursuit of higher earnings growth'.[4] As an example of this discipline and focus it's worth noting that very few companies ever set their management teams a dividends target as a way of calculating their bonuses – the cynic might note how difficult it is to manipulate the dividends stats compared to earnings.

Dividends by contrast are boring and steady. Table 4.1 comes from a study by French bank BNP Paribas and looks at both US and European dividend growth over the very, very long term. It's the highlighted number for the US figure that really matters in this analysis – using long-term data from the US stockmarket, this study suggests that US equities have not only risen consistently faster than inflation but have increased by a fairly steady 1.4% per annum in compound annual terms. An extra 1.4% every year, compounded, makes a huge difference to returns data, as we shall discover.

table 4.1 UK long-term nominal and real dividend growth (all figures in %)

Average	Dividend growth	Real dividend growth	Inflation rate	Earnings growth	Payout ratio	Dividend yield	Ten-year bond yield
US: 1871–2008	3.5	1.4	2.1	2.7	63	4.5	4.7
UK : 1970–2008	8.4	1.9	6.5	9.7	56	4.4	8.9

Source: Equity Derivatives Strategy (EDS): Dividends 18 May 2009, Significant Upside to 2010 and 2011, Euro STOXX 50 Dividends, BNP Paribas Research Report.

Turning to the academic research it's clear that the long-term case for dividends and their importance to private investors rests on all these factors – the dividend payout itself, the rating attached to a high yielder and the stable growth in the dividend payout over time – but it's the reinvestment of these dividend payouts that really makes the huge difference over time. The hard spade work on this analysis comes from the London Business School (LBS) Professors Elroy Dimson, Paul Marsh and Mike Staunton – featured regularly in their Credit Suisse Global Investment Returns Yearbooks. Like many analysts they break the long-term returns from equities down into four components:

■ the actual yield itself (usually compared to the risk-free rate of return from holding cash or index linked gilts)

---

[4] Quoted in 'The Safest Dividends', by David Stevenson, *Investors Chronicle*, 3 April 2009.

- the growth rate of real dividends (increased dividends above the inflation rate)
- the way that the market rewards a company because of its dividend, i.e. the rating it will give the shares via a measure like the price to dividend ratio, and last but by no means least
- the reinvestment of the dividend using schemes like the dividend reinvestment investment plans (or DRIPs).

According to Dimson *et al.* 'the dividend yield has been the dominant factor historically' and they add that 'the longer the investment horizon, the more important is dividend income'.[5] The LBS analysis is subtle. The authors suggest that in fact the long-term real dividend growth rate is actually only about 1% per annum and this low growth can't make that big a difference while the re-rating of a stock based on its multiple to dividends is also very variable over time, and also doesn't appear to make that much of a difference. As the authors note 'dividends and probably earnings have barely outpaced inflation'.[6]

But the actual payout is dwarfed by the importance of reinvesting those dividend cheques. Looking at the 109 years since 1900, Dimson *et al.* suggest that the average real capital gain in just stocks plus the dividend payout is about 1.7% per annum (an initial $1000 would have grown six-fold), but over the same period dividends reinvested would have produced a total return of 6% per annum (or a total gain of 582 times the original $1000, i.e. $582,000). Dividend reinvestment *really* matters and luckily most big progressive dividend payers have their own easy to use dividend reinvestment plans (see the box on DRIPS in Chapter 7).

City-based analysis of dividends

This academic research into dividends has been tested over shorter, more recent periods of time, by a number of leading investment bank economists, but particularly Tim Bond at British bank BarCap and Andrew Lapthorne at SG.

Tim Bond is the author of the hugely influential annual *Equity Gilts Study* by Barclays Capital – a definitive work on long-term returns used by many

---

[5] Dimson, E., Marsh, P. and Staunton, M. (2009) *Credit Suisse Global Investment Returns Yearbook 2009*, Credit Suisse.
[6] Ibid.

analysts as their default reference guide. A large part of that study focuses on the relative returns of equities versus gilts but dividends feature prominently. Tim Bond summarises the conclusions of this study thus:

Between 1925 and 2004, dividends provided 27% of total US equity returns. In the UK, from 1899 to 2004, dividends provided 31% of total returns. Both calculations assume the reinvestment of dividends, a practice which provides a very sizeable element of long run equity returns, just as coupon reinvestment provides much of the return from bonds. To illustrate this point, consider that £100 invested in 1899 would be worth just £9,961 today without reinvestment, but a cool £1,103,668 if dividend income had been reinvested. Without reinvestment of dividends, equity returns barely beat inflation. In real terms, the £100 invested in 1899 would now be worth £170 without dividend reinvestment, but £18,875 with reinvestment.[7]

Bond's long-term comprehensive market data very much backs up the conclusions of the LBS team, although his data suggests that dividends play a less important role over the short term. But Tim Bond also bangs the drum of dividend reinvestment – without constant reinvesting back into shares, equities barely hold their own against bonds.

However, Bond's analysis also reminds us that dividend's importance varies hugely over time – in recent years dividends have mattered much less:

The contribution of dividend income to total UK equity returns fell to an all time low in 2000, at the peak of the bubble, as payout ratios drifted down and investors focused on the rampant price gains delivered by soaring valuations. At the margin, changes in the UK tax treatment of dividends for pension funds in 1997 reduced investors' preference for dividend income, whilst changes in corporate taxation had much the same effect in the late 1980s in the US.[8]

The Barclays Capital analysis (see Figure 4.1) has one other crucial observation worth noting – dividends are a good hedge against inflation, i.e. they tend to increase in inflationary periods. Bond observes that:

Annual changes in dividends display a moderately positive correlation with inflation, averaging 38% over the 1950–2004 period in the UK and 26% in the US. When changes in dividends and inflation are considered over longer periods of time, the correlation improves, as would be expected from a volatile series. Over five-year periods, the correlation is 54% in the UK and 52% in the US, whilst over ten years the correlation is 56% in the UK and 70% in the US.[9]

---

[7] Quoted in 'Global speculations Dividend delights, *Asset Allocation* 7 September 2005.

[8] Proprietal client research, www.scribal.com/doc/19586723/Barclays-Capital-Dividend-Delights

[9] Ibid.

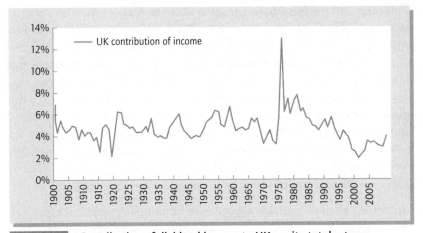

figure 4.1 Contribution of dividend income to UK equity total returns
(1900–2009) *Source: Barclays Equity Gilt Study.*

Andrew Lapthorne at French bank SG has echoed many if not all the conclusions of both Tim Bond and the LBS team. His key observation over the
post-war period is that real returns have not been from share price appreciation but almost exclusively dividends and their subsequent growth and
reinvestment. He summarises his case for what he calls income investing
through dividends, thus:

1 *The bulk of historical real returns have come from re-invested dividends. Using
   data back to the 1970s, this ranges from 56% of total returns in Japan to 96%
   in the UK.*

2 *A strategy of buying above-average yielding stocks has strongly outperformed
   buying those with below average yields.*

3 *With bank deposits currently earning very little interest, many will be pushing
   equities (with their higher yields) as a more attractive (albeit far riskier)
   proposition.*

4 *Dividend yields are easy to calculate. Dividends are also far more stable than
   earnings during downturns – annual earnings growth has historically been 2.5
   times more volatile than dividend growth.*

5 *Dividend payments should encourage management discipline. The retention of
   a too-high proportion of earnings can encourage unnecessary M&A (and often
   wasteful) investment in the pursuit of higher earnings growth.*[10]

---

[10] 'Rock steady income? Seeking an optimal income investing strategy', *The Global
Income Investor*, SG Quantitative Research, 3 February 2009.

Lapthorne and his quantitative team at SG have focused their analysis on data from global markets since 1970. Their analysis has some different twists and turns compared to that of both BarCap and the LBS study – the SG team reckon that the actual dividend yield represented just 30% of the nominal returns versus 70% for dividend growth, with their analysis suggesting that trend real dividend growth has been closer to 1.2% over the period. Looking at the UK, the SG team reckons that of total annualised equity returns since 1970 of 11.4%, the actual dividend yield accounted for 4.3% per annum, dividend growth 8% per annum, and multiple expansion (a higher or lower share price to dividend yield) –1.1%, i.e. high yielding shares were actually rated lower by the market – see Figure 4.2.

Lapthorne's analysis contains a number of other hugely important insights. His team's analysis looked at the relationship between earnings and dividends. Most investors commonly assume that there's a very close relationship between profits and dividends but according to Lapthorne's team that relationship is not in reality that strong. His quantitative analysts looked at the volatility of earnings growth compared to dividend growth – earnings were hugely more volatile, with earnings growth oscillating between –35% and +40%, against dividend growth which has stayed between a range of –7% to +19% – see Figure 4.3. In overall terms the SG team concluded that annual earnings growth has been 2.5 times more volatile than dividend growth.

Crucially when they used a measure called beta to look at the sensitivity of dividends to earnings, they discovered relatively low numbers (0 indicates

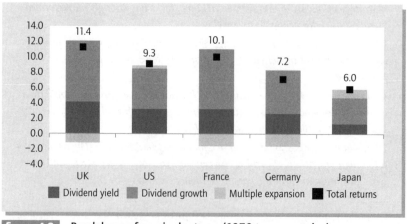

figure 4.2 Breakdown of nominal returns (1970 to present day)

Source: SG Quantitative Research.

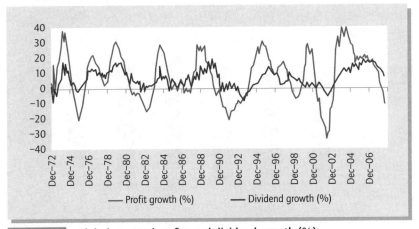

figure 4.3　Global reported profits and dividend growth (%)

Source: SG Quantitative Research, MSCI.

no sensitivity while 1 implies absolute sensitivity) of between 0.12 and 0.50 for nearly all major equity sectors with the exception of healthcare, building and construction, and travel and leisure. The point here is that dividends don't change as much as earnings and that that markets value that consistency.

Citi on dividends

It's worth commenting on the analysis of one last team of investment bank strategists – those at American bank Citi led by Rob Buckland. Yet again Buckland and his team declare that dividends matter, observing that:

They have been an important contributor to historical equity market returns. Since 1970 they have made up 30% of the annualised total return from global equities [see Figure 4.4]. Contribution to individual markets has been greater. In the UK it was 37% of the return. But their importance increases dramatically during periods of equity market weakness. In the 2000s they contributed 144% of global equity return (i.e. the capital return has been negative). While in the 1970s it was nearly 60%.[11]

The Citi team make one crucial additional point – that stock selection built around high yielding stocks has also been a very profitable strategy.

---

[11]　Buckland, R. (2008) *Global Equity Strategist: Dividend Resilience*, client research, Citibank.

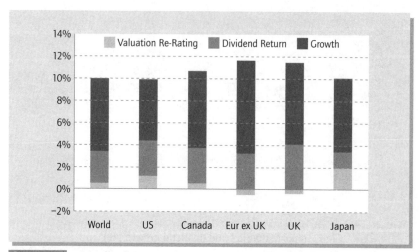

figure 4.4 Contribution to equity market returns (period covered 1 January 1970–30 August 2008)
Source: MSCI, Citi Investment Research.

From an investment perspective dividend yield strategies have also proved profitable for investors. For example, since inception the MSCI World High Dividend Yield Index has fairly consistently outperformed the MSCI World, both through good and bad times [see Figure 4.5].[12]

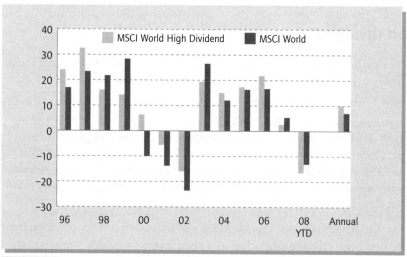

figure 4.5 MSCI high dividend yield index performance (%)
Source: MSCI, Citi Investment Research.

---

12 Ibid.

This point is rammed home in Figure 4.6 which looks at different regions around the world and their relative strength in making a dividend payout. Buckland observes that the table 'shows that regions with the strongest dividends have outperformed, with the best overall market up by an average 18% relative. *It hasn't paid to own the dividend laggards.* All have been associated with price underperformance.'[13]

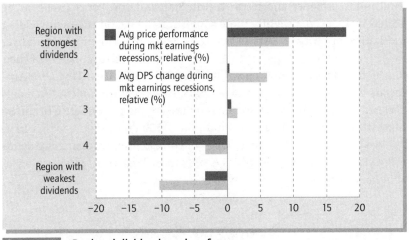

figure 4.6 **Regional dividends and performance** *Source*: MSCI, Citi Investment Research.

Strategies for capturing dividend performance

Investment analysis may well loudly proclaim that dividend matters but how can private investors go about capturing this hugely important insight using simple to implement strategies? One simple solution is to find a broad index that is weighted towards high yielding stocks – an idea discussed in greater detail in Chapter 12 on fundamental indexing by Rob Davies, who runs a dividend weighted, index tracking fund called Munro.

The FTSE index group has certainly championed its own take on an easy to understand dividend weighted index called the FTSE UK Dividend Plus. This index is constructed by taking the universe of FTSE 350 stocks and then weighting the composition of the index based solely on dividend yield. It's a simple concept but in recent years this strategy has sadly

---

[13] Ibid.

resulted in rather too many bank stocks which in turn have helped destroy returns. Figure 4.7 shows prices from 2005 for the exchange traded fund (ETF) from iShares which follows this index – this ETF was until recently hugely popular with many planners and advisors.

But the relative under-performance of this index and the accompanying ETF (see Figure 4.7) hasn't stopped rivals trying to come up with similar ideas.

Rival index provider and research firm Standard and Poors (S&P) in the US has introduced a slightly more sophisticated take on the high yielding index idea, but with a novel twist – consistency of dividend payment over time. This index only picks stocks that have consistently increased their dividend yield over time – it's called the S&P High Yield Dividend Aristocrats index and was launched in 2005. At launch the index developers declared that the index is 'designed to measure the performance of the 50 highest dividend yielding S&P Composite 1500 constituents which have followed a managed dividends policy of consistently increasing dividends every year for at least 25 years',[14] i.e. only those large companies paying an above average yield, consistently over time.

figure 4.7 iShares UK dividend plus

Source: www.ShareScope.co.uk

---

[14] Dash, S. (2005) 'The S&P High Yield Dividend Aristocrats Index', Standard & Poors Research Paper, www.sandp.com

For a share to get into the index, the company must pass a simple set of tests which include the following:

- the index is weighted by indicated annual dividend yield
- the stock must also have a minimum market capitalisation of $500m
- the company must have increased dividends every year for at least 25 years.

In reality, although the thresholds seem simple and basic, only a tiny number of companies actually pass. According to S&P this 'selectivity results in less than 2% of U.S. listed companies qualifying as Aristocrats'.[15] But what a short list it is as many of the companies tend to be boring, solid, conservative... and profitable. According to S&P, constituent companies boast a return on equity (a measure of profitability compared with capital invested in the business) which is usually well above the average (15% compared to under 12% for the S&P 500), while their credit ratings (this measures the reliability of their debts as measured by agencies like S&P) are consistently above the average. A grand total of 62% of the Aristocrats have investment grade debt and just 8% have a junk rating. Unsurprisingly, this elite group also tend to sport juicy dividend yields. According to S&P the Aristocrats index has consistently delivered yields in the range of 3.2%–4.2% over the past five years, well above average US yields which have been closer to 2.5% over the past few decades.

The acid test of this 'progressive' dividend strategy has to be returns and S&P has indeed tested it out thoroughly but only over two key periods – it back tested the strategy between 2000 and 2005 after which point it launched the index in full. In the back tested period S&P found that the strategy produced an annualised return of over 14% compared to –1% for the wider S&P 500 benchmark index. The risk inherent in these returns – as measured by something called standard deviation – was also much lower than the S&P 500.

As we'll discover in this book back tests are of limited value to investors – what really matters is the live implementation of a strategy. Luckily the US variant of this index seems to have been relatively successful in action – the most recent analysis at the end of September 2009 revealed that the 'live' index had fairly consistently beaten the S&P 500 benchmark index, with much less risk (see Table 4.2, overleaf) for the returns and constituents of the index).

---

[15] Ibid.

table 4.2	S&P US Aristocrats index portfolio statistics						
Index performance	3rd quarter 2009	YTD to 30/09/09	12 months	3 years	5 years	10 years
S&P 500 Dividend Aristocrats	19.29%	19.84%	0.56%	−1%	4.04%	2%
S&P 500	15.61%	19.26%	−6.9%	−5.43%	1.02%	0.51%
Standard deviation	3 year	5 year	10 year			
S&P 500 Dividend Aristocrats	19.18%	15.32%	14.7%			
S&P 500	19.68%	15.96%	16.24%			

Table 4.3 shows the top ten companies in the Aristocrats index.

table 4.3	Top ten companies in the S&P High Yield Dividend Aristocrats index in September 2009	
Name	Weight	Sector
Gannett Co Inc	2.51%	Consumer Discretionary
Walgreen Co	2.14%	Consumer Staples
Abbott Laboratories	2.12%	Healthcare
CenturytelInc	2.09%	Telecom Services
Chubb Corp	2.02%	Financials
Questar Corp	2.01%	Utilities
Kimberly-Clark	2.01%	Consumer Staples
Clorox Co	2.00%	Consumer Staples
Avery Dennison Corp	2.00%	Industrials
Sigma-Aldrich Corp	2.00%	Materials

Source: S&P Global Strategies Report, September 2009, avaiable at
http://www.standardandpoors.com/indices/sp-500-dividend-aristocrates/en/us/?indexId=spusa-500dusdff--p-us----

Standard & Poors have also recently launched a European version of this index – called the S&P Europe 350 Dividend Aristocrats.[16] This features a slightly different strategy – with just two key measures:

1   Each company must be a member of the S&P Europe 350 index of largest blue chip companies on the mainland and the UK.

2   Each must have increased dividends for at least ten consecutive years.

The resulting index is equal weighted and constituents are reviewed annually in December – the constituents from this index at the end of September 2009 are shown in Table 4.4.

table 4.4   Top ten companies in the S&P Europe 350 Dividend Aristocrats index

Name	Weight	Sector	Country
Legal & General Group	2.99%	Financials	UK
Man Group	2.82%	Financials	UK
Novartis AG	2.73%	Cons Stpls	Switzerland
Misys	2.72%	Info Tech	UK
Gas Natural SDG SA	2.71%	Utilities	Spain
Daily Mail & General Trust	2.71%	Cons Discretionary	UK
AbertisInfraestructuras	2.69%	Industrials	Spain
Essilor Intl	2.67%	Healthcare	France
KBC Group NV	2.62%	Financials	Belgium
Scottish & Southern Energy	2.61%	Utilities	UK

Intriguingly, returns from this European strategy have been noticeably less impressive – the returns are in Table 4.5 (overleaf) and they don't make terrifically impressive reading! Although results in 2008 and 2009 were impressive, returns for the first three years were very poor with significant underperformance.

---

[16] Soe, A.M. (2008) 'S&P Europe 350 Dividend Aristocrats', Standard & Poors Research Paper, www.standardandpoors.com

table 4.5	S&P European Aristocrats index portfolio statistics				
Index performance	3rd quarter 2009	YTD to 30/09/09	12 months	3 years	5 years
S&P European Dividend Aristocrats	25%	42%	12.88%	−3.5%	6.18%
S&P Europe 350	23.21%	31%	2.6%	2.92%	7.08%
Standard deviation	**3 year**	**5 year**			
S&P European Dividend Aristocrats	25.22%	20.67%			
S&P Europe 350	25.76%	21.54%			

The UK members of the S&P 350 European Dividend Aristocrats index are show in the box below.

UK members of the S&P 350 European Dividend Aristocrats in 2008

Barclays	Hammerson	Centrica
Cobham	Legal and General	Next
Capita Group	Misys	Pearson
CRH	National Grid	Rexam
Daily Mail	Scottish and Southern Energy	Royal Dutch Shell
MAN Group	WPP	Tesco
Enterprise Inns	British American Tobacco	Vodafone Group
FirstGroup	British Land Company	

Investment strategies focused on yield

Yet another take on a high yield strategy has recently been proposed by Andrew Lapthorne's team at SG who've looked at what's worked in terms of income strategy in various major developed markets in the past few decades. His team then developed a clever strategy that's based on the payout as a yield plus an all-important additional factor, namely balance sheet strength.

Before looking in detail at this strategy it's worth delving into SG's regional market research. The SG team's first step was to screen the major world developed markets for a threshold level of dividend yield – including only those stocks that paid out more than 100% of the market/benchmark yield. That threshold level was progressively raised from 100% to as much as 200% but the results of this ratcheting up varied markedly between regions. In most regions – bar mainland Europe – pushing the level up to 200% substantially reduced returns. Lapthorne's team settled on a figure of around 110% for most markets. The results are shown in Table 4.6.

table 4.6 Back testing dividend yields by region since 1988 (long only returns, annualised %)

	US		Europe (ex. UK)		UK		Japan	
Dividend yield greater than	Annual return	Maximum drawdown	Annual return	Maximum drawdown	Annual return	Maximum drawdown	Annual return	Maximum drawdown
100	11.3	54	10.3	58	9.1	57	5.1	53
110	11.1	55	10.3	59	9.4	59	5.5	53
120	11	55	10.3	59	8.9	64	6.2	53
150	10.4	57	11.4	63	8.1	73	· 7.8	57
200	9.6	61	12.6	67	6.1	79	8.3	58

Source: SG Client research at www.sgbcib.

The SG team then took these returns and mapped them out over time. In Figure 4.8 (overleaf) you can see how a strategy of only picking stocks paying at least 110% of the average market yield performed from 1987 onwards. What's immediately apparent is that in most regions this simple screen delivered very decent results – anything over the base of 1 implies relative out performance. Yet here in the UK the performance of this simple screen – only pick stocks paying out 110% of the market yield – was hugely under-whelming with total returns much lower than a simple strategy of buying the FTSE 100 regardless of yield.

Emboldened by this research the SG team realised that in some markets they had to add an additional filter to sift out the poorly performing stocks being caught within this simple yield based screen – a move that would also narrow down the number of companies identified, making it easier to operate as a strategy. Lapthorne's team looked at a total of six measures in all – many of which we'll encounter in some detail later in this book. These filters consisted of the following:

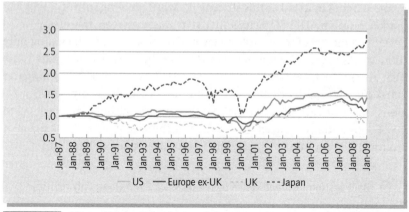

Source: SG Quantitive Research

figure 4.8 The relative performance of the above dividend yield portfolio versus the market (cumulative total returns indexed to 100)

- price momentum – top quintile based on six-month relative price momentum (for more details on this measure see Chapter 8)
- EPS momentum – top quintile based on three-month change in EPS forecasts (see Chapter 6)
- balance sheet risk – top quintile based on highest distance to default – the Merton model (see Chapter 5)
- quality – those stocks with a Piotroski F-score ≥ 7 (see Chapter 5)
- earnings cover – top quintile of stocks with the best earnings cover based on EPS over DPS
- growth – top quintile of stocks based on the five-year historical dividend growth rate (see Chapter 6).

After running these screens across all the major developed world markets, Lapthorne's team decided to focus on just one additional measure, namely balance sheet strength! Their chosen measure was based on an established idea borrowed from the global bond markets – the Merton model – which looks at balance sheet strength and indebtedness. Adding this extra measure seemed to substantially improve long-term returns, particularly in the UK but without taking on any extra risk. Over the 20 years to 2008, this two-step screen would have produced an annualised return of 12.3% per annum compared to just 8.4% for a simple 110% of the market average dividend threshold (see Table 4.7).

table 4.7   UK annualised long only returns when filters applied (% best for each period), 2009

Period	Above yield portfolio	Balance sheet strength	Earnings cover	Price momentum	Earnings momentum	Quality	Growth
Last year (2009)	−47	9.4	−34	−16	−26	−21	−27
Last 5 years	−0.2	14.8	8.2	12.4	11.2	9.5	10.9
Last 10 years	6.2	9.8	8.1	6.2	3.9	7.3	7.5
Last 20 years	8.4	12.3	11	10.6	12.1	11.3	11.9

Source: SG Research.

The UK SG stock screen companies in 2009 are:

- BHP Billiton
- Cable and Wireless
- Centrica
- Sage Group
- United Utilities
- AstraZeneca
- British American Tobacco
- National Grid
- Pearson

Graham Secker, a strategist at top American bank Morgan Stanley, has also developed a number of dividend weighted strategies that target high yielding stocks. In the UK his favourite yield-based strategy is something called FTSE 100 DPS-Based Reliable Growth Screen. In this strategy Secker builds a basket of shares using three factors:

1 The median quarterly percentage change in consensus 12-month forward DPS estimates since 1995 – in this measure he's trying to capture shares where analysts have constantly been increasing their estimates of dividend growth.

2 The standard deviation of these quarterly percentage changes in 12-month forward DPS over the past five years – Secker uses the standard deviation measure as a way of excluding companies where the change in dividends is volatile.

3 The probability that a quarterly percentage change is positive based on data since 1995 – Secker's team have developed a probability-based measure that looks at the pace of dividend change over time.

According to Secker this strategy has been hugely successful since it started running early in 2005 – capital price-only returns over time have beaten the main market yet the dividend payout has also increased over time (see Figure 4.9).

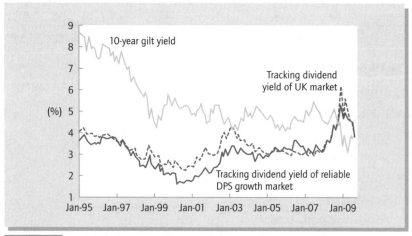

figure 4.9 Stocks in Morgan Stanley reliable DPS growth basket have the best track record yet yield the same as UK market and gilts, i.e. no premium for superior growth!

Source: Morgan Stanley.

Progressive Dividend Heroes

The problem with many of these strategies (and the special strategy-based indices) is that the markets are so fluid and volatile that everything can literally change overnight. To understand this, take a look at the earlier S&P list of British Dividend Aristocrats, for instance, and you'll notice banks like Barclay – which stopped paying its dividend in 2009 – as well as property companies like British Land and Hammerson. To survive in volatile markets investors need to take both a backwards look at dividend consistency *and* a forward look at projected dividend growth, otherwise they could find themselves investing in companies like GKN and AngloAmerican where the dividend has been stopped despite many years of heroic consistency.

We've tried to build this thinking into a simple filter called the Progressive Dividend Heroes – this looks at the FTSE 100 universe and then systematically excludes any company that doesn't fit the following criteria:

- We looked at the more recent past – the last eight years for instance – and excluded any company which hadn't increased its dividend year on year over those eight years.
- Crucially we looked at forward projections of dividend growth by analysts and only included those where dividends are set to increase. Bear in mind though that this is only an *estimate* and that analysts could have got it wrong!
- We've also only included companies where there is a stated dividend policy. This will usually consist of a simple commitment to growing real sterling dividends (Pennon for instance is committed to growing it at 3% per annum), or the company might commit to paying a fixed percentage of earnings.
- Only companies with a proper dividend reinvestment plan have been included.

We'd also suggest that investors carefully scrutinise a range of wider issues including:

- The potential FX risk – examine how much of the business is conducted outside of the UK. If a large portion of turnover is derived in dollars and euros this opens the company up to some risk if the exchange risk goes against it (the opposite has been happening in the past six months). Most companies will aggressively hedge away this exposure but it's estimated that upto 60% of the entire earnings flow in the FTSE 100 is based on foreign earnings.
- We've also included a measure for cash flow per share in the most recent accounts – this shows you how much the dividend per share is covered by operating cash inflows. As long as it's above 1 the company can afford the payment and anything above 2 is pretty safe.
- We've also noted any pensions scheme liability, where disclosed. The pensions regulatory body has already warned that it would expect companies to sacrifice their dividends before they cut pensions payments so a company with a high deficit is potentially risky. None of our shortlisted dividend heroes seems to be in too much trouble.
- Last but by no means least we've also included the level of gearing – this could be an indicator of future trouble if the SG analysis is correct,

although it's worth cautioning that many utilities have high levels of regulated debt that are comfortably backed by both real assets and growing earnings.

When this screen was first run in September 2009 for the *Investors Chronicle* magazine the resulting shortlist comprised just 16 companies in the FTSE 100 (see Table 4.8). Intriguingly this slightly more complex take on a progressive dividend strategy also seems to have delivered some decent returns over the past eight years. Over the time span the FTSE All Share index had declined by just over 11% in total return terms (dividends included) yet our Progressive Heroes have returned to investors an average gain of 30% in total. But that average total return increases to an impressive 61% if you had reinvested the dividends paid out by our heros – you'd have doubled your total returns by reinvesting through the companies' dividend reinvestment plans.

The Weiss Income Screen

An alternative take on a dividends-based strategy comes from an investment writer based in the US called Geraldine Weiss. Editor since 1966 of newsletter, *Investment Quality Trends*, she's been dubbed 'the Grande Dame of Dividends' and has promoted one simple message – dividends don't lie. She was once quoted as saying: 'My father told me that he would never buy a stock unless it paid a dividend. He believed that companies that did not share profits with stockholders in that way were not worth investing in.'[17]

Her belief is that the level of a stock's dividend yield shouldn't just be seen as an income stream (though there's nothing wrong with that per se), but as a measure of valuation. For that reason, she targets stocks with dividend yields at the high end of their historic ranges, and trading at comparatively low prices. But Weiss wants more. Her chosen stocks must also have other favourable characteristics, such as a dividend that is well protected by earnings of some sort, plus a relatively low level of debt. But the key measure for her is something called the *dividend cover* – the company can't be paying out more in dividends than total earnings. Her logic is undeniable: if a company isn't making money, it stands to reason that it will have trouble paying dividends. That means a dividend cover of at least 2 is absolutely

---

[17] Brill, M. (2003) 'Duchess of Dividends', Financial Advisor website, www.fa-mag. com/component/content/article/650html?issue=29&magazinedID=1&Itemid=27

table 4.8	The Progressive Dividend Heroes shortlist

Company name	EPIC*	Close	Cash flow per share (p)	Cash cover on dividends	Net gearing (%)	Total gain without reinvesting (%)	Total gain with reinvesting (%)	Pension deficit
BP PLC	BP	4.5475				5.33	26.60	$301m deficit
British Land Co PLC	BLND	4.02	58.6	1.67	74.4	25.80	38.75	n.a.
Centrica PLC	CNA	2.5975	50.9	4.4	26.6	20.47	40.78	£97m surplus
Diageo PLC	DGE	8.3	63	1.83	186	33.14	65.51	£477m deficit
FirstGroup PLC	FGP	2.6675	87.3	5.13	320	33.97	58.39	£89m surplus
GlaxoSmithKline PLC	GSK	11.06				19.31	34.73	£285m UK deficit
ICAP PLC	IAP	2.065	43.7	2.79	7.18	65.22	104.42	£1m deficit
Imperial Tobacco Group PLC	IMT	16.6	141	2.23	184	65.98	155.81	£105m deficit
Marks & Spencer Group PLC	MKS	2.51	59	2.62	128	41.23	67.39	
National Grid PLC	NG	6.19	212	6.42	388	27.11	55.22	
Pearson PLC	PSON	6.33	64.9	2.05	28.4	13.03	24.42	n.a.
Pennon Group PLC	PNN	4.28	67.6	3.41	275	56.57	129.98	£58m deficit
Sage Group (The) PLC	SGE	1.66	19.4	2.69	41.6	6.96	11.77	n.a.
Schroders PLC	SDR	7.01				13.24	23.66	n.a.
Scottish & Southern Energy PLC	SSE	11.27	134	2.21	123	51.18	111.97	£211m deficit
Vodafone Group PLC	VOD	1.2265	19.5	2.6	32.7	13.92	25.06	
					Average	30.78	60.90	

Over 8 years to 1 March 2009

* Stockmarket code for the stock, also known as the ticker.

essential, i.e. that for every £1 dividend there's £2 of earnings. She's also a fairly unashamed blue chip investor and usually insists on a minimum market capitalisation of at least $100m or even $500m. Weiss also stipulates that the share price must not exceed 2× book value, and it must sell for 20× earnings or less.

To get into her elite final selection a stock also has to meet one last crucial criteria – the company has to have raised its dividends at a compound annual rate of at least 10% over the past 12 years.

It's a very tough set of measures but according to analysts at the *Hulbert Financial Digest* – the oracle newsletter for analysis of US investments – it seems to work. Since 1986 *Hulbert* reckons that Weiss's recommended stocks gained 12.2% beating the 10.9% annualised gain of the Wilshire Index over the same period. Crucially *Hulbert* reckons that Weiss's picks were 27% less volatile than the index, and her newsletter's selections, performed better than each of the 42 others tracked by Hulbert over the period on a risk adjusted basis.

But Weiss's methods are increasingly not suited to a (US) market that believes dividends are a signal of failure. Over the past decade yields have been steadily falling as companies have stopped paying them. Their defence? Better to take surplus profits and reinvest them in the business to grow profits. As yields tumbled below 6% and then 3%, Weiss grew increasingly bearish. Since the end of the 1990s Weiss has argued that the whole market was overvalued and advised her readers to put as much as 70% of their money into cash. That meant they'd have missed the crash of 2001 and 2008 but also the subsequent massive rallies and bull markets, missing out on some huge profits! And Weiss hasn't changed her view since the 1990s. In one recent interview she noted that although 'the yield profile of the Dow has evolved... There could certainly be a new paradigm for the Dow in which a 1.5% yield signals overvaluation and a yield of 3% would mean undervaluation.'[18] To describe this as a tad bearish is perhaps the understatement of the century. Her view also crucially ignores the increasing importance of share buybacks in the US which some analysts maintain could,[19] if added to dividends as a measure of shareholder returns, double the yield again bringing it back within the normal historical range.

---

[18] Ibid.

[19] Dillow, C. (2004) 'Op Ed' column, *Investors Chronicle*, 1 October.

A strategy for finding Weiss blue chips

Running a Weiss screen in the UK is fairly straightforward, but does involve a few minor alterations from her US-based approach. Investors should focus on a number of key measures or screens:

- The dividend yield should be above the average for the market.
- Dividend cover should be at least 2 – that is dividends are covered at least twice by earnings.
- The minimum market cap should be at least £100m.
- The PE ratio should be at least positive and there should be some evidence that the firm has been growing earnings per share over the past three to five years, on average.

Turning to the balance sheet Weiss suggests a number of other crucial measures:

- Net gearing should be less than 50% to avoid companies with too high a level of debt.
- There should be some evidence of positive cashflow at the operating level.
- The current ratio should be above 1.
- The share price should be no more than twice the level of tangible assets.

Armed with an initial shortlist, Weiss then recommends that investors investigate the successful companies in much greater detail, in particular examining whether that crucial dividend payout is viable. According to Weiss investors need to see five years of continuous dividend payments that have been increasing year on year. Weiss wants stocks that simply won't vanish. She wants stability and stature. That means she also wants some evidence that the big institutions like the stock. Her suggested requirement is that at least three big institutions hold above 10% of the stock, or ideally 50%. This last requirement can be a little daunting but most stocks that have passed all these demanding requirements will have heavy institutional backing anyway.

The cavaets – what to watch out for!

Dividends may have a great many obvious attractions but they are not without their challenges and concerns. Rob Buckland from Citi reminds his clients that:

Any dividend-based analysis should recognise that attitudes to dividends vary between both markets and companies. Companies in some regions place little emphasis on dividends, either because they can't pay them or because they believe investors will be better served through cashflow being reinvested into the business. Furthermore, taxation legislation may mean that stock buybacks are a better and more flexible way to return capital to shareholders (this was the case in the US in the late 1990s when capital gains taxes were only 20% (long-term) versus a 39.5% income tax rate on dividends). Also, buyback programmes can be abandoned more easily than dividend payments. The UK, on the other hand, has a strong dividend paying culture, despite the fact that taxation on dividends is onerous.[20]

Dividends can also change over time – at least three major FTSE 100 companies slashed their dividends in 2009. According to a report from Buckland's team at Citibank Research, 'the key swing factors in the [FTSE 100] dividend are the oil price, the dollar/sterling exchange rate and the state of the financial system'.[21] Research from ING Wholesale Banking also looked at 59 large-cap European stocks that had declared dividends by the middle of the year. The researchers found that nearly half had either cut their dividends or omitted them entirely – many in France also cut back cash payments and brought in scrip payments where the dividend is paid out in cash instead.

That sudden decline in dividend payments, not unnaturally, caused much concern in the financial markets – and especially in a niche market that trades swap financial instruments which track the estimated dividend payout in any one year. At the end of 2009 this specialist market was pricing in a 31% drop in European dividends from 2008 to 2009, and then a 48% drop from 2009 to 2010. These might seem like disastrous numbers but stockmarket historians are always quick to remind us that previous bear markets have also taken their toll on dividend payouts. As the world reeled from the 1973 oil shock, for example, dividends from companies in the benchmark S&P 500 index fell from more than 60% of earnings in 1970 to 37 per cent in the second quarter of 1974. So although dividends may not be as volatile as earnings, investors shouldn't under-estimate just how quickly dividend payments can evolve… or even vanish!

The total dividend payout for all FTSE 100 companies over the time period shown in Table 4.9 illustrates the following trend.

---

[20] Citi research client paper, 'Global Equity Strategist: Dividend Resilience', 30 September 2008.
[21] Ibid.

table 4.9   Total dividend payout for all FTSE 100 companies

	Forecast (£)	Exchange rate (£)
Dec-07	72377	2.0434
Jan-08	68475	1.9587
Feb-08	69886	1.9484
Mar-08	71202	2.0125
Apr-08	71349	1.9746
May-08	70582	1.9608
Jun-08	71451	1.9538
Jul-08	71330	1.9773
Aug-08	72702	1.9127
Sep-08	74881	1.7596
Oct-08	68402	1.6975
Nov-08	66735	1.5626
Dec-08	67329	1.4834

Source: Rob Davies, the Munro Fund, www.themunrofund.com/

However, it's not just falling or vanishing dividend payouts that investors need to be wary about – they also need to be incredibly careful about an undue concentration on just a few big companies, nearly all of which earn most of their profits in foreign currencies, with more than a few focused on oil (another toxic asset class). According to research from Citibank again, *just seven companies contribute half of the total UK dividend base in 2009*. The Citibank analysis suggests that of the total dividend base 37% is paid in dollars, while about 25% is from the oil sector. Citibank's bottom line: 'A sharp fall in oil price below $40 a barrel would make the sustainability of the dividends questionable.'[22]

And as for a quick and sudden strengthening in the sterling rate against the dollar – the consequences could be cataclysmic! GlaxoSmithKline noted in its 2008 annual report that every 10 cents movement in the cable rate (ster-

---

[22] Ibid.

ling versus dollar) has a direct 3.5% effect on earnings, even after extensive hedging operations. With just £620m of its £19bn sales made in the UK, one can understand that caution – a run on the dollar which pushed cable back to $2 could directly hit EPS by between 15% and 20%, with possible knock-on effects on the dividend.

If all this wasn't bad enough the UK pensions regulators have chipped in with their own (negative) thoughts on the future of the dividend. David Norgrove, the Pensions Regulator, told managers of defined benefit schemes that: 'There is no reason why a pension scheme deficit should push an otherwise viable employer into insolvency. But the pension recovery plan should not suffer, for example, in order to enable companies to continue paying dividends to shareholders.'[23] So in the regulator's view, the dividend ranks as less important than the pensions deficit – investors in outfits like the BT Group with huge pensions deficits and equally chunky dividends (even after some recent cuts) might want to consider just how safe their payout really is.

Investors using a dividend-based stock selection strategy also have to be aware of one last very significant, structural risk – sector bias. Typically, most dividend-oriented portfolios or index funds are dominated by two sectors, Financials and Utilities. For example, the Dow Jones Select Dividend index and the Mergent Dividend Achievers 50 index have nearly 60% and 80%, respectively, in these two sectors. According to an S&P note on its US Dividend Aristocrats 'this is because companies in these sectors have traditionally been the biggest dividend payers, and portfolios focused exclusively on high yields tend to be concentrated in these sectors. While this approach enhances current yield, it poses significant sector risks. Traditionally, Financials and Utilities have done well in stable and low interest rate environments.'[24] This constant bias towards specific sectors can be seen in Figure 4.10 which tracks the composition of one of S&P's own dividend-based indices in Europe – the S&P Europe 350 Dividend Aristocrats.

The bottom line? All these threats to a strategy focused solely on companies that pay out a fat dividend cheque should remind investors that equity is risk capital: their role is to stand first in line when losses are realised. And that means the first thing to go when a company is in trouble is usually the dividend!

---

[23] See www.tltsolicitors.com/resources/publications/pensions/pensions archive/contingentassetsmar09

[24] Standard and Poor's research paper, 'The S&P High Yield Dividend Aristocrats Index' by Srikant Dash, www.standardandpoor.com

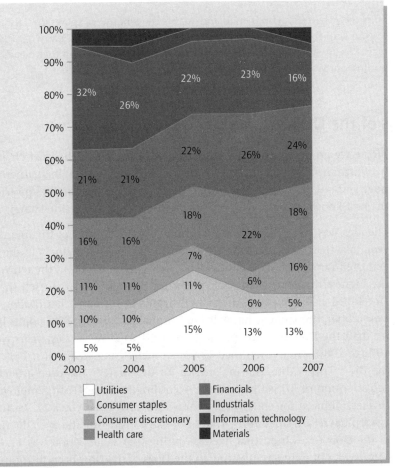

figure 4.10   S&P Europe 350 Dividend Aristocrats: sector composition of the Aristocrats over time

Source: Soe, A.M. (2008) 'S&P Europe 350 Dividend Aristocrats Analytical Contacts', S&P Research Paper, December, www.sandp.com

Dividend reinvestment plans

DRIPs as they're inelegantly called are the great unsung heros of the modern investment world. These are incredibly simple schemes – you just contact a big share registrar like Equiniti (www.shareview.co.uk/products/Pages/applyforadrip.aspx) and download a DRIP form. This form tells the registrar about your holding of shares in the underlying company held via your stockbroker. When a dividend is issued the company then buys some of its own shares on your behalf and credits the amount of shares directly to your broker holdings at no extra cost. These services by company registrars are free but you have to apply to join the scheme and that means finding out which registrar handles the forms.

Dogs of the DOW

Before we go on to investigate value-based strategies in the next chapter it's worth mentioning one last, dividend-based strategy that has garnered a huge amount of publicity – it's called the Dogs of the Dow and it's probably the best known attempt to apply dividends to a stock selection strategy.

The idea was and is devastatingly simple. On the last day of the financial year, take the Dow Jones Industrial index of the 30 largest stocks in the US and then rank them by their dividend yield. Invest $1000 in the ten with the highest dividend yield. Hold them for one year and then sell them. Developed and refined by Michael O'Higgins in his best-seller *Beating the Dow* (2000), this strategy has delivered annual performance 5% points better than the Dow over the period from 1961 to 1995. Its best years were 1973 to 1989, when it returned 17.9% annually compared to just 11% for the Dow. This enthusiasm in America for the strategy has even attracted the attention of British journalists. According to *MoneyWeek*: 'Employing this technique at the end of each year would have given you a 17.7% average annual return since 1973. That's not bad considering the overall return of the Dow Jones Industrial Average during that same period was 11.9%. Moreover, not only has investing in the Dogs of the Dow been historically more profitable than buying all 30 Dow stocks, it's also been safer.'[25]

British investment writer Peter Temple has also taken these ideas and devised a homegrown variation of this model for the *Financial Times*. This involves using a slightly obscure index – the FTSE 30 – which covers the 30 largest stocks in the UK and is probably the nearest equivalent to the Dow. This Beat the FT30 strategy is essentially a copy of the Small Dogs of the Dow strategy (see below) and involves investing in the five companies with the highest dividend yields.

---

[25] www.moneyweek.com/investment-advice/how-to-invest/the-dogs-of-the-dow-an-investors-best-friend.aspx

A number of equally important variations have also emerged in the US. Another version suggested by O'Higgins involves taking the ten highest yielding stocks in the Dow, and then picking the five with the lowest share prices and buying these five in exactly the same way. This is called Beat the Dog (BTD 5) or Small Dogs of the Dow. Yet another variation has the catchy title of PPP or Penultimate Profit Prospect. This involves taking the five Small Dogs and then picking the one with the second cheapest share price.

The Motley Fool website devised its own take on the Small Dogs and PPP strategy. Called the Foolish Four this takes the four highest yielding stocks in the Dow, ignoring the cheapest share, and then investing twice as much in the second cheapest share (that PPP) and then the rest equally in numbers 3, 4 and 5. This last strategy returned a 25-year compounded average annual return (1973–1997) of 23.17%, well above the return of the Dow.

Does it work?

The idea behind all these iterations of the same strategy is relatively simple – the market eventually rediscovers the importance of high yielding big stocks and starts bidding up share prices. We'll explore a wider range of strategies built around this concept in the next chapter.

Sadly results for this strategy haven't been quite as impressive in recent years. For the ten years up to 31 December 2008 the Dogs were up 1.9% while the Dow was up 3.3%. As analyst and investment newsletter analyst Mark Hulbert observes, 'the strategy worked as well as it did historically because, far more often than not, these stocks' high yields came down because their prices went up. But, as the recent bear market reminded us, there's another way for high yields to come down: for the dividends to be cut'.[26]

Economists have also attacked the system – they claim the basic Dogs strategy is a classic example of dangerous 'data-mining', confusing workable systems with logic behind them with statistical freaks or outliers. More to the point most economists reckon the Dogs has stopped working as a strategy. In a paper entitled 'Do Dow Stocks Offer a Value Premium?' Jeong *et al.* investigated long-term returns and found that 'the dividends value portfolio earned significant excess returns during May 1983–April 1995, while the earnings value portfolio significantly outperformed during May 1995–April 2007'.[27]

---

[26] www.marketwatch.com/story/recent-performance-of-dogs-of-the-dow-2009-08-26

[27] Jeong, J.-G., Lee, Y. and Mukherji, S. (2009) 'Do Dow Stocks Offer a Value Premium?', *The Journal of Wealth Management*, Vol. 12, No. 3, pp. 95–103.

Conclusion

Dividends make a huge difference to investors over the long term – there's plenty of academic evidence to remind us that without dividends and their subsequent reinvestment, equities would be a much less attractive proposition compared to bonds.

Focusing your stock selection on high yielders can be hugely productive – as long as you're very aware of the risks in bearish markets where dividend favourites like banks tend to be disproportionately badly hit. Also investors are advised to focus their search for high yielding stocks using more than just one measure – not just an above average yield. Some sense of the consistency of the payout and its growth over time is essential while a focus on the balance sheet strength is also probably a good idea. Ideally dividends shouldn't be seen as operating in isolation from the wider balance sheet and cash flow statement. As we'll discover in the next chapter many value-based strategies tend to include some measure of dividends as a key component.

If I had to offer some general advice to investors I'd suggest bearing in mind the following simple principles:

- Look at the frequency and consistency of the dividend payment itself! Most analysts look for a consistent dividend payout, preferably increasing over time.
- Dividend cover is also hugely important. This is the ratio between the earnings per share and the dividends per share – if a company produces £2 of earnings and pays out £1 in dividends per share, the dividend cover is 2. Most analysts regard a dividend cover of 1 as the bare minimum, less than 1 troubling (the dividend isn't covered by earnings) and over 2 positive.
- Last but by no means least, some analysts prefer to look at cashflow per share at the operating level (after depreciation but before tax, capex and dividends) and then compare this to the dividend payout, rather than focus too much on stated earnings per share.

5

Deep value investing: the world according to Tweedy, Browne and Graham

Many shall be restored that now are fallen and many shall fall that now are in honour. Horace's *Ars Poetica*

Introduction

Many aeons ago a senior and respected investor confided to the author of this book that 'there was something rather peculiar about buying cheapo, value stocks'. He maintained that investing in equities was about risk and adventure, about chasing those capitalist high fliers and bagging your own shooting stars that would provide your portfolio with huge returns. It's a concept that we'll return to in the next chapter when we examine the various strategies devised to hunt down quality companies with decent growth profiles, but at a reasonable share price. My City insider maintained that this hunt for the elusive GARP – a company growing, at a reasonable price – stock was what equity investing was all about! 'Investing should be about taking risks to get rewards otherwise you may as well invest in bonds', he noted. 'Value investing strikes me as slightly anti-capitalist – in effect you don't believe the management's predictions on profits and the only thing you trust are hard fixed assets and cash.'

Another investor – this time a fund manager – offered an alternative view on why there was something wrong about value investing. Hunting down stocks with a low share price relative to the asset base of the business – a brutal summation of value investing in its purest form – was akin to 'actually turning around and saying that you like shopping at Aldi or Asda. We all know that given a choice we'd actually rather shop somewhere more aspirational like Waitrose which looks nice and feels expensive. Why would you consciously choose to spend so much time hanging out in bargain basement places?'

One can only guess at the fund manager's weekly shopping bills but some readers will see his point – cheap stuff makes rational sense but it's no substitute for something more luxurious feeling, with brand cachet and a better class of customer, all delivered for a small extra price. As we noted earlier in this book, most investing is firmly anchored in various behavioural vices, wedded to mental concepts designed to make you lose money including an inner voice that tells investors they too can make more money by trading more often or that something that is sexy and growth orientated deserves a higher price. Value investors, as we'll discover in this chapter, believe in a very different set of values and worldviews. This book isn't meant to be the definitive guide to the different styles of investing (value vs growth, with GARP in the middle) and in particular value investing, but in this chapter we will sketch out this world view and see how it can be summed up in simple to understand strategies that help with stock selection. We start this journey through value investing with the first of a long line of financial gurus who we will encounter over the next few pages. His name is Benjamin Graham and for most people proper investing starts with 'Ben'.

BG and AG

I once jokingly described to a seminar that modern investing should use the terms BG and AG – Before Graham and After Graham. The deadening silence of the audience reaction and the slightly embarrassed looks on audience faces convinced me that I was in a room full of Christian investors who didn't appreciate the simile with the son of god or Ben Graham acolytes, who think of the 'great man' as the investing equivalent of a saint.

Graham believed that the market gets it wrong because of its obsession with growth at all costs. By now you'll be more than familiar with the prognostications of the Sage of Omaha himself (the eponymous Warren Buffett) who's famously gone on record as saying that modern day markets seem to irrationally over-price 'OK' stocks with decent growth prospects and underprice solid stocks with almost as good growth prospects. Periodically he warns private investors of irrational exuberance, famously refraining from investing during what he perceived to be mad phases of rising share prices.

Buffett believes, like Ben Graham, his first great mentor, that you make money by focusing. The path to true riches lies with a relentless focus on good value and a margin of safety. When he, or you for that matter, chooses to invest hard-earned money in a share (which for Buffett and Graham means a real world business not just a piece of paper) he wants to be sure that it – company and shares – are cheap.

Cheap means a great many things in the lexicon of value investors. It might mean on a surface level that the vital statistics, the fundamentals, of the share price are cheap in relation to the wider market or alternatively that the PE ratio is low, or the ratio of sales to the share price unreasonably high.

But cheap means much more than simple ratios. It also means that there is a margin of safety built into the shares. Graham, Buffett and the Holy Church of the Value Investor believe that there is some kind of intrinsic value in a company. Look at its balance sheet and consider the asset backing of the shares – is it cheap in relation to these assets? Other investors take a more dynamic view and like to look at future prospects as well and consider whether future profits growth and cash generation will add to the intrinsic value of the business.

But it gets better. Value investors are rigorous folk and they make the effort to acquaint themselves with other measures of shareholder wealth. In particular they love dividends – as we discovered in the last chapter a juicy dividend can make a big difference to total shareholder returns over the long term. You might not only benefit from an increase in the capital value of the shares following a re-evaluation by the market of the intrinsic value of the business but you'll also get all those lovely dividend cheques. Add it all up and you could make above average returns.

The bottom line is this – the market all too frequently gets it wrong by under-valuing decent companies with good prospects. One great value investor and Graham disciple Mario Gabelli, nicely summed up the core of this philosophy in Peter Tanous's book on great investors, *Investment Gurus*:

We're buying a business and a business has certain attributes... as surrogate owners there are certain characteristics with regard to the franchise, the cash generating capabilities of the franchise and the quality of the management... You also have a notion of price. Where are you buying that stock within the context of what I call 'private market value' – what others might call intrinsic value? And within that framework, Mr Market gives you opportunities to buy above that price and below that price, that intrinsic value.[1]

---

[1] Tanous, P. (1997) *Investment Gurus: A Road Map to Wealth from the World's Best Money Managers*, Prentice Hall Press.

Gabelli is rightly famous for his own version of intrinsic value, namely something called private market value. Arguably in our private equity, leveraged buyout driven world this variation on the definition of intrinsic value has more relevance than ever. If you ask what an informed industrialist or even private equity house might pay to buy this business, you're probably asking the same question the VC and private equity boys are asking. Like all good value investors you'll be looking at the summation of business value – the cash, the receivables, the inventory as well the goodwill, the earnings power, plus some modicum of future value potential. If it all adds up to something that can be viewed as cheap, you stand a better chance of making a profit.

Ben Graham and the art of investing

Ben Graham famously once suggested a stock picking strategy based on the idea that you should 'Fish where the fish are'. What he meant by this was simple. If there are lots of seemingly cheap companies in a particular sector, start fishing (and investing) because some of those stocks will probably be what they say they are – cheap.

According to Greenwald *et al.*[2] the core to understanding Graham's value approach is that 'over the long run, performance of both companies and share prices generally reverts to a mean' – in the spirit of Horace's poem, the lowly priced cheap stock no-one seems to like will eventually rise in price as the market comes to love its low intrinsic value in relation to the share price. At the core of Graham's investing style is a belief that despite wild speculative variations, shares do have a fundamental economic value that are relatively stable and can be easily measured by use of the term intrinsic value. Put simply investors should only buy shares when their market price is significantly below that of the calculated 'intrinsic value'.

Graham actually specified what he meant by intrinsic value in the following equation.

$$\text{Value} = \text{current (normal) earnings} \times (8.5 + \text{twice the expected annual growth rate})$$

where the growth rate should be that expected over the next seven to ten years.

---

[2] Greenwald, Kahn, Sonkin, and Van Biema, *Value Investing*, Wiley.

A literal translation of this equation is perhaps simpler to understand – the intrinsic value of any investment is determined by the present value of the distributable cash flows that the asset supplies its owner, the shareholders.

As you'd expect subsequent analysts have varied this understanding of intrinsic value. One of the more radical was offered by Mario Gabelli who used an alternative we've already mentioned, namely something called the private market value. This measures the real value of a company to trade buyers and private equity houses, and is equal to the underlying intrinsic value plus a premium for control. As Gabelli puts it the PMV (private market value) equals 'the value an informed industrialist would pay to purchase assets with similar characteristics'.[3]

Cheap stocks backed by a clear free cashflow and a good asset base will make a perfect takeover target for trade buyers and private equity houses who will realise the 'real hidden' value in the shares. These 'insider' buyers will already have realised that assets and cashflow are much more reliable than 'earnings' – assets can be sold to pay for the purchase while cashflow can be milked to pay for continuing debts.

James Montier, former house strategist at SG and now asset allocation guru at fund management firm GMO is another Graham acolyte (it's Montier who reminds us of Graham's nickname as Dean of Wall Street) who's tried to keep the master investor's ideas current. Montier, summed up his take on Graham's view thus:

At the heart of Graham's approach was the concept of an appropriate margin of safety. That is to say, investors should always seek to purchase securities with a large discount between intrinsic value and market price. ... Indeed, Graham's own best loved criterion was a price less than two-thirds of net current assets.[4]

Montier fleshes out his take on Graham's approach to shares by defining a screen or strategy that should be able to identify specific stocks – ten criteria in all, listed back in the 1970s in the *Journal of Portfolio Management*.

In order to qualify as a value opportunity Montier reckons Ben Graham would have been looking for the following measures:

---

[3] Quoted in Calandro, J. (2008) 'The Sears acquisition: a retrospective case study of value detection', *Strategy & Leadership*, Vol. 36, No. 3, pp. 26–34. ISSN: 1087–8572, DOI: 10.1108/10878570810870767, Publisher: Emerald Group Publishing Limited.
[4] Montier, J. (2008) 'Mind Matters – What would Ben think? Or, how low can we go?, *Valuations – a bottom-up perspective*.

1 A trailing or historic earnings yield greater than twice the AAA bond yield. Remember that the trailing earnings yield is simply the PE ratio for the last years expressed as a percentage, i.e. a PE of 10 equates to a yield of 10%.

2 A PE ratio of less than 40% of the peak PE ratio based on five-year moving average earnings. Graham was very insistent that investors should look beyond just the last year's earnings figures and instead focus on the moving average of the past five years.

3 A dividend yield at least equal to two thirds of the AAA bond yield.

4 A price of less than two thirds of tangible book value. Graham had a preference for looking only at tangible assets rather than intangible assets – buildings and equipment can be sold in distressed circumstances whereas brands can devalue almost overnight and have no real value at all!

5 A price of less than two thirds of net current assets.

6 Total debt less than tangible book value.

7 A current ratio greater than 2.

8 Total debt less than (or equal to) twice net current assets.

9 Compound earnings growth of at least 7% over the past ten years.

10 Two or fewer annual earnings declines of 5% or more in the past ten years.

(If you're not sure about any of these terms remember to check Chapter 2 on measures or Appendix 2 on the tools of the trade.)

According to Montier:

The first five criteria are all methods of trying to ensure the margin of safety is large on any purchase. They are all deep value conditions. The next three criteria are concerned with balance sheet strength. They are essentially solvency measures. After all, it is no use buying a cheap stock if it's about to go belly up! The final two elements of Graham's screen try to incorporate an element of growth and stability (quality measures if you like) into the screen.[5]

Montier also suggests that if you can't get any companies which meet the full list of ten measures – he calls them Graham net nets – you should focus instead on measures 1, 3 and 6:

---

[5] Ibid.

Criteria 1 and 3 are effective valuation constraints, [while] criterion six ensures that there is likely to be some equity value even in the event of liquidation. Thus the overall screen looks for extremely rare, cheap, non-bankrupt, quality stocks… every investor's dream. Given the deep value nature of this screen we won't really ever expect to see masses of stocks appearing.[6]

Montier's former colleagues at French bank SG have tested this strategy in great detail – measuring both risk and return for the US markets between 1950 and 2008. The average annualised return for a strategy built around a Graham screen is just under 16% per annum while more expensive stocks – called growth stocks – delivered under 10% per annum but with even greater risk. And the SG analysis is backed up by countless other studies of Graham stock selection strategies including the American Association of Individual Investor's own stock screening programme since 1998. The AAII's two screens based on Graham's ideas (a defensive one and an adventurous one) have delivered 517% and 767% respectively since 1998, a massive premium to the S&P 500. There's even a Ben Graham index – see the box on pp. 144–6 – which has distilled Graham's ideas into a constant basket of stocks that is tracked in turn by an exchange traded note which has also consistently beaten the wider market.

The Graham Defensive Screen

Montier's version of a Graham net net screen is one take on a series of measures articulated by the Dean of Wall Street over the post WW2 period in a number of books, but most importantly the classic *Intelligent Investor* (2003). Graham himself wrote eloquently about his own style and although his views changed over time, he did spell out two distinct strategies, namely a defensive investor screen as well as a slightly more adventurous, enterprising screen for those willing to take more risks.

Graham's more cautious defensive screen spells out the margin of safety he is looking for – protection against further share price falls and the opportunity for reward in the long run when the market realises the true intrinsic value. For Graham that's nearly all about asset backing. His measures for a defensive strategy or screen include the following:

---

[6] Ibid.

1   Graham set a rather arbitrary minimum capitalisation rule of annual sales of not less than $100m. He was concerned, he says, to exclude small companies which may be subject to more than average vicissitudes especially in the industrial field.

2   Graham wanted a stock with a very strong financial backing. The current ratio – the ratio between current assets and liabilities – should be at least 2, implying that current assets were at least twice as large as current debts.

3   Some earnings stability in each of the past ten years.

4   Uninterrupted payment of dividends for at least the past 20 years.

5   A minimum increase of at least one third in EPS over the past ten years.

6   A reasonable PE ratio probably not much more than 15 over the past three years.

7   The current share price should not be more than 1.5 times the book value.

8   As Graham has a specific stock selection system for utilities, he excludes all utilities.

In reality there are very few companies in our modern age that would satisfy all of Graham's tough criteria. Of the just under 1900 companies in the ShareScope Data Mining database – we'll look in greater detail at this particular system and how to use it in Chapter 11 – there are actually 600 companies with tangible assets of over 1.5 times the share price. Add in all the other criteria in that list above and the actual numbers drop to just one, a plantations company based in Asia! Remember that Graham is looking for companies with superb asset backing as well as reasonable profits *and* dividends, a tall order indeed.

An alternative take on a Graham screen in the UK market

To make this work for the UK market most investors would probably have to make some subtle alterations to the model. We've been running a version of this screen for some years at the *Investors Chronicle* (until recently through its *Stockscreening Newsletter*) and in that screen we've made some small modifications.

■   It seems reasonable to set the minimum market cap at about £100m, instantly excluding more than half the total market.

- The current ratio of 2 is fairly easily applied but this removes at least three quarters of most stocks in any screen. If you apply these two screens you should still end up with at least a few hundred stocks.

- A PE ratio of below 15 isn't too demanding in most markets but it will exclude the vast majority of smaller growth stocks: but then again Graham is no enthusiast for equities that promise a lot but no real cash or asset backing. Defensive investing, in his view, has to be about controlling risk.

- We can also fairly easily apply Graham's demand that the share price be no more than 1.5 times the current book value – PBV is 1.5 or below. This very tough requirement cuts down the number of passing companies fairly dramatically but you should still have a fairly long list of candidates. It's the next bunch of criteria that are the more difficult.

- Some earnings for the past ten years is a very tough requirement for British companies and very difficult to screen for – data for more than ten years isn't included in most mass market software programs. A realistic variation on this requirement could be some profits (normalised) for each and every one of the past five years. Likewise for the dividend.

Armed with our shortlist it's probably worth examining each company in more detail.

- Look at the five-year record of dividend payments and EPS figures. There must be a minimum five years of continuous EPS and dividends – if there's ever been a break in dividend payments exclude the stock immediately.

- It might also be worth adding one other quite strict qualitative criterion – look at the cashflow and make sure that it's positive at the very least and that it can easily afford the capex and dividend payments.

But we're not done yet. *The next stage of the screen is to look at EPS five years ago and current EPS figures – current figures should be at least one third higher than five years ago.*

In this modified version of a Ben Graham defensive strategy we're looking for a company with a solid reputation for producing profits and dividends. We're not actually that bothered about it increasing profits next year or the year after!

At the end of this fairly exhaustive process you should be left with a fairly small list of about a dozen or so stocks. Be aware also that this list may also be dominated by just one or two key sectors. If we had run this test in February 1998, for instance, we'd have had a shortlist of 16 companies, most of which would have been builders or property companies, i.e. companies that nearly went bust a decade later!

In fact this paucity of stocks and the consequent reliance on just a few key, 'cheap' sectors presents us with a problem. A Graham screen could all too easily turn into a strategy for simply buying property and construction stocks and this is absolutely not what risk and safety obsessed Graham had in mind. He was keenly aware of the risks of over-concentrated portfolio's and the lack of diversification. One solution to this problem might be to only pick one share from each sector, ranked by PBV. So if you've got five builders that all pass the test, rank them by book value, and then pick the one with the lowest PBV.

A little bit of growth but at a reasonable cost... the enterprising investor

Many value investors can rightly be characterised as growth pessimists – they tend to be openly dismissive of talk about future prospects for growth. But it's probably wrong to characterise Graham as someone who didn't care about the growth potential of a company. Graham was in fact concerned with growth and even went so far as to articulate a stock picking strategy for 'enterprising investors'. But this definition of growth bears very little relation to the growth stocks idealised in our later chapter on the subject – growth only has value within a protected franchise, i.e you know that there's a decent chance the prospect of growth will be delivered through a strong business franchise or regulated position.

And it's important to understand that when Graham talks about the enterprising investor he doesn't necessarily mean that this kind of investor will take greater risks for greater reward. His definition of greater reward derives instead from the amount of time the slightly more knowledgeable, more experienced investor is willing to take to look far and wide for shares – an enterprising investor will be adventurous in the sectors and size of stock. They'll also use more measures and be even more discriminating about the stocks they'll buy.

In fact Graham thinks the really smart enterprising investor will be very focused and spend lots of time hunting down particular types of company – a sniper's approach to investing.

■ He suggests that the enterprising investor might be particularly interested in unpopular companies with a low PE ratio although Graham does warn against being fooled by low PE ratios found amongst cyclicals in their good years, since the market recognises that those high earnings will not be sustained. To avoid this cyclicals trap, Graham suggests an additional requirement that the price be low in relation to past average earnings.

■ Graham particularly likes what he calls 'bargains' amongst smaller stocks. These might be stocks selling at 50% or less than their 'indicated' value. Most obviously this means a stock selling at less than its net working capital alone – in essence, the investor would be purchasing a company without paying for its plants and machinery or any intangibles.

■ Graham also looks for companies with reasonable stability of earnings over the past decade with no years of negative earnings and enough financial size and strength that would allow the firm to survive any future setbacks. The same logic applies to hunting down firms with a very long dividend record, with a high yield, probably well above the market average or median.

■ Last but not least he's after a company with a strong financial condition – low debt, good cashflow – and, as he puts it, 'a low price in relation to the previous high [share] price'.[7] Graham recommends that the stock also have a high quality analysts' rating, which tends to imply that more than one analyst covers the stock and they rate at least a hold.

Putting this into action means that some of the measures will be similar to a defensive screen. The PE ratio for instance has to be reasonable – Graham is clearly looking again for firms with a below average PE ratio. One simple way of doing this is to only pick firms in the lowest quartile according to the PER. An alternative might simply be to set the maximum PE ratio at a decent historical average of about 15 or less.

The firm's financial condition is also important. Like the defensive screen above Graham wants a safe current ratio, this time down to 1.5, but is also

---

[7] Graham, B. (2003) *The Intelligent Investor*, HarperCollins.

clear that he wants debts to be under control and manageable (net gearing below 50% is reasonable). Also look for evidence of positive cashflow with the PCF measure being at least positive.

But this screen is defensive in a number key respects:

- Instead of a full five-year record you might want to look instead for just three years of profits and again profits in the current year must be greater than they were three years ago.

- If you want to be especially demanding you could demand that the current EPS figures be at least 20% higher than three years ago.

- Also whereas the defensive screen set a minimum market cap of £100m, this screen allows in all companies valued at £30m or more.

- This reduced three-year requirement and acceptance of smaller companies introduces greater risk. The shortlisted companies don't have quite the same conservative, almost blue chip status as in the defensive screen so investors probably need to be especially demanding with the last two measures.

- The share price relative to the book value threshold is slightly lowered to 1.2 from 1.5 – this more adventurous strategy wants lots of asset backing for taking on riskier investments.

- And this enterprising strategy also dictates a dividend yield that is above that of the defensive investor. That means a yield which is in the top quarter of the market at least. And that dividend payment has to be covered at least twice by earnings (dividend cover 2 or above).

Again, as with the defensive screen, Graham would stress the need for a broad diversified portfolio at a minimum of ten holdings but probably would prefer a larger group consisting of 30 of the best prospects in each sector, with no one sector dominating. In reality these criteria are actually even more demanding than the defensive screen and you'd be doing well to end up with more than five candidates!

The perfect Graham stock

Until the beginning of 2008 such a screen would probably have produced a fairly short list, dominated by Britain's builders! For most of the past 20 years they've been making huge margins by sitting on a restricted land supply, making excess profits out of selling dream homes that seem to cost more with every passing year (or month as the case may be).

Firms like Taylor Wimpey and Persimmon kept periodically popping up on a Graham screen – defensive or enterprising. Until 2008 they had sound finances, very little debt, great profit margins, fantastic balance sheets. The managements of these companies also believed in paying out to their investors solid, chunky, well-covered dividends. But there was one small problem, hinted at by their lowly rated share prices relative to those bountiful earnings – the shares were dirt cheap. Investors clearly couldn't quite understand why this sector was so profitable and worried about a massive house price boom turning into a bust. And those sceptical investors were of course right. In 2008 the unthinkable happened and the housing market froze up, profits collapsed and the likes of Taylor Wimpey and Persimmon nearly went bust and were forced to raise hundreds of millions in share placing to shore up their battered balance sheets. By 2008 it became apparent to any observer that although these companies had oodles of asset backing this was largely based on massive land banks that collapsed in value almost overnight! Inevitably a more nuanced view has emerged since the travails of 2008 and 2009.

First, think long and hard about diversification. We've already mentioned that a risk averse investor might only want to choose one or maybe two stocks from each sector. This is especially true for builders that remain heartily cyclical and vulnerable to sudden changes in interest rates – but be aware that the fortunes of a sector can change astonishingly quickly.

The example of builders also highlights another of Graham's admonitions. He was asked about how investors should manage their portfolio of value stocks. His view – in the early 1970s – was to take your profits at 50% and only hold for two years. Perhaps Graham was being a bit defensive on the upper limit for profits but he was right to be worried about holding on too long to value stocks. Perhaps he was more aware than most of value stocks' inherent vulnerability, with many boasting a very cyclical profile that made valuations vulnerable to the ebb and flow of the wider economy.

Sound investing principles

It's worth taking one quick detour before we leave Graham, repeating the four guidelines he set for private investors at the end of his most recent edition of *The Intelligent Investor* – they're all laudable and should inform every determined value-based investor:

■ *Know what you are doing – know your business… do not try to make business profits… that is returns in excess of normal [capital] and dividend income.*

■ *Do not let anyone else run your portfolio unless you can supervise his performance with adequate care and comprehension.*

■ *Do not enter upon an operation unless a reliable calculation shows that it has a fair chance to yield a reasonable profit. For enterprising investors [this means] profit should be based not on optimism but on arithmetic.*

■ *Have the courage of your knowledge and experience… you are neither right nor wrong because the crowd disagrees with you. You are right because your data and reasoning are right.*[8]

Index tracking Ben Graham style

In Chapter 12 we'll examine in much greater detail a compelling alternative to active stock selection based on value ideas – this innovative concept is called fundamental indexing and it looks to avoid the risk of picking a concentrated portfolio of shares by building a diversified index of stocks weighted by measures like share price relative to the book value of the company assets. An American research firm called Nuveen Hyde Park has taken this concept and added a novel twist – it's taken Ben Graham's ideas and then turned them into an index. This echo's John Bogle's observation that Ben Graham would have been an index investor if he'd been alive today! It's a fascinating idea and investors can track it via something called an exchange traded note marketed by a company called *Elements*. These notes are in effect derivatives-based contracts between a big investment bank and the investor – the bank takes the money, promises to pay out the return on the index at maturity and in return issues something called a swap contract which sits at the heart of the note. Crucially this note doesn't copy the index by buying all the constituents or companies – it just promises to make the payment.

It's a novel concept and allows funds managers to issue unusual ideas like this – a note that tracks a basket of ideal Ben Graham-like stocks. It's a new idea – the index was only launched a few years ago – but recent performance (as of December 2009) has been hugely impressive, as detailed in the returns on the ETN in Table 5.1 opposite.

The downside with this index is that the developers – in this case Nuveen Hyde Park – haven't disclosed the exact details of their Ben Graham strategy or the filters/screen used. In the filing documents though

---

[8] Ibid.

table 5.1	Returns as of market close 21/12/2009						
Timeframe	3 mo	6 mo	YTD	1 yr	3 yr*	5 yr*	Since note inception
Russell 1000 Total Return Value Index	3.45%	23.55%	20.00%	22.73%	−8.80%	−0.11%	−13.96%
Benjamin Graham Large Cap Value Index − Total Return	N.A.	N.A.	N.A.	N.A.	N.A.	N.A.	−2.54%
Benjamin Graham LC Value ELEMENTS ETNs (Indicative Value)	6.98%	25.00%	46.21%	49.15%	N.A.	N.A.	−3.50%
Benjamin Graham LC Value ELEMENTS ETNs (Market Price)	6.06%	22.08%	49.38%	63.33%	N.A.	N.A.	−3.80%

*3yr and 5yr represent annualised returns. The performance quoted represents historical performance.

they have given some specifics about the index that are worth looking at in some detail. According to Nuveen the index 'seeks to identify businesses with strong, liquid balance sheets that trade at a discount to their implied intrinsic value, implementing the investment principles of Benjamin Graham through a quantitative, objective process utilising modern portfolio theory and statistical analysis. The methodology consists of four steps: (i) Universe Screening, (ii) Stock Selection, (iii) Semi-Annual Re-allocation, and (iv) Annual Reconstitution.'[9]

Nuveen does go on to list the seven major factors used in its index:

1 Earnings Quality – a quantitative analysis that seeks to measure a company's reported earnings as compared to an assessment of its true economic earnings.

2 Valuation – an examination of the ratios of a company's share price to certain financial metrics, including historical earnings and book value.

3 Forward P/E – a ratio of price to consensus estimates of future earnings. Such estimates will be based on data obtained from one or more vendors who provide consensus earnings estimates.

4 Dividend Yield – the ratio of a stock's dividend to its share price.

---

[9] http://www.nuveen.com/HydePark/Products.aspx

▶ 5 Profitability – an evaluation based on measurements of a company's return on capital.

6 Debt and Liquidity – an analysis of a company's current assets as well as its ability to service debt.

7 Measurements Relative to Industry Peers – key measurements of valuation and performance compared to average levels within a given stock's industry.[10]

Crucially this innovative approach to index investing seems to have worked over the past calamitous few years. Table 5.1 shows data on the indices and the ETN funds for the past few years.

A quick Tweedy Browne primer on screening for value shares

There's a weighty body of evidence to suggest that by the 1960s and 1970s Ben Graham was modifying his approach to shares – according to Vanguard founder and investor champ John Bogle he even remarked that index tracking funds might be the best solution for most private investors. It certainly seems that Graham became aware that applying his strict standards were becoming next to impossible – his great disciple Warren Buffett tried to apply them through the post war period but by the late 1960s had virtually given up. The Graham net nets and defensive just didn't seem to be that common anymore!

All of which presented a difficult challenge to those professional investors charged with carrying on where Graham had left off! How could any big fund manager apply the thinking behind Graham's value investing to modern markets obsessed with growth? Cue the seminal and still highly profitable New York-based fund management firm Tweedy Browne. Graham may be the patron saint of most value-based investors, but it's Tweedy Brown who are the Jesuits – the brains behind the scene who bother to work it all out and put it into practice. A select group of Graham acolytes and value enthusiasts, they've been in the investment management game for more than four decades. They also boast two other characteristics that makes them especially compelling. The first is that they take investing seriously and if the management of a company they're invested in messes up, they'll make sure the management is removed. A great example of this

---

[10] Ibid.

ethical approach to investing is their pursuit of Conrad Black and the alleged 'mismanagement' of his newspaper empire which helped to land him in jail. They are value orientated shareholder activists par extraordinaire. Their second even more endearing feature is that like Ben Graham they think long and hard about why value investing makes sense, checking the evidence and then constructing careful strategies – and then communicate these ideas to a large army of dedicated followers.

A few years ago in pursuit of what Tweedy Browne perceive to be the truth, they put out what has to be the simplest and most comprehensive manifesto of value investing ever produced. A paper entitled 'What has Worked in Investing'[11] listed a number of the key characteristics of their hugely successful long-term portfolios. Self-consciously borrowing on the musings of their former partner – a certain Ben Graham – the pamphlet lists 'the criteria and characteristics [that] have been utilized by Tweedy Browne because they pointed, like clues, in the direction of truly undervalued companies; appealed to common sense; and because the partners have always believed that undervaluation, which is associated with low risk, would be associated with satisfactory returns'.[12]

What follows is a study that also refers to 44 different academic studies that backed up their value investing world view. It's a compelling review but a number of key themes emerge – according to the partners at Tweedy Browne, successful companies spotted by their strategy need to have:

▪ A low share price in relation to their asset value. Stocks that sell for below their book value are great while stocks that trade below their net current asset value (cash and easily realisable assets) are even better.

▪ A low share price in relation to the PE ratio. If we turn the PE ratio around and express it as an earnings yield – i.e. a PE ratio of 10 becomes an earnings yield of 10% – their contention is that the earnings yield should be at last twice that of the yield obtained by investing in triple AAA rated corporate bonds. But investors shouldn't forget about the potential for growth in earnings (they paraphrase Warren Buffett by saying that 'value' and 'growth' are joined at the hip) as long as the PE ratio remains low. They're also on the lookout for high dividend yields and generous cash inflows at the operating level.

---

[11] 'What has worked in Investing – studies of investment approaches and characteristics associated with exceptional returns'. A PDF is freely obtainable from Tweedy Browne's website (www.tweedy.com).
[12] Ibid.

■ They love evidence of the directors buying in their company stock.

■ True contrarians, Tweedy Browne go out of their way to look for stocks where the share price has dropped back recently finding that, more often than not, companies whose recent performance has been poor tend to perk up and improve.

■ Last but not least Tweedy Browne focus on small cap investing – they find that investing in small caps produces better long-term results.

As their review puts it 'each characteristic seems somewhat analogous to one piece of a mosaic. When several of the pieces are arranged together, the picture can be clearly seen: an undervalued stock'.[13]

The rest of the paper goes on to detail academic study after academic study that, in their minds at least, proves beyond all reasonable doubt that value stocks out perform. Table 5.2 highlights a small number of the studies, but the cumulative impact is overwhelming – if you'd have screened for stocks using a combination of these criteria, you'd have yielded significantly above average returns over the past 50 years.

table 5.2 Academic studies cited by Tweedy Browne

Net current asset values Oppenheimer's study on using net current asset values in stock picking.[1]	From 1970 through to 1983 Henry Oppenheimer screened the US market for companies with a low ratio of net current assets to market value. A portfolio of low ratio stocks gave an average return of 29.4% per year against 11.5% for the wider market.
Low price to book value Ibbotson's study of returns from shares with a low share price to book ratio.[2]	Roger Ibbotson looked at returns from shares between 1967 and 1984 which boasted a low ratio. He found that the lowest 20% stocks yielded compound annual returns in excess of the market of 8.91% per annum.
Low price to book value One further study looked at whether these excess returns were the result of higher risk and volatility[3] while another paper looked to see whether the out performance of low price to book value was true globally.[4]	Low price to book value stocks produced consistently above average returns even in the best months of US stockmarket returns. Turning to global comparisons Barton Biggs looked at Morgan Stanley's own global database of stocks and found that the lowest 10% of low price to book value stocks delivered excess market returns of 5.1% between 1981 and 1991.

---

[13] Ibid.

table 5.2   Academic studies cited by Tweedy Browne (cont.)

Low PE ratios

Sanjoy Basu from McMaster University looked at six portfolios with varying PE ratios.[5]

Between 1957 and 1971 the portfolio with the lowest PE ratio stocks returned an annual average of 16.3% while a portfolio with the highest median PE ratio (about 35.8 for the median) produced just 9.3% per annum with greater risk.

The dividend yield

Michael Keppler's study of high yielding dividend stocks globally.[6]

Keppler found that annual investment returns for countries with the highest yielding quartile produced 18.49% annual returns while the lowest quartile produced annual returns of just 5.74% per annum.

Low price in relation to cashflow

In a separate study Keppler went on to examine global returns from shares with a generous cashflow backing.[7]

Globally (using the Morgan Stanley Worldwide index) between 1970 and 1989, investments in the quartile with the lowest share price to cashflow produced a 19.17% annual compound return against those with the highest price to cashflow which produced a 4.37% compound annual return.

Poorly performing share price

Poterba and Summers looked at how poorly performing shares performed during later time periods.[8]

They concluded that stock returns throughout the world tend to revert to the market average after a long period of time i.e. more than one year. Current low investment returns tend to be associated with lower investment returns in the future.

---

[1] Oppenheimer, H. (1986) 'Ben Graham's Net Current Asset Value: A Performance Update', *Financial Analysts Journal*.

[2] Ibbotson, R. and Cooper, G. M. (1972) 'Risk-Return Classes of New York Stock Exchange Common Stocks, 1931–', *Financial Analysts Journal*, March/April, pp. 46–54, 81, 95–101.

[3] National Bureau of Economic Research (1993) 'Contrarian Investment, Extrapolation and Risk', Working Paper No. 4360.

[4] Biggs, B. (1991) 'Ben Graham would be proud', Morgan Stanley, April.

[5] Basu, S. (1977) 'Investment Performance of Common Stocks in relation to their price/earnings ratios', *Journal of Finance*, June.

[6] Keppler, M. (1991) 'The Importance of Dividend Yields in country selection', *Journal of Portfolio Management*, Winter.

[7] Kepler, M. (1991) 'Further evidence on the predictability of international equity returns', *Journal of Portfolio Management*, Fall.

[8] Poterba, J. and Summers, L. (1989) 'Mean Reversion in Stock Prices: evidence and implications', NBER Working Paper.

A Tweedy Browne strategy in action

Tweedy Browne are of course in the business of making money from managing assets that are deployed using their distinctive approach, thus they're sensibly cautious about revealing their own detailed stock picking strategy. But based on their analysis we can construct a simple version of their strategy that seems to tick most of their analytical boxes.

■ First off investors probably need to narrow down the potential universe of stocks by focusing on the top quartile of the market based on book value relative to the share price – in practice most of the time that means a PBTV level well below 1. In some depressed markets you might be able to pull that threshold down to as low as 0.6.

■ The balance sheet also figures in our next two measures. Borrowings are acceptable as long as they're under control but a sensible net gearing ratio of 50% or less should weed out most troubled companies. Also a current ratio of 2 or over appears sensible.

■ The team at Tweedy Browne are also probably looking for a juicy, well-covered dividend. This is not a strict income strategy but it does seem sensible to derive a healthy dividend to help compensate for taking on the extra risk of investing in equities. Additionally logic would suggest that investors should be demanding about that dividend payment – you need to be absolutely sure that it can comfortably carry on paying out those dividend cheques, so look for dividend cover (the amount of times dividend payments can be funded out of earnings) of at least 2.

■ Turning to company size, set a limit on both the upside and downside for market capitalisation. A lower limit of £10m will only really exclude the tiny market minnows while an upper limit of £100m firmly marks this screen out as a small cap value strategy.

■ You should also be looking for a reasonable PE ratio – below the market average or in our case the market median – and some strong evidence of cash generation at the operating level. Experience suggests that the PCF measure should be well above the average (or median) for the market. Be under no illusions – this screen will produce cheap, unloved, cashflow rich firms turning out a reasonable profit.

Table 5.3 summarises the screen.

table 5.3	The screen in summary
Step one: screens	■ Upper quartile (lowest) for PTBV (e.g. less than 0.79 in Feb 1999)
	■ Current ratio above 2
	■ Net gearing below 50%
	■ PER in upper (lowest) quartile
	■ Prospective dividend above median market for the market
	■ Price to cashflow below median for the market
	■ RS 1 month and 3 months negative
	■ Market cap below £100m and above £10m
	■ Dividend cover above 1
Step two: screens	■ *Eliminate* any company with significant clusters of directors selling
	■ *Buy all* stocks with evidence of directors' buying
	■ Favour share price below net asset value
	■ *Eliminate* loss makers in the coming year

The new king of value

Both Ben Graham and his colleagues at Tweedy Browne can lay claim to being the true pioneers of value investing and adherents of a 'deep value' approach that is deeply suspicious of any measures that don't suggest strong asset backing and a decent dividend. Most value investors in the new millennium, by contrast, have evolved and adapted to the changed markets, moving on to newer interpretations.

In particular a certain Joseph Piotroksi – an accounting professor at the University of Chicago – has quietly emerged as a new champion within the firmament of this kind of 'deep value' investing. Crucially he's a link between the mainstream academic world who are largely dismissive of stock selection strategies and active private and institutional value investors who think the market is not always terrifically efficient at pricing shares. More to the point, like most modern value investors, he's keenly aware that the world has moved on since Graham's days and that dirt cheap firms selling well below their asset base are increasingly hard to find. His great innovation is to refocus attention not on the earnings and dividends statements but on the *balance sheet*.

Crucially the model that Piotroski constructed was not the result of 'endless back testing but a selection of characteristics that he (and previous research) had identified as improving expected stockreturns'[14] as one commentator puts it. 'The model is also not dynamic or optimised using historical returns and, as such, one of its main appeals is its simplicity,'[15] suggests quantitative strategist Andrew Lapthorne.

Piotroski undertook a huge research study that found that the performance of conventional value stocks is wildly skewed, with a few big winners and lots of losers. Emboldened, he devised a system using points for 'good behavior' that would spot these unloved gems. But Piotroski noticed something else – economists generally define boring value stocks as those in the bottom 20% when companies are ranked according to PE ratios. Crunching the numbers he found that the long-term performance of this group is anything but boring: *the mean return earned by high book value companies increased by at least 7.5% annually over the average for all stocks.*

At the core of Piotroski's approach are two simple, classically value driven ideas. First, financial assets are what matter – in this he echoes Ben Graham in his unbending belief that the route to above average returns is through finding companies that have solid asset backings relative to the market valuation.

Piotroski is also convinced of a second equally important canon of value investing philosophy – that the market singularly fails to adequately price all that solid financial backing into the current share price, i.e. the market consistently under-values some company shares. At the core of this analysis is the belief that markets are too swayed by the wild gyrations and ephemera of speculative investing. Investors, institutional and private alike, are victims of their own short-sightedness – they react to every bit of rumor and gossip and neglect the hard evidence of past returns and strong finances.

High BM – book value to market value – firms by contrast represent 'neglected stocks where prior poor performance has led to the formation of "too pessimistic" expectations about future performance'.[16] According to Piotroski this pessimism unravels in the future periods,[17] as the company begins to get itself back on its feet helped by strong internal cashflow generation and sound finances.

---

[14] Lapthorne, A. (2008) 'Piotroski's F-score – Helps to pick the winners while identifying potential losers', *Global Quantitative Strategy*, SG.

[15] Ibid.

[16] Ibid.

[17] Ibid.

Why doesn't the market wake up to this market inefficiency, and start to revalue these 'neglected' companies? The problem is that these neglected stocks tend to be 'thinly followed by the analyst community and are plagued by low levels of investor interest'.[18] But these firms are also out of the loop in another key respect – they're not plugged into 'the "informal" networks of rumor, gossip and analysis'[19] and so the only way of really appraising their true value is to fall back on the one thing that can be trusted (and is neglected by the wider community) – their financial statement.

Piotroski believes that investors should stick to the hard facts represented by the reports and accounts. They should scrutinise the P&L, the cashflow statement and the balance sheet carefully making full use of the full range of financial measures including specialised measures such as the current ratio. When he applied the analysis to the US stockmarket, the results (published in the *Journal of Accounting Research*) were compelling. The better a firm fits his criteria – we'll talk about his filtering system below – the better its shares perform. In fact an investment strategy that bought the expected winners and shorted the expected losers generated a 23% annual return from 1976 through to 1996. Applying just a long strategy – only buying stocks not selling or shorting stocks – also produced above average returns. A portfolio of high scoring BM firms produced average returns of at least 7.5% beyond the market over the same time frame.

A Piotroski screen in action

Piotroski's work has one other big plus for private investors – he spelled out his approach in great detail so that it could be widely copied. This analytical model consists of a set of binary financial tests based on profitability, leverage, liquidity and operating efficiency. The more tests a stock passes the better the investment is said to be. So a stock that passes all the tests (an F-score of 9) would be an excellent investment whilst a stock with a score of 0 or 1 should be avoided.

The Chicago professor kicks off his analysis by focusing on a number of key themes, but with one key threshold built around the share price relative to book value of the company's assets.

---

[18] Ibid.
[19] Ibid.

Piotroski searches for companies with a high BM value although in the UK we tend to use the reverse measure, something called the price to book value or PBV. Where Piotroski looks for a high BM value, we would tend, by contrast, to look for a low PBV value. In reality Piotroski is only interested in the bottom 20% of firms measured by their book value – that is the 20% of firms with the lowest price to book value ratio. In most markets that means a PBV of well below 1, and in some depressed markets this cut off point might slip below 0.6.

With this initial threshold in place, Piotroski then uses measures grouped around three key themes – profits, the balance sheet and operational efficiency.

- Looking at *profitabilty*, Piotroski notes that many value stocks become 'cheap' through deterioration in their business model, that they're less profitable than they once were, or non-profitable, and as such the decline in share price is simply reflecting that. Avoiding firms where earnings generating capability is poor would seem sensible.

- He also suggests focusing on a measure called return on assets (ROA) which is simply the net income before extraordinary items divided by total assets. Likewise focusing on cashflow from operations – the CFO measure he uses comprises cashflow from operations divided by total assets. If ROA is positive, the firm is profitable, so the firm scores 1, otherwise it gets 0. The same idea applies to CFO. Piotroski also wants the trend in the return on assets to be upwards or improving over time – the year-on-year change in that ROA should be positive.

- Piotroski focuses much of his attention on the *balance sheet* and the use of assets including cash. He looks at measures like the change in gearing – this is the annual change in a company's gearing which is the year-on-year change in the ratio of long-term debt to total assets. He also looks at the annual change in the current ratio (the ratio of current assets to current liabilities), believing that an increase in the current ratio indicates the ability to service debt costs, whilst a decline could indicate potential short-term funding problems. Piotroski's key concern is that the firm is not being overwhelmed by a poor capital structure.

- Piotroski is rightly scornful of companies that constantly raise fresh dollops of capital by issuing new shares. As quantitative analyst Andrew Lapthorne notes in his review of Piotroski's work 'issuing stock ultimately costs the existing shareholder, either in cash or dilution. A deeply discounted rights issue at depressed prices is particularly irritating, especially given that many of the companies currently raising funds were actually buying back stock several months earlier at significantly higher levels!'[20]

▦ The final bundle of measures centres on *operational efficiency,* namely the operating margin. Piotroski wants an increase in the operating margin year on year – and something called the annual change in the asset turnover. This last measures shows how sales have increased relative to the size of the asset base. According to Andrew Lapthorne 'increasing sales at a greater speed to the change in asset base implies that a firm is generating more business from existing assets rather than simply making acquisitions'.[21] This last bunch of measures show that Piotroski is deeply concerned with the way in which the firm is sweating its operations, to generate new efficiencies. Are they increasing their margin at the point of sale and are those assets being worked hard enough?

All these concepts are turned into a relatively easy to understand points system.

▦ One point is awarded for a positive return on assets – this is defined as net profits before exceptional items divided by the total assets of the firm.

▦ One point is awarded for a positive cashflow.

▦ One point is awarded for an improvement on return on assets over the past year.

▦ One point awarded for a company where cashflow from operations exceed net income. This should be the case as depreciation and non-cash expenses normally reduce the net profits but have no impact on cashflow.

▦ One point is awarded if the measure of financial leverage, ratio of total debt to total assets, declined in the past year.

▦ One point is also given if the current ratio (working assets or current assets divided by current liabilities) increased over the year.

▦ One point comes with companies that have not issued any new shares in the current financial year – firms that issue too much debt might be struggling to manage liquidity and running short of funds.

---

[20] See note 14.
[21] Ibid.

■ One point for an increase in gross margin.

■ One point if asset turnover (total sales divided by total assets at the start of the financial year) has increased during the year.

Piotroski's research may be fairly easy to understand but that doesn't make it easy to apply. Trying to point score an initial universe of stocks that may run into the low hundreds is going to take a quite considerable amount of your time. Even the most overpaid of analysts might rebel when faced with trying to screen a market to find a share with the perfect 9 score – assuming that you'll even find one! Piotroski says he's after stocks with a high 9 (a perfect score of 9) although most subsequent commentators tend to be a little more relaxed, suggesting a score of 5 points or more.

Also many analysts have revised Piotroski's screening criteria and points system and a few have even gone so far as to include some new measures. Chief amongst these revisers is Peter Sturm of *Smart Money* magazine (a veteran stock screener and value investor) who suggests including one other key measure – insider buying of shares by directors. Sturm's reasoning is that any firm that qualifies highly under a Piotroski screen is likely to be cheap but backed by a solid asset base. The one group of people likely to be in 'the loop' about this under-valuation is the management. Analysts and institutional investors may be woefully ignorant but the managers will be well aware the firm has a great asset base, solid cashflow generation and a potentially bright future. If they're selling the stock that is terrible news – even they, the insiders, have no confidence in the future. Conversely, a management that is buying the stock is a great sign of insider knowledge and confidence in the future.

Bringing all these revisions together into a relatively simple mechanical screen isn't too difficult.

■ The first process is a quantitative screen that quickly narrows down the number of stocks in your universe. The key measure is share price to book value. As Piotroski's research suggests, try to immediately narrow this down to the *cheapest quarter of the market by PBV*.

■ Then set the market cap filter. Piotroski is quite a fan of small caps but experience using this screen suggests a small tweak. Set *the market cap at a minimum of £35m* to avoid really tiny minnows that no-one in the marketplace is really watching.

■ The return on capital employed, or *ROCE measure, should be at least positive and trending upwards in the past few years*. This means the company is efficiently working its equity and capital base.

- Also make sure that *interest cover on debts is more than 2 and that net gearing is less than 50%* – two sensibly conservative measures.
- At the cashflow level make sure the *PCF measure is at least positive* and that like the ROCE, it has been trending upwards in the past few years.
- As for profits, the PE ratio is really rather incidental but experience suggests that any shortlisted companies should at very least be producing profits, so *set the PER above 3*.
- Also one last little measure – stipulate that the *earnings per share must be covered at least once by operating cashflow*.

Drilling down

This first screen through the market should drastically reduce the number of stocks deserving further analysis. The next, more qualitative step is to look for stocks where the management has been buying the shares on a fairly consistent basis – a strong sign of confidence in the future by insiders. At this stage it might also be worth screening out companies where the total net borrowings are trending upwards in recent years – a financially strong firm should be using its cashflow to pay down debts not take on more loans. Last but by no means least make sure that on certain key measures – like ROCE or net margin – the shortlisted stock compares well with its peers from the sector. If the average ROCE of the market is say 10%, a stock with a figure of 15% might sound superficially exciting. But what happens if the sector's average ROCE is a mighty 20%? Suddenly our share looks a lot less appealing.

Testing the model

Piotroski tested out his system on US stocks in his paper and suggested that his points scoring system – subsequently called the F Score system by most analysts – seemed to be successful at producing above average returns.[22] The AAII has also taken his ideas and applied them to a US-based screening system – with equally spectacular results since 1998 with total returns of 1861%!

In Europe and the UK much of the testing of this system has been undertaken by big investment banking houses and particularly the quant team at

---

[22] See note 14.

SG, although Graham Secker's team at Morgan Stanley have also tested the system and even market their own fund that uses the F Score to select shares.

The SG team have applied this system across a global universe from 1985 onwards – each year building a portfolio which was held for that year, with the shares sold at the end of the year. Their model also excluded financial stocks and introduced a market cap limit 'that was proportional to the total market cap of the country index, so for example the global universe would currently include stocks down to around US$1bn'.[23] Crucially the SG team applied this screen as both a *long only* strategy (using it to generate shares to buy) and a *short/long* strategy – suggesting shares to buy and also shares to short.

Applying this strategy over the 23 years since 1985, the SG team found that 'on average, just 4% or fewer stocks in the global universe score three or less, whilst 43% manage a score of higher than seven. This clearly makes the strategy quite difficult to execute on a long/short basis, as the stocks highlighted by the model as a short are typically relatively few in number. Given that distressed stocks also tend to be smaller and more volatile, they are often prohibitively expensive to short. This hardly strikes us as surprising. If you own a stock which has a high risk of going bust, you are probably less willing to want to lend it to anyone to short!'[24]

Looking at total returns (see Table 5.4), Lapthorne and his quant team found that: 'A long strategy of buying high F-score stocks performed well in most years – with the exception of the strong rebound years of 1999 and 2003. The strategy outperformed on average in North America by 200bps, in Europe by around 260bps and in the UK by 370bps. Only in Japan were the results a little disappointing, with annual outperformance of 70bps.'[25]

What is the magic behind the system?

The Piotroski screen is a classic value screen, with a dash of contrarianism, and it's exactly those kinds of 'cheap' stocks that in general have done pretty well over the past decade. As Lapthorne concludes: 'Piotroski's system really isn't rocket science. He's looking to find neglected companies with good prospects that should start turning themselves around with astute manage-

---

[23] Ibid.

[24] Ibid.

[25] Ibid.

table 5.4   Returns by F score since 1986 (global universe, absolute one year ahead total returns)

F score	75th percentile performance	Median performance	15th percentile performance	Of stocks with positive performance
1	−53.6	−25.5	102.4	40
2	−56	−11	21.3	42.9
3	−28.4	−5	25.9	45
4	−22.4	1	27.3	51.2
5	−17.2	3.4	27	54.8
6	−15.4	5	28	56.5
7	−13	6.9	29	59
8	−11.4	8.2	32.1	61.1
9	−8.6	10.7	32	64.9
Low score (0–3)	−28	−4.8	26.7	45.7
High score (7–5)	−12	7.7	30.7	60.3

Source: SG Quantative Research

ment. This turn around will, over a time frame of a few years, start to be reflected in the share price'.[26]

The Piotroski screen is very demanding and tends to identify a much smaller shortlist of shares than most other value screens. Smaller portfolio size implies greater focus which can mean greater rewards but also greater risk. And it's true that this strategy does take on more potentially highly risky, small cap stocks than other screens that tend to focus on safer large caps. But that risk is not actually hugely increased compared to racier growth screens for instance. At the core of this out performance is the points system and the insistence on low book value accompanied by decent operating efficiency and in some versions of the F-score system, evidence of directors buying the shares. It's a tough test and makes big demands on the shortlisted shares but delivers well run companies that are unloved by the market for a short period of time before they eventually come back into favour.

---

[26] Ibid.

Alternative value-based approaches – Neff and O'Shaughnessy

No account of value investing could finish without mentioning two hugely influential value investors, both of whom have actually run big money funds, practising what they preach – John Neff and James O'Shaughnessy. Both of these guru-investors have broadened out value investing, bringing in some ideas and measures used by 'mainstream' investors, namely the share price performance relative to the stockmarket (this measure features in O'Shaughnessy's analysis) and earnings growth (Neff).

We've already noted that many value investors have a slightly detached relationship with the concept of earnings growth – they recognise, as Graham did, that profits are hugely important and that they need to expand over time, but equally as a group, value investors are suspicious of headline earnings growths results (and forecasts), and are particularly concerned that they are easily manipulated by senior managers to impress investors. Nevertheless earnings growth cannot be ignored – Ben Graham certainly embraced the idea of long-term organic growth in profits – and John Neff puts profits growth at the heart of his analysis.

Neff's approach to stock picking is to focus on hunting down cheapo shares that also boast solid growth prospects *and* a decent dividend. Sadly John Neff is nowhere near as famous as other much flashier, more worshipped American investing legends such as Warren Buffett or Peter Templeton, but he's no less successful. Investors might look on him as an American version of Fidelity's Anthony Bolton or Invesco Perpetual's Neil Woodford, only bigger and better.

The core of his appeal can be summed up in just four words – the Vanguard Windsor fund. To describe this hugely successful brand as a brand in itself is to do it a disservice. Quite simply, it's widely regarded as the most consistently successful fund ever marketed in the US. Little wonder then that its manager was nicknamed 'the professional's professional', because many fund managers entrusted their money to him in the belief that it would be in safe hands.

Professional fund managers picked Neff for one very simple reason – he was hugely successful. For more than 30 years, the Windsor Fund routinely featured in the top 5% of all US mutual funds.

Here's just a small list of Neff's achievements with this fund.

▪ The average annual total return from the Windsor Fund during Neff's 32-year tenure was 13.7%, against a return from the S&P 500 index of 10.6%.

▪ These results mean that during his 32 years at the helm, Neff beat the market by more than 3 percentage points each year he earned an extra $175,000 on every $5000 invested in his fund!

▪ His fund beat the market in 22 out of his 31 years as manager.

At the core of Neff's huge success was his consistent value approach and his obstinate contrarianism. Neff bet big time on his investing ideas – for instance in 1984 he wagered a huge portion of his fund on US car maker Ford, when everyone feared it might go bust and the PE ratio had sunk to 2.5! He paid an average price of under $14 for a share. Within three years, the price had climbed to $50, making Windsor profits of $500m.

At the core of Neff's success was a consistent stock picking approach – he describes himself as 'a low price-earnings investor'. He used a series of strategies that allow him to filter or screen through the huge US market and find shares that fitted his 'cheapo' approach. He wanted to buy decent companies with relatively cheap share prices that also boasted decent growth prospects. Luckily his ideas on investment are admirably simple and easy to understand. They've also been copied by outfits like the AAII which has been running its own version of a Neff screen for nearly a decade now with total returns of 682%.

Neff summed up his strategy using seven simple criteria:

▪ low PE ratio

▪ fundamental earnings growth above 7%

▪ a solid, and ideally rising, dividend

▪ a much-better-than-average PE ratio

▪ no exposure to cyclical downturns without a compensatory low PE

▪ solid companies in growing fields

▪ a strong fundamental case for investment.

In reality two key measures explain nearly all of Neff's success. In his book *John Neff on Investing* (1999) Neff gave away his first big market-beating secret: 2 of those 3 percentage points above the market for the 32 years came from dividends. So while he worked hard to buy cheap stocks, much of his success came from finding shares that also happened to pay a very decent dividend. Neff understood that firms that pay healthy dividends offered up return potential that was more certain and consistent. Neff valued this consistency and, in part, this steadiness has helped dividend-paying stocks out perform the market over the long term.

Neff's second big secret was a measure he used called the total return ratio (TRR) also known as the dividend-adjusted price-earnings relative to growth (PEG) ratio. This served as the foundation of his stock screening process and is defined as:

$$\text{Total return ratio} = \text{(analysts' expected earnings} \\ \text{growth rate + dividend yield)/PE ratio}$$

The TRR ratio – also called the dividend adjusted PEG ratio – is designed to look for companies that have a low relative PE ratio in comparison to their relatively high earnings growth rate in the next few years.

Neff argued that the TRR should be compared with that of the wider stock-market. He liked to hunt down shares whose ratios were at least 50% greater than the market's. In doing so, he believed that he increased his chances of finding a stock that would give him greater returns than the market turned in while taking on less risk.

Building a Neff screen in detail

The dividend-adjusted PEG

There should be strong evidence that recent growth rates, and projected growth rates in the next two years, are above 6% but below 20% per annum. Neff likes growing companies but not ones growing too fast or unsustainably.

Low PE ratios

The cornerstone of any value investing approach is a low PE ratio – anything way above the market should be ignored. In the current climate a PE – based on historical returns – of much above 20 would be regarded as extortionate.

Dividend yield

The results of a low PE ratio strategy often include companies with high dividend yields – low PE ratios and strong dividend yields normally go hand in hand. Aim for a yield above 4%.

Sales growth

If a company isn't growing sales substantially it's in trouble. Neff strongly believes that investors needs evidence of both earnings growth and sales growth of more than 6% per annum or more (sales growth of 20% or more is regarded as suspect by Neff).

Free cash flow

Free cash flow refers to the operating cash left over after paying out on capex. Neff searched for companies that would use this excess cash flow to pay dividends and also fund future expansion.

Operating margin

Neff also looked for a share where the operating margin was better than current industry average or even better the median. In particular, Neff was insistent that the company's operating margin is compared with sensible peers, not from the wider market, but from within its own sector.

O'Shaughnessy and the importance of price to sales as a key measure

Research guru James O'Shaughnessy caused a stir back in 1996 when he published his bestseller, *What Works on Wall Street*.[27] In an heroic struggle documented in the book he back tested 44 years of stockmarket data from the comprehensive Standard & Poor's Compustat database to find out exactly what had worked – and what had been a huge failure! The study stretched 43 years, from 1951 through 1994, probably the longest period ever used to examine investment strategies. He evaluated each strategy by using it to select 50 stocks at the beginning of a test year, and then calculated the return of those 50 stocks if they were sold 12-months later. To take just one small example of this rigorous approach – focusing on the PE ratio he selected the 50 stocks with the lowest PE ratios at the beginning of each of the 43 test years and then tabulated the return realised by selling the 50 stocks at the end of each test year.

To the astonishment of many he discovered that classic value-based measures such as the PE ratio were almost completely pointless as predictors of share price growth and that small company stocks, contrary to popular wisdom, as a group didn't have an edge on large company stocks.

---

[27] O'Shaughnessy, J. (1996) *What Works on Wall Street*, McGraw-Hill.

The best results were achieved by using a combination of three factors;

■ share price/sales ratio

■ one-year share price performance relative to the stockmarket, and lastly

■ year-to-year earnings growth.

We'll look in detail at the importance of earnings growth in the next chapter but it's the first two measures which captured the most attention. Most value investors are hugely uninterested in the relative movement of the share price – as contrarians they tend to assume that no-one would love a value stock until after they'd made their purchase. To suggest that momentum in the share price, relative to the market, seemed to be important was almost heretical!

But it was the first of this trinity of measures that was the most influential and innovative – *the price to sales ratio*. O'Shaughnessy concluded that the price to sales ratio (this measures the ratio between the share price per share and total turnover per share) was what he liked to call 'the King of Value Factors'. His exhaustive, back-tested analysis concludes with the following:

*Low price to sales ratio beat the market more than any other value ratio and did so more consistently in terms of both the 50 stock portfolios [a screened shortlist] and the decile analysis [the market as a whole broken down into decile groups]. **Low PSR stocks from both the All Stocks [any stock regardless of market cap] and Large stocks groups beat the universe every decade** [emphasis added].*[28]

But why are sales so important? Intriguingly O'Shaughnessy's ducks a detailed explanation of why this measure is so crucial, choosing to cite another well known guru, Ken Fisher, who says that a stock's PSR 'is an almost perfect measure of popularity', warning that 'only hope and hype will increase the price of a stock with a high PSR'.[29] Fisher himself is admirably clear about why the price to sales ratio is so important. He says:

It is rare to see a Super Company [the target of Fisher's analysis] have a truly substantial sales decline. It is quite common to see one suffer from severe earnings reversals. The increased relative stability of sales, in relation to other financial yardsticks, allows you to use sales as an anchor in the process of securities valuation.[30]

---

[28] Ibid., p. 134.

[29] Ibid., p. 121.

[30] Fisher, K. (1990) *SuperStocks: The Book That's Changing the Way Investors Think*, McGraw Hill Companies.

Now it's important to understand the origin of Fisher's and thus O'Shaughnessy's analysis. Both are fundamentally value-based investors – they like using fundamentals-based measures to find cheap companies. But Fisher in particular is also excited by companies where the potential for growth above trend is substantial. Thus his 'SuperStocks' term which he uses to define a 'company [which] is a business... that distinguishes itself because it can generate internally funded growth at well above average rates'.[31] He then goes on to point to another bunch of characteristics of this kind of stock which include:

- growth orientation
- marketing excellence
- an unfair competitive advantage
- good financial controls.

Fisher adds up all these factors and then implores his readers to go in search of stocks that seem good value but where there's been a glitch of some sort, where the PSR is low, and where's there's some new product or service on the way that will act as a catalyst for future growth.

We'll encounter this form of best of both worlds investor – buying growth stocks at a reasonable price – again in the next chapter but suffice to say that O'Shaughnessy was convinced. Better to have a company where the top line sales were growing but the margin was still relatively subdued as opposed to a company with declining sales but high operating margins. In the first example good managers could increase the margin and thus boost the share price while in the second shareholders are facing terminal long-term decline. O'Shaughnessy also liked to focus on the price to sales ratio (PSR) because although earnings often fluctuate dramatically, sales tend to follow consistent trends.

By focusing on the PSR O'Shaughnessy knew he was on to a winner – his hunch was that if you bothered to screen for shares in companies backed by loads of top line sales relative to the share price alongside some evidence of a strong share price you'd make good money. He was right. Testing out this strategy over the period 1951 through to 1996, he found that a share with a low price to sales ratio *and* high relative strength produced a return of 23% per year, consistently beating each and every benchmark. His conclusion? Buy cheap shares that are hitting new 52-week highs but absolutely never, ever buy shares that are hitting new 52-week lows, no matter

---

[31] Ibid.

how cheap they are! Don't try and fight the market in a contrarian way as it rarely ever pays off!

The Cornerstone Strategies

Based on all this exhaustive his research, O'Shaughnessy developed two key investment strategies: 'Cornerstone Growth' and 'Cornerstone Value'.

Despite its name, Cornerstone Growth is in fact a value orientated stock selection strategy – it channels the investor into finding relatively good value stocks that have begun to move up in price terms. According to O'Shaughnessy, the Cornerstone Growth approach returned more than 18% per year over the 43-year test period, compared to an overall market returned of less than 13% annually during the same time-span. The key measures in this strategy consisted of share price relative to sales and the share price performance over the past 12 months relative to the market. O'Shaughnessy discovered that shares with the highest price performance increased the most in value during the previous 12 months. He also added one last measure – an earnings growth requirement which simply called for some profits growth over the previous year.

In O'Shaughnessy's view the ideal company would be one that churned out lots of sales, and was making half way decent profits but with some progress in the business recognised by the stock market via the relative out-performance of the share price.

The Cornerstone Growth screen

■ Find all stocks that have increased earnings in the past year.

■ They must have price to sales ratio below 1.5 (but above 0.1).

■ The price to book value must be reasonable.

■ Select the 50 best stocks with the best 12-month relative share price performance.

The resulting 50 shares (he suggests that you have to buy all 50 to avoid any behavioural bias creeping into your screening), should out perform the market. By the way, if you don't want to buy all 50 stocks and want to avoid any behavioural bias you could choose to only buy the top stock in each sector or industry.

The Cornerstone Value strategy shares some measures with its racy sibling – it too looks for companies with strong sales, but it chooses to focus instead on two additional measures, namely the company cashflow and the dividend yield. This strategy is very appropriate for income investors looking at total shareholder returns that include generous dividends. Again, if you don't want to buy 50 stocks, just order the stocks by dividend and then pick one stock from each sector. Whatever you do, don't arbitrarily pick a few stocks at the top of the list. This could massively increase risk as you could end up with an undue concentration of shares from one or two sectors – in the UK you'll probably end up with a portfolio stuffed full of retailers and food producers.

One final word of caution: like many gurus, O'Shaughnessy's success at putting his own research and wisdom into an actual, live fund has been at best lukewarm in recent years. After the release of his book he established a Cornerstone Value and Growth mutual fund but performance over the past five years has been slightly disappointing (see Tables 5.5 and 5.6).

table 5.5   Average annual total returns – historical performance as of 30 September 2009

Fund/Index	YTD	1 Year	3 year	5 year	10 years	Since inception 1/11/96
Cornerstone Growth	2.06%	−20.76%	−14.54%	−3.84%	5.79%	7.4%
S&P Index	22.43%	−9.55%	−4.57%	2.41%	4.88%	5.94%

Source: http://www.henessyfunds.com/cornerstone_growth_fund.html

table 5.6   Year by year total returns

	2000	2001	2002	2003	2004	2005	2006	2007	2008
Cornerstone Growth	5.3%	12.15%	−4.71%	45.82%	16%	11.96%	10.42%	−2.18%	−43%
S&P 500	−9.1%	−11.8%	−22%	28.68%	11%	4.91%	15.80%	5.49%	−37%

Source: http://www.henessyfunds.com

The big caveat – value investing doesn't always work

Once an investor embraces the logic of buying cheap, selling high, the stigma attached to investing in dog stocks evaporates. No wonder so many leading hedge funds, including world-class outfits like Third Point in New York, embrace some aspects of value investing. In fact at times it's seemed like value investing has moved from being a renegade ideology into the mainstream with hundreds of value and contrarian funds chasing investor's money.

Sadly many of those investors will have discovered an uncomfortable truth that awaits all value investors – that although study after study has suggested over the very long term value investing does pay off in terms of rewards that is absolutely no guarantee of success over much shorter periods.

To understand this paradox – that long-term success is no indicator of short-term rewards – look at Figure 5.1. This is from a series of indices that started in 1969 and were compiled by index firm MSCI Barra. The graph shows returns for the MSCI UK index through to 22 December 2009. The top line is for the value version of this index and clearly shows massive long term out performance compared to the mainstream core UK index.

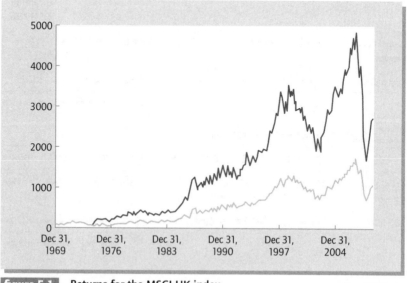

figure 5.1 Returns for the MSCI UK index

Source: MSCI Barra.

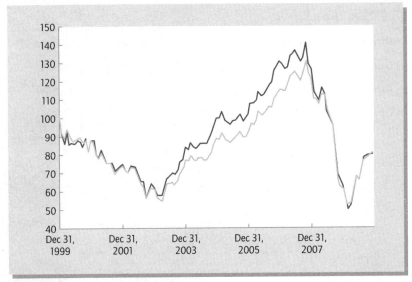

figure 5.2 Returns over the past ten years *Source: MSCI Barra.*

Figure 5.2 shows returns over the past ten years. Again the top line is nearly always the value index while the lower one is the UK core index. So far so good.

Figure 5.3 (overleaf) covers the past four years through to the end of 2009 – the results here are startling. We've now included another line for the alternative growth version of this UK index. The line on the top is always the growth version of the index while the line nearly always on the bottom in terms of performance is the value version of the index.

These dreadful recent returns are echoed in Table 5.7 which shows annualised returns for this index series (plus the US version) for the past ten years. Almost without exception the value version of this index in the UK has underperformed both the main core index and the growth version of the index.

table 5.7 MSCI Index returns by style – annualised returns

Country index	1 year	3 year	5 years	10 years
UK Growth	41%	−7.84%	0.59%	−2.08%
UK Value	29%	−15%	−4%	−2.20%
UK Core	31%	−9%	0.86%	−0.36%

table 5.7 (cont.)

Country index	1 year	3 year	5 years	10 years
US Growth	38%	−3.46%	0.31%	−4.44%
US Value	19.8%	−10.9%	−3.02%	−1.59%
US Core	29%	−7.16%	−1.28%	−2.82%

Source: MSCI Barra

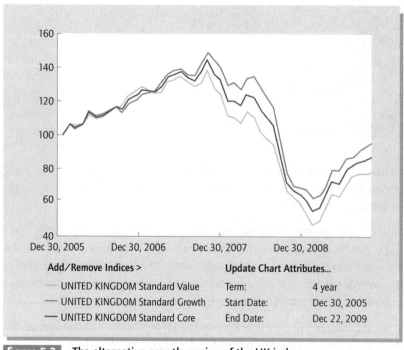

figure 5.3 The alternative growth version of the UK index *Source*: MSCI Barra.

Recent under-performance

Jeremy Grantham of Grantham, Mayo, Van Otterloo & Co. summed up this systematic recent under-performance brilliantly:

Value stocks have been bid up to a level where they may not even have an appropriate risk premium far less an excess return. For value investing has always had a hidden but serious risk: the sixty-year flood. The so-called price/book effect (and the small stock effect) sound like a free lunch, but in 1929–33, 20% of all companies went bankrupt. They were not the large, high-quality blue chips but small 'cheap stocks' with low price/book ratios. To add insult to injury, the data indicates that the best growth managers add more to growth than the best value managers can add to value, probably because the fundamentals and the prices are more dynamic for growth stocks.[32]

The SG team led by Andrew Lapthorne suggested in 2009 their own narrative for recent under-performance by value stocks:

The poor global economic environment is creating some dramatic downward moves in stock prices. … Some of these will represent a buying opportunity, but many will not. Value investing has proved to be an expensive pursuit during the last 12 months, with low price-to-book, low P/E and high dividend yield strategies suffering in most regions. With earnings uncertainty high, dividends under pressure and balance sheets being wrecked by write downs it is difficult to know on what basis many of the poorly performing stocks should be measured.[33]

According to Lapthorne's team, simply buying shares with the lowest PE ratio was the worst performing investment style, during 2008 especially: 'collapsing confidence in both historical and forward profit measures undermined the meaning of most valuation measures'.[34] Simple dividend strategies also started off badly but by the second half dividends began to be cut at the weaker companies.

Over at the *Investors Chronicle* our own version of a particular strategy – based on Piotroski's ideas – performed equally abysmally in the volatile year of 2009. An article from that year noted that:

At the beginning of this period, at the end of January 2008 for instance, our core value screen based on the ideas of Chicago accounting professor Joseph Piotroski had been running for three years to date and had delivered a total return of 5.94% but by the end of January 2009 that overall return was down to a loss of 12.9% (after allowing for new additions and some sells within the portfolio), a turnaround of just under 20%.[35]

One key theme emerges – in the recent sell off of 2008 and 2009 value stocks massively under-performed. Many analysts suggested a series of causes at the time – value-based strategies for instance end up picking small

---

[32] Quoted at http://deanlebaron.com/book/ultimate/chapters/val_inv.html

[33] www.sgcib.com, proprietary research.

[34] Ibid.

[35] Stevenson, D. (2009) 'Dash to trash bypasses Piotroski', *Investors Chronicle*, 14 May.

caps. Sadly small caps suffered disproportionately during the sell off as investors have fled what are perceived of as risky sectors. The starkest indicator of this meltdown has been the 40% decline in the FTSE Small Cap index and 42% decline in the FTSE Fledgling index in the 12 months up to the middle of 2009. Traditional defensive sectors such as utilities – beloved of many dividend hungry value investors looking for steady cashflows – also performed relatively poorly in 2008 and 2009. It's also worth noting that simplistic value strategies also didn't work in the stressed years of 2008 and 2009. Focusing exclusively on a low PE ratio or a very high yield without taking into account the strength of the balance sheet produced some woeful results in 2008, especially in the first half of 2008. All too often these strategies simply ended up focusing on companies with lots of debt or banks!

Is value investing fading away?

Some academics have even gone so far as to suggest that value investing *was* a strategy that appeared to work but only applied to specific decades. Efficient markets theorist Eugene Fama raised the possibility in a paper from 1998 that the observed return differential – academic argot for superior returns – during the past 30 years was what was called a 'time-period specific regularity'[36] that had been uncovered by researchers but had no systematic underlying explanation.

There's no definitive answer to these objections, unless one can avail oneself of a crystal ball and look into the future. Many value orientated academics simply make two objections – the first is that value stocks have significantly out performed over long time spans and indeed since the inception of most major indices. The point seems to be that value investing starts to outpace its growth-based rivals after a 10–20 year time frame.

Also a great many studies suggest that in previous decades, value as a style has under-performed only to bounce back in later years – in effect a simplified version of mean reversion seems to be at work with markets and styles moving in 10 to 20 year cycles.

These rebuttals haven't silenced the value critics within mainstream academia – they've launched another attack which avoids focusing on par-

---

[36] Quoted in Chan, L.K.C. and Lankonishok, J. (2004) 'Value and Growth Investing: Review and Update', *Financial Analysts Journal*, January/February.

ticular decades. Instead they've suggested that the proven long-term out performance of value stocks over the past 50–100 years is in fact entirely real but accounted for by the extra risk. In effect these analysts suggest that value strategies have delivered extra returns but that's because they're especially risky!

Again efficient markets theorist Eugene Fama has been at the forefront of this critique suggesting that cheap stocks measured by the price to book ratio 'captures a priced element of systematic risk, and that the observed differences in returns between value and glamour stocks reflect a fair compensation for risk'.[37] This bold assertion is far from being a consensus though – in a recent review on the literature in this space academics Louis Chan and Josef Lakonishok conclude that the:

Evidence from a variety of indicators, including beta and return volatility, suggests that value stocks are not riskier than growth stocks. Indeed, using the popular risk indicator that focuses on performance in down markets, we found that value stocks suffered less severely than growth stocks when the stock market or the overall economy did poorly. Under any but a metaphysical definition of risk, therefore, the superior performance of value stocks cannot be attributed to their risk exposure. A more convincing explanation for the value premium rests on characteristics of investor behavior and on the agency costs of delegated investment management.

In particular the writers point to research from Lakonishok, Shleifer and Vishny which advances 'an alternative possibility that high book-to-market firms' stock prices are temporarily depressed because investors overreact to prior poor performance, and maintain expectations about future performance that are "too pessimistic"'.[38] This theory is consistent with Joseph Piotroski's own analysis of high book to market firms.

Academic critics of value have also tried to suggest that the data pointing to past long-term value out performance is a by-product of the business cycle. In this argument value stocks simply become surrogates for cyclical stocks like banks or industrials – companies that boom when the economy moves ahead, but collapse in share price terms as the business cycle moves into a recession. Researchers suggest that because so many value stocks are cyclical in nature, investors should be careful about timing their investment.

---

[37] Ibid.
[38] Lakonishok, J., Vishny, R.W. and Shleifer, A. (1993) 'Contrarian Investment, Extrapolation and Risk', NBER Working Paper, National Bureau of Economic Research.

Academics Kwag and Lee look at this trend, concluding forcefully that this supposed extra risk from the business cycle is not relevant:

This research investigated the relative performance of value investing to growth investing. Empirical evidence suggests that value investing based on high valuation ratios (that is, book-to-market ratio, earnings-to-price ratio, cash flow-to-price ratio, and dividend yield) tends to outperform growth investing based on low valuation ratios. This superior performance is robust for all economic conditions, meaning that investors will be better off investing in stocks with high valuation ratios versus stocks with low valuation ratios regardless of economic conditions. The benefits of value investing are even greater during periods of contraction than during periods of expansion.[39]

The lesson from Japan

There's obviously no way of knowing whether value will power back into pole position over the next few decades or stay becalmed! But there is one useful pointer that suggests that value may eventually triumph. It comes from Japan where the local stockmarket has been undergoing a punishing multi-decade long bear market, punctuated by frequent bull market rallies. Sadly these rallies are soon submerged under a tidal wave of bad debt, massive system wide deleveraging and a separate but related long-term demographic meltdown.

The SG team have looked at different styles in the Japanese markets over the past decade and concluded that if anything has worked – and equity investing has been a dismal pursuit for more than 20 years – then it's value (see Figure 5.4). According to Andrew Lapthorne's team in an economy suffering from 'anaemic growth and a deflationary environment, value performance actually *improved*, especially when the metric used did not incorporate a measure of earnings'.[40] Their bottom line on the measures to use – forget earnings as a measure. By contrast Lapthorne's team found it difficult to isolate the effect of debt on Japanese share price returns but buying stocks with high dividend yields and strong balance sheets did absolutely produce strong returns. In particular, picking stocks with a low price-to-book versus their history proved to be a winning strategy.

---

[39] Kwag, S.-W. (A) and Lee, S.W. (2006) 'Value Investing and the Business Cycle', *Journal of Financial Planning*, January.
[40] See note 33.

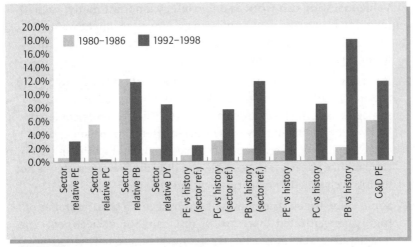

figure 5.4 Before and after performance of a selection of value styles in Japan

Source: SG Quantative Strategy Research

Lapthorne's bottom line:

The evidence from Japan suggests that most growth plays will eventually disappoint anyway and better protection against anaemic growth and ensuing deflation is to buy the cheap stuff. A value strategy, especially those based on not profit related measures such as price to book or dividend yield… makes sense. Finally dividend yield coupled with balance sheet strength also outperformed.[41]

Conclusion

We'd venture a number of concluding observations at the end of this long chapter on value investing and strategies to find cheap stocks.

◼ **Value investing doesn't always work**: the evidence on the long-term success of value investing is fairly conclusive despite the more recent criticisms. Most respected value orientated academics and analysts such as Rob Arnott from RAFI point to inevitable mean reversion and the eventual return of value investing. But investors need to be observant, look at the data and understand the risks of underperforming the index over long periods of time – it can happen and it could destroy your portfolio!

[41] Ibid.

- **Value investing can work as one strategy amongst many**: value investing needn't be your only strategy – investors might want to consider running another strategy (momentum-based ones for instance) alongside a value-based strategy.

- **If we had a preference we'd opt for a Piotroski strategy**: we're reasonably convinced by the evidence from both academics and strategists that the ideas articulated by the Chicago professor are the best way of finding quality value stocks with decent balance sheets and cheap share prices. We suspect that although the thinking behind Graham-like screens is impeccable and difficult to argue with, it's not terribly well suited to modern stockmarkets

- **Some value-based strategies will only suggest a small number of highly concentrated shares**: we've run many value screens over the past decade and in most cases these strategies have only tended to produce a shortlist of maybe 5–10 shares, many of them from similar, unloved sectors. There's nothing specifically wrong with this but it does increase your risk. Be alert to this risk and control your exposure to certain sectors

- **Consider using a value-based index as an alternative**: in Chapter 12 we'll look at the idea that maybe a better way of capturing the value anomaly is not through specific shares but rather through a specially created index that weights something like the FTSE towards 'cheaper' shares. We're not convinced such a strategy will deliver massive out-performance – as some contrarian value-based screens can – but over a 10- or even 20-year time frame we think it can deliver year on year out performance when measured against a benchmark index.

Interview

James Montier of GMO

Back in the early part of 2009 we interviewed James Montier at SG, the French bank. He's recently moved to asset management firm GMO. Montier has always been a wonderfully articulate exponent of both behavioural finance and value investing, with classic textbooks on both subjects to his name. When he's not travelling around the world talking to investors, Montier spends nearly all his time staring at charts and data developing an approach based around the rigorous, contrarian, interrogation of data. He's an exponent of what he calls evidence-based investing, but investing with a value bias. But is value investing still a workable idea? Aren't too many investors trying to implement Ben Graham's ideas in a market that's fundamentally changed? Hasn't value investing turned into a bubble in the past decade, forcing up prices and forcing down returns?

Interviewer: Do you think that value exists any longer, or do you think it's a bit of an artefact?

James Montier: I think it still exists. To my mind it's the only sensible way of approaching investment, regardless of the environment. I think you have to be careful how you define value and one of the hallmarks of what we've seen in the past few years has been rather simplistic approaches to value – PEs, price to books, a lot of the quant guys moving in and just using very simple metrics.

I think the market we've been through in the past 18 months suggests that actually we need to reconsider the role that Ben Graham then put front of centre of his approach, which is that balance sheets and trying to think about value without the context of the balance sheets side of the equation, to my mind, is pretty meaningless. So integrating or reintegrating analysis of balance sheets and capital structures into the investment process seems to me to be the way in which value is still meaningful. The other way in which value is perhaps still meaningful in these markets is it's a multi-asset trait. It isn't necessarily all about equities and there is a tendency, given the nature of our industry, to just obsess about what's happening in equities. But if you broaden value out, there's no reason why you can't find value outside of equity space.

Interviewer: So a classic example might be bonds?

James: Exactly! How you think about the valuation of bonds, corporate bonds – you can think about forms of cheap insurance, which again have a valuation consideration in them, because you only want to pay as little as possible for that insurance. So I think value is far from dead – it's tempting to try and go down that line but I think it's a dead end.

Interviewer: One of the hallmarks of classic value, and certainly its derivation which is equity income, has been the emphasis around dividends. Now that hasn't been very productive has it? Because the problem is that it's all based upon a figure which is the dividend yield, the dividend payout, and that has been, not declining, but in many cases vanishing, literally abolished overnight. Now that is a core component of most value investors' process. They might add other bits onto it but dividends will be a big bit. But dividends are horribly unpredictable at the moment and seem to be vanishing very quickly. I mean one doesn't know whether not to trust the FTSE 100 yield at the moment.

James: I think you are absolutely right. The problem with the dividends that we've had is again they ignore the balance sheet, so people have been happy to take the income stream, forgetting it's being generated by over-leveraged institutions. As soon as they are forced to deleverage the first thing that goes is the highest risk part of the capital structure, which is the shareholder, therefore the dividend gets cut. Whereas you can find stocks with strong balance sheets, that still pay good dividends, so again it brings you back to the way in which we've moved away from understanding balance sheets and we've become focused on profit/loss accounts. Whereas if you read *Security Analysis*, I think there are only something like three chapters on income statements and about seven on balance sheets.

Interviewer: That book is by Ben Graham isn't it?

James: Yes. So I think you can account for some of the dividend problems by thinking about the way in which we failed to understand the role of leverage and the use of the balance sheet in that equation.

Interviewer: Do you think here in the beginning of 2009 we're in a perfect Ben Graham like market? Ben Graham was writing about the 1930s where there were loads of companies with low book value, there were loads of companies still paying dividend yields. And there is now as we look at the market. You've said many times before, that over the past 30 years or even 20 years it's been impossible to find those stocks. But does it seem that we are entering that kind of market here in 2009?

James: I think we're returning to it. If you look at the sort of stocks that Graham would like, the net-net things that are trading below two thirds of their current assets minus total liabilities. You can find a large number of such stocks – the Japanese small caps market is littered with them. So I think we are returning to a world in which Ben Graham would be a lot more familiar with what's going on. He certainly wouldn't have ever approved of all the financial engineering and leverage, so I think the deleveraging process is throwing up the kinds of stocks that Graham would recognise as true bargain basement issues.

Interviewer: Could this be a very good time to be an equity income-based, dividend-orientated stock picker?

James: Yes. I think it could be. As long as, and this is the huge caveat, you have a sufficiently long-term view because there's no guarantee that this won't get worse in the short term, and one of the great institutional constraints that we suffer is, of course, that everybody obsesses about short-term performance. If you could buy a set of stocks today and bury them for five years, you'd be laughing. But the trouble is there's very few institutions who can behave in that fashion.

Interviewer: Time spans are critical – pick the wrong 20-year time span, and if you're an investor – institutional/private – you're basically stuffed... and that matters to investors because quite often they have a life cycle approach to investing. Pick the wrong cycle of decades, and you're in desperate trouble. Now the problem, of course, is a lot of value people say, 'Ah in the long run it will all work out. Equities in the long run, do always work out,' but there are a lot of time spans where actually investors would not have done alright, even if they had been phenomenally patient, and had waited five, ten years, they'd still have been down.

James: Yes. The problem is that they've bought at the wrong point. They bought when the market was expensive. So if you'd bought in 2000, yes, you'd be screwed... buying now is a totally different evaluation backdrop, and the primary determinant of your long-term returns is the valuation environment that you purchase in... so buying when markets are expensive is a bad idea, buy in markets when they are cheap, provided you are patient, is actually a long-term good idea.

Interviewer: Aren't investors thus forced to market time?

James: I think there's a difference between what I would call market timing, which is trying to guess the short-term outlook, and having a sensible valuation driven approach to asset allocation, which I think is perfectly sensible, and is generally an under-exploited area of the market, because people aren't so petrified of the concept of market timing. You don't actually have to try and time markets. I'm not trying to guess the future, all I'm doing is saying, I won't buy when they're expensive, I will buy when they're cheap, which is no different to what a stock picker does on an individual level. I don't see why it shouldn't transfer into an aggregate level concept.

Interviewer: What about buying shares and holding them for the long term? Simply buying and holding on a monthly basis through an investment plan, might not work?

James: I think that's right. There's a whole set of presets and rules that are used, that we have to rethink. The entire capital asset pricing model goes out of the window. Diversification needs to be rethought. Buy and hold, which is a bi-product of the efficient markets because it's all about cap weighted indices, all of these things go out of the window. The simple truth is they were never true. They are artefacts of very dubious theories. Unfortunately we have a very bad habit of taking theories as a substitute for fact, and just following simple advice. Actually I think you need to go back and sort of reconstruct finance from first principles, and that can lead you to some very different conclusion. So, yes, buy and hold doesn't work, so you have to become more strategically flexible in your allocations.

Interviewer: What about momentum investing – according to plenty of scientific evidence it works?

James: I don't find that comfortable although the evidence is very clear – momentum strategies do work. I find them intellectually rather unsatisfying, which is a terribly snobbish thing to say. I hate buying simply because anybody else is buying – it's never struck me as a terribly good rationale! It's the same psychology that leads you into believing a whole load of other stuff that is rubbish, because you just copy other people's behaviour. I think a value orientated approach is much more robust and prevents you getting trapped. You know, the great fear of momentum is you're the last man in. You are the greater fool. Buffett always talks about playing poker and if you can't work out who the patsy is, it's you! That's the great danger of momentum investing, as far as I can see, so I prefer a value approach combined with a long duration. So I'm much happier to buy cheap and forget about it for long periods of time.

Interviewer: But maybe markets really have changed? Maybe momentum is the future! A permanent moderation with occasional small bubbles!

James: There's two things that are worth noting. One is from J.K Galbraith [the American economist], who said that financial markets are characterised by the extreme brevity of memory, and the other was from Jeremy Grantham [Head of fund management firm GMO] who when asked what we would learn from the current crisis, said, 'In the short term a lot, in the medium term a little, and in the long term, absolutely nothing at all.' You know, the more people think it changed, the more it stays the same. You know, you look at the patterns of bubbles over history; they are always exactly the same. The details change but the general process of the bubble inflating, and then bursting, remains very, very constant. So we will see future bubbles and busts, because each new generation greets them with a degree of arrogance and overconfidence that is befitting of youth.

6

Quality and growth... of wide moats and GARP

Successful long-term investing involves more than just identifying solid businesses, or finding businesses that are growing rapidly, or buying cheap stocks. We believe that successful investing also involves evaluating whether a business will stand the test of time. Morningstar.com

You too can have it all!

As we've seen in the last chapter value investing can be enormously appealing especially to the more cerebral and contrarian investor who makes a point of tracking down shares – or strategies even – that stand out against the mainstream. Sadly, as we also discovered towards the end of that chapter, value investing can fail to produce the desired returns for extended periods of time.

In Table 6.1 (overleaf) we've repeated returns from a widely used index, namely the MSCI UK (and US) index, broken down for value and growth stocks. As established earlier, value in the broadest sense of the term has actually been a very poor performing strategy over the past decade and specifically since 2006.

table 6.1	MSCI Index returns by style – annualised returns			
Country Index	1 year	3 year	5 years	10 years
UK Growth	41%	−7.84%	0.59%	−2.08%
UK Value	29%	−15%	−4%	−2.20%
UK Core	31%	−9%	0.86%	−0.36%
US Growth	38%	−3.46%	0.31%	−4.44%
US Value	19.8%	−10.9%	−3.02%	−1.59%
US Core	29%	−7.16%	−1.28%	−2.82%

Source: MSCI Barra – MSCI World Indices.

These poor returns have, not unsurprisingly, been picked up on by many investors and fund managers who maintain that value investing is a dangerous pursuit. The *Investors Chronicle* columnist and house economist Chris Dillow recently remarked that value investing was virtually crypto 'Marxist'! He was referring to the cynical, slightly bearish tone of most value investors who think that capitalism, especially in its current earnings obsessed incarnation, is not to be trusted entirely and that the only way of surviving is to run against the trend and seek shelter and value in hard assets.

Chris Dillow only gives voice to a wider band of professional investors who maintain that value investors are too focused on a small subset of measures and poorly equipped to navigate their way around modern markets which trade in recent decades at much higher multiples than much of the 20th century. Even acolytes of Ben Graham, such as the mighty Warren Buffett, have remarked that the Dean of Wall Street's strategy ultimately proved frustrating. His partner Charlie Munger reminded him that simply bottom fishing was proving an increasingly difficult exercise as the amount of money he managed exponentially grew in size. Both Munger and Buffett concluded that there just weren't enough sufficiently cheap shares for the vast amount of money under their management. Better, Munger suggested to Buffett, to switch their mutual attentions to finding solid, decent, quality companies with great businesses where earnings were steadily advancing.

Buffett's switch to a different style of investing has been mirrored across the fund management industry – not everyone can be a contrarian when there aren't many cheapo stocks! But fund managers can get investors excited about a different type of share – quality, growing companies with a reasonable share price. While the focus of the next chapter might be on finding the elusive fast growing tenbaggers – shooting stars that will zoom up in share price terms, making investors vast profits – the strategies discussed in this chapter focus more on finding strong, reliable businesses that would make Warren Buffett and his business partner Charlie Munger proud.

This alternative view of investing has its own acronyms – we'll encounter GARP shortly for instance – and its own buzz words such as quality stocks and wide moats of competitive advantage. But at its heart is a simple desire – investors can have it all! They can buy great stocks for the long term, cheaply. This best of both worlds approach – a bit of value with a topping of growth – is also the mainstream for the massive global funds management industry, outnumbering the value fiends and contrarians by a massive margin. Private investors, it seems, also love a quality stock and what better story to sell them than a portfolio jammed pack full of these high-quality stocks all purchased at a great price!

As is the way with so much of investing, a great financial guru helped define this style of investing – he's regarded as a rival to Ben Graham and was one of the very best fund managers in the US. His name is Peter Lynch and he's renowned for overseeing Fidelity's prestigious Magellan Fund from 1977 to 1990. Lynch grew his assets from a paltry $18m to more than $10bn by the time he retired. Astoundingly, he held more than 1000 individual stock positions and his fund averaged an annual 29.2% return over the course of his management.

He defined his favoured investment style for mainstream investors in simple terms. It was, he suggested, good practice to pay no more than one times the growth rate of earnings per share over the past three to five years as well as the projected earnings over the next three to five years. This simple earnings-based strategy is clearly very different from that of most value investors. Lynch insisted that earnings growth both in the past and in the future mattered enormously and shouldn't be submerged under talk of strong balance sheets and massive dividend payouts. Lynch also suggested paying close attention to the share price and he liked to focus in particular on shares where the managers and directors were buying in shares – he believed that investors needed to play close attention to the relative performance of the share price. He also liked to invest in companies where better than expected news was likely to result in an increased share price as market enthusiasm continued to build over time.

A great company can be a great investment

Until fairly recently all this breathless talk of great, quality companies would have produced mirth amongst most professional academic economists brought up on the efficient markets hypothesis. They'd have suggested that there are indeed great quality companies on the UK and the US markets and that these companies do indeed see their share price increase in value over time – but trying to spot these companies in advance was, and is, next to impossible. For every Google spotted as a precocious upstart and then tracked through to mega-capdom, investors would probably be suffering from a gaggle of Netscapes. According to academic critics quality, growing companies with great businesses are much easier to spot with the benefit of hindsight!

But by the beginning of the noughties a rival group of academics had sprung up suggesting that the task of spotting great companies with decent growth prospects was in fact an entirely reasonable proposition. Leading the pack were two Californinan economists, Jeff Anderson and Gary Smith with their paper 'A Great Company Can be a Great Investment'.[1] Like many of their colleagues they'd been brought up on the prevailing orthodoxy that warned against confusing a great company with a great stock. They even noted in passing Andrew Tobias's classic account of a lunchtime discussion with an executive for a bank managing billions of dollars during the Nifty Fifty mania in the 1970 – a period where the mania for 'quality' fast growing large caps ended in disaster as shares drifted lower and lower over many years. Here's Andrew Tobias's description of that encounter:

> [He] told me that it was his bank's policy to invest only in companies whose earnings they expected to grow at an above-average rate. What about companies they expected to grow at only an average or subaverage rate? No, he said, they did not buy stock in such companies. Regardless of price? Regardless of price. Was there any price at which the bank would buy stock in an average-growth company? This question made the money manager uncomfortable. He clearly wanted to answer no, because he clearly would be damned before he would buy stock in such a company. But he couldn't come right out and say that, because he knew that, theoretically, there must be some price at which he should choose the stock of the mediocre company over the stocks of his nifty fifty.[2]

---

[1] Anderson, J. and Smith, G. (2006) 'A Great Company Can be a Great Investment', *Financial Analysts' Journal*, Vol. 62, No. 4, pp. 8–93.

[2] Ibid.

The Californian academics also repeat economist John Maynard Keynes's warning from the 1930s that 'day-to-day fluctuations in the profits of existing investments, which are obviously of an ephemeral and non-significant character, tend to have an altogether excessive, and even absurd, influence on the market.'[3]

And just to ram the point home Anderson and Smith repeated research from Lakonishok, Shliefer and Vishny[4] which provides formal evidence that 'if investors generally do not understand regression to the mean, they are likely to overestimate a company's "true greatness" and pay too much for the company's stock, a decision they will regret when measures of the company's greatness regress to the mean'.[5]

It's against this backdrop of open academic contempt for spotting great, quality companies in advance – *before* the stockmarket wised up and pushed share prices higher – that Anderson and Smith tested a simple concept. They wondered whether simply buying the ten best companies every year identified by *Fortune* magazine in the USA might be a clever stock picking strategy – they tested the period 1983 through to 2004. This *Fortune* exercise involved a survey of 10,000 executives, directors and securities analysts who rate the companies in their industry on a scale of 1 to 10 in eight areas of leadership: innovation, financial soundness, use of corporate assets, long-term investment, people management, quality of management, social responsibility, and quality of products/services. According to Anderson and Smith:

The 10,000 participants are then asked to name the companies they admire most in any industry from a list that included the two companies with the highest average scores in each industry and companies whose vote totals were among the top quartile the previous year.[6]

Figure 6.1 (overleaf) shows the simple result of an uncomplicated stock selection strategy i.e. buy the companies in the short list. To the academics' surprise the results demonstrated significant out performance.

According to Anderson and Smith:

---

[3] Ibid.

[4] Lakonishok, J., Vishny, R. and Shliefer, A. (1993) 'Contrarian Investment, Extrapolation, and Risk', NBER Working Paper, National Bureau of Economic Research.

[5] See note 1.

[6] Ibid.

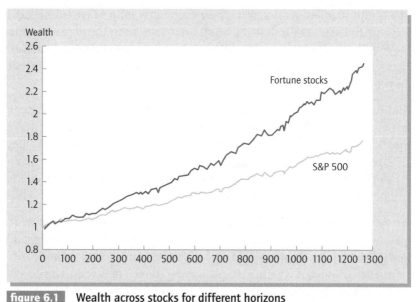

figure 6.1 **Wealth across stocks for different horizons**
Source: Anderson, J. and Smith, G. (2006) 'A Great Company can be a Great Investment', *Financial Analysts Journal*,
Vol. 62, No. 4, pp. 8–93.

The Fortune *strategy beats the S&P 500 by a margin that is both substantial and statistically persuasive... annual returns of 17.7%... It is unlikely that this observed difference in returns is some sort of risk premium since the companies selected as America's most admired are large and financially sound and their stocks are unlikely to be viewed by investors as riskier than average. A portfolio consisting of the stocks identified annually by* Fortune *magazine as America's most admired companies outperforms the S&P 500, whether the stocks are purchased on the publication date, or 5, 10, 15, or 20 trading days later. This is a clear challenge to the efficient market hypothesis since* Fortune's *picks are readily available public information.*[7]

The importance of earnings

This *Fortune* strategy – never actually replicated by a fund manager, curiously – highlights two crucial factors. The first is that the markets don't always correctly price well-respected market leading companies – this failure eventually translates through into opportunity for the careful stock picker willing to focus on a quality company.

---

[7] Ibid.

This study also hinted at another truth that's only now slowly dawning on academics – the collective power of informed investors. Efficient market adherents have always by default accepted the wisdom of crowds if only because their decisions, in aggregate, are in effect the market's day-to-day prices. But for most mainstream economists that insight into collective behaviour stops there – lots of investors swarm on to the exchange, in aggregate make their decisions and a price emerges. The *Fortune* strategy suggested that different crowds of investors, even experts could swarm together (via a survey) and collectively a judgement could emerge of the attractiveness of a company and thus its stock. And that consensus could, in fact, be right for much of the time!

In the next chapter we'll look again at how this collective intelligence could work as a strategy but for now another group of experts suggested themselves to academic researchers – equity analysts. Surely their collective judgements could also influence not only sentiment but ultimately pricing of a share? A first stab at an answer came in a paper – 'Analyst Recommendations, Mutual Fund Herding, and Overreaction in Stock Prices' – by Brown, Wei and Wermers.[8] The academics wanted to analyse 'mutual fund trading behaviour during the 1994 to 2003 period by focusing on instances of fund herding... we are especially interested in the tendency of funds to herd in... sell-side analyst recommendation revisions. We believe that mutual funds pay particular attention to analyst recommendations, perhaps even herding in the process'.[9]

Brown *et al.* had already built into their analysis a sense of crowd or herd like behaviour but they were especially interested in the reaction of fund managers – mutual fund managers in the US – to analysts' recommendations i.e. should the analysts' clients respond directly to the buy or sell recommendations.

Their conclusion:

Our analysis during 1994 to 2003 shows that mutual funds are more likely to herd on the buy-side following a consensus analyst upgrade, and (especially) to herd on the sell-side following a downgrade... We also find that stocks bought by herds experience a sharp increase in price during the herding measurement quarter, followed by a decrease during the following year, while stocks sold by herds experience the opposite pattern... All of the above-noted results are similar when we substitute analyst earnings forecast revisions for analyst recommendation revisions.[10]

---

[8] Brown, N.C., Wei, K.D. and Wermers, R. (2009) 'Analysts Recommendations, Mutual Fund Herding, and Overreaction in Stock Proces', available at www.ssrn.com/abstract=1092744

[9] Ibid.

[10] Ibid.

The authors also observe that this herding behaviour may have been growing in strength in recent decades: 'We find evidence that mutual fund herding impacts stock prices to a much greater degree during our sample period (1994 to 2003) than during prior-studied periods.'[11]

It's a fascinating paper that firmly establishes the power of crowd behaviour and its ability to produce stock selections which can 'beat the market', if only for a short period. The paper also begins to explain why this herd like behaviour occurs. The authors suggest 'reputational concerns':

Since managers of losing funds are more likely to focus on the short-term to avoid being fired, we would expect them to overinvest... in the common signal represented by analyst revisions.[12]

Woe become the fund manager who fails to follow the actions of his competitors!

The last piece of the puzzle is that signal, namely the actions of the analysts. Brown *et al.* firmly point to something called 'consensus revision in analyst recommendations'. These analysts are usually employed by large banks and brokers and spend their time looking in detail at a company's P&L and balance sheets but with a particular focus on one key measure – earnings. The consensus estimate for earnings in the next period is a widely used term by fund managers and simply refers to the average of all the analysts' estimates. If it increases, it's a strong indicator that the crowd of experts (otherwise known as analysts!) think that the company is growing fast. This, Brown *et al.*, conclude is frequently followed by a sharp increase in the share price.

There is one last caveat from the authors though – that increase in the share price over the short term is not sustained as fund managers tend to over-react to these upgrades:

Mutual funds appear to overreact when they follow analyst revisions... upgraded stocks heavily bought by herds tend to underperform their size, book-to-market, and momentum cohorts during the following year, while downgraded stocks heavily sold outperform their cohorts.[13]

---

[11] Ibid.

[12] Ibid.

[13] Ibid.

Quality, earnings and experts matter

The two academic studies above indicate a number of important themes that will be examined in greater detail in this chapter.

The *Fortune* study suggests that spotting quality companies in advance is possible and certainly profitable while also telling us that certain expert crowds can have some 'inside knowledge' that can be exploited by investors.

The paper on analysts' recommendations additionally tells us that one group of experts can absolutely move a share price – analysts. Their influence is most pronounced on earnings estimates – and the faster growing the increase in earnings estimates across the pack of analysts, the faster the share price seems to rise.

One last term also emerges from this discussion – share price momentum. Once the herd of mutual fund managers rally behind a stock where estimates of earnings growth are increasing, the faster the share price seems to move forward. This suggests a distinct momentum effect – the shares of the lucky, profitable company are moving ahead faster, in relative terms, than the wider market. In the next chapter, on growth strategies, we'll look in detail at the importance of share price strength – it is core to understanding any growth-based strategy. But the influence of momentum and relative share price strength has also been noted by many of the investment thinkers in this chapter. Even value biased investors have come to accept that fighting the market's judgement in terms of the share price is futile. Surely, they've concluded, it is better to develop a strategy that focuses on shares where the share price is moving ahead of the market? And wouldn't it be even better if this company with a strong relative share price was reasonably valued using key fundamental measures such as the PE ratio *and* was increasing its earnings over time, i.e. you could buy a growing company at a reasonable price. As fund manager Mario Gabelli puts it, the ideal share is a growth stock selling at below its intrinsic value. Welcome to GARP investing or the art of buying growth at a reasonable price.

The world according to GARP

A typical GARP strategy asks the investor to focus on companies where earnings are growing steadily but the shares are reasonably priced. If we can find companies growing at a steady rate whose share price is cheap we'll hopefully SWAN (sleep well at night), another term associated with GARP investors.

At its core is a simple desire – to benefit from a double whammy of growing earnings and a growing PE ratio that reflects this growth of earnings (see Figure 6.2).

Here's how this double transformation process could work. As the company's earnings per share grow, the price to earnings ratio of the company will fall, if the share price remains constant. But faster growing companies usually receive a premium rating from investors – remember that investors like the look of fast growing, 'shiny' companies that are enticing. So an astute GARP investor not only benefits from a rising share price prompted by the increasing earnings (the PE stays constant) but also benefits from a rerating, upwards, as investors reclassify the once boring stock as growth and *increase* the PE ratio, i.e. all those analysts start to suggest that Quality Company X can now safely trade at 20× (growing) earnings rather than the previous 15× earnings.

This mechanism helps explain why GARP investors like to see positive earnings numbers over the past few years, coupled with positive earnings projections for upcoming years. Yet GARP-based investors can never entirely

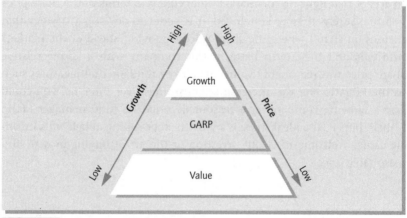

figure 6.2   **The GARP philosophy**

escape what is in many cases a value-based training – they're also highly sceptical of companies that are growing too fast, with earnings accelerating at an unsustainable rate! For GARPers these kind of companies – shooting stars growing at a fast pace – are too risky and unpredictable. Better for GARPers if the company's earnings growth is ticking along at a nice, steady 10–25% per annum rate.

GARPers also like to reassure themselves by making certain that this 'sustainable' growth is also reflected in the cashflow statement and that means they'll be looking for positive cashflow at the operating level to accompany earnings increases. But that's not all – cashflow needs to be greater than earnings, indicating that the firm is throwing off cash at a generous rate.

If a firm is growing at this 'sustainable' rate GARPers are probably more likely to accept a higher PE ratio than traditional value investors. They may be unwilling to buy into firms with a PE ratio of 40 plus – clearly that's not a reasonable price by any historical measure – but they're probably more than happy to accept a PE ratio of between 15 and 25, a level which is far too pricey for classic value investors.

GARP investors also tend to home in on 'out-of-favour' shares, i.e. where market conditions are not favourable or the financial community does not properly perceive the true worth of such companies. They then tend to hold the stock until there's been either a fundamental change in the company's nature or it has grown to a point where it will no longer be growing at a faster rate than the economy as a whole.

Truth be told, it's hard to quibble with this strategy of 'best of all worlds' investing: it's simply telling us to find the best companies at cheap share prices. This is reasonable enough except that such mythical beasts are actually rather hard to track down, especially in the large cap universe.

In reality most GARPers tend to focus on medium and small cap stocks. Whereas the market does a pretty good job of pricing in expectations of future growth for large companies, with much smaller companies there's a great deal more inefficiency. Only a small number of brokers may actually cover the stock, which means that the big institutional players may not have accurate information on which to base their share buying decisions. This kind of market inefficiency – imperfect knowledge – can produce stunning price anomalies.

But this focus on smaller stocks also brings with it a greater potential risk. Many smaller stocks do have limited analysts' coverage and sometimes actual coverage is limited to just one 'house broker' who is effectively employed by the company to make forecasts. That means your estimate of 'future' sustainable growth is based on a slightly dubious source, not the dozens of relatively objective estimates you'll find with larger companies.

Nevertheless, despite these risks an enormous number of fund managers and private investors do follow this strategy as their core – many with stunning results. Perhaps the clearest way of examining the relative success of this strategy is to look at an index that simulates such a strategy. Index research firm IndexIQ has developed – like Nuveen for Ben Graham's strategy – a specific index that looks to focus exclusively on GARP shares in the US market. The precise details of the underlying strategy aren't spelt out by Index IQ but its developers do state the following: 'A GARP strategy emphasises picking stocks that have historically demonstrated solid earnings growth, are expected to continue to exhibit strong future growth characteristics, yet are undervalued today'.[14] Table 6.2 suggests that over the ten years this strategy has been tested, GARP shares have consistently beaten the wider market – in this case the S&P 500 – but with one big exception, 2008.

table 6.2 Performance (as of 30 November 2009)

Index history (%)	YTD	1 year	3 year	5 year	10 year
IQ GARP Index	32.70	34.12	−4.41	5.21	10
S&P 500 Index	24.07	25.39	−5.79	0.71	−0.2
Russell 1000 Growth Index	33.09	35.50	−2.76	1.80	−2.6

Figure 6.3 shows discrete annual performance – in 2008 this GARP index lost 45% compared to just 37% for the S&P 500.

---

[14] http://www.indexiq.com/indexes/inaw/infundgarp.html

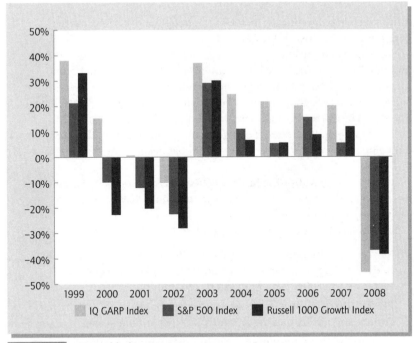

IQ GARP Index   S&P 500 Index   Russell 1000 Growth Index

figure 6.3   Annual index returns

A simple GARP strategy

What could a very simple GARP strategy look like in a screen? Our GARP screen is a hybrid, combining a number of simple to understand ideas, all designed to find solid, reliable, growing companies with cheap share prices.

At its very core is the idea that earnings have been growing steadily over the past few years, indicating sustainable growth. That means, in practice, that GARP-based screens should be looking for growth in earnings in the 10–20% per annum range – we're after a company growing relatively fast but in a sustainable manner.

But what about the size of company? Because this screen targets small to medium sized caps – we've set the minimum at £10m and the maximum at £1bn – we run the risk of finding stocks that the market will ignore even though growth prospects are reasonable. As a result we've added one key additional criterion – some evidence of relative share price strength in the past 12 months. As long as this figure is at least positive, then there's some hope that the market might rediscover its enthusiasm for the stock.

A negative figure by contrast increases the potential risk of the market neglecting the intrinsic value of the stock.

We've also added some criteria which address internal efficiency and profitability. Many GARP investors wouldn't bother with the net profit margin – they're happy with a growing EPS figure – but there's always a concern that although profits may be growing, the margin may be falling. This could be the result of growth at the bottom line accompanied by decline at the top line (sales). So, if you can, set one criterion that screens out companies where the operating margin has been falling over the past few years.

It's also worth scrutinising just how effectively the company is exploiting its capital base – in our screen we've set a minimum ROCE (return on capital employed) of at least 15%.

In summary here's our first, main GARP screen:

- Market capitalisation should be above £10m but no more than £100m to exclude large companies. The minimum market cap could be increased to £500m if it's found to be too limiting

- EPS growth over the past three to five years should be above 10% per annum and ideally moving around a 20% per annum average.

- Growth in EPS for the current year and the coming year should also be above 10%.

- ROCE should be at least 12% if not 15% and, crucially, trending upwards over the past few years.

- The net operating margin should also be trending upwards over the past few years indicating a company that's improving its profitability.

- The PE ratio should be reasonable and no more than 20.

- Last but definitely not least it would be nice if there was some relative strength (RS) in the share price against the market average for the past 12 months.

This first screen should probably then be refined by an additional screen that looks at the earnings growth figures. Examine the last five years of EPS growth figures and try and narrow your choice down to firms where earnings growth has been steady – not too many rapid moves up or down – progressively upwards, and not unsustainably fast.

The small number of stocks you'll be left with should probably be a fairly hardy bunch of 'steady as they go' cheap growth stocks. They probably won't out perform the market in a boom phase but they should be solid stocks capable of delivering growth over the long term.

The Magic Numbers

The GARP approach we've looked at so far puts earnings growth very much at the core of its approach – a company with long-term, steadily rising, sustainable earnings growth, with a reasonably rated share price, is the absolute ideal. But the strategy we created to capture this in the box above would strike some analysts as far too complicated. They'd suggest honing in on measures that look at how efficiently the company uses its capital: are the company's managers generating enough in the way of profits and earnings to justify the investment in equity (and debt) in the company? This relatively simple approach has been championed by Joel Greenblatt.

The 'Little' book (*The Little Book that Beats the Market*) has been a huge success both in the US and the UK where RBS have even introduced an index based on this approach. Even ultra-cautious financial analysts and researchers have taken notice, curious to see if Greenblatt's novel approach really can deliver huge returns moving forward.

With the 'Little' book, Greenblatt set out to develop an approach that was apparently simple enough for his children to understand and use, yet that also reflects the core values used by Greenblatt to manage his portfolio.

The result is an easy-to-understand approach that relies on two simple rules:

- Seek out companies with high return on invested capital, based on the generation of decent profits.
- A low share price, a low PE ratio and a high earnings yield (the PE ratio expressed as a percentage).

These two concepts – buying a good business at a bargain price – make up what Greenblatt calls the 'magic formula'.

Identifying good businesses

The first key foundation to Greenblatt's approach is to identify the strength of a business by examining the return on capital. This measures the operating profit of the total investment (equity and debt) used by the company to generate a profit. If a company is able to earn a high return – say 25% or more – then it's a desirable business.

The key point here is that Greenblatt uses a very particular measure, namely return on capital invested. Most investors use alternative measures like return on equity (ROE, net profit divided by equity) or return on assets (ROA, net profit divided by total assets) to assess the profitability of a business. He determines return on capital by dividing earnings before interest and taxes (EBIT) by the tangible capital employed (net working capital plus net fixed assets).

Turning to the share price, Greenblatt takes the popular PE ratio and inverts it – he calculates the earnings yield by dividing earnings before interest and taxes (EBIT) by enterprise value. The enterprise value is a new measure in this book but it's easy to understand – it's all the equity invested in the business plus all the debt.

Finding magic formula companies

Using these basic principles Greenblatt then goes on to run a very simple screen. The key measures include the following:

- He eliminates foreign companies.
- He also eliminates banks, finance firms and utilities.
- Greenblatt suggests that it's costly to trade less liquid, micro-capitalisation stocks, so he only looks at the 3500 largest companies. This size cut-off is roughly equal to a market capitalisation minimum of $5m.
- He then runs a screen based on return on capital and ranks them from 1 to 3500, based on that measure.
- That 3500 is then ranked again this time using the earnings yield where the share with the highest earnings yield is ranked number 1 and 3500 is assigned to the stock with the lowest yield.

These two rankings are then added up, giving you a magic number with the lowest combined rank bought. Thus a share with a rank of say 100 for return on capital and an earnings yield rank of 431 would have a combined rank of 531.

Does it work?

Greenblatt says he's tested his system in enormous detail. Buying the 30 best-ranked companies, holding that portfolio for a year, and then repeating the screening process the next year would have returned 30.8% annually over the past 17 years. By contrast, the S&P 500's annual return over the same timeframe was only 12.4%.

According to analysts at the American Association of Individual Investors (AAII) if you had limited a screen to the largest 2500 companies (market cap above $200m) you would have reduced the annual rate of return to 23.7%, while using just the largest 1000 companies (market cap above $1bn) resulted in a 22.9% annual rate of return.

The great risk with any *simple* system like this is what some critics call the garbage in, garbage out syndrome. Just because two numbers seem to produce a series of correlated returns doesn't mean there's an actual, real world mechanic at work; some method within the numbers that hints at a real cause for the out performance. Statisticians frequently warn of these data mining risks but to be fair to Greenblatt the value ideas behind this approach are easy to conceptualise – you're buying a company that is efficient, works its assets hard, produces good profits and has cheap shares. In essence the Magic Formula approach is about banking on smart money eventually waking up to the potential of quality companies and then driving up the share price. If this approach piques your interest you can see the screen in action over at Greenblatt's website at www.magicformulainvesting.com. (You have to register for free, then identify the level of return on capital you want, and then select the 25 best shares that fit the bill.) The data on the site is updated daily and is licensed from Standard and Poor's. We've put the full list of recommended US stocks from the end of 2009 in Table 6.3 (overleaf).

table 6.3 Top 30 companies with a minimum market capitalisation of $50 million, price data (22 December 2009)

Company name	Ticker	Market cap ($m)
CF Industries Holdings Inc	CF	4,198.41
Cherokee Inc	CHKE	143.4
Chicago Bridge & Iron Co. NV	CBI	1,962.14
Corporate Executive Board Company (The)	EXBD	764.39
Cytokinetics Inc	CYTK	173.59
Deluxe Corp	DLX	760.89
Dyadic International Inc	DYAI	52.82
EMCOR Group Inc.	EME	1,801.65
EarthLink Inc	ELNK	878.4
Endo Pharmaceuticals Holdings Inc	ENDP	2,358.73
Forest Laboratories Inc.	FRX	9,747.04
GT Solar International Inc	SOLR	843.09
Immunomedics Inc	IMMU	257.15
InterDigital Inc	IDCC	1,127.93
KHD Humboldt Wedag International Ltd	KHD	410.33
Lorillard Inc	LO	12,662.65
Net 1 Ueps Technologies Inc	UEPS	888.96
PDL BioPharmaInc	PDLI	814.95
PRG-Schultz International Inc	PRGX	127.62
Pervasive Software Inc	PVSW	86.94
Pre-Paid Legal Services Inc	PPD	443.24
Questcor Pharmaceuticals Inc	QCOR	277.18
Sturm Ruger & Co Inc	RGR	194.16
Synta Pharmaceuticals Corp	SNTA	186.54
USA Mobility Inc	USMO	242.83
United Online Inc	UNTD	591.33
Universal Travel Group	UTA	142.96
ValueClick Inc	VCLK	839.85
Versant Corp	VSNT	53.4
j2 Global Communications Inc	JCOM	858.66

Source: www.magicformulainvesting.com

A Greenblatt strategy for the UK

Running this strategy in the UK is a little more problematic, if only because Greenblatt uses his own version of key measures like ROCE – but it is possible to adapt his thoughts and use the following simple steps:

■ Screen for companies in the top quartile for return on capital employed. Most of the time that's above 25%.

■ To screen for the earnings yield, reverse it, and use the PE ratio – we prefer using the forward PE ratio but you could use the historic one instead. Again look for the lowest quartile which usually translates to under 15, or even 13. We'd also apply a lower cut off of 5 or below – most companies with abnormally low PE ratios are statistical freaks that are usually in deep trouble.

■ Exclude foreign stocks and banks and utilities.

■ Award a rank for the PE ratio – the lowest one gets 1 and so on. Then award a rank for the ROCE. If you can export screens as spreadsheets this is easy to do – simply apply a filter or sort by the measure. Add the two ranks up.

With your final long list, only select the top 25 or 20 shares.

The gospel according to Buffett

Many of the great investors encountered in this book think we're perhaps a little too obsessed with magic numbers and simple maths! What we actually need to do is use other ideas in our decision-making process, ideas that echo the logic behind the *Fortune* survey we mentioned earlier in this chapter.

Like that great value investor Ben Graham, they think that as an investor you're buying into real world companies, with real businesses which also have real products that need to influence which stocks you pick. These great investors – characters like Peter Lynch and the Sage of Omaha himself, Warren Buffett – reckon that private investors have a huge advantage in this respect because you can actually go out on to the high street and see what's selling well. As Peter Lynch puts it: 'Wall Street thinks like some of the ancient Greeks did. They'd sit around for days and debate how many teeth a horse had. The right answer is go check a horse.'[15]

---

[15] Lynch, P. and Rothschild, J. (1994) *Beating the Street*, Simon & Schuster.

Peter Lynch suggest that you go out and look at the products of any company under analysis, see how consumers react to them, and kick the 'tyres' to see if the products feel solid, well built. If the company's products seem great, then that'll probably mean the company has a great future, even if Wall Street or the City thinks otherwise.

Peter Lynch sums up this school of real world investing by suggesting that:

There's a 100% correlation between what happens to the company and what happens to the stock. The trick is that it doesn't happen that way over one week, or even over six or nine months and that's terrific. Sometimes the fundamentals are getting better and the stock is going down. That's what you're looking for. The stock market and the stock price don't always run in sync.[16]

Warren Buffett has spent most of his investing career trying to spot the very few companies where this relationship is out of sync. His success in finding these companies is now legendary. Using his own secretive strategy, Buffett has delivered huge profits for investors in his Berkshire Hathaway group. Book value per share has grown at a compounded annual rate of more than 20% over the past 37 calendar years. What's even more surprising is that screens based on his ideas also seem to work. Analysts at S&P/Business Week have been running a Buffett screen since February 1995 (see the box below). From 13 February 1995 through to 17 January 2008, the screen had an annualised return of 14.9%, vs. 8.2% for the S&P 500.

The S&P/Business Week Buffett screen

American business magazine *Business Week* likes to kick off its new year with its own take on a Warren Buffett strategy. The screen was developed by S&P's top quant, Howard Rosenblatt, and is in turn based on investment criteria attributed to the Sage of Omaha. According to *Business Week*, Buffet uses five investment criteria

1 Free cash flow (net income after taxes, plus depreciation and amortisation, less capital expenditures) of at least $250m.

2 Net profit margin of 15% or more.

3 Return on equity of at least 15% for each of the past three years and the most recent quarter.

---

[16] Ibid.

4   A dollar's worth of retained earnings creating at least a dollar's worth of shareholder value over the past five years.

5   Ample liquidity. Only stocks with a market capitalisation of at least $500m are included.

The analysts at S&P add one last criterion to eliminate overvalued stocks:

6   Over-priced stocks are identified by comparing the five-year discounted cash flow (DCF) estimate with the current price.

Table 6.4 sets out S&P's 'Buffet Screen' for January 2009.

table 6.4	S&P's 'Buffett Screen', January 2009
Company	**Ticker**
Alcon	ACL
America Movil	AMX
Autodesk	ADSK
Baxter International	BAX
Becton, Dickinson	BDX
BG Group	BRGYY
British-American Tobacco	BTI
Brown-Forman	BFB
C.R. Bard	BCR
Canadian National Railway	CNI
Companhia Vale do Rio	RIO
Frontline	FRO
Genentech	DNA
GrupoTelevisa	TV
McDonald's	MCD
Noble Energy	NBL
Novo-Nordisk	NVO

Precisely because he doesn't spell out his exact criteria or likely investment targets (that is, after all, how he makes his money) it's left to his acolytes and followers to spell out the gospel according to Buffett, or more particularly his stock selection strategy!

Two main schools dominate. The first are the Buffettologists, led by Warren's former daughter in law, Mary, and his old friend and colleague David Clark. The rival camp is led by Robert Hagstrom, the author of three popular books on Buffett including his 1994 bestseller, *The Warren Buffett Way: Investment Strategies of the World's Greatest Investor*. This latter methodology is used by *Business Week* and S&P in their own screen.

Both sets of acolytes articulate a classic Buffett philosophy – take your time to find the right stock, use painstaking research and screening, and then stick with the share until its intrinsic value is realised. As Buffett would say, 'buy great companies not great stocks' – that means you should approach buying a single share as if you were buying the entire business.

At the heart of Buffett's analysis is his dislike of what he calls commodity-based firms – firms where price is king and the cheapest firm and products always wins out. These firms are characterised by low profit margins, low returns on equity, little brand name loyalty, excess capacity within the industry and erratic profits.

Consumer monopolies on the other hand are very much Buffett's forte. He likes firms with significant pricing power, partly through strong brand recognition or significant intangible but unrecognised value. These 'monopoly' firms can easily build shareholder value by making the 'intrinsic value' in the company become more open.

A Buffett strategy in practice

Buffett is a very discriminating investor who bothers to research his 'businesses' (his view is that by investing you end up owning a bit of the business) in great depth. He's not one of those investors who runs a few quantitative screens – low PE, high dividend yield – and then goes away and buys all the stocks identified. In as much as we can guess a typical Buffett screen, based in part on the various studies of his methodology, we can probably say with some certainty that it will involve many different layers and many different themes:

■ First and foremost investors need to examine the underlying *profitability* of the business. For Buffett that doesn't mean taking for granted the gloss of the modern P&L account and the quarterly EPS figures. These quarter-on-quarter figures, miraculously showing a steady increase, tells someone like Buffett very little about the business and its underlying profitability. Ultimately he wants to discover the underlying intrinsic value of the business and the only way to start this is to dig deep and find out what the underlying profitability of the business really is. Earnings of course matter when you start to investigate a business. You are looking for companies that, at a minimum, produce profits over the medium historic term. That probably means you're looking for companies with steady earnings growth over the last three and five years – that growth need not be excessive but it must be above the average for the market. Buffett would probably also examine loss making firms where there is a record of underlying profitability and the opportunity to unlock hidden asset values, but for the average private investor the key is to start by targeting profitable businesses that have grown relatively steadily.

■ Like many investors who started off as a value investor Buffett does appear to care about the *current PE ratio*. Judging by his sage-like pronouncements before the dotCom meltdown he doesn't really like firms with a high PE ratio, and so any strategy probably should have a maximum PE value. Anything much above twice the market average or median is likely to be a bit too rich for Warren. But in truth, earnings matter very little for the Warren Buffett's of this world. What really matters is hard cash.

■ Does the business produce the cash you'd expect it to? Look at the *cashflow* statement – can it fund its growth sustainably and pay dividends as well as the capex? Take some time to look at how easily the earnings are covered by this cashflow – the ratio of cashflow to EPS should be at least 1. Also drill a bit deeper and look for a company producing current positive cashflow (set a target of a positive share price to cashflow or PCF) and then screen for companies where the cashflow trend is positive, implying an improving cashflow position.

■ Just as cashflow is a positive way of examining underlying profitability, so is *return on equity*. Buffett watchers suggest that the Sage probably prefers a RoE or RoCE of at least 12% though some suggest it could be as high as 15% per annum – and he likes that RoCE rate to be consistent in historical terms with a trend upwards if anything. One implication of high returns on equity is a net margin that is likely to be well above average.

■ Returning to Buffett's 'training' in value investing – remember that he was trained by Ben Graham – you probably also need to look at the *balance sheet* to check the asset backing of the firm. Buffett is a good deal more liberal that his mentor Ben Graham in using measures like

PBV – he has to invest his giant mountain of money in stockmarkets where a share with a PBV below 0.5 is almost unheard of.

▨ Buffett is also suspicious of excessive *debt* – when looking for a quality business examine the net gearing and interest cover as your best measures of 'affordability' of debt. A net gearing rate above 100% is likely to trigger alarm bells and interest cover of at least 1 is pretty much essential.

▨ Last but not least Buffett is only likely to be impressed by firms that have some stature and some clear profits and earnings visibility – a *market cap* much below £50m is likely to fail any elementary Buffett screen.

All these measures can probably be used in a quantitative screen which will in turn yield a relatively small number of potential shares, but this is only the start of any Buffett-style investigation:

▨ In the second stage, investors should examine the performance of the firm compared to its sector or industrial *peers*. A RoE of 12% or a net profit margin of 10% might look great compared to the whole market but compared to its peers, it might actually be 'sub-average'. Compare key measures like ROCE, margin, gearing and PCF against sector (or industry) peers – your chosen few Buffett stocks need to be at least average in most if not all these key measures.

In the last stage investors also need to figure out if the future growth in the company (and the shares) is going to be enough to compensate you for the extra risk you're taking on by investing in the shares.

Effectively what we're examining in this third stage is your margin of error – if the company manages to sustain past growth rates into the future, will the appreciation in the share price be large enough to compensate you for any risk undertaken? This risk can be measured against something called the risk free rate, which is the interest rate you would have received if you had invested in a gilt or treasury bond. Add that interest up over the next few years and you have a 'measure' of the risk free alternative.

The underlying idea here is one we encountered in our earlier chapter examining company accounts and the use of different financial models – the discounted cash flow model where growth rates are projected forward and then related back to returns in excess of the risk free alternative. Buffett notably repeats John Burr Williams's equation for value, which is summarised as:

The value of any stock, bond or business today is determined by the cash inflows and outflows – discounted at an appropriate interest rate – that can be expected to occur during the remaining life of the asset.[17]

Warren Buffett and Charlie Munger in their own words

Law professor Lawrence Cunningham has performed an enormous service for all those time strapped investors eager to understand Warren Buffett and partner Charlie Munger's accumulated wisdom – but impatient enough not to read through his various letters to shareholders at Berkshire Hathaway and his bestselling books. He's condensed all their thoughts, key letters and conversations into one 219-page online PDF document – you can download it from the internet at http://www.monitorinvestimentos. com.br/download/The%20Essays%20Of%20Warren%20Buffett%20-%20 Lessons%20For%20Corporate%20America.pdf.

In this compelling summary you can begin to see the evolution of Buffett's investment philosophy from its roots in value investing. Buffett is wonderfully honest about this journey – he started out looking for Graham's increasingly mythical net net bargains but found them almost impossible to find as the decades wore on. 'It must be noted that your Chairman [of Berkshire Hathaway], always a quick study, required only 20 years to recognize how important it was to buy good businesses. In the interim, I searched for "bargains" – and had the misfortune to find some. My punishment was an education in the economics of short-line farm implement manufacturers, third-place department stores, and New England textile manufacturers)'.

Put simply, for Buffett and his business partner Charlie Munger, there just weren't enough bargains out there. 'If you buy a stock at a sufficiently low price, there will usually be some hiccup in the fortunes of the business that gives you a chance to unload at a decent profit, even though the long-term performance of the business may be terrible. I call this the "cigar butt" approach to investing. A cigar butt found on the street that has only one puff left in it may not offer much of a smoke, but the "bargain purchase" will make that puff all profit.'

'Unless you are a liquidator, that kind of approach to buying businesses is foolish. First, the original "bargain" price probably will not turn out to be such a steal after all. In a difficult business, no sooner is one problem solved than another surfaces – never is there just one cockroach in the kitchen. Second, any initial advantage you secure will be quickly eroded by the low return that the business earns.'

▶

---

[17] Williams, J. B. (1936, reprint 1997) *The Theory of Investment Value*, Harvard University Press, 1997 reprint Fraser Publishing.

Buffett and Munger adapted their new strategy in the 1960s and 1970s – their goal became that of finding 'an outstanding business at a sensible price, not a mediocre business at a bargain price'.

It's important though to understand that when Buffett, and Munger, speak about their target businesses, they distinguish two different types of proposition. The first are those businesses they take control of, i.e. buy through Berkshire Hathaway and then operate on a long-term private equity model. Yet most public attention is actually focused on their open market investments where they buy a stake as investors, which the duo call their marketable holdings. With the controlled businesses 'we get to allocate capital, whereas we are likely to have little or nothing to say about this process with marketable holdings'. For their marketable or trade investments they want a business '(a) that we can understand; (b) with favourable long-term prospects; (c) operated by honest and competent people; and (d) available at a very attractive price.'

Buffett and Munger do become more specific over time in the measures they use when picking which marketable business to invest in – they are for instance clearly concerned with *capital usage* and thus by default the return on equity employed in a business: 'Leaving the question of price aside, the best business to own is one that over an extended period can employ large amounts of incremental capital at very high rates of return. The worst business to own is one that must, or will, do the opposite – that is, consistently employ ever-greater amounts of capital at very low rates of return.'

Earnings are clearly an important measure for the Berkshire Hathaway duo: 'Put together a portfolio of companies whose aggregate earnings march upward over the years... Our look-through earnings have grown at a good clip over the years, and our stock price has risen correspondingly'.

Buffett and Munger also spell out their concept of a quality business – one with real longevity based on the business model. 'We are searching for operations that we believe are virtually certain to possess enormous competitive strength 10 or 20 years from now. A fast-changing industry environment may offer the chance for huge wins, but it precludes the certainty we seek.' They go on to define these companies using the term 'The Inevitable' – outfits like Coca-Cola and Gillette. 'Forecasters may differ a bit in their predictions of exactly how much soft drink or shaving-equipment business these companies will be doing in 10 or 20 years.'

The Berkshire Hathaway duo doesn't delve into any more detail on their selection criteria or spell out a screen. But Buffett and Munger do clearly articulate a *growth at a reasonable price strategy*, one which combines the best of both the value and growth worlds:

In our opinion, the two approaches are joined at the hip: growth is always a component in the calculation of value, constituting a variable whose importance can range from negligible to enormous and whose impact can be negative as well as positive. In addition, we think the very term 'value investing' is redundant. What is 'investing' if it is not the act of seeking value at least sufficient to justify the amount paid? Consciously paying more for a stock than its calculated value – in the hope that it can soon be sold for a still-higher price – should be labelled speculation (which is neither illegal, immoral nor – in our view – financially fattening). Whether appropriate or not, the term 'value investing' is widely used. Typically, it connotes the purchase of stocks having attributes such as a low ratio of price to book value, a low price earnings ratio, or a high dividend yield. Unfortunately, such characteristics, even if they appear in combination, are far from determinative as to whether an investor is indeed buying something for what it is worth and is therefore truly operating on the principle of obtaining value in his investments. Correspondingly, opposite characteristics – a high ratio of price to book value, a high price earnings ratio, and a low dividend yield – are in no way inconsistent with a 'value' purchase. Similarly, business growth, per se, tells us little about value. It's true that growth often has a positive impact on value, sometimes one of spectacular proportions. But such an effect is far from certain. For example, investors have regularly poured money into the domestic airline business to finance profitless (or worse) growth. For these investors, it would have been far better if Orville had failed to get off the ground at Kitty Hawk: the more the industry has grown, the worse the disaster for owners.'

Buffett and Munger conclude with some sage advice for private investors on how to build a sensible portfolio. They start by reminding private investors that 'Most investors, both institutional and individual, will find that the best way to own common stocks is through an index fund that charges minimal fees. Those following this path are sure to beat the net results (after fees and expenses) delivered by the great majority of investment professionals.' If investors insist on picking individual shares Buffett and Munger suggest: 'Your goal as an investor should simply be to purchase, at a rational price, a part interest in an easily-understandable business whose earnings are virtually certain to be materially higher five, ten and 20 years from now. Over time, you will find only a few companies that meet these standards – so when you see one that qualifies, you should buy a *meaningful amount of stock* [emphasis added].' And of course never forget their demand that you ignore the siren calls of both the deep value investors looking for a bargain and the growth nuts with their talk of tomorrow's tenbaggers: 'It's far better to buy a wonderful company at a fair price than a fair company at a wonderful price.' Always remember Ben Graham's advice on a margin of safety: 'We insist on a margin of safety in our purchase price. If we calculate the value of a common stock to be only slightly higher than its price, we're not interested in buying.'

Source: Buffett, W.A., ed. Lawrence A. Cunningham (2009) *The Essays of Warren Buffett: Lessons for Corporate America.*

A British guru – Jim Slater and the Zulu principle

So far our discussion of GARP investing has exclusively been articulated through American academics and investors – but there is one British investor turned commentator who has also developed a clearly thought through strategy for picking decently priced growth stocks: Jim Slater, a former banker and fund manager turned commentator. He's eloquently argued for a 'growth at reasonable cost' investment philosophy for many years now, with much success. The clearest definition of his approach came in his book *Beyond the Zulu Principle: Extraordinary Profits from Growth Shares* (2000) which is pretty much basic textbook reading for British investors. His obsession with screening through the stock market also led him to set up the CompanyREFS information system.

Slater is a classic growth at a reasonable price investor, with a slightly Buffett-like conservative temperament. His key measure is the PEG factor or PE growth factor – he thinks it's the best indicator of reasonably priced growth. As Slater himself says in the guide to his REFs system: 'The PEG is a much more sophisticated measure [than PER] because it relates the PER of a company to its future earnings growth rate and gives a better indication of value.' It's a dynamic measure and changes over time but Slater reckons that 'over the long term, it has paid to buy the market on a PEG of one or below'.[18]

Slater uses his own PEG factor in a very distinctive fashion. In his Company REFS system he only gives a PEG to a company where there's at least four years' evidence of earnings per share growth. Companies that pass this test are classic growth companies with real evidence of earnings stability and sustainable growth.

Slater goes on to spell out in great detail his own take on the classic growth at a reasonable price screen. He uses the metaphor of 'a quiver full of arrows' to describe his approach of using a large number of measures. His core concern is earnings consistency and momentum. That implies that the company must have four years of consecutive EPS growth and that each of the past five years must have been profitable, although a period of poor performance is allowed if the following four periods show a consistent upwards trend. Slater likes to see earnings through the prism of the PEG measure, which he thinks shouldn't be above 1 although Slater does cau-

---

[18] www.companyrefs.com

tion that low PEGS (below 1) work best with companies where the PE ratio is in the 12–20 range and EPS growth rates are between 15 and 30%.

To make this focus on earnings work Slater adds a number of important caveats:

- There must be a number of broker forecasts available, preferably more than one. The important point here is that Slater bases much of his analysis on 'expected' earnings growth and if only one broker covers the stock that figure may be deeply unreliable, especially if it is a 'house broker' with a relationship to the company management.
- Slater thinks investors should be very careful with companies in the micro-cap UK FTSE Fledgling Index. They generally tend to only have one broker following the stock. Most fans of the Slater approach tend to restrict their screens to firms with a market value of at least £10m and in most cases £3m.
- Cashflow per share should exceed EPS for the last reported year and for the average of the previous five years.
- You must exclude the whole property sector and most companies in the building construction/materials sector.

Slater also uses a great many measures based on traditional value investing:

- The interest cover should be reasonable.
- There should be a current ratio of 2 or more.
- Gearing should generally be no more than 50%.
- ROCE excluding intangibles should be above average for the sector and the trend should be upward.
- Low price to sales ratios are desirable and an 'added attraction' but not absolutely necessary.
- Slater doesn't require a dividend but he says it's 'preferred' and in reality most stocks that pass a Slater screen will pay dividends anyway.

Last but most definitely not least Slater wants some reassurance that our cheap growth stock is actually capable of share price momentum. That means making use of a measure that looks at the relative strength (RS) of the share price (relative to the benchmark index such as the FTSE 100). According to Slater investors should look for positive figures for both the last month, and the last 12 months. Slater is also, like many gurus featured in this book, deeply suspicious of heavy insider selling (regarding it as a strong sell signal) and hugely motivated by *heavy insider buying* which he conversely regards as a strong buy signal.

Slater also goes into detail about how a portfolio of 'Zulu' stocks should be managed. He favours a tight portfolio of 10–12 shares with no share occupying more than 15% of the total portfolio by value. He's also a classic buy and hold investor who thinks investors should only sell if the 'story has changed' and the PEG for instance has shot up beyond a reasonable level. In other words, that selection is more important than timing. He also reckons that investors should 'run with [their] profits and cut your losses'[19], i.e. don't sell at the first sign of profits but be prepared to cut losses quickly if the shares fall by more than say 20%.

A Slater Zulu screen in summary

Jim Slater suggests a series of screens, starting with an initial quantitative screen built around the following measures:

- PER below 20.
- PEG below 1 if not 0.75. Taking this ratio down from 1 will dramatically narrow your likely shortlist – in most screens you'll instantly lose 70–90% of all stocks as you screen below 1.
- EPS growth rate in coming year above 15%.
- Cash flow per share to EPS 1 or more.
- Net gearing 50% or less.
- ROCE above 12%.
- RS in the past 12 months is positive.
- Margin should be above the median or average for the market, or at least 8%.
- Market cap should be between £10m and £1bn although investors should consider tightening this range so that its starts at £30m and finishes at £250m.
- PSR should be below 10.
- The dividend yield should be at least positive, i.e. you get a dividend.

The second stage of this screen is designed to exclude shares where the directors are selling a lot of stock. That means excluding any shares where there's either persistent (more than two) or very large scale (£100k or more) selling of stock.

---

[19] Slater, J. (2000) *Beyond the Zulu Principle: Extraordinary Profits from Growth Shares*, Texere Publishing.

The last stage is the most detailed and qualitative and involves the investor running their own due diligence process. In this last screen investors are looking for evidence of an increase in the growth of earnings over time:

▧ Check that the current EPS growth rate is higher than it was three years ago, i.e. earnings growth is accelerating. If this is present award one point.

▧ If there's evidence of persistent buying of shares award another point.

▧ If RS is positive for the past three months and last 12 months add another point.

To make the grade companies should really score at least two points in this final screen. This is a very demanding screen and truth be told very, very few companies will actually pass it.

Martin Zweig and the ultimate GARP stock

Martin Zweig is another leading US investor and commentator who's taken a slightly bolder position on tracking down stocks in companies growing fast, all detailed in his bestselling book *Winning on Wall Street* (1997).

The American Association of Individual Investors (AAII) has a screen based on his methodology that has delivered performance that is little short of astonishing – cumulative gains of over 1172% since inception back in 1998. The reason for this success? Zweig is a classic growth at a reasonable price investor in that he doesn't like over-paying for shares he regards as exciting. Zweig's primary purpose is to identify high growth firms at a reasonable price or, as Zweig himself puts it, 'reasonable gains in sales and earnings'. He likes chasing fast growing companies where earnings are consistently rising – sustainable earnings growth and its recognition by Wall Street analysts is absolutely at the core of his approach. It's worth repeating that word consistency again – for Zweig everything is about consistent fast growth, quarter on quarter, year on year that is also sustainable and is backed up by a share price showing some recent strength. But what makes him different from many of his racy, growth orientated peers such as as Bill O'Neil (he's developed a methodology called CAN SLIM that we'll encounter in the next chapter) is that he also thinks value investing has a role to play – investors should never over-pay for poor fundamentals.

In sum Zweig wants earnings growth but not at any cost. He likes companies with positive growth in quarter-over-quarter earnings, positive year-to-year growth in annual earnings and strong price movement over the

Martin Zweig – an investing life in summary!

Martin Zweig was editor of *The Zweig Forecast*, the top market advisory fund publication for 15 years, from 1980 to 1995, returning 16% annual returns. It's clearly made him a very rich man – he owns the most expensive apartment in Manhattan, a $70m triplex penthouse on Fifth Avenue! One US website has helpfully captured some of his key thoughts on modern investing:

■ In a strong market, pick those companies that are outpacing and continue trending with higher highs and higher lows.

■ Cut losses and run with profits.

■ Either be in the market or out of it. Market timing is relevant. Look at factors such as the Prime Rate Indicator, the Fed Indicator, and the Installment Debt Indicator. 'In the stock market, as with horse racing, money makes the mare go... the monetary climate – primarily the trend in interest rates and Federal Reserve policy – is the dominant factor in determining the stock market's major direction.' Or as he more succinctly put it, 'don't fight the Fed'.

■ The two greatest fundamentals of a company are its earnings trend and the PE ratio: 'If a company can show nice consistent earnings, I don't care if it makes broomsticks or computer parts.'

Source: http://sumofsome.com/stock-market-strategies/martin-zweig-investment-strategy/

past 26 weeks. But that search for growth shouldn't be compromised by paying too much for the stock – he also wants PE ratios that are not too far above the average for the market. One last crucial caution before we examine a Zweig screen in detail. Zweig is obsessed with short-term earnings momentum and he bases a lot of his analysis on quarter by quarter results. These aren't mostly available for British investors so you should rely instead on six-monthly figures.

A Zweig screen in practice

Like many GARP investors Zweig is looking for evidence of earnings acceleration. Over whatever period you choose to concentrate on – quarter by quarter basis, or six monthly – he's after companies that are increasing earnings above trend. He wants the earnings holy trinity of:

■ earnings stability (not overly influenced by seasonal factors)

■ earnings persistency (persistent rising earnings) and

■ earnings momentum (growth over the short and long term).

Zweig details how this holy trinity might be identified by suggesting we look for companies where earnings are growing faster than they were:

- a year ago during the same period
- in the preceding three quarters, and
- over the preceding three years.

For Zweig the same period growth last year – taking the equivalent period in the previous year – is crucial as it strips out seasonal factors and gets to the heart of how a business is responding to change. What Zweig wants is a fast growing company which has been growing earnings pretty much consistently for the past five years.

But Zweig is also profoundly interested in two other key measures – sales growth and share price momentum. He specifically demands that sales should be growing as fast as or faster than earnings – in this he echo's James O'Shaughnessy from our previous chapter – because cost-cutting and other non-revenue producing measures alone can't support earnings growth forever. That sales growth should be at least 15% per annum.

Zweig also doesn't want to fight the market. Although he cares about paying over the odds for a stock he ideally doesn't want to pay more than three times the market average PE ratio. He's also concerned that you only buy shares where sentiment is positive, hence his requirement that whatever your measure of momentum – relative strength against the index for instance – it should at the very least be positive over the past six months.

This quantitative level of screening is only the first and most basic stage for Zweig. He uses the metaphor of the 'shotgun and rifle' approach, i.e. the quantitative screen is only the broad screening measure whereas the rifle approach is to then zero in on the shortlisted companies, and use much more detailed qualitative analysis.

A Zweig screen in detail

Zweig's main emphasis is on quarterly earnings growth which can be a little tricky for British investors as most companies only report twice a year. One modification for the UK market might be to focus EPS growth for a six-monthly and yearly basis.

- EPS growth in the current year is at least 20%.
- EPS growth over past three years is at least 15%.

> ▶ ■ EPS growth over past five years is at least 10%. With all these three figures put them side by side and look for evidence of earnings acceleration, i.e. current EPS growth rate more than the three-year and preferably more than five-year rate.

■ Sales per share should be up at least 10% if not 20%. Also look at the last two sets of annual sales and check that sales growth has been accelerating.

■ One idea suggested by the investment writer Peter Temple is that the margin trend should actually be negative. His thinking is that if sales are supposed to be growing faster than earnings, a slip in the margin trend is obvious and probably a good thing.

■ The PE ratio is between 5 and 43. Most Zweig enthusiasts would probably reduce that top PE figure down to 25 for the UK.

■ Screen out firms whose relative share price strength over the past month, three months and six months is negative.

Last but not least investors should consider applying a number of important thresholds suggested by Zweig to miss out poorly traded firms, small caps with no real analysts' coverage and companies with poor balance sheets:

■ Exclude firms where the shares are illiquid, i.e. low trading volumes.

■ Compare the company's debt position with that of its industry peers. Try and concentrate on companies where the 'relative debt levels' are low.

■ Look for insider selling of shares. Exclude companies where there's been director selling in the past three months. If there have been three insider buys in the past six months that constitutes a strong buy signal.

A cavaet on Zweig

Before we leave all this breathless talk of fast expanding companies with amazing earnings machines and rocketing share prices it's worth noting one important caveat to Zweig's record: funds that have applied his methodology haven't been a great success in recent years. Although the AAII screen based on Zweig's writings may have clocked up returns of over 1000% in 2009 it fell a nasty 23%. That loss was much worse than the 5.2% return on a fund based on his strategy, called the Phoenix-Zweig Strategy Fund Class A, one of six Zweig funds marketed by Phoenix Investment Partners. According to Phoenix, Martin Zweig doesn't pick individual stocks, but he does determine the fund's asset allocation and develops models for stock selection. According to a report on US website Morningstar, Phoenix-Zweig

Strategy Fund missed the boat because Zweig's models were frequently bearish during the 1990s. As a result, the fund often held big cash positions: 22% in 1998, and an incredible 43% in 1999. The fund's manager admits: 'Marty was being cautious because interest rates were rising, and there was too much optimism in the market... The past five years [through to 2007] weren't friendly to our style of investing.'[20] This fund management company also offers some listed closed end funds on the US exchange that implement various aspects of Zweig's analysis, including the Zweig Fund which has pretty consistently under-performed the S&P 500 since the late 1990s – see Figure 6.4.

| **figure 6.4** | The Zweig Fund Inc vs. the S&P 500 | *Source*: www.ShareScope.co.uk |

Pulling it all together – quality companies

How should investors pull together all these differing thoughts about how to spot a GARP stock. Should they focus largely on earnings growth, as Martin Zweig and Jim Slater suggest, or should they instead follow Warren Buffett's more cautious advice on finding companies with a great business franchise and competitive 'wide moat' of advantage? We're going to finish

---

[20] www.morningstar.com

this chapter by looking at a number of attempts to synthesise these ideas into coherent strategies – all influenced by thinking at some of the big investment banks in the UK and the US. These institutions attempt to take all this big picture thinking and turn it into a trading strategy that actually makes money for their investors!

Quality is a much used and widely abused word in the lexicon of City analysts and researchers. It's taken to mean anything from fantastic fast growing small to medium-sized companies through to boring, worthy, almost value defining large stocks with quality balance sheets. In fact there's good grounds for banishing the word altogether as a term singularly lacking in any clarity, was it not for one unsettling fact – quality companies using a fairly narrow set of parameters could be the best place to be over the next few turbulent years for private investors. Or that at least is the view of analysts like Graham Secker at Morgan Stanley, a respected stock strategist with a strong GARP outlook.

In 2009 Secker cited a series of startling observations which he thought made the case for his own definition of what constitutes a quality stock. For Secker a quality company is one that persistently increases earnings over multiple parts of the economic cycle. Secker highlighted his own shortlist (we'll look at the companies that passed this strategy in the box below) and suggested that in late 2009 his 'growth basket' of shares are at 'an all time valuation low versus the UK market'.[21]

Secker's analysis back in 2009 was especially compelling because of the mismatch in that year between the euphoric rise in poor quality companies and their share prices and those of what Secker defined as quality stocks. To understand this unique moment – and opportunity for Secker and his quality strategy – consider the following statistics taken between 19 May 2008 (when the FTSE 100 peaked at 6376) and 3 February 2009 (a low point of 3512 based on close of day trading). Over this period the FTSE 100 fell by more than 34%. But over these 204 trading days a grand total of 1400 stocks on the wider London market fell by more than 75%. It's worth noting that over 90% of these companies also boasted the worst fundamentals with poor balance sheets and dreadful earnings growth profiles.

Flash forward to the period between 4 February 2009 and 16 October 2009 and the FTSE 100 has increased by 22% yet those companies with falls of more than 75% over the previous period had risen by an average of 180%!

---

[21] Secker, G. (2009) 'UK Strategy: Reliable Growth Has Never Been Cheaper', www.morganstanley.com

That massive cyclical rebound had been fairly evident to almost any sentient human being at the time – sectors that were perceived to traditionally benefit from a sudden uptick in global demand performed the best. Using the two time frames from the analysis above (the downturn leg between 19 May 2008 and 3 February 2009, with the upturn from 4 February through to 16 October), it's clear that sectors like industrial metals, cars and car parts, basic resources and mining were the star performers (all up by more than 75% over the upturn and all down by more than 60% over the downturn)! On a stock level just two companies sum it all up perfectly – both Vedanta and Kazakhmys (global mining companies) were down over 79% in the crash but both had ticked up massively in the upturn (279% and 348% respectively).

But if smart investors had filtered through this raw set of data, another story begins to emerge – that companies any sensible person would define as quality had been producing steady returns that augured well for 2010 and beyond.

Over these two legs of the bust/boom cycle of 2008 and 2009, a remarkable 272 companies had increased their EPS and were still forecast earnings again in the forthcoming year (based on analysts' earnings). This group of very simply defined quality companies saw their share prices fall by 29% over the downturn (May 2008 to February 2009), a full 5 percentage points less than the FTSE 100 over the same period, yet they saw their share prices increase by a perfectly respectable 56% in the upturn.

That increase was considerably more than for the FTSE 100 as a whole (up 22%) but clearly not a patch on the return from cyclical stocks such as Kazakhmys and Verdanta. That relative under-performance resulted in what Secker regarded at the time as a unique opportunity. According to Secker, in October 2009 his gaggle of quality reliable growth stocks underperformed the market by 12% since March 2009, and were at the all time low in valuation terms (based on price to earnings ratios) relative to the UK market, and producing a higher dividend yield ('the same as the 10 year gilt yield – in March 2000 it was 4× lower').[22]

So what's Secker's definition of quality? For him it's ultimately defined by persistent earnings growth both in the past and in analysts' forward projections, although yield and a reasonable share price are also relevant.

Looking first at earnings, Secker is looking for evidence of earnings per share growth over the past in a fairly consistent fashion but not necessarily in a

---

[22] Ibid.

straight line fashion. Analysts like Secker are rightly cautious about miracle companies where earnings per quarter or half yearly manage to magically increase by a steady 4 percentage points regardless of the economic cycle. Secker points to Rentokil Initial as one example where EPS was a steady upwards trajectory... until it suddenly announced a fall in profits growth, prompting a massive share price sell off!

Many analysts like Secker prefer an alternative measure for earnings consistency – they look at past earnings reports for big changes and then convert that change into standard deviation measures. This measure highlights companies where earnings have moved up and down sharply over time, indicating companies with poor earnings growth consistency.

Secker and his colleagues at Morgan Stanley are also looking for evidence of earnings growth over the near future – remember that academic evidence from earlier in this chapter suggested that companies where earnings forecasts are being consistently upgraded by analysts tend to show the strongest share price growth. Secker doesn't ignore balance sheet strength and debt levels either – like many GARP analysts he looks for evidence that debt levels are manageable, that current liabilities aren't growing too fast, and that too much money isn't being sunk into capital expenditure that isn't boosting profits.

Lastly, Secker has a penchant for dividends, although it's not a determining factor in his strategies. Add these all up and Secker's GARP strategy managed to shortlist 31 stocks in the FTSE 100 that passed all his tests and still boasted an average forward PE ratio at the time of just 12.3× earnings

Graham Secker's quality strategy in summary

Secker uses three main measures as a focus for his strategy:

- The median quarterly percentage change in the consensus estimates of analysts following a stock as they estimate future earnings – this is for a 13 year period since 1995 and shows the companies that have consistently grown earnings.
- The standard deviation – a measure of variability around an average – of these quarterly changes in 12-month forward EPS over the past five years. With this measure he's focusing on past volatility in earnings results. The higher the volatility the lower the score.
- The probability that a quarterly change is positive is then calculated based on data since 1995.

The highlighted shares from the Morgan Stanley strategy are shown in Table 6.5.

table 6.5 The highlighted shares from the Morgan Stanley strategy (October 2009)

Company	% quarterly change in 12-month forward EPS		SD of % quarterly change				Probability of positive EPS change (%)	12-month forward PE	12-month prospect of dividend yield (%)
	Average	Median	2yr	5yr	10yr				
Serco Group	4.6	4.2	1.8	1.4	2.2	95	15.2	1.4
Capita Group	6.1	5	0.9	1.9	2.9	100	16.5	2.7
Sage Group	4.8	3.9	2.8	2.2	3.7	90	12.8	3.6
Cobham	3.6	3.5	2.2	2.5	2.6	91	10.7	2.9
Reckitt Benckiser	2.3	3.3	2	1.7	2.2	87	15.8	3.2
Intertek	4.1	3.8	2.7	3	3.4	87	14.4	2.1
Tesco	2.6	2.8	1.8	1.6	1.5	91	11.9	3.6
Imperial Tobacco	3.5	3.1	4	2.7	3.1	91	10	4.8
WPP	3.1	3.2	3.2	2.8	4.3	87	11.6	3.1
Bae	3	3.8	2.7	3.4	7.1	75	7.7	5.1
Next	3.5	3.9	5.5	5.2	4.8	84	11.4	3.3
BAT	2.2	2.4	1.6	2	4.9	82	12.4	5.8

Source: Morgan Stanley

The *Investors Chronicle* own take on quality stocks

In October 2009 we ran our own take on a quality strategy for the *Investors Chronicle*. It was inspired by Graham Secker's strategy but used measures that were more readily available to private investors.

What surprised us at the time was the sheer quantity of what we perceived to be quality stocks – in fact dozens of companies passed the test so we decided to increase the market cap barrier from £50m to £250m to reveal a smaller but potentially higher quality sample, but still 16 mid to large cap stocks passed (see Table 6.6)! This was then focused down to a top ten, but we've also included a smaller number of also-rans who narrowly failed. (Most of the companies were mid cap stocks but there were four FTSE 100 stocks (plus Irish large cap Kerry Group) including classically defensive companies such as GlaxoSmithKline and Reckitts, both of which payed more than 3% a year in dividends at the time.)

The measures used in the screen included the following:

- Don't over-pay for your quality stocks – the PE ratio based on current or future earnings shouldn't be over 25.
- Look for companies where capital is used efficiently. Most analysts reckon that 10% or more is a fair threshold.
- Cashflow is also important – a quality company lives or dies by the ability of its trading companies to generate cash at the operating level and many analysts also look to focus on the trend in cashflow, with a preference for some growth in that positive cashflow.
- Debt – loans and bonds are not necessarily a bad thing if they can be paid. Most analysts would agree that any company with 200% net gearing probably deserves very close scrutiny – utilities with their regulated business franchise might survive but most other companies would be viewed as too risky.
- Compare with their peers. Measures like the profit margin and the return on capital employed are valuable in and of themselves but they're much more powerful when compared to their sector peers. Use the operating margin and ROCE as measures and look for companies in the top quartile of their sector.
- Last but no means least *earnings growth* – both in the past and in the future. Look over a relatively short period of six years and excluded companies where there had been sudden reversals in earnings growth in more than one year.

table 6.6 The smaller sample in detail

Name	EPIC	Projected PE	Capital (£m)	Projected yield (%)	ROCE (%)	Close	Broker consensus	Forecast EPS growth
ASOS PLC	ASC	19.82	256.5		59.1	3.51	Buy	33.56
ITE Group PLC	ITE	10.07	320.1	4.13		1.29	Weak buy	37.74
Synergy Health PLC	SYR	15	334.3	1.96	14.7	6.15	Buy	29.17
Halfords Group PLC	HFD	11.34	847.1	4.23	58.9	4.028	Buy	8.89
Chemring Group PLC	CHG	12.15	912.4	1.77	27.9	25.83	Buy	72.87
Rotork PLC	ROR	16.86	1010.7	2.54	68.9	11.68	Hold	12.41
Intertek Group PLC	ITRK	17.53	2113.4	1.75	40.5	13.32	Hold	20.51
Sage Group (The) PLC	SGE	14.33	3101.2	3.16		2.362	Hold	29.87
Kerry Group PLC	KYGA	12.13	3192.3	1.25	34.4	19.9	Buy	2.08
Reckitt Benckiser Group PLC	RB.	16.32	22030.3	3.03		30.82	Buy	18.4
GlaxoSmithKline PLC	GSK	10.9	66026.3	4.88	45.8	12.725	Weak buy	5.92
The also rans								
Petrofac Ltd	PFC	17.12	3433.6	2.01	64.5	9.94	Hold	3.83
Fidessa Group PLC	FDSA	20.44	438.9	2.38	74.4	12.27	Buy	16.86
MITIE Group PLC	MTO	14.02	886.6	2.99	87	2.519	Weak buy	10.58
Spice PLC	SPI	11.23	311.7	1.86	82.3	0.885	Buy	44.85
United Drug PLC	UDG	9.65	494.9	3.36	19.6	2.095	Buy	10.08
Average		14.30688	6606.894	2.753333	52.15385			22.35125

In search of alpha: the Goldman Sachs' approach

An influential quantitative analysis team at Morgan Stanley's rivals, Goldman Sachs, has developed its own approach to identifying quality stocks with great potential but at decent prices!

In a paper from 2004 the team focused on a number of fundamentals led strategies that produced above average returns. The result, *Fundamentals Drive Alpha*,[23] back tests a number of these key measures all the way back to January 1993. The paper's main conclusion is that investors need to use traditional value-based measures like book value, alongside other measures like relative share price strength (momentum) and the ebb and flow of analysts' estimates.

In all the Goldman Sachs team identify six key factors:[24]

■ Valuation. Is the share price reflecting the intrinsic value? 'All being equal, cheaper stocks are more attractive than stocks selling at high multiples.'

■ Profitability. Are the returns on capital sufficient? 'The stocks of companies that earn higher margins and use their assets more efficiently outperform the stocks of their lower margin, less efficient industry counterparts.'

■ Earnings quality. The 'cash component of earnings... is highly persistent' while the remorseless build up of EPS figures, year on year, is more 'transitory'.

■ Management impact. 'Well managed companies don't waste assets on unprofitable investment opportunities or on empire building, but instead return excess capital to shareholders.'

■ Momentum. Stocks with some momentum in their share price tend to outperform as investors slowly wake up to the potential for the firm.

■ Analyst sentiment. Analysts who are slow to change their estimates create 'trading opportunities for investors who buy on upward revisions... as stock prices later adjust to reflect the information conveyed by the consensus signal'.

Add all these key measures up and you have a classic GARP synthesis – look on it as a primer for private investors looking to copy the very best (thus the

---

[23] Alford, A., Jones, R., Lim, T. and Litterman, B. (2004) *Fundamentals Drive Alpha*, April, GS Asset Management.
[24] Ibid.

alpha of the title) of investment managers. Now of course the Goldman Sachs team aren't offering a simple, easy to use way to screen the market – their aim is to lay out the methodology that lies behind their 'computer-optimised research enhanced' (or CORE) perspective. The idea is to run a 'shadow' portfolio of stocks for each measure – a bunch of stocks with high earnings quality for instance – in each major national market and then see which fundamental measure wins out over the decade (starting in 1993). Their overall project is in essence a rigorous quantitative exercise to find out which fundamental variables drive 'alpha' (top quartile risk adjusted) performance.

But they're also careful to apply varying weights to each virtual portfolio of measures – not all alpha fundamentals are created equal after all. All this talk of weights and 'CORE' alphas gives you a hint that the average investor is unlikely to be able to perfectly replicate Goldman Sachs' extremely powerful approach, but a couple of simple thoughts do flow from their analysis.

You should, on paper at least, be able to combine the GS key alpha drivers in a strategy that attempts to track down cheap stocks boasting some share price momentum plus a consensus from analysts that earnings are likely to rise.

The limitations of such a screen will also be obvious. Run this screen and you're likely to rule out vast swathes of the market. (In the box below we've developed a version of the strategy that involves at least 15 different screening measures.) Very few companies are likely to survive this rather exhaustive process and even fewer 'cheap' stocks will survive the last key hurdle – some relative strength, some momentum in the share price.

It's also worth pointing out that the GS study is a global one and that what may be true for the UK is probably not true for the US or any other market for that matter. Correlation between markets may be increasing but that doesn't mean that markets and shares react in the same way to key changes in say analysts' sentiment. Some markets for instance look upon a change in analyst sentiment as one of the most important 'events' that can happen on a daily basis – there's some evidence that the Australian and Canadian markets in particular are hypersensitive to collective sentiment. Others markets such as the Japanese one display a much more cynical attitude, perhaps borne out of a decade's long disenchantment not only with equities per se but with analysts' ability to predict the future. When markets keep grinding lower, as they have done in Japan, it's easy to become cynical about any predictions of future growth. Here in the UK, by contrast, there does not seem to be any one particular set of measures or factors that are overwhelmingly dominant: earnings growth and momentum seem to be important but then again analysts' upgrades and changes in collective sentiment are also crucial. On that last point it is worth adding that some UK based hedge funds such as Marshall Wace have set up specific strategies and funds built around changes in the consensus of analysts.

A very simplified version of the GS strategy

There are a huge number of ideas at work here but it is possible to construct a strategy that attempts to reflect the 'alpha' drivers the Goldman's team discusses. It's a complex, multi-stage screen but it should reveal companies whose shares are cheap, where analysts are starting to become more optimistic and where earnings are growing at a sustainable pace.

Looking at each of the alpha drivers, it's probably best to start with simplest, most value driven measures:

- Ideally the price to book value (PBV) is less than 3.
- To screen out companies with lots of intangible asset backing (some of which may not actually have any 'real' value), try and make sure that every company has a price to tangible book value (PTBV) of under 3.
- The PE ratio should be no more than 20.

Moving on to profitability there are three crucial measures:

- The return on capital employed (ROCE) is more than 15.
- Profit margin. Rather than use some market wide average for profits, it's best to be a little more specific and demand that the profit margin certainly be in the top quartile of all companies when you run the screen.
- Whatever the profit margin, it should be increasing over the past few years.

Turning to earnings quality, the key theme here is that the profits being generated by the business are backed up by real operating cash inflows:

- Price to cash flow (PCF) should be at the very least 5, i.e. the company is producing solid cash inflows relative to its share price.
- Cashflow per share in relation to EPS should be at least 1. That means the cashflow per share must be above earnings per share.

Goldman's 'management impact' alpha is defined as follows: 'Well managed companies don't waste assets on unprofitable investment opportunities or on empire building, but instead return excess capital to shareholders.'[25] Most

---

[25] Ibid.

screening systems won't allow you to screen for share buybacks but you can screen for the next best thing – dividends. A company that hands a lot of its profits back to its shareholders through a generous dividend policy should fit the bill. This key alpha is reflected in the following two measures.

- The dividend yield should be enough to be useful – in historic terms that means a yield above at least 3%. Traditionally a yield above 3% is seen as generous, while anything below that is regarded as a bit miserly. This could be revised up to as much as 3.5% or even 4%.

- That dividend payout should be affordable. That implies a dividend cover of at least 2.

Last but not least we need to look at the momentum in the share price. The paper's authors believe that momentum is a key variable and should definitely not be ignored by investors. But which measure to use? A simple measure worth using is called 12 month RS – relative strength measured against the wider benchmark index:

- RS over the past three months is at least positive.

The next stage of this screen involves a great deal more detail. You're likely to be looking out for companies where analysts' sentiment is improving and consensus estimates are rising. But that growing consensus of increasing earnings has to be very strong – there should be at least two brokers giving out estimates and ideally a lot more:

- More than two brokers provide estimates of earnings or EPS.

- The consensus for those earnings should be increasing (if only marginally) over the past three months and the past month.

This stage of the screen is hugely important because you're looking for a 'convincing' story of rising earnings expectations. That means we're looking for real evidence that the shares are beginning to 'turn' and that sentiment (or at least brokers' sentiment) is also improving.

As the authors clearly state: 'Analysts are conservative: they change their views gradually, so that a revision in one direction is often followed by similar revisions in the same direction. In addition, the market under-reacts to revisions in consensus earnings forecasts and stock ratings. The combination of conservatism and under-reaction creates trading opportunities for investors who buy on upward revisions and sell on downward revisions, as stock prices later adjust to reflect the information conveyed by the consensus signal.'[26]

---

[26] Ibid.

> In our last, third, screen we need to look at the company in comparison with its peers. If you can examine it on a 'sector' or 'industry' basis make sure that on a number of key measures like ROCE and profit margin the company is at least average. If you can't get this kind of information, just pick two other competitors, and then compare them using this criterion:

■ On a sector or peer basis the ROCE and profit margin should be at least average if not better.

Sector specific strategies – Mike Murphy's bargain tech stocks

Before we conclude this chapter on GARP strategies it's worth looking at one last, practical and very focused strategy. How about applying a reasonably priced growth strategy to a *particular sector*, in this case the technology sector where the idea of a cheap growth stock was until recently an almost laughable proposition?

Hi-tech companies have always been notorious for ludicrous valuations, based on equally ludicrous financial projections and even more ludicrous business plans. And then the dotcom bubble burst and suddenly the whole technology sector – both in the US and in the UK – went into reverse. Share prices crumbled before our eyes and whole swathes of the technology sector – and especially technology investment companies – vanished.

And then something strange happened – contrarian investors, many of them with a strong GARP bias, started investing in tech stocks. Very soon this quiet movement found an articulate voice in American investor Michael Murphy, editor of the *California Technology Stock Letter*, a highly-regarded and well-followed investment advisory newsletter that tracks and makes recommendations on technology stocks.

Murphy articulate's two simple observations about tech stocks that are hugely compelling. The first is that despite all those dotcom shenanigans, the technology sector is still the powerhouse of the global economy and that means that investors absolutely need to buy into the sector without over-paying for fast growing companies with astronomic share prices. His fairly unique approach is to identify technology shares that are most likely to be future leaders, and then buy these shares when they become under-valued relative to their growth potential.

The philosophy

Murphy contends that the American economy is in the midst of what he calls a 'paradigm shift' – a 'once-in-a-century revolution' that is creating huge wealth as well as destroying whole sectors too slow to keep up. The result of this shift, says Murphy, is that the technology sector is the fastest-growing sector of all and will quickly dominate most other sectors – as is painfully apparent on the US market where the net worth of tech companies like Google, Microsoft and Cisco dwarfs whole industrial sectors.

But Murphy has cottoned onto something even more interesting. As the tech sector has grown it's also become much, much more varied, both in terms of size (enormous global Leviathans are surrounded by a legion of young start-ups) and in terms of sub-sector. There are, in Murphy's view, already seven major industry groups in existence and every few years the number of sectors within the industry keeps growing (nanotechnology will probably emerge as a discrete sector within the next decade for instance).

Yet Murphy believes that the stockmarket has by and large not recognised this massive change. Most investors, he says, are underinvested in technology stocks. Although technology receives a lot of coverage in the media, Murphy says that fewer than 10% of Wall Street analysts cover technology stocks, and only a few big investment funds specialise in the sector.

Murphy also believes that the 'back-to-basics' theme of the past few years – only invest in what you can understand and see – is entirely misguided. He absolutely rejects the ideas of investing gurus like Peter Lynch who say that investors shouldn't invest in things that can't be easily understood. According to Murphy, investors don't need to understand the underlying technology, only the company and its competitive environment. Investors aren't required to understand how oil companies can drill in difficult places using special technology to invest in oil companies so why should this rule be applied only to tech stocks? Investors simply need to understand the opportunity and be able to quantify the risks.

Luckily Murphy has a very detailed strategy for nascent technology focused GARPers. His core idea is to invest in

- companies with a great range of products, and
- whose shares are cheap, in relative terms.

Call it value investing with a technology bias.

'Investing is a two-step process', maintains Murphy. 'The first step is to identify situations – managements, products and markets – with which you would like to associate your capital. The second step is to decide what price you are willing to pay to associate your capital with those situations. [Investors should] focus on a small list of superior companies with rapid growth and excellent financial ratios. Then wait for each of them to get knocked down.'[27] Tracking down the perfect Mike Murphy share involves two, relatively straightforward steps.

The first step is to filter through, or screen, the technology sector for five, key measures:

- **Research and development – as much as possible!** According to Murphy the only reliable way to gauge whether a company really is involved in this technology 'paradigm shift' is to look at how much money it's spending on R&D. According to Murphy the most reliable way of doing this is to divide the company's earnings by its R&D spend. Murphy says that a tech company should spend a minimum of 7% of revenues on R&D spending.

- **Return on equity (earnings divided by shareholders' equity) of 15% or more.** This measure indicates that a company is capable of financing its own growth without resorting to outside financings that dilute earnings.

- **Are they producing new products?** Does the company turn out a steady stream of new, successful products? Murphy also suggests calling a prospective company and asking what percentage of revenues today come from products introduced in the past three years. If the company's research is productive, the answer should be over 50%.

- **Sales growth of at least 15% per year.** Murphy regards this as a crucial test and suggests that companies failing this are not worth pursuing.

- **Pretax profit margins (net income divided by revenues) of 15%.** Fast growing sales, high spending on R&D and strong return on equity are great but the net operating margin – the profit margin – needs to be chunky.

Your second step is to work out if the shares of these shortlisted companies are 'cheap', as Murphy doesn't believe in paying any price for growth.

---

[27] http://www.worldinvest.com

Murphy's problem is that traditional valuation approaches – such as the PE ratio – are misleading. R&D spending directly cuts into a company's current earnings, which means that the more a company spends on R&D the worse its earnings appear, which in turn will push up the PE ratio. But from a shareholder's viewpoint, earnings invested for tomorrow in the form of R&D are as important as reported earnings today.

Murphy deals with this problem by adding together the R&D spending (R&D spending divided by the number of shares outstanding) per share to the normal earnings per share to work out what he calls the company's 'growth flow'. The final step in the stock-picking process is to divide the current share price by this growth flow per share to provide what's called the price-to-growth-flow ratio. In Murphy's view, tech shares are 'fairly priced' when the price-to-growth-flow ratio is around 10 to 14; anything under 8 is cheap and below 5 is a real bargain; 16 and over is too expensive.

Building a technology portfolio

Murphy is candid about the risks involved with tech investing. He realises that prices will move up and down quite sharply and that technology cycles wax and wane. The best way of controlling this risk is to diversify your holdings amongst seven major sub-sectors:

- semiconductor equipment producers (companies that make the equipment that makes semiconductors)
- semiconductor producers
- business-level computers
- PCs
- software
- communications, including data communications (computer-to-computer data) and telecommunications
- medical technology, including both biotechnology and medical devices.

Murphy suggests that investors build a portfolio of at least ten stocks, with companies from each of the seven industry groups. To keep the portfolio to a manageable size, add proportionately to existing holdings when adding new money to your portfolio, rather than buying new stocks. If you feel you must buy a new stock, sell your least attractive stock.

Murphy also believes that his approach will only work if it's aggressively followed by investors. He suggests that these cheap tech stocks should amount to a high proportion of total assets: 100 minus your current age. That means that if you're 50 years old you should invest upwards of 50% of your total assets in these tech stocks.

Does it work?

The most accurate – and objective – analysis of Murphy's methodology comes from the AAII. It's been running a screen based on his ideas since 1998 and to date the results have been hugely variable.

In good years – bull markets where growth stocks with a small cap bias do well – the screen has delivered some pretty spectacular returns. In 1999 the AAII Mike Murphy screen produced a mammoth 139.7% return while in 2004 tech stocks also bounced back giving their Murphy portfolio a hugely impressive 108% return. But in bear years the results have been poor with a violent swing against what are perceived as high risk, small cap stocks. In 2002 the return was a disastrous: –80%, a very poor result compounded by an equally bad 2003 with losses of 34% (against gains of just under 50% for the NASDAQ). In overall terms though this strategy has been a poor performer at the AAII with a cumulative loss of 63.3% since inception in 1998.

It should also be noted that Murphy runs his own newsletter called *New World Investor* (which is apparently the top performing investment newsletter in 2009, according to research firm Hulbert Financial Digest) and in the last available year his strategy was up 70.7% compared to a fall of 6.4% for the broad Wilshire 5000 US index (stats are for year to end September 2009).

So, what's the bottom line with these very volatile returns? It appears that when stockmarkets are bullish this kind of focused, sector specific GARP strategy can deliver extraordinary returns but the risk of equally sizeable losses is obvious and ever present. There are also some broader concerns with this unique approach. Spending on R&D for instance might be an inefficient measure of value creation. Using R&D as a proxy for generating shareholder wealth is fine in theory but in reality an awful lot of R&D is wasted and produces poor returns. Just because a company spends countless tens of millions on clever research doesn't automatically mean it will produce best selling profits or even profits. The best example of this is tech innovator Xerox which has over decades spent billions on cutting edge research but whose shares have consistently under-performed its peers.

There's also a very real concern about the lack of diversification for UK-based investors who might use this strategy. Murphy sensibly calls on investors to try and contain risk by diversifying across different sub-sectors within technology but here in the UK that's hugely difficult. In the US there are hundreds of tech firms whereas in the UK there are no more than a few hundred companies in total of which only a couple of dozen actually generate any profits at all! More importantly most UK tech companies are based around one of three sub-sectors – biotech, telecoms and software. Diversification might be hugely problematic in the UK.

A Murphy technology strategy in summary

▪ R&D spending of at least 7% of revenues.

▪ Sales growth of at least 15% per year.

▪ Pretax profit margins of 15% or better.

▪ Return on equity (after tax profits divided by shareholders equity) of 15% or more.

Valuations

Use a company's price to growth flow ratio to determine value:

> Per share R&D + EPS = growth flow
> Price ÷ growth flow = Price to growth flow ratio

Guidelines for judging price-to-growth-flow ratio:

▪ Fair: 10 to 14

▪ Cheap: below 8

▪ Expensive: 16 and above.

Concluding thoughts on gilt edged glamour!

It's clear from this long chapter that there is in fact a very broad school of beliefs and strategies that encompass what might reasonably be called growth at a reasonable price investing. Many classic GARP investor such as Warren Buffett are philosophically much closer to value investing than others such as Martin Zweig or Jim Slater.

That massive diversity is also reflected in the choice of key measures to use. Should they stick with a key measure like the return on equity (as suggested by Joel Greenblatt) or should they instead prioritise earnings growth as Martin Zweig suggests? Warren Buffett's ideas about finding great quality businesses are fine on paper but maddeningly difficult to specify in detail – the concept behind his inevitables such as Coca-Cola or Gillette is truly wonderful but how do you find these companies before Warren?

This discordant range of voices all seem to want to find the same kind of company – that mythical GARP beast. But isn't the real risk here the most obvious? That by the time most of us have dug around and found these very small number of mythical beasts, the market will already have priced in that success with an over-rated share price?

This concern mirrors a wider attack on growth stocks from analysts such as Rob Arnott. These wonder stocks may exist but the market inevitably ends up over-paying for the shares. In the next chapter we'll look in more detail at this criticism as well as another profound challenge based on the reliability of forecasting earnings growth. Most of our GARP strategies are based on the concept of finding companies with consistently growing bottom line earnings, with estimates for future growth integral to popular measures such as the PEG. But as we shall see there's a mountain of evidence that suggests that those estimates, based on analysts' work, is fatally flawed and that nearly all forecasting is a work of fiction.

It's also worth repeating the observation of academics Lakonishok, Shliefer and Vishny, who noted that if investors 'generally do not understand regression to the mean, they are likely to overestimate a company's "true greatness" and pay too much for the company's stock, a decision they will regret when measures of the company's greatness regress to the mean'.[28] The learned academics remind us that growth companies don't always stay fast growing and that they eventually go 'ex-growth' with the inevitable effect upon share price.

Surely investors are better off cutting to the chase – instead of trying to second guess future growth patterns in earnings why not admit that what really matters is what the markets think? If the shares of a company are shooting ahead – displaying positive momentum relative to the market –

---

[28] See note 4.

then maybe we should ignore all those siren voices about a reasonable price and simply invest in the hottest, sexiest stocks?

In the next chapter we'll explore this idea of momentum as a strategy and link it back to spotting pure growth stocks – developing strategies that don't worry about the relative value of a share but only focus on finding the stars of tomorrow.

All out for growth: small caps and the momentum effect

Envision a snowball rolling down a hill: as it rolls along, it picks up more snow, which causes it to move faster, which causes it to pick up even more snow and move even faster. Wayne A. Thorp, CFA

The search for the elusive tenbagger

There's an old adage in the movie business that nine in ten movies in a studio's portfolio of releases will lose money – but the one in ten that is a huge success will probably more than pay for all those losses combined and still leave the cigar smoking media magnates with a tidy overall profit.

This apocryphal one in ten success rate finds something of an echo in a more esoteric term, that of the Pareto principle. Otherwise known as the 80/20 rule or law of the vital few, this is widely used in business to describe how a small number of successful phenomena can produce a disproportionately large total impact. Many a management seminar has been built around the idea that 80% of your company's sales come from the top 20% of customers.

The same principle could be applied to investors' portfolios – many professional investors such as George Soros or even Warren Buffett admit that much of their long-term success can be accounted for by a small number of stunningly successful, hugely profitable investments.

For most private investors this translates into one much used, and abused, word – the wonderfully elusive tenbagger of stock market lore! Peter Lynch coined this term to describe the kind of share that goes up by more than ten times – a curious origin for the term given that Lynch was far from being a spivvy, growth orientated investor. Undeterred by his reputation as a value orientated investor Lynch famously listed his key criteria for finding those elusive tenbaggers. His list of factors included:

- Look at small companies. Lynch asserts that big companies don't have big stock moves. Instead you get your biggest moves in smaller companies.
- Look for fast growers where earnings are growing by more than 20–30% per year.
- Look for insider buying and share buybacks.
- Diversify and hold plenty of stocks and different kinds of risk in your portfolio.

But Lynch had two final criteria waiting in the wings, criteria not so widely referred to today by breathless growth fiends:

- Buy stocks from dead industries with dull products and dull names.
- Buy stocks from sectors where analysts don't bother looking.[1]

Given Peter Lynch's background in value orientated investing these last two criteria shouldn't have surprised anyone – but it's fair to say that very few growth investors bother with them. Yet the search for the tenbagger has taken on added urgency in today's volatile, ultra-short-termist markets and the elusive creature is today more likely to be discovered at the tech sector watering hole. At some point in the mid-1990s investors woke up and noticed two inter-related phenomena occurring within modern capitalism; namely the rapid growth of the technology sector which was in turn fuelling rapid increases in corporate productivity (or at least that's the myth), and profitability aided by outsourcing, restructuring, refocusing and greater emphasis on shareholder returns.

A whole new kind of super growth company – the shooting star that produces that tenbagger return – had emerged, with most of the candidates being based in the USA. The most articulate guide to finding these tenbaggers is the big daddy of private investor friendly websites, Motley Fool.

In 2004 David Forrest, co-founder of the site (which by the way boasts a superb bulletin board on screening strategies and a great US screener at

---

[1] Referred to by Harry Domash in *The Basics: How to invest like Peter Lynch* at http://moneycentral.msn.com/content/Investing/Findhotstocks/P87270.asp

http://caps.fool.com/Screener.aspx) defined precisely what he meant by something he liked to call 'high octane investing'. Forrest is always a hugely illuminating writer and his column singled out that one of the best ways to track down fast rising stocks is to find, well, find... fast rising stocks. His point is that investors who are buying stocks where the share price is rising fast are trying to tell us something and that something is that the company is growing fast. The key measure here is something called relative strength (RS) and in Forrest's case he was interested in developing a version of the measure of RS used by a US newspaper called *Investor's Business Daily*. We'll run into this publication later in this chapter when we examine the CAN SLIM methodology.

The point of Forrest's investigation was to come up with ideas for tomorrow's tenbaggers. But as Forrest wryly observed 'its never entirely clear if the companies achieving high RS status [IBD has a big, closely watched ranking system for RS] are here because the underlying business is performing exceptionally well and the stock is rising [the theory behind growth investing] or if the somewhat self-fulfilling prophecy of momentum madness is at work'.[2]

Regardless of his justified suspicions Forrest persevered and soon came up with his own shortlist of stock ideas. One company in particular shows that the idea behind a tenbagger, namely the fast growing technology stock has not entirely vanished even after the dotcom meltdown at the beginning of the past decade. The company was, and is, Netflix. It's an internet-based rival to the bricks and mortar video rental outfits like Blockbuster and over the past decade has grown at an astonishing rate! Netflix is an archetypal super-growth stock, a shooting star, and for investors who bought at the right price, a tenbagger! Floated on NASDAQ in 2002 at around $8 it's kept on increasing in price throughout the first decade of the new millennium even while most other technology stocks sank into oblivion, finishing the decade at around $56. But many investors had ignored its IPO price and had picked up the shares in the $3 to $6 trading range back in 2002 and 2003 – bagging more than ten-fold increases by the end of the decade.

That massive increase in the share price was largely a result of one simple inescapable fact – here was a company that was inexorably turning its innovative business model into a huge profits machine in the same way as predecessors such as Amazon and Google. The business was, and is, simple. You log onto www.netflix.com, pay a monthly fee and in return Netflix

---

[2] Forrest, D. (2004) 'High Octane Investing', www.fool.com, 10 February.

sends you DVDs through the post. In 2002 Netflix boasted sales of just over $200m and a pre-tax loss of $21m – by the end of 2008 sales were $1.3bn and profits had hit $131m, with most analysts expecting another big increase in the 2009 financial year.

This inexorable rise in profits also prompted another feedback loop – as it grew in scale and profitability, more and more analysts started following the shares, prompting in turn more and more institutional interest. Suddenly brokers' notes started emerging that suggested a rapid increase in earnings over the next few quarters and years. Table 7.1 is taken from the US technical analysis website www.clearstation.com (09/12/2009) and shows the average or consensus estimates for brokers covering Netflix in 2008 and 2009 on a quarterly basis. You'll immediately notice that the brokers' estimates are constantly growing but the actual earnings produced continued to smash these forecasts. The last column measures the earnings surprise – the difference between the consensus estimate and the actual earnings produced, and every quarter the figure is positive.

table 7.1 Average or consensus estimates for Netflix

Quarterly earnings surprises	Estimate	Actual	Surprise (%)
Quarter ending 09/2009	0.46	0.52	13.04%
Quarter ending 06/2009	0.51	0.54	5.88%
Quarter ending 03/2009	0.32	0.37	15.63%
Quarter ending 12/2008	0.34	0.38	11.76%
Quarter ending 09/2008	0.31	0.33	6.45%

Note: EPS excludes non-recurring items; see earnings per share in profile for EPS including non-recurring items. EPS is undiluted.

Source: www.clearstation.com.

Needless to say with this kind of seemingly perpetual growth, the analysts keep on increasing their rate of growth in earnings to catch up. The net effect of all this growth was obvious – the shares continued rising throughout 2008 and 2009 as first earnings grew and then the PE ratio attached to the shares also increased as investors scrambled into the stock pushing up its market ratings multiple.

Figure 7.1 shows the share price of Netflix for these two years through to mid-December 2009 relative to the S&P 500 index, which is the dotted line at the bottom, a dotted line that spent much of 2008 and 2009 going nowhere! The straight thin line in the middle shows the 200-day moving average: Netflix shares were constantly smashing through this barrier, indicating enormous relative strength. Over the past few years the PE ratio for this stock has also varied hugely, moving within a 20 to 50 PE range, indicating that at varying points the market was willing to pay as much as 50× earnings for this shooting star.

But it would be wrong to assume that this kind of astonishing growth only ever happens in the US – these super growth stocks also occasionally pop up in the UK as well. If the success of Netflix finds any echo here in the UK, it's probably with another internet-based sensation called ASOS (it used to be known as As Seen On Screen). This internet-based fashion store has been an astonishing success: it truly is a veritable tenbagger, floated in 2001 at around 23p a share, a long way from its end 2009 price of just under 500p. Figure 7.2 tells the story of ASOS and its shares. After a quiet few years through to 2004, the shares began to pick up momentum at the beginning of 2004, moving into veritable over-drive in the summer of 2007 at which

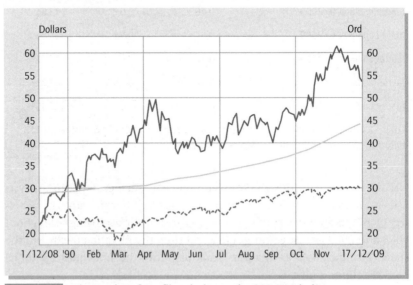

figure 7.1 Share price of Netflix relative to the S&P 500 index

Source: www.ShareScope.co.uk

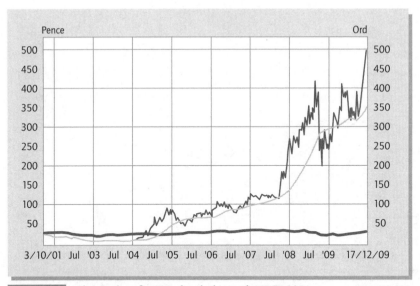

figure 7.2   Share price of ASOS plc relative to the FTSE 100
(3/10/01 to 17/12/09)   *Source*: www.ShareScope.co.uk

point the shares shot above 115p to hit a peak of over 400p just over 12 months later. The big thick line at the bottom by contrast is the progress (of sorts) of the FTSE 100 index!

Before we look in detail at the cause of this momentum it's worth dwelling just a bit longer on that pick up in momentum. Figure 7.3 (overleaf) shows ASOS shares from 2001 through to summer 2004. The big thick line on the top is the FTSE 100 index benchmark while the thin straight line in the middle is the 200-day moving average. As you can see ASOS shares under-performed the wider market for most of this period. However, by the summer of 2007 this relative under-performance had vanished (see Figure 7.4, overleaf) and there was quite literally nothing to stop ASOS – even a disastrous warehouse fire in Hemel Hempstead in 2008 only dented the shares' progress for a few months!

This strength in the share price was also mirrored in another crucial measure used by analysts – the volume of shares traded on a daily basis. Figure 7.5 (overleaf) shows how trading volume in the stock almost completely mirrored that of the share price – one long upwards trend!

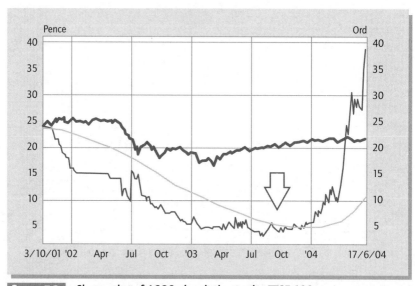

figure 7.3 Share price of ASOS plc relative to the FTSE 100 (3/10/01 to 17/6/04)

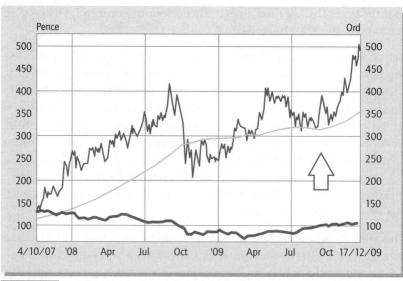

figure 7.4 ASOS plc relative to the FTSE 100 (4/10/07 to 17/12/09)

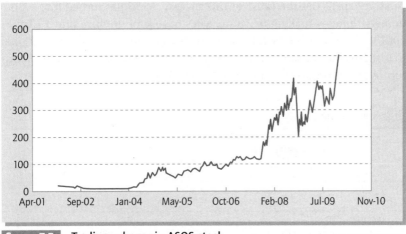

figure 7.5　**Trading volumes in ASOS stock**　*Source:* Investor Ease

In recent years this retailer has even managed the not inconsiderable feat of outpacing the mightiest retailer in the UK (and no slouch in the internet business itself) Tesco. Figure 7.6 shows the relative performance of the ASOS share price and that of Tesco (the thin dotted line at the bottom).

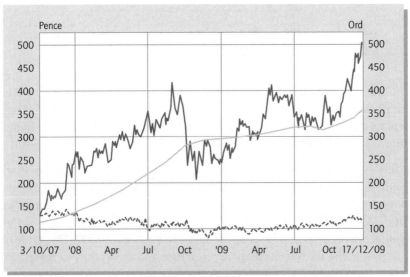

figure 7.6　Relative performance of ASOS plc share price against that of
Tesco plc　*Source:* www.ShareScope.co.uk

Table 7.2 spells out the cause of this success. ASOS has turned into a phenomenal money making machine. Sales have shot up from under £1m in 2001 to £165m in 2009 while profits have leapt up from a loss of £500,000 to £14.1m over the same period. In every year between 2001 and 2009 both turnover and profits have increased year on year.

table 7.2 ASOS analysis

EPIC	Close	Price (%)	Share price (p)	Price (%) 1 year ago	Price (%) 5 years ago	Capital (£m)	Net asset value price (p)	ROCE (%)	PCF
ASC	4.87	−3.6	1.17	95.58	476.33	356.2	34	59.1	26.9

Projected PE	Forecast EPS Growth	EPS 2009	2008	2007	2006	2005	2004
26.89	36.58	13.6	6.95	3.4	2	1.3	0.99

Turnover (£m) 2009	2008	2007	2006	2005	2004	2003	2002	2001
165.4	81.04	42.61	20.37	14.42	8.956	4.104	1.702	0.335

Profit (£m) 2009	2008	2007	2006	2005	2004	2003	2002	2001
14.1	7.31	3.37	1.405	0.88	0.26	−1.7	−1.11	−0.49

It's little wonder then that analysts have woken up to the potential of this small cap. Table 7.3 shows broker earnings estimates for ASOS at the tail end of 2009. The consensus is a buy, with earnings predicted to increase from 13.6p in 2009 to 17p in 2010.

ASOS is perhaps an even better candidate for true tenbagger status than Netflix, but there is one crucial difference – while Netflix has consistently beaten the estimates for earnings established by analysts following the stock, ASOS has been something of a laggard. Table 7.4 (overleaf) shows the change in earnings estimates in the first five years after 2000. This table is taken from the software package Investor Ease and shows the change in EPS estimates between 2002 and 2005. Notice how the actual earnings outcome has consistently lagged behind broker estimates.

table 7.3		ASOS – broker consensus earnings (December 2009)			
Broker name	Opinion	Date forecast	Forecast dividend	Date confirmed	Forecast EPS
Investec Securities	Buy	02/11/2009		12/11/2009	16.86
KBC Peel Hunt Ltd	Buy	11/09/2009	2	11/11/2009	19.7
Numis Securities Ltd	Buy	30/09/2009		10/11/2009	17.5
SG Securities	Buy	13/10/2009		10/11/2009	18.11
Shore Capital	Buy	06/07/2009		06/11/2009	19
Arden Partners	Buy	27/07/2009		03/11/2009	18
Singer Capital Markets Ltd	Buy	06/07/2009		03/11/2009	16.7
Evolution Securities Ltd	Buy	30/06/2009		02/11/2009	19.2
Seymour Pierce	Buy	07/08/2009		02/11/2009	17.9
Altium Securities	Hold	06/10/2009		30/10/2009	17.1
Fyshe Horton Finney Ltd	Hold	28/07/2009		28/07/2009	
Consensus	Buy				17.71

Using both ASOS and Netflix as examples, it's worth dwelling on the broad similarities – and probing the common forces at work.

In both cases the primary driver of growth has been the establishment of a successful brand – online and with a loyal and growing army of customers. This has in turn fed through into an almost perpetual growth engine for both sales and bottom line earnings – with both Netflix and ASOS, net operating margins have also held relatively steady even as total sales have increased.

That earnings growth engine has then fed through into perhaps the sexiest game in stock picking, the analysts' estimate game, with a larger number of analysts following the stock as its prominence has increased. In the case of Netflix those analysts have clearly failed to grasp the speed of the increase in earnings quarter on quarter, producing a constant series of surprises. In

| table 7.4 | ASOS: change in earnings estimates in first five years after 2000 |

	Consensus at	Date	Profit (£m)	+/−%	EPS (p)	+/−%
Actual		31/03/05	0.88	−20.00	1.30	−3.70
Forecast	05/07/05	31/03/05	1.10	−15.39	1.35	−27.81
Forecast	13/05/05	31/03/05	1.30	−15.03	1.87	−10.53
Forecast	09/02/05	31/03/05	1.53	4.08	2.09	2.45
Forecast	10/12/04	31/03/05	1.47	−0.68	2.04	−0.97
Forecast	05/11/04	31/03/05	1.48	1.37	2.06	8.42
Forecast	01/10/04	31/03/05	1.46		1.90	
Actual		31/03/04	0.67	−43.70	1.00	−42.53
Forecast	14/06/04	31/03/04	1.19	21.43	1.74	19.18
Forecast	19/03/04	31/03/04	0.98		1.46	
Actual		31/12/03	0.12	−72.73	0.19	−69.84
Forecast	14/06/04	31/03/03	0.44	25.71	0.63	18.87
Forecast	19/03/04	31/03/03	0.35		0.53	
Actual		31/12/02	−1.70		−2.80	
Actual		31/12/01	−1.11		−2.60	
Actual		31/12/00	−0.49		−1.70	

Source: Investor Ease

the case of ASOS the analysts have possibly been too cautious and there haven't been too many surprises, although the shares have continued to head north regardless.

As the success of the business model becomes well known the 'herd' of fund managers and professional investors piles into the stock, pushing the share price inexorably higher – the sheer volume in the shares bears testament to this trend. As that momentum gathers pace, investors less fixated on the fundamentals (which are beginning to look rather expensive compared to the share price) start to take an interest – as they see the 'technicals' of a share strengthen, these shorter-term traders also start to buy the stock in the belief that the shares will continue to beat the wider market in relative terms. This last engine of momentum also helps explain why investors are suddenly willing to attach a much higher multiple – based on the PE ratio – to the shares!

In the previous chapter on growth at a reasonable price investing, we examined the connection between earnings and analysts' estimates. In this chapter on growth stocks we'll examine the other key foundation of growth stocks, namely the phenomena of momentum. As we'll discover, a large number of academics have examined why companies with a strong share price relative to the market have continued to experience even greater price strength. For some leading thinkers such as Eugene Fama – the father of modern efficient markets thinking – this momentum effect is the last great missing piece in the efficient markets hypothesis, the one risk factor that seemingly can't be explained but is of huge importance. It even has its own label – the 'premier anomaly'.

The premier anomaly – the momentum machine

Professors Elroy Dimson and Paul Marsh remind us in their 2009 edition of the *Credit Suisse Global Investment Returns Sourcebook* that economists Fama and French had struggled to explain the momentum effect and thus attached the term 'premier anomaly' to the effect. Dimson and Marsh mention this because it seems clear from the academic literature that momentum is alive and well even if value investing is looking a tad anaemic. Analysts have questioned the small cap effect and even the value premium but the momentum effect still seems to be powering ahead. In Dimson, Marsh and Staunton's earlier 2008 yearbook (this time for ABN Amro) they test out the momentum effect using one simple strategy. In their analysis they define the anomaly thus: 'pure momentum strategies involve ranking stocks into winners and losers based on past returns over a *ranking period*. One then buys the winners and short-sells the losers, over a *holding period*. To ensure implementability, there is usually a *wait period* before investing. Strategies are thus described as "r/w/h". For example, a 12/1/1 strategy ranks returns over the past 12 months, waits 1 month, and then holds for 1 month until rebalancing'.[3]

---

[3] The ABN Amro 2008 report is available at http://www.london.edu/assets/documents/facultyandresearch/786_GIRY2008_synopsis%281%29.pdf

Dimson *et al.* proceed to test out this simple 12/1/1 strategy. According to the authors: 'winners (defined as the top 20% past returns) beat losers (bottom 20%) by 10.8% per year across the entire UK equity market from 1956–2007 (the period for which comprehensive data is available). £1 invested at start-1900 in the winner portfolio would have grown to more than £4¼ million (15.2% p.a.). £1 invested in the losers would have grown to only £111 (4.5% p.a.).'[4] The LBS academics go on to make a few tweaks to their model:

■ 'With equal, rather than capitalisation, weights, the index of momentum stocks produce an even greater difference at 12.0%.

■ And with winners/losers defined as the top/bottom 10% (rather than 20%), the gap was greater still.

■ The winner-minus-loser (WML) gap was smaller at 7.0% p.a. when investment was limited to just the Top 100 UK stocks. However, within this group of highly liquid stocks, the strategy was much easier to implement.'[5]

See Figures 7.7 and 7.8.

Dimson *et al.* conclude: 'The momentum effect, both in the UK and globally, has been pervasive and persistent. Though costly to implement on a standalone basis, all investors need to be acutely aware of momentum.

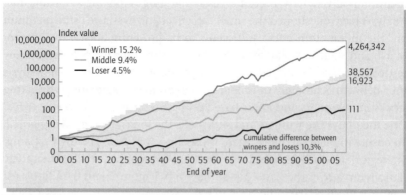

figure 7.7 Annual value-weighted momentum portfolio returns for the top 100 UK equities 1900–2007

---

4 Ibid.

5 Ibid.

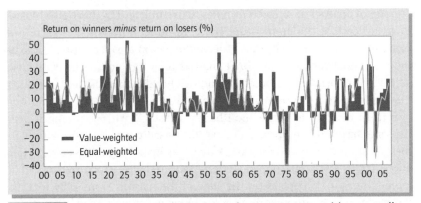

figure 7.8 **Return on winners minus losers for top 100 UK equities, annually 1900–2007**

Even if they do not set out to exploit it, momentum is likely to be an important determinant of their investment performance.'[6] There is one caveat though – they declare that there are 'numerous periods when winners underperform losers, sometimes by a dramatic margin. Pure momentum plays are not for the faint hearted'.[7] Trading costs can also eat into returns – transactions costs can seriously dent performance – but even allowing for this, the returns are consistent, across many different stockmarkets around the world.

In 2009 the LBS academics repeated the exercise – with similar results for a Credit Suisse report.

We limit portfolio constituents to relatively liquid stocks (the largest 100 companies) and study a market (the UK) and sample period (109 years) that has not previously been investigated. For a universe of the top 100 stocks as at the start of each year, from 1900 to 2008, the winners outperformed losers by 10.7% per annum, i.e. a cumulative difference between winners and losers of 10.7% per annum... Momentum investing was profitable in all 17 markets – the momentum premium was substantial... averaging more than 0.80% per month.[8]

---

[6] Ibid.

[7] Ibid.

[8] Credit Suisse Global Investment Returns Yearbook 2009 by Elroy Dimson, Paul Marsh and Mike Staunton, available at http://www.london.edu/facultyandresearch/news/2009/02/Credit_Suisse_Global_Investment_Returns_Yearbook_2009_by_Elroy_Dimson,_Paul_Marsh_and_Mike_Staunton_942.html

A group of analysts at research firm Research Affiliates LLC have also looked in great depth at the momentum effect, to understand whether there is a consensus and what might cause the 'anomaly'. In a paper entitled 'A Synthesis on Stock Momentum'[9] RAFI analysts Bing Han and Jason Tsu review all the major academic studies (including the LBS analysis) and conclude that a relative strength strategy (summarised as 'buy stocks with high returns over the prior three to twelve months and sell stocks with poor returns over the same past horizon') produces near 'universal' positive results, although they do note one important caveat that is echoed in the LBS study. They quote a 2003 study by Cooper, Gutierrez and Hameed which suggests 'that momentum profits depend on the state of the market. From 1929 to 1995 the mean monthly momentum profit following positive market returns is 0.93% whereas the mean profit following negative market returns is negative 0.37%'.[10]

The analysts also warn that momentum 'slowly dissolves over longer horizons – for example the portfolio formed on the basis of returns realised in the past 6 months generates an average cumulative return of 9.5% over the next 12 months but loses more than half of this return in the following 24 months'.[11]

Han and Tsu also review explanations for why the momentum effect is so powerful – concluding that a number of studies believe that momentum is strong with companies 'below the institutional radar in terms of coverage and ownership', with the extra returns likely to be a compensation for the extra risks taken on. They also suggest that investors build in systematic biases towards growth into their expectations for both the share price and underlying earnings: they under-react to firm specific information regarding short-term prospects and over-react when they buy past winners and sell past losers!

Academics, and especially those investigating behavioural finance, continue to probe the momentum effect anomaly but it's fair to say that there are a number of simple conclusions that fall out of all the studies:

■ Momentum does work – focusing a strategy on buying shares with relative strength vs. the market is likely to pay results.

---

[9] Available at http://www.researchaffiliates.com/ideas/pdf/A_Synthesis_on_Stock_Momentum.pdf

[10] Gutierrez, R.C., Cooper, M.J. and Hameed, A. (2003) Market States and Momentum, available at http://ssrn.com/abstract=299927

[11] Ibid.

▇ Momentum seems to be especially strong with smaller companies below the institutional radar that are fast growing.

▇ And, in particular, superb earnings growth and consequent earnings upgrades by analysts who start to follow the stock seems to be a powerful effect as evidenced by the success of both ASOS and Netflix.

Over the past few decades a number of investment theorists and writers have tried to combine the best of both the momentum effect and the search for the fast growing tenbagger. Some have tended to focus on share price strength above everything else – the CAN SLIM approach featured next – while others have preferred to focus on smaller cap stocks where earnings growth is strong and persistent.

CAN SLIM

Most British investors will probably never have heard of William O'Neil, author of *How to Make Money In Stocks*. More's the pity – according to the American Association of Individual Investors (AAII), its version of a classic O'Neil screen called CAN SLIM has delivered returns of over 2700% since its launch in 1998. That success has even carried on through 2009 – delivering an astonishing 97% return while most other strategies have struggled to return much above 40%.

Much of that success may be because O'Neil is in a prime position to study what's required to make both a successful company and share. He's been in the business of providing stockmarket data to institutional investors since the 1960s through his *Investors Business* daily publication that has built up a vast database containing fundamental and price information on thousands of public companies. Using this, he tracked the 500 biggest gainers in the 40 years between 1953 and 1993. As O'Neil himself puts it, finding growth stocks is all about examining 'winners of the past to learn all the characteristics of the most successful stocks'.[12] The fruits of this research are contained in the CAN SLIM approach which can be examined in greater detail at his website (http://www.canslim.net/).

The important thing to remember about O'Neil is that he has no love for value investing. He passionately believes that stocks sell for what they are worth and stocks with low PE ratios are probably correctly priced by the

---

[12] O'Neil, W. (2009) *How to Make Money in Stocks*, McGraw-Hill Professional.

market – in fact O'Neil has gone on record as saying that the PE ratio really doesn't matter! He is also not especially interested in balance sheets or intrinsic values – what matters for him is that the firm you're buying is growing fast and that the markets recognise this fact.

For O'Neil the key test of quality is earnings – he's looking for a minimum increase of 18–20% in quarterly earnings compared with the same quarter last year. He's specifically looking for shares where a kind of earnings growth engine is kicking in, and where new products or services are about to be launched.

Before spelling out in detail O'Neil's strategy it's worth making one crucial point – he's addicted to studying quarterly figures. His approach demands that you scrutinise recent quarterly results in great detail – an easy approach in the US but a good deal more difficult in the UK. Most British investors will probably have to make do with comparing either half yearly results or annual results – it's not perfect but you have no real choice in the vast majority of cases.

A typical CAN SLIM screen might include the following screens:

- C as in current earnings. The key here is to look for companies experiencing major percentage increases in current quarterly EPS when compared to the quarter from the year before. According to O'Neil, 'among all big gainers between 1970 and 1982, 86% reported higher earnings in their most recently published quarter and 76% were up over 10%.' Applying his penchant for quarterly earnings growth of at least 18% to 20%, in the UK you might look for year on year (or same six months compared to the previous six months) reporting period EPS growth of at least 20%. Sales should also increase by at least 30% in the last reporting period compared to the previous period. Remember you're looking for shares where earnings growth is accelerating in each reporting period.

- A as in annual earnings. There should be meaningful growth over the past five years with the four- to five-year annual growth rate between 20% and 50% per annum. But there's one very important caveat – 'beware... companies with outstanding five-year growth records of 30% per annum but whose current earnings in the last two quarters have slowed significantly to 15–10%... [these] should be avoided in most circumstances'. This might practically mean setting the five- and three-year growth rate at at least 20%.

- ■ N as in new products. O'Neil reckons it is a new product or service that causes the big earnings acceleration. He cites innovations like Rexall's new Tupperware division, in 1958, which helped the stock go up from $16 to $50.

- ■ S as in supply and demand of the shares. If there are not many shares in circulation, a small amount of buying could push prices up quickly, so in the US investors should look for companies with 5–25 million shares outstanding. Also watch out for companies that split their stock two or three times in just a year or two – this splitting creates a large overhang of shares and may weaken the share price.

- ■ L as in leader or laggard. O'Neil thinks Graham's faith in cheap stocks is entirely misplaced. He passionately believes that 'expensive' shares are worth it because they carry on rising in value, whilst those shares that seem cheap usually get even cheaper. Relative strength in the share price matters. According to O'Neil 'the 500 best performing stocks from 1953 to 1990 averaged a relative price strength of 87 (in a scale of 1–99) just before they began their major advances in price. Avoid laggard stocks and look for genuine leaders'.

- ■ I as in institutional ownership. O'Neil likes some, but not too much, institutional ownership. Look for 5–25% institutional ownership.

- ■ M as in market direction. Very few stocks go up when the market is going down. According to O'Neil investors should buy individual stocks only when the market as a whole (S&P 500 index) is going up.

O'Neil summed up his philosophy thus:

We're buying companies with strong fundamentals, large sales and earnings increases resulting from unique new products and services and trying to time [those] purchases at a correct point as the company emerges from consolidation periods and before the stock runs up dramatically in price.[13]

It's also worth saying that O'Neil doesn't think you'll be inundated with potential stocks – the point is to be very discriminating and buy the right stock. As O'Neil himself said of his early days as a speculative day trader: 'I learned that your objective in the market was not to be right but to make big money when you were right.'[14]

---

[13] Ibid.
[14] Ibid.

A CAN SLIM approach in the UK

So how might British investor's use the CAN SLIM strategy? You'll probably need a two-step screen with the first screen very much focusing on earnings. We'd suggest the following five measures comprise the first screen:

- Current year EPS growth should be at least 30%.
- Earnings growth over the last three and five years should be at least 25% per annum.
- Still on the earnings theme you could also demand that the PEG be below 1 although this could easily be left out if you want.
- The share price should be showing some real forwards momentum. The RS for the last one month and last three months should be at very least positive.
- Contrary to first appearances O'Neil is moderately interested in what the balance sheet has to say and in his book he's careful to warn about the dangers of debt. That means possibly putting in a screen that requires net gearing to be below 100 or 50%.

Our next screen involves us looking for real evidence of the earnings acceleration we talked about above. Look at the recent accounting periods – the past four six-month periods and the past three annual figures – and look for evidence that the recent EPS growth rate is above that of the past five or three years. The bottom line is that earnings really do need to be taking off – if that growth isn't constantly increasing, exclude the share.

Also look at the ownership structure and see if there is some evidence of institutional ownership (maybe owning 10–20% of the stock) and that the management has fully bought into the growth story by buying the stocks (big directors' sales clustered together is a big no-no) and that they own at least 5% of the shares.

As O'Neil himself predicts, you won't be inundated with companies that fit the bill. The brutal truth is that there aren't that many real tenbaggers out there and the few that do exist are maybe unnoticed or have little institutional backing which would worry any CAN SLIM enthusiast. These issues should make UK investors cautious – this screen will turn up some familiar 'growth' stories peddled by the tip sheets and some not so familiar ones. Expect a lot of technology companies, business services outfits and leisure companies.

But it's worth repeating yet again that this exercise won't reveal dozens and dozens of winners. That's not what it's meant to do. The primary use of a CAN SLIM style screen is not as a way of telling you how to build an entire portfolio, rather it's a way of flagging up undiscovered gems that may turn into tomorrow's tenbaggers.

Small cap investing

Another way of finding shooting stars, or super growth stocks, is to start in the most obvious place – amongst fast growing small caps with the potential to turn into tomorrow's Google or Netflix. This approach is based on a huge weight of detailed academic research that suggests that, in the past, small cap stocks – companies with a small market capitalisation usually in the range of between £10m and £500m – have delivered superior returns.

The most potent piece of evidence comes in the shape of yet another London Business School analysis (jointly with ABN Amro) run by Professors Elroy Dimson and Paul Marsh.[15] Over the past few decades they've developed a unique UK small cap index called the Hoare Govett Small Companies Index, also known as the HGSC index (there's also a sister index called the HG1000 index). The HGSC index represents the bottom 10% by market capitalisation while the HG1000 represents the bottom 2% by market cap. Both have been 'live' for over 20 years but Dimson and Marsh have pushed their analysis way back to 1955.

The conclusions of this study on small caps in this index are startling. Both the HGSC and the HG1000 have out performed the FTSE All Share by 3.5% and 5.7% per annum respectively on an annualised return basis for more than 40 years. In simple terms that out performance means that £1000 invested in 1955 into the HGSC would today be worth £1.8m, vs. £400,000 with the FTSE All Share (with dividends reinvested in both cases). If you had opted for the HG1000 index your returns would be even greater – £4.6m.

And what seems to work in the UK also seems to work globally. James O'Shaughnessy in his research for his book *What Works on Wall Street* found that really tiny stocks, measured by market value and called microstocks, deliver by far the biggest returns. In the 45 years between 1951 and 1996 these microcaps delivered a compounded annual return of 35% (see Table 7.5, overleaf)!

Even after adjusting this return for the much greater risk taken on board (he uses a measure called the Sharpe adjusted risk return) microcaps delivered the biggest return by far. But his analysis also clearly shows that any

---

[15] The Hoare Govett Small Companies Index 2005 An Analysis for ABN Amro. Downloaded at faculty.london.edu/edimson/assets/.../Hoare_Govett_Book_4th_proof.pdf

table 7.5 Micro-stock returns

31 December 1996 value of $10,000 invested on 31 December 1951 excl. microcaps in millions		Sharpe adjusted risk return index by market cap
	Compounded annual returns	1951–1996 (higher is better)
All stocks	2.7	14.97%	49
Large stocks	1.6	13.11%	48
Small stocks	3.8	16.30%	50
S&P 500	1.7	13.39%	48
> $1 billion	1.6	13.18%	48
500m to 1 bn	1.9	14.04%	47
250m to 500m	3.4	15.90%	50
100m to 250m	3.4	16.51%	46
25m to 100m	7.8	19.75%	48
Microcap	NA	35.93%	64

Source: O'Shaughnessy, J. (2005) *What Works on Wall Street*, McGraw-Hill Professional.

stock with a market value below $250m delivered returns well in excess of the 'All stocks' universe.

Figure 7.9 shows the returns on UK equalities ranked by market capitalisation.

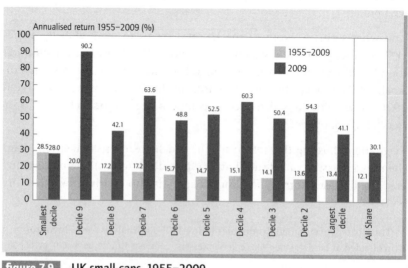

figure 7.9 UK small-caps, 1955–2009

Source: E. Dimson and P. Marsh, *The RBS Hoare Govett Smaller Companies Index 2010*, Royal Bank of Scotland 2010.

Small caps grow faster...

What's behind this consistent out performance? The best answer is probably the simplest – it's much easier for a small company to grow really fast than a huge company. The hard evidence comes in Table 7.6 from something called the CompanyREFs guide – we'll encounter this in a later chapter on how to run a stock screen. Table 7.6 shows the average growth rates of companies in different indices – ranging from the microcaps of the FTSE Fledgling through to the FTSE 100.

What's interesting is that small cap shares consistently out perform both the FTSE 100 and FTSE 250 sector, both in projected earnings growth for the coming year and over the last three and five years. But the Fledgling index – the one that contains really very small companies – has produced much lower returns. These classic microcaps have turned in some decent five-year EPS growth rates, but over the last five years, average EPS growth has been *negative*! It's all about risk... and containing it.

table 7.6   Average growth rates of companies in different indices (all figures are median figures)

Measure	Market	FTSE 100	Mid 250	Small cap	Fledgling
Prospective EPS growth rate % current year	8.62	9.02	10.6	11.3	5.31
3 year EPS growth rate	14.7	11	8.68	12.9	11.3
5 year EPS growth rate	7.91	5.54	7.29	7.35	−1.33

Source: CompanyREFS, Hemington Scott, 2008.

The huge variation in earnings growth between the relatively bigger, small caps index, and those from the really tiny microcaps is of course easily answered – risk. Microcaps tend not to have an enormously proven business trading record and many fail completely – Figure 7.10 (overleaf) clearly shows that every year an inordinate number of small caps and especially microcaps (those from say the Fledgling index) simply vanish without trace.

Returns can also be hugely variable. Since the HGSC went live there have been negative returns in five years, and positive returns in 13. There are also some other less obvious problems with investing in small caps – small caps

for instance suffer from a distinct sector bias. Because small caps are by definition valued at no more than £500m in the UK there are very few banks or
tobacco companies. There are also remarkably few utility stocks, life assur-
ers and there's even a paucity of oil and gas stocks. James O'Shaughnessy
himself adds another warning – the small cap returns he obtained in his
analysis can be 'chimera' because the only way to achieve those returns was
to invest a few million dollars in over 2000 stocks.

O'Shaughnessy has tried to address this issue of risk by developing his
own strategy for picking fast growing small caps – he called it his Tiny
Titans strategy. Over the past few decades he's mined stockmarket data from
around the world for stock screening strategies that work and in his latest
book *Predicting the Markets of Tomorrow: A Contrarian Investment Strategy for
the Next Twenty Years*,[16] he reckons he's found the answer. He argues that
you can second guess market trends by testing the historical data using key
fundamental measures. O'Shaughnessy studied data stretching dating back
to the late 1790s and found that equity markets tend to move in trends of
about 20 years. According to this pattern, a 20-year trend began in early
2000 during which time greater returns will be earned by small- and mid-
cap stocks and large-cap value stocks. How to find these small caps with the
greatest potential? Step forward his Tiny Titans. This strategy searches for
cheap small cap stocks with upward price momentum.

O'Shaughnessy believes there are many advantages to investing in really
small, tiny microcap stocks. Few analysts cover these small stocks and this
lack of coverage leaves much room for upside potential when good stocks
are largely unnoticed. Also microcap shares in the US at least have a low
correlation with other market capitalisation strategies. These tiny stocks,
however, are highly volatile and best suited for investors who can handle
the dramatic swings that a portfolio of these shares will produce. To find
rewarding, potentially successful microcaps O'Shaughnessy suggests focusing on the following key measures:

- Market capitalisation. O'Shaughnessy's Tiny Titans screen looks for
  shares with a market capitalisation between $25m and $250m.
- Price-to-sales ratio. Shares must also have a price-to-sales ratio that is
  less than 1.
- Relative strength. Finally, the 25 stocks with the greatest 52-week
  relative strength are picked for the portfolio.

---

[16] O'Shaughnessy, J. (2006) *Predicting the Markets of Tomorrow: A Contrarian
Investment Strategy for the Next Twenty Years*, Portfolio.

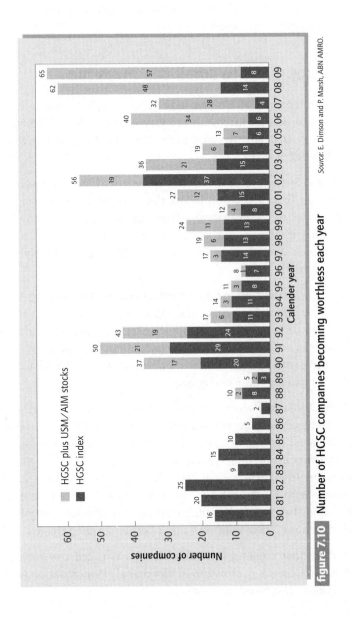

figure 7.10 **Number of HGSC companies becoming worthless each year**

Source: E. Dimson and P. Marsh, ABN AMRO.

Does it work? The AAII has run this screen for the past few years and the answer is a resounding yes! In the past year, their Tiny Titan's 25 have produced an average return of 24.6% while over the past 9 years, returns have totalled an astonishing 1960%!

The Foolish approach to small cap investing

An equally interesting, alternative, take on spotting fast growing small caps comes from those ever insightful analysts at Motley Fool. They've identified a strategy that aims to spot early stage small cap stocks with huge potential ahead of them.

Like James O'Shaughnessy they take the view that many hugely interesting small cap firms exist well below the radar of most analysts. In fact for Motley Fool that's great news – that's the opportunity. Analysts, news organisations, influential magazines – they're all obsessed by fast growing big companies. According to Motley Fool these experts barely mention small companies.

As Motley Fool expert Brian Graney observes 'a look at *Business Week's* archives over the past five years shows 19 cover stories devoted to just six different companies – Microsoft, Apple, AT&T, General Electric and Sun. The number of cover stories on small companies over that span? Three. To boot, all three small companies' issues were promoted with the flashy "Hot Growth Companies" title. Go figure.'[17]

But Motley Fool also realises that much of this ignorance is based on sensible fear. Many of the conventional valuation metrics don't stack up when it comes to small caps. Again Graney notes that although one in four $500m plus companies in the US have returns on equity of over 15%, that falls to just over one in eight for small caps (defined as $500 million in sales or less). Analysts find it difficult to use many conventional valuation metrics and also find that proper research on small caps takes up a lot of time for not much reward. Their solution – don't bother covering them.

The strategy that emerges from this analysis is called the Foolish eight and it features eight key measures in its original US incarnation. These are grouped under two broad headings.

17 'Buy Small' by Brian Graney at www.fool.com/foolish8

First there are business specific fundamentals such as:

1 earnings and sales growth of at least 25%

2 net operating profit margins of at least 7%

3 operating cash flow must be positive

4 evidence of insiders such as the directors buying into the shares (Motley Fool suggests they hold at least 10% of the stock).

The second set of measures are 'market specific' and are designed to catch well traded, liquid stocks, with reasonable volume and RS. They are:

5 stocks with a $1m to $25m daily volume

6 stocks with a minimum $7 share price

7 stocks with strong RS.

The eighth measure is a slightly odd one:

8 exclude all firms with revenues of over $500m (Motley Fool are deadly serious about their small cap bias).

Applying this screen to the UK isn't all plain sailing. The first set of measures are easy enough to apply but the second set are a bit trickier. Volumes of small cap shares in the UK are considerably lower than in the US and a minimum share price of say £4 (the rough equivalent of $7) might be a little odd considering that most UK stocks trade of any size in the pence range not pounds.

A UK version of the Motley Small Cap strategy

Our version of the Foolish 8 features eight measures in the first screen but all of them are slightly different in emphasis and tone. It's very much our 'own label' version of a Foolish 8 strategy.

The measures used include:

▪ RS in the last three months is in the top quartile for the market. This is a tough yardstick and shows clearly that the firm's shares are motoring ahead.

▪ The net profit margin must also be in the top quartile for the market. In practice this means well above the 7% suggested by Motley Fool and tends to be in the 10–15% range.

▪ A share price that is more than 10p. This is designed to avoid the difficult to trade and highly volatile penny stocks of old (daily trading volumes can also be very low).

▶

▶ ▪ Market cap should be in the £10m to £100m range.

▪ The price to cashflow measure should be at least positive. This helps to narrow down our shortlist to those that will have positive operating cash flow.

▪ Earnings per share over the past three years should be in the top quartile for the market and earnings for the current year should be growing by at least 25% over the year.

▪ Our last measure is a bit unorthodox and is not mentioned by Motley Fool but it's ROCE. This is designed to answer Motley Fool's own observation that one of the shortcomings of small caps is their frequent inability to keep up with large caps when it comes to key measures like return on equity or ROCE. We've picked ROCE because if our small cap is going to grow bigger – along with the share price – analysts will need to know that the company is sweating its capital base efficiently. In reality it's not an overly demanding target as most fast growing small cap companies boast very high ROCE rates. We've set this filter at 15%.

The second screen is much more qualitative and looks at more company specific issues. These are:

▪ Sales growth at the top line should be at least 25% in the last year.

▪ There should be strong evidence of 'insider ownership' – management – with a suggested minimum of 10% of the entire equity.

▪ ROCE of 15% should be present for at least the last two years.

▪ A sales maximum of £500m. In practice this could easily be set lower – at around £200m.

▪ Make sure that the cashflow at the operating level can easily pay for capex and dividends.

Run the screen and like CAN SLIM you won't find yourself overwhelmed with candidates. You'll get maybe 12–20 shares shortlisted, all of which will need further investigation.

Directors' dealings

Buying of shares by directors in the company has long been regarded by analysts and investment writers as one of the most positive signals for investors – if directors reckon that it's worth spending a small fortune on the shares of their company, shouldn't private investors follow their lead? Legendary British investor Jim Slater certainly believes this is the case and includes directors' dealings as one of his key measures in his own screens of the market.

In his guide to CompanyREFS[18] Slater mentions a leading City study (by Smith New Court in August 1993) which he suggests demonstrates that an investor can out perform the market by following directors' dealings. According to Slater there are a number of key points to consider when analysing directors' dealings:

- Directors' buying is a clearer signal than directors' selling. Directors decide to sell shares for a variety of reasons, such as buying a new house, to meet a tax obligation or simply to maintain a high standard of living. When a director buys a share, he or she is expressing the belief that the company's shares are a better investment than cash. The director also usually believes that the share is under-valued. The exceptions are when a director buys qualification shares on appointment, buys shares to take up an option that is expiring or when a director with a major shareholding buys a further trivial number of shares to excite interest in the company.

- There is no doubt that there is comfort in numbers. Three or more directors buying a significant number of shares is a far more powerful indicator than an isolated transaction.

- Directors' dealings need to be related to the number of shares already owned and the amount of money involved. The sale of 20,000 shares by a director owning one million shares worth £1 each is of no great significance. However, the sale of an entire shareholding of £20,000 worth of shares owned by a director can be a cause for alarm.

- The identity of the buyer or seller of shares can be significant. The chairman, managing director or finance director are usually the three directors with the most intimate knowledge of a company's affairs. The transactions of other directors can be meaningful, but they are a little less likely to have the full story.

- There are, of course, close periods when directors cannot sell shares. It is useful to know when they are, but I do not regard proximity to them as a particularly meaningful indicator.[19]

Slater is not alone in suggesting that directors' dealing have strong predictive power – many growth-based investors such as William O'Neil and Richard Driehaus also closely scrutinise director buying as an indicator, but a London investment firm has taken this approach to a whole new

---

[18] Available online at http://www.companyrefs.com/Guide/guideIndex.htm
[19] Ibid.

level. Mayfair based Knox D'Arcy Investment Management Limited has developed an enormously sophisticated methodology built around directors' dealing – the system has even found its way into a listed investment trust. The analysts at Knox D'Arcy suggest that directors are better informed than the market and that following their lead produces out performance verified by independent research. Crucially they've built this thinking into a quant-based strategy – although not untypically the firm hasn't fully disclosed all the workings of its system. It has suggested though that its system is built on a database with 14 years of directors' trading information, over 7.1 million data observations and 182,000 directors' trades. What we do know about the strategy is that it looks at a number of different elements based on directors' trading:

- motivation for trade (e.g. purchase, options, rights)
- type of director trading (e.g. executive, by role)
- market timing of trade around results and corporate news
- trade size and value – absolute and relative size
- type of company traded – size, FTSE classification
- clustered trading.

Using these filters Knox D'Arcy have then focused their funds on UK listed stocks, based around a portfolio of 40–80 individual stocks with a strong mid to small cap bias (although they don't invest in any companies with a market cap of less than £25m). The firm has also helpfully back tested its strategy between 1994 and 2007 – the generally impressive results are in Table 7.7, although it's worth mentioning this 'test' is a back test and not based on actual live trading strategy.

table 7.7   Investment performance 1994–2007

Simple strategy	Average 120 day out performance	Annualised 120 day out performance	Number of trades	Average 240 day out performance	Annualised 240 day out performance	Number of trades
All purchases	2.01%	4.22%	93,300	3.71%	3.87%	89,250
Strategy 1	4.29%	9.13%	2876	8.46%	8.83%	2074
Strategy 2	4.34%	9.20%	2323	9.21%	9.61%	2240
Strategy 3	4.90%	10.40%	2281	9.72%	10.14%	2194
Strategy 4	6.2%	13.39%	1144	10.79%	11.26%	1115

Source: Directors' Dealing Trust.

Crucially the Knox D'Arcy analysis suggests that the predictive power of directors' buying peaks over a specific holding period (for the directors buying the shares) of between 200 and 240 days, i.e. it's best to focus your purchase of shares on those companies where directors have held the share for more than 6–8 months.

Figure 7.11 shows that the fund has out performed the small cap index in seven out of eight periods. While Figure 7.12 shows an average annual out performance of 14.3% the fund has out performed the index by 167% over the period.

But, and there is a very big but here, this strategy hasn't yet proved itself in an actual fund over a sufficiently robust enough period of time. In 2009 Knox D'Arcy were successful in an attempt to take over a small cap investment trust called Eaglet, despite considerable opposition from some rival fund managements groups. The fund changed its name to the Directors' Dealing Investment Trust and since the spring of 2009 the managers have been attempting to sell down the old investments and reinvest according to the new strategy.

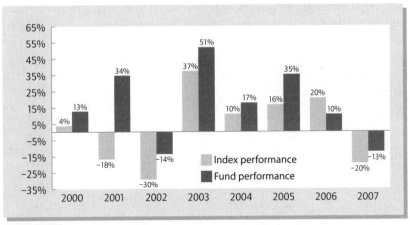

figure 7.11   **Fund performance by year**   *Source*: Knox D'Arcy.

Notes (i) Fund simulation period from 1 Jan 2000 to 31 Dec 2007 (ii) Excluding dividends (iii) Fund start value £50m (iv) Returns stated after deduction of trading costs but prior to deduction of investment manager fees (v) Sample strategy STP500

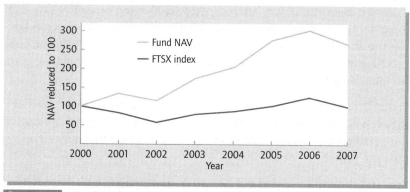

figure 7.12 **Fund performance against the index** *Source*: Knox D'Arcy.

Notes (i) Fund simulation period from 1 Jan 2000 to 31 Dec 2007 (ii) Excluding dividends (iii) Fund start value £50m (iv) Returns stated after deduction of trading costs but prior to deduction of investment manager fees (v) Sample strategy STP500

Figure 7.13 shows the performance of the fund versus the UK Small cap index since Spring 2009 – the FTSE Small Cap index is the thick line. The fund has managed some out performance in price terms but not to any demonstrable degree, especially as it is still holding a large number of legacy stocks. It's also worth observing the conclusions of one academic study in this area which noted that although companies with heavy directors' buying did indeed display subsequent out performance (especially in smaller companies), once an

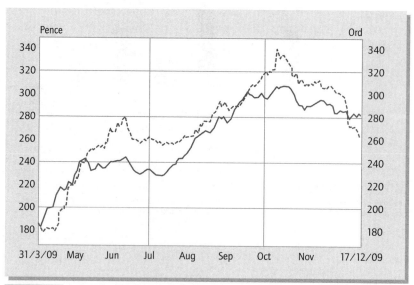

figure 7.13 The Directors Dealing Investment Trust plc against the FTSE Small Cap

Source: www.ShareScope.co.uk

appropriate benchmark is used it was 'found that the significance of the abnormal returns is substantially reduced, with the implication that directors' trading does not yield particularly high profits to either directors themselves or to an outside investor mimicking those trades'.[20] This analysis reminds us of the curse of many quantitative-based strategies – what seems sensible on paper doesn't always work in the real world especially once trading costs are factored back in! Nevertheless, even though a strategy exclusively based on directors' dealing has yet to be proven, there does seem to be some logic to monitoring buys and sells as part of a wider strategy.

Concluding thoughts on why growth strategies are so risky

The risks with pure growth stocks and the screens that find them are obvious. They are by their nature risky – it's stating the obvious but it needs constant repeating! One small example should demonstrate this point.

At the end of 2009 we ran a simple screen that looked back five years beforehand and set simple parameters for earnings per share growth. It excluded all companies where EPS growth over the previous three years had not been above 10% per annum – on average the shortlisted 71 companies on the London market had produced over the three years previous to December 2004 EPS growth of between 30% and 40% per annum. It's also important to note that this was no group of tiny small caps – the average market cap of the 71 companies that passed this simple GARP screen was over £3bn. Care to guess the returns over the subsequent five years to the end of December 2009? The FTSE All Share returned 13.29% in price terms, yet our 71 companies returned an average loss of 9.29%. Here was an elite of earnings enhancing stars and yet on average they failed to beat the FTSE All Share! We make no great claims to this slightly spurious piece of data mining but the same relative under-performance was noted if we pushed the sample back ten or even 15 years. Past evidence of earnings growth is absolutely no guide to future potential!

Chasing the market and looking for stocks with above average share price strength is a dangerous game. Sooner or later that share price growth has to slow down – the power of mean reversion over sufficiently long periods of

---

[20] Gregory, A., Matatko, J., Tonks, I. and Purkis, R. (1994) 'UK directors' trading: the impact of dealings in smaller firms', *The Economic Journal*, www.jstor.org

time is astonishing, suggesting that what goes up must, eventually, come down! Trying to keep earnings powering ahead at rates of 50% or more, every year, year on year, is back breaking stuff. Management eventually trip up and earnings come crashing back down to earth, along with the share price!

Mean reversion is one danger, but there's another even bigger threat lurking – even when we do correctly spot tomorrow's shooting stars, we systematically end up over-paying for the privilege of 'glamour' and 'growth'.

The founder of research firm Research Affiliates Rob Arnott in particular has spent a great deal of time examining the allure of growth stocks – and the resulting high stock price. In an article for the *Financial Times* based on his research Arnott introduced the newspaper's readers to his concept of clairvoyant stock selection or value. Suppose, he suggested 'we could see all future dividends that all companies pay, and the eventual price of those that are acquired. We could easily calculate the fair value of these companies. We could simply calculate the net present value of these future distributions'.[21] But surely this would mean seeing into the future:

Au contraire. *We can see the future – for any time in the past. Suppose, for example, we wanted to know what IBM or BP were truly worth to the clairvoyant investor in 1980. We can see the distributions from 1980 until today. And, while we don't know what the distributions will be from tomorrow onward, we can use today's price as the market's best guess at the value of those remaining future distributions. By discounting all of these back to 1980, we can know what a clairvoyant would have been willing to pay in 1980... We can compare prices of companies with eventual true value and extract remarkable findings.*[22]

By using this extraordinary concept Arnott was able to suggest that some 20% of the value of a typical stock is based on future distributions that lie 50 years or more in the future: 'How do we know this? Simple, 20% of the fair values of 1958 are embedded in the 2008 price of the companies that survived that long.'[23]

Using this analysis Arnott proceeded to explore whether the premium companies were with the extra price: 'we can compare the valuation multiples (for instance, price/earnings ratios or price/book value ratios) of the past with the fair valuation multiples that a clairvoyant would have paid. We find a 50–60 per cent correlation between the premium or discount in past market prices and fair premium or discount that future distributions would have

---

[21] Arnott, B. (2009) 'Future tips from past clairvoyants', *Financial Times*, 9 August.
[22] Ibid.
[23] Ibid.

justified.'[24] This relatively high percentage suggests to Arnott that the 'market does a brilliant job of discriminating between future winners and future losers, paying a substantial premium for the former and a deep discount for the latter'.[25] But did the market over-pay? Arnott's conclusion is clear – yes! 'On average, a clairvoyant would have paid about 50 per cent more for the companies with lofty expectations than for the companies where stasis or disappointment is expected. But the market pays an average of about 100 per cent premium for the former, relative to the latter. The market overpays for future growth – relative to its ability to correctly anticipate that growth – by about two-to-one'.[26] Switching to late 2009 Arnott updated his analysis – he suggested that growth stocks are no longer twice the multiple attached to value stocks but 2.5 times the multiple: 'This is three times the premium that a clairvoyant investor would have willingly paid in the past!'[27]

The SG team have examined the same theme – with similar results. In a paper for the French bank James Montier[28] looked at the degree to which investors over-pay for growth stocks relative to the company's actual growth rates. Table 7.8 shows the annual performance of the various categories. Consistent with the idea that investors over-pay for the hope of growth, the stars turn out to be disappointing relative to both the dogs and the overall market (under-performing by 6% and 3% respectively).

table 7.8 Return performance (% p.a.); US 1985–2007, market = 13.4%, Europe 1998–2007, market = 14.3%

	Expected growth	
Past sales growth	Low	High
Low	Dogs US 14.9% Europe 19.5%	Old dogs, new tricks US 13.2% Europe 14.9%
High	Fallen angels US 13.2% Europe 12.2%	Stars US 9.9% Europe 12.4%

Source: Montier, J. 'Learn to love your dogs, or, overpaying for the hope of growth (again!)', *Mind Matters*. Published in Montier, J. (2009) *Value Investing*, John Wiley & Sons .

---

24 Ibid.

25 Ibid

26 Ibid.

27 Ibid.

28 Montier, J. (2009) *Value Investing*, John Wiley & Sons.

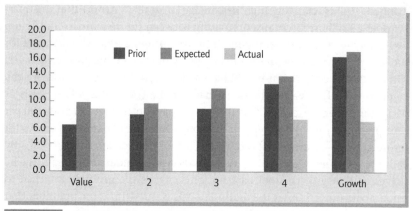

figure 7.14 **Growth: past, expected and actual (US 1995–2007)**

Source: SG Global Strategy Research.

Figure 7.14 – again from the SG team – has a slightly different take on the same theme. It shows the estimated growth rates chalked in by analysts in the US for a range of value and growth stocks. The value stocks don't quite hit their expected growth rates but the mismatch between expected growth rates (based on analysts' data) and actual growth rates for the growth cohort is massive. Growth stocks usually fail to deliver! As Montier concludes: 'It is also noteworthy that there is a 0.98 correlation between past growth and forecast growth, and a –0.9 correlation between forecast growth and actual delivered future growth.'[29]

This last example introduces us to the other big issue with growth stocks – many growth stocks are only worth that extra premium based on estimates of future growth rates by analysts. Many of our previous strategies for selecting stocks have future earnings growth built into the screen – these estimates are absolutely crucial.

Unfortunately, as the SG team has already hinted at in the example above, the actual relationship between earnings and analysts' estimates is woeful, even in the very short term. Using data on 498 of the S&P 500 companies from the third quarter of 1999, one analyst estimate service, First Call, found that earnings came in, on average, 3% above analysts' estimates. The AAII ran a similar exercise and found that as of 28 January, 2000, the median earnings surprise for the 4328 companies with earnings surprise data was 2.4%. The bottom line – analysts consistently under-estimate earnings

---

[29] Ibid.

growth in the short term, allowing companies to frequently 'surprise' the market! To be fair to analysts this may not entirely be their fault – we also need to look carefully at the role of senior managers and directors in 'guiding' those estimates. In one academic paper a Buffalo School of Management accounting researcher Weihong Xu looked at more than 11,000 firm-quarter observations. She found that managers often underestimate the implications of their past forecasting errors when forecasting earnings. Unsurprisingly her research suggested that this 'underestimation of past errors' can affect how the market responds to a new earnings forecast. In particular it seems to result in what's euphemistically called 'post-earnings announcement drift' – share prices continue to drift in the direction of the initial price response to an earnings announcement. Weihong Xu also suggests that: 'Managers under-estimate the information in their prior forecast errors to a greater extent when they make earnings forecasts with a longer horizon.'[30]

The longer time horizon for earnings estimates is also likely to introduce another much simpler but even more devastating problem – notably that analysts like nearly all professionals are terrible at predicting the medium to long term. This observation doesn't probably need too much evidence although it's always worth reminding ourselves of Torngren and Montgomery's 2004 research project (mentioned by James Montier in *Behavioural Investing*). Students and finance professionals were asked to select a share they thought would out perform each month from a pair of stocks. According to Montier's retelling of the story 'all the stocks were well known blue chip names and players were given the name, industry and prior 12 months' performance for each stock. Overall the students were around 59% confident in their stock picking abilities; however the professionals averaged 65% confidence. The bad news is that both groups were worse than sheer luck. That is to say you should have been able to beat both groups just by tossing a coin!'[31] What was even worse, according to Montier, was that the professionals were 100% sure they were correct whereas in fact they were actually correct less than 15% of the time!

Montier's colleagues at SG generously place this systematic over-estimation of forecast growth by analysts within a concrete example – mining stocks. Over the very long term most mining stocks have managed to increase earnings

---

[30] 'Evidence that management earnings forecasts do not fully incorporate information in prior forecast errors' by Weihong Xu can be accessed at http://www.physorg.com/news177062971.html

[31] Montier, J. (2007) *Behavioural Investing: A Practitioners Guide to Applying Behavioural Finance*, John Wiley & Sons.

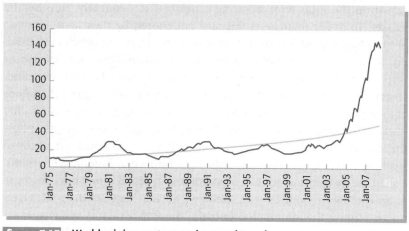

figure 7.15 World mining sector earnings and trend *Source:* SG Global Strategy Research.

at a rate of about 5% per annum – Figure 7.15 shows the cumulative trend of earnings estimates for the sector, with the nice 'straightish' line showing actual long-term trends in those earnings. The mismatch is truly horrendous!

If all this talk of the fallibility of earnings estimates isn't enough to scare off most cynical investors, there's also the tricky issue of making momentum work. All those academic studies we mentioned earlier in this chapter may be very insistent that over the long term momentum works wonders but that doesn't mean it works all the time – or even much of the time.

This important warning finds support in modern trading-based strategies designed to capture momentum. Algy Hall in the *Investors Chronicle* for instance has been running a simple implementation of a momentum strategy, based on a simple quarter by quarter monitoring exercise. According to Hall, his basic strategy 'is to go long on the best 10 performing FTSE 100 stocks of the previous three months and short on the 10 worst performing stocks'.[32] In the middle of December 2009 Hall noted that the strategy was hardly a glorious one in 2009 and 'finished the year on a suitably wobbly note. Since December 2008 the long portion of our momentum portfolio has had a fairly decent run (up 56%)... that said the long portfolio produced a disappointing return in the most recent quarter (4th) falling by an average of 3.8%'.[33] But this wobbly relative success was killed stone dead by the

---

[32] Hall, A. (2009) 'Momentum's Mixed Message', *Investors Chronicle*, 18 December.
[33] Ibid.

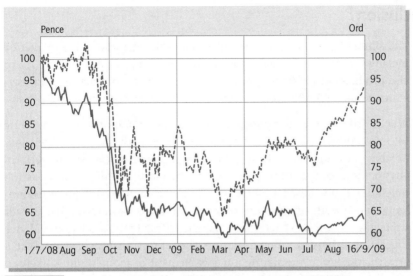

figure 7.16 Eclectica UK Relative Momentum against the FTSE 100

Source: www.ShareScope.co.uk

disastrous performance of the short portion of the portfolio – this particular strategy 'would have turned a £10,000 investment on 15 December 2008 into a measly £1,875 now – and that's before taking into account of any dealing costs'.[34]

Some asset managers have even tried to develop the ideas behind momentum and turn them into successful, simple to administer retail funds. Back in 2008, hedge fund Eclectica, headed by Hugh Hendry, launched a UK Relative Momentum product that used a relative share price scoring system. Launched in the summer of that year this screen-based strategy fund failed to take off. Figure 7.16 shows returns from the fund through to its closure in September 2009, with the thick line returns from the FTSE 100. Over virtually every quarter of its short life, this relative momentum fund failed to beat a FTSE 100 tracker – momentum may be one of those great academic principles that actually proves next to impossible to operate on a day in day out basis!

---

[34] Ibid.

Conclusion

The allure of growth stocks – the glamour of being ahead of the market by picking tomorrow's Google – has obvious psychological attractions. It can also produce extraordinary profits if you do manage to enact these ideas as a successful, replicable strategy but there are a great many potential pitfalls.

It's clear that systematic strategies – where a pot of money is run according to certain principles, year in, year out – in the growth space are hugely vulnerable to the market cycle. In other words, growth stocks tend to perform abysmally in bear markets as investors abandon anything that looks too much like equity based 'boosterism'! It's also clear from our quick encounter with real world applications of momentum-based strategies that growth strategies can also have terrible years where despite the academic evidence suggesting otherwise, momentum crashes! Most analysts suggest that a growth strategy incorporating a heavy element of momentum is likely to work best in relatively stable mid to high peak bull markets with relatively low volatility. The best summary we've encountered on momentum in fact comes from one of its biggest intellectual opponents Rob Arnott. In an interview for a later chapter he suggests that:

Momentum works in the short run, it doesn't work in the long run. And also momentum works until it doesn't work. And when it doesn't work, it bites you very hard. The problem with momentum is it doesn't work at market turns. And so what we find is that if something has performed brilliantly, yes, momentum may carry it higher. But there's no harm in trimming it. And continuing to trim it, and continuing to trim it. Because eventually it will turn. And so what we find is, momentum works in spans measured in months, and anti-momentum works in spans measured in years. What has performed brilliantly over the last five years, for instance, is highly unlikely to be brilliant the next five years. Highly unlikely. And so momentum is a short-term phenomena, but it is powerful.[35]

It also seems clear to us that growth-based strategies need to be ruthlessly applied with no sense of emotion or emotional commitment – when a stock goes ex growth, sell it! The likes of William O'Neil and Richard Driehaus are insistent on this point – don't stick with losers. Once the reasons for including your growth-stock vanish, sell the shares. Also investors operating a growth-based strategy need to be aware of the risk levels in their portfolio – most growth-based thinkers suggest strict application of stop losses and constant monitoring of positions.

---

[35] In an interview with the author.

We also suggest that growth strategies tend to work by taking much more of a sniper-based approach – the strategies outlined in this chapter probably work best in identifying a shortlist of stocks which can then be researched in detail with just a few shares making it into the final portfolio. Broader-based, momentum-based strategies – picking lots of stocks displaying positive relative strength – can work some of the time but the risk is that they become too difficult to monitor on a regular basis for a time strapped private investor and trading costs from a constantly churning portfolio could eat into returns, especially if private investors don't get the best dealing commission rates and suffer from wide spreads! This suggests to us using certain growth-based strategies in a sparing, selective way, as a tool for further research and only as part of a much broader portfolio with different strategies that could run alongside a commitment to finding tomorrow's tenbaggers!

part

two

Putting it into practice

8

How to investigate a company
Paul Darrall Dolman

In this part of the book we're going to turn our attention to how an investor starts to use some of the ideas discussed. How does a private investor construct a stock screen? What exactly constitutes good value in a share? Which measures should investors choose to prioritise? In this first chapter in the Putting it into Practice part we've asked private investor and broadcaster (for the *4WiseMonkeys* online TV programme) to focus in on one company he likes and then run a proper due diligence process – using both the measures we've already introduced and the concepts that influence an investor looking to hunt down a growing company with a reasonable share price. What follows is Paul's very individual – and successful – approach to company analysis, due diligence and stock screening.

A great story

Behind every great investment there is a story. It may be the world-class management, that must-have product, a new company acquisition or sudden economic change that will drive the share price higher. We revel in the success of our find before seeing the results, rushing to invest in case the shares rise the very next day.

Speed is regarded as a key advantage by investors, driven by a constantly moving share price and the fear of a missed opportunity. Research is limited to the article that tipped the share and a glance at the charts to ensure the price is going in the right direction or is rightfully due a recovery. In our desire to exploit the benefits of speed, we are blinded to the benefits of spending time on research.

There has never been a greater abundance of information. Private investors now have access to live and historic prices, the ability to search newspapers and magazines, discuss our latest gem on bulletin boards and browse company websites. This has not led to improved decision making. Fast information and the ability to act have led to an increase in speculation, as seen by the ever-increasing volumes of trades.

Investment is not just an investment of money but also time. Every company does have a story to tell but if you are to be successful you cannot expect to jump to the end and be rewarded. Bernard Baruch, famous for his investment skills long before the Information Age, said that the principal mistake investors make is to have an inexact knowledge of the securities. Basically, they know too little about a company's management, its earnings and prospects for future growth.

One hundred years after that sentiment, less than 5 per cent of investors use annual reports, either for prospective investments or even when the report is mailed to their home as a current investor. But this is where the real story about a company is contained, including management discussion and analysis, the company strategy and the financial accounts. The latest reports can be downloaded in a split second and can be analysed along with the historic reports to build up a year by year picture. All newspapers, magazines and broker reports ultimately rely on this information. By carrying out your own research you can be sure of its validity. You know that no corners have been cut. This can be the difference between understanding why you have made a good investment and keeping you away from a bad one.

Great investors including Warren Buffett, Jim Rogers, Jim Slater and Benjamin Graham all did their own research, placing the greatest importance on the annual report. It is this that can give you an edge over the vast majority of private and professional investors, but it requires time.

During this chapter we are going to examine some key steps that allow you to examine a company, looking both at the quality of the company and how to arrive at a valuation. The chapter will guide you through identifying the purpose of the company, how well it is performing and its ability to build competitive advantage. Financial ratios will be used to decipher that performance before using all of this information to produce a company valuation using a method called discounted cashflow.

The annual report

Listed companies in the United Kingdom are required to produce an annual report available on the internet. Throughout this chapter I shall be using the London Stock Exchange Group Plc as a working example (www.londonstockexchange.com). All investment ideas begin with a spark, an initial interest. This company has benefited from ever increasing volumes due to stock speculation. This gives us a potential story, an investment, but we currently lack research and evidence.

The London Stock Exchange Group Plc's corporate website contains 13 years' worth of historical annual reports showing a commitment to providing investor information and a perfect example of best practice. Our main focus will be on the 2009 annual report. All the research and evidence provided will be solely from the annual accounts and official company updates.

The annual report is a comprehensive report on the company's activities throughout the preceding year. It is important to understand these reports are not written exclusively for shareholders but designed to satisfy the information needs of many different groups of people.

Typical contents

Typically annual reports will include:

- chairman's report
- CEO's report
- auditor's report on corporate governance
- mission statement
- corporate governance statement of compliance
- statement of directors' responsibilities
- invitation to the company's AGM

as well as financial statements including:

- auditor's report on the financial statements
- balance sheet
- statement of retained earnings
- income statement
- cashflow statement

■ notes to the financial statements

■ accounting policies.

By law, companies must have their accounts examined by independent auditors, according to standards laid down by their regulators. The auditors' report to shareholders is an important safeguard: it contains their opinion on the company's financial position and the procedures used to prepare the accounts.

Past, present and future

Annual reports traditionally begin with a review of the year from the company's chairman and chief executive and larger companies will always have a longer and more detailed review of the performance of the business. Investors are often advised to skip these bright, colourful sections full of photographs which compare well to a holiday brochure (you never know 'til you get there) and start at the back with the financial information. Annual reports are a tale of two shares, one with the public relations spin that helps form your story, your reason for investing. The second provides you with audited information to support or end that story as regards your investment. Annual reports can give you a view of the past, present and future.

As investors in a business, we want to identify those companies that will be superior at producing profits and excess cash (free cashflow) allowing for timing and risk. These companies are better than the competition and are in the right industry, building advantages that protect them throughout the many cycles of the economy and the markets. The free cashflow of these companies can be valued to try and identify companies below their intrinsic value.

Warren Buffett once described investing as 'simple, but not easy'. When investigating investment opportunities, it is important to avoid quick assumptions even to the simplest of questions. For example, the London Stock Exchange Group was selected due to 'its ever increasing volumes'. This assumption could quickly be turned into an investment, and yet the annual report shows that despite revenues from trading services relentlessly increasing, trading represents less than half of the revenues of the company. Dig further into the detail and you can see volumes have been falling in the short term. The annual report contains most of the answers you need to assess a company but it does not have the questions.

Investors should never be short of a question, preferring them to assumptions. Understand how a company operates both internally and compared with the competition. Identify the existing and emerging trends that could propel a company to further profits or limit its potential. As we examine the London Stock Exchange Group, potential questions will be raised and any one of those questions may lead to a possible red flag to investment.

Competitive advantage

Competitive advantage is a key differentiator in the long-term performance of companies and share prices. Warren Buffett referred to the link between competitive advantage and profits as an 'economic moat'. Companies capable of creating significant competitive advantage defences are able to reward investors with higher returns. By building up a view of the company and using competitor reports to build up a view of the industry we can take a judgement on the opportunities and risks faced by a company. There are four key questions upon which we can build all of the analysis.

1   What are the goals of the business?
2   How does the business make money?
3   How well it is doing?
4   How does it compare to its competitors?

Bull and bear

Even the worst investments can be justified if you are only searching for reasons to buy. Investments need to be made on the balance of evidence. When investigating a share it is good to imagine yourself both as a bull (looking for the reasons to buy) and a bear (looking for the reasons to sell). Highlight the key bull and bear points of the annual report for further investigation. Annual reports will focus on positive stories and present negative factors in a good light.

Analysis requires you to recognise trends, make decisions and consider the impact on the company. Will the difficult environment continue? What is the impact of the difficult environment on revenues and profits? Does, as the chairman suggests, this offer opportunities to the company?

The London Stock Exchange Group: annual report overview

What are the goals of the business?

Facilitate access to capital, a wide range of products for investors, market efficiency to lower cost of capital, trading and investment.

We then need to consider whether it makes sense for the company to be aiming for these goals.

How does the business make money?

The London Stock Exchange has four primary sources of revenue

- Issuer Services £90m (annual fees £41m, admission fees £28m; RNS News Services £21m)

- Trading Services £275m (equity £184m; fixed income £26m; derivatives £25m; others £40m)

- Information Services £183m (data charges £114m; others £69m)

- Post Trade Services £104m (clearing £53m; settlement £17m; custody £34m).

You need to ask yourself whether you really understand the sources of these revenues and whether these revenues are increasing?

How well is the business actually doing?

Every area of revenue has increased year on year for the past five years according to the annual report.

Chairman's statement

- Group's markets have been affected by the crisis (negative).
- Good underlying performance (positive).
- Robust cash flows (positive).
- Markets (*the product*) have become ever more essential (positive).
- £484m goodwill charge connected to Borsa Italiana Acquisition (negative).
- Acquisition has led to strong post trade services growth (positive).
- Strategic partnerships key to growth, progressing well (positive).
- Dividend increased, but remain cautious (negative).
- Chief executive changing (positive or negative).
- Group companies will continue to seek equity funds (positive).
- Market conditions are expected to remain testing (negative).

Chief executive's statement

- Resilient business model (positive).
- Busy year integrating (positive or negative).
- Cost synergies from merger on target (positive, keep monitoring – this may fail).
- Record equity raised (positive).
- Promoting international equity – new customers (positive).
- Equity trading weakened in second half (negative).
- Daily value traded has fallen (negative).
- Number of trades continues to rise (positive).

Investing in speed and capacity of trading platform (positive, keep monitoring – this may increase costs).

- Derivative volumes increased (positive).
- Information services increased (positive).
- Drop in professional terminals (negative).

Review of market trends

- Financial crisis, impact on GDP (negative).
- Re-equitisation, repaying of debt and increasing equity (positive).
- The central role of exchanges and efficient post trade services (positive).
- Benefiting from diversification (positive, keep monitoring – are the core services of the business still growing?).
- Technology, efficiency, new types of trading (positive, but may increase costs).
- Succeeding in an evolving industry (negative, may increase competition).

Business review

- Reduction in IPOs – significant drop (negative).
- Total number of companies down (negative).
- Equity order book value traded down in both Italy and London (negative).
- Mixed order book bargains (postive or negative).
- Lots of evidence of new products to target customers (positive, keep monitoring – were they successful?).
- Number of terminals down (negative).
- Number of post-trade contracts traded down (negative).

▶ ▦ Pre-settlement instructions down (negative).

▦ Amount under custody down (negative).

Financial highlights

▦ Revenue up (positive).

▦ Operating profit up (positive).

▦ Overall profit down due to goodwill impairment (negative).

▦ Earnings per share before goodwill impairment only slightly up (negative).

▦ Earnings per share down (negative).

▦ Cash generated from operations up (positive).

▦ Long-term credit rating improved (positive).

▦ Administrative expenses up considerably (negative, keep monitoring – linked to acquisition).

▦ Two goodwill impairments (negative).

▦ Net debt reduced (positive).

▦ Share buyback programme (investigate if in the interests of shareholders).

Principal risks and uncertainties

▦ Economic environment could reduce demand for services and for customers to meet obligations (negative).

▦ IPO activity may not return to record levels for some time (negative).

▦ Increased regulation expected (negative).

▦ Implementation of the Markets in Financial Instruments Directive (MiFID) may lead to low price competition (negative).

▦ Technology will lead to reduced costs of trading and lower fees (negative).

▦ Price pressure from customers (negative).

▦ Significant pressure from technology (negative).

▦ Strong brand name (positive).

▦ Capable of financing investment using internally generated funds (positive).

▦ If further capital is required, may not be able to raise it (negative).

▦ Partnership/joint ventures crucial to growth (positive, keep monitoring).

This is just a summary of the information available in the London Stock Exchange Group Annual Report. You can see that the lists above are far more comprehensive than a typical newspaper article, providing many areas to be considered before making an investment.

Questions

- Negatives mentioned in an annual report are significant – what is their impact?
- Identify the trends of the company – what direction will they go in over the next few years?
- Will the company win customers?
- Use each key statement as a question. For example, will the new technology and efficiency benefit the London Stock Exchange or the competitors? Will it make more profit or bring more cost?
- How does the business compare to its competitors?

The competitors named in the annual report are Deutsche Borse, Nasdaq, Euronext and the NYSE.

Annual reports don't tend to refer to the competition, the best way to understand the competition is to get a copy of each competitor's annual report. Selecting the right industry can make a significant difference to your investments and investigating the competition can provide further questions that may impact the performance of the London Stock Exchange Group. It is interesting to note that the London Stock Exchange faces competition from other providers including Turquoise and Chi-X. Basically, understanding the market share of the industry on all of the key revenues is the best way to identify the competition.

Classic management thinking says that competitive advantage can be achieved through cost advantage (the cheapest ability to deliver goods and services) or differentiation advantage (unique and difficult to replicate goods and services). The London Stock Exchange annual report has the goal of being the most efficient place for accessing capital. This goes beyond cost advantage. Whilst having the vast majority of British companies on a single market offers scale advantage in providing services, it also offers other types of competitive advantages. The market acts like a network, its value is increased for both new and existing customers as more people use the market, providing liquidity. This is a very powerful competitive advantage providing an explanation as to why this stock exchange has existed for more than 300 years.

Competitive advantages are rare, companies are always trying to capital-ise on market opportunities and therefore it is common to have many similar products or services. This impacts growth and profits, and leads to the high failure rate of companies. The vast majority of companies live a relatively short life, either failing, shrinking or being swallowed up by the competition. Less than a quarter of the companies listed on the original FTSE 100 25 years ago are still a part of it today. When analysing your stock, immediately presume the company has no advantages until you can prove otherwise.

Types of advantage

These can be any of the following:

- the lowest cost goods or services, often leading to scale and market share
- unique goods or services aimed at a specific customer within the market (e.g. luxury, special requirements)
- high switching costs, making it hard for customers to leave
- limiting competition by creating high barriers to entry or high barriers to success
- intangible assets (brands and patents are the most significant, but be careful not to overvalue them).

True competitive advantage lasts a decade, often longer than the latest must-have product, and is something that is more intrinsic to the company. When considering if your potential investment has a competitive advantage, con-sider whether the company would still have it in ten years' time.

Ask yourself:

- What is the competitive advantage?
- Will it last for more than ten years?
- How long will the competitive advantage last for?
- How competitive is the industry?

Annual reports will always contain evidence of competitive advantage. The financial accounts will show high product margins, high returns on capital employed, high returns on shareholder equity and strong profitability. These numbers, combined with evidence of a sustainable source of revenues, and how many and how vicious the competitors are in attacking any advantage, can be used to decide the strength of the competitive advantage.

The London Stock Exchange Group: competitive advantage (a quick look)

The London Stock Exchange demonstrates the advantages above, but these are all under threat from the competition.

Lowest cost goods or services

The Exchange is committed to price reduction, but the annual report does indicate that lower cost services are a threat. In the global market, the London Stock Exchange is not the biggest and therefore may lack the scale and market share to compete.

Unique goods and services

A number of services are unique to the Exchange, as is the information related to the Exchange. The annual report refers to product innovation as offering 'a wide range of products'. The core product is not unique and is offered by other exchanges.

High switching costs

Companies already on the Exchange would suffer from high switching costs and those using services like information and news are relatively tied into the service. However, a substantial quantity of turnover comes from raising new capital – these customers could consider other options.

High barriers to entry or high barriers to success

The industry is highly regulated, and the Exchange has a good brand name, offers a significant array of services, the benefit of a networked advantage and localisation of markets. There are definite barriers to entry and to success.

Intangible assets

These are the brand and the market itself, which are good intangible assets.

Five forces model of competitive advantage

Michael Porter developed an analytical framework for assessing the risks posed by competitors and their behaviours. This model can be used to provide a wider perspective on the industry. The more aggressive the threat posed by the five forces of competition, the higher the competitive advantage required by the company to be able to defend its profits. Whilst some speculators will be able to make profits from temporarily holding stocks for a short period of time, the rewards are greater by identifying companies that have distinct competitive advantages that they can maintain within their industry. If perfect competition exists, then all the companies in that industry will be unable to make profit.

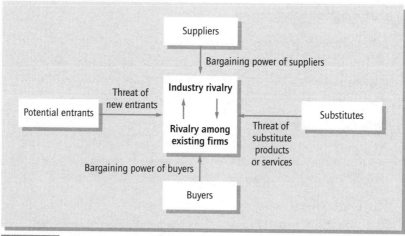

figure 8.1   The competitive elements

The London Stock Exchange Group: the competitive elements (a quick look)

Consider the following in conjunction with Figure 8.1.

Potential entrants

The globalisation of markets and new threats like Chi-X (mentioned on the Exchange's website) shows there is the potential to enter the core trading markets of the London Stock Exchange Group. However Chi-X makes limited profits and does not offer a full array of services (access to capital). The reliance upon the London Stock Exchange to continue to be the market that sets the price indicates that potential entrants have several barriers to overcome. Low price competition and strategic partnerships/alliances are raised as two key risks and these point to either new entrants or increased industry rivalry.

Buyers

The risks section of the annual report refers to buyers demanding lower prices. The London Stock Exchange depends on its large customers (other financial organisations) and again Turquoise (another start-up competitor) shows that the buyers can link together to force the London Stock Exchange to review its fee structure.

Suppliers

Not referred to within the risks section, so not a significant factor.

Industry rivalry

The NASDAQ failed takeover is not referred to in the Exchange's 2009 annual report, but is referred to in other investor relations information. This shows that rivalry among existing firms is increasing. Product innovation as referred to in the report is also a sign that there is competition to win customers. The industry rivalry is not as high as other sectors but global alliances and the dependence on them for growth shows that the large companies will be competing for smaller markets. Consolidation of the sector looks very likely as shown by the London Stock Exchange Group purchasing Borsa Italiana.

Substitutes

Whilst debt is an alternative way of raising capital, the key trend of deleveraging is mentioned in the report. The annual report refers to the need for markets more than ever and there is no real substitute to that need at this time.

Management

The board of directors makes significant decisions on behalf of the company and members are responsible for delivering sustainable shareholder value. Supported by professionally written gleaming résumés in the annual report and experience as demonstrated by their involvement often in more than one company, they are fundamental to the success of the company and the investment. Private investors have little opportunity to look directors directly in the eye to ensure they will make the right decisions and yet they can be the difference between a great investment and absolute failure.

Professional investment companies argue that the opportunity they have to visit management in person, ask the tough questions and receive guidance on profits, means their advice contains a considerable advantage over what the private investor can achieve. Competence and integrity are the key two attributes required to trust management. Judging this on the previous actions of the company is the best approach, and possibly more reliable than the words and promises being made to visiting analysts of professional companies.

The London Stock Exchange Group is excellent at providing clear communication about the business. (Whilst writing this chapter it has been easy to gather information from its website.) The company has also provided clear information about its business. Beyond the annual report, the company provides web-casts, presentations, interim reports, fee information, an enquiry service and information dating back over a decade. This shows its commitment to providing information. However there are key questions that are worth asking that cover areas like management remuneration and acting in the interests of shareholders.

Key questions: good signs

The answers to the following questions could be good signs for the investor:

- Has the company been buying back shares? Has this been in the best interests of the company (buying the shares below intrinsic value)?
- Does the company focus on core activities which have not varied over time?
- How has management dealt with problems in the past?
- Does the management have a conservative approach to debt and liquidity?
- Has the company consistently grown earnings and the rates of return (assets and equity)?
- How has the company allocated capital? Have acquisitions made sense and been successful for the company?
- Has the company got clear communication with its shareholders and has it always been to the highest standards of timeliness and clarity, including even to the smallest investors? How easy has it been for you to get the information you need from the annual report?
- Does the CEO own a significant stake in the company (including options)?

Key questions: bad signs

The answers to the following questions could be bad signs for the investor:

- Does the company continue to have write-offs?
- Is the chairman of the board and the chief executive the same person?
- Has the board engaged in significant related party transactions that cast doubt on its ability to act in the interests of all shareholders?
- Has the board agreed to a compensation structure that rewards management merely for being employed, rather than enhancing value for shareholders?
- Are there managers who pursue growth for growth's sake, irrespective of the value of that growth to the company?
- Are there any 'vanity' acquisitions, that don't represent a good return for shareholders (often involving using the stock of the company or significant debt)?
- Over the past three years, has the company given away more than 3% of shares annually as options?

The London Stock Exchange Group: management (a quick look)

Despite the excellent information provided by the London Stock Exchange, working through the above questions does highlight some concerns.

Buybacks

The share buyback programme has ended, according to the annual report, but the company purchased its own shares when it was trading at record highs during which time a takeover was a possiblity. This does not suggest the company was purchasing below the intrinsic value, but does not benefit long-term shareholders.

Acquisitions

The goodwill impairment indicates that the company may have overpaid for the Borsa Italiana. This was also announced during the period in which a takeover was a possibility, though as a merger it may have benefited shareholders by using stock worth above its intrinsic value rather than purchasing in cash.

Annual bonuses

Annual bonuses were paid despite minimal growth in earnings per share. The potential takeover temporarily boosted total shareholder return. This will have boosted returns for management.

> My concern would be around how well you felt management handled the potential NASDAQ takeover. Did they act in shareholders' interests? Were they valiant in defending shareholder value, or did they defend the company regardless of being offered considerably more than the shares are worth today? Time will tell, but as a potential investor you need to consider the impact of management very closely.

Financial accounts

If you want to understand a business, the financial statements are critical. The income statement summarises the performance of the company: did it make a profit over the period, did it improve its business compared to last year? The balance sheet shows you the financial health of the company – how much the company owns (assets, both value and type) and how much it owes in debts (liabilities), and difference between the two. The cash flow statement is arguably the most crucial, as cash acts as the lifeblood of a company. This will show you how much cash went into and out of a company during the period.

Income statement

Key questions to ask include:

- Are revenues increasing?
- How are revenues recognised (revenue recognition policy)? Has the company received the cash?
- Are gross profits showing the company can make a good markup on its sales?
- Are profits (operating and net income) increasing? What has an impact on profits? How does this increase compare to previous years?
- Are earnings per share increasing? How does this increase compare to previous years?

Balance sheet

Key questions to ask include:

Assets

- How much cash and short-term investments does the company have?

- How much do customers owe (accounts receivable)? Does the company have good credit control?
- Does the change in inventories present any problems?
- Does the company have any significant long-term investments? If so, does this present a risk?
- How much does the company spend on property, plant and equipment? Will this need to be replaced?
- Does the company have lots of goodwill (showing that it overpaid for previous aquisitions)?

Liabilities

- How much does the company owe in short term liabilities (this will impact cashflow)?
- How much does the company owe other companies? Obviously paying late is beneficial but the company must also be in a position to pay.
- How much does the company have in debt, can it afford to pay and will this impact shareholder returns? How does this compare to competitior debts?

Cashflow

- Does the company have free cashflow?
- How does cashflow vary from the profit and loss account? What is the reason behind these differences?
- How much cashflow is spent on capital expenditure?
- How is the company financing its activities? Is it dependent on raising capital?

Financial ratios

Investors use ratios to understand the relationships between the differing numbers offered by the three financial statements. These ratios help to make clear the performance and condition of the company, and also allow you to compare it to other companies. Trends and changes in the ratios on a year to year basis can provide historical context. The ratios can indicate if the company is getting worse (higher risk) or better (lower risk). There are four major types of ratios: efficiency, liquidity, leverage, and profitability. Not all of the ratios will be relevant to all companies, for example, the

London Stock Exchange Group does not really have inventory, additionally CCP numbers (related to their clearing business) have been excluded in most instances as these are less relevant to the running of the company. All accounts will have some anomalies.

Efficiency ratios

Efficiency ratios measure the effective use of assets and how well the company manages its liabilities.

Inventory turnover = cost of sales/average inventory

This measures how well the company manages its inventory. Too low and there are potential issues with sales. A higher inventory turnover is better.

This ratio is not relevant to the London Stock Exchange Group.

Accounts receivable turnover = revenue/average accounts receivable

This measures how effective the company is at receiving money from its customers. Too low and there are potential issues with collecting money, or being generous with credit. A higher receivable turnover is better.

For the London Stock Exchange we have £671m/£72.3m = 9.28. This is healthy and improving, though credit impairments have been rising.

Accounts payable turnover = cost of sales/average accounts payable

This measures how effective the company is at managing its own bills. Too high and there are potential issues with agreeing favourable terms with suppliers. A lower payable turnover is better.

For the London Stock Exchange we have: £332m/£41.2m = 8.05. This figure is less relevant for the London Stock Exchange.

Total asset turnover = revenue/average total assets

This measures how effective the company is in using its assets. Too low and there are potential issues with effective management of assets. A higher total asset turnover is better.

For the London Stock Exchange we have: £671m/£1943m (CCP figures excluded) = 34.5%. This figure is improving; the company is getting a good return on its assets.

Liquidity ratios

Liquidity ratios measure whether the company is able to reach its short-term obligations and continue operating. Even profitable companies go out of business and investors often fail to understand that the clues exist in these ratios.

Current ratio = current assets/current liabilities

This measures how the company can meet short-term liabilities with its short-term assets. A ratio of >1 shows the company should be able to meet its short-term liabilities.

For the London Stock Exchange we have £37,617m/£35,807m = 1.05. Figures here include the CCP numbers which balance out. The current ratio is only just above 1: this rises to 1.8 if you exclude CCP.

Quick ratio = (cash + accounts receivable + short-term or marketable securities)/(current liabilities)

This measures how the company can meet short-term liabilities with its most liquid assets (a tougher test).

A ratio of >1 shows the company should be able to meet its short-term liabilities with cash, equivalents and uncollected sales.

For the London Stock Exchange we have: £257m/£128m = 2. Figures here exclude the CCP numbers. The quick ratio is fine.

$$\text{Cash ratio} = (\text{cash} + \text{short-term or marketable securities})/$$
$$(\text{current liabilities})$$

This measures how the company can meet short-term liabilities with just cash (the toughest test).

A ratio of >1 shows the company should be able to meet its short-term liabilities with cash.

For the London Stock Exchange we have: £143m/£128m = 1.11. Figures here exclude the CCP numbers. Even on the toughest measure the company can cover short-term liabilities with cash.

Leverage ratios

Leverage ratios measure how much debt a company has on its balance sheet. It is sensible for most companies to use debt to improve the efficiency of the company, but it increases the risk to shareholders as those who are debt holders get first priority on the cash flow of the company.

$$\text{Debt/equity} = (\text{short-term debt} + \text{long-term debt})/\text{total equity}$$

This measures how much of the company is financed by debt compared to shareholders. Higher ratios indicate higher risk to shareholders. A lower debt/equity ratio is lower risk.

For the London Stock Exchange we have: £625.3m/£1053m = 59%. This looks reasonable.

$$\text{Interest coverage} = \text{operating income/interest expense}$$

This measures how the company can cover the cost of interest by using its income. Shareholders only benefit from free cash flow; debt costs money (interest). The closer the coverage is to 1, the more likely a company will have issues paying its interest. Higher interest coverage is better.

For the London Stock Exchange we have: £338.6m/£38m = 10.1. The interest cover is more than sufficient.

Profitability ratios

Profitability ratios measure how good the company is at running its business.

$$\text{Gross margin} = \text{gross profit/sales}$$

This measures how much the company keeps per sale, comparing the cost of producing or delivering the good/services to the price received. Higher margins are preferable but these can vary considerably from company to company. Compare the gross margin to previous years to identify a trend.

This is not relevant to the London Stock Exchange Group as operating margin is used instead.

$$\text{Operating margin} = \text{operating income or loss/sales}$$

This measures how much profit/loss per sale the company makes including all operating costs. Higher margins are preferable but these can vary considerably from company to company. Compare the operating margin to previous years to identify a trend.

For the London Stock Exchange we have: £338.6m/£671.4m = 50.4%. This is a very healthy margin, and margins have also been improving from previous years. The company is able to leverage its assets.

$$\text{Net margin} = \text{net income or loss/sales}$$

This measures how much profit/loss per sale the company makes including all operating costs. Higher margins are preferable but these can vary considerably from company to company. Compare the net margin to previous years to identify a trend.

For the London Stock Exchange we have: £208m/£671.4m = 30.9%. A very healthy margin, which has also been improving from previous years. The company is able to leverage its assets.

Free cash flow margin = free cashflow/sales

This measures how much revenue can be turned into free cashflow. Shareholders benefit from free cashflow and the higher the better. Compare this margin to previous years to identify a trend.

For the London Stock Exchange we have: £205m/£671.4m = 30.5%. An excellent free cashflow figure.

Return on assets = net income + interest expense/average total assets

This measures the ability to turn assets into profits.

For the London Stock Exchange we have: £208m + £38m/£1943m (CCP figures excluded) = 12.6%. The number is quite low considering the high margins. The purchased intangible assets arising on consolidation represent customer relationships, brands, software and licences relating to Borsa Italiana and EDX. These intangible assets have reduced the return on total assets.

Return on equity = net income/average shareholders' equity

This measures the ability to turn assets into profits and can be improved, often by funding coming from sustainable debt.

For the London Stock Exchange we have: £208m/£1053m = 19.7%. The retained profit/loss is negative, meaning the group has recorded losses in the past. Instead, in the present year, the company announced significant losses connected to the Borsa Italiana. The return is not as strong as you would expect considering the other strong measures.

Company valuation

The London Stock Exchange Group Plc is a great company by most measures, but that does not make it a great investment. All the information we have produced is in the public domain and even for the smallest company is calculated by both professionals and private investors. Identifying great companies is a key part of investment, but the vast majority will also have a share price that reflects the quality of the company. The aim is to identify great companies that are available at a reasonable price. This concept of reasonable price is important, as finding great companies below their book value (current value of assets minus liabilities) as suggested by Benjamin Graham identifies few opportunities. There will, however, be several opportunities to purchase great companies at 20–30% below a fair discounted cash flow value and occasionally as much as 50% below. With the benefits of compounding, these can become great investments. Even companies with the highest sales, the highest margins and/or a world changing product are eventually brought down to earth when sales and growth slow and the share price reflects the future potential of the company. Overpay for this potential and this can have a significant effect on your investment performance.

There are several different methods for valuing a company, one of the most popular is the price/earnings (PE) ratio. However some of the best value investments have had high PEs and some of the worst, low PEs. Whilst it is preferable to pay a lower price for earnings, the current calculated PE does not include any information on the future. A high PE may just be reflective of the strong potential of a company. These ratios also have to be compared to other companies and the market to give an indication of expectation.

Buying shares is buying a small part of a business, to value it we need to understand the expectation of profit and growth in the future. The trend picture that has been built from the annual report is key to understanding this expectation. The future is only easy to predict with hindsight and this explains why we want to identify companies below a fair value – this reduces the risk of our investment.

Shareholders benefit from the cashflow of the company. Companies either continue to invest this for higher returns or pay the cashflow to shareholders in the form of dividends. Shares are only worth what can be paid to shareholders in dividends, the further away in time the dividend the less that dividend is worth. You can then compare the share price of the company to these discounted cashflows to determine whether the company offers value. Calculating and estimating the future cashflows of a company requires more time and effort, and this explains why it is not a popular method. However the information it provides is one of the most valuable methods that exists in investing.

Predicting

Predicting future trends of the company and turning this into a financial picture is difficult. To be able to estimate the expected cashflow of the company we have to make assumptions regarding the revenue growth rate, net operating profit margin, income tax rate, required investment and incremental working capital. The most important is predicting the future sales of the company and the profit margins that will be achieved from those sales. Competitive advantages are attacked over time, so it is not as simple as calculating the current growth and current profit margins as these are likely to reduce over time.

Sales prediction is driven by the needs of the customer: consider the opportunities for new products, customers buying more of the same or an increasing supply of new customers. These can all lead to increasing sales as opposed to businesses that sell their product only once to the customer. Examine the trend of current sales and try to identify where the customers of the future will come from. Will they have a choice to purchase elsewhere or are they tied into the company?

Profit margins will be driven by the costs the company incurs delivering the goods/service and the ability to pass those costs onto the customer should they be rising. Has the company been able to improve its margins over a period of time? What in the past has impacted them? Are the costs of the company mainly fixed, meaning it can improve its margins if it is able to achieve higher sales?

Discounting cashflow

Once the free cashflow of the company has been estimated, it is then necessary to discount that cashflow to allow for the ravages of time as cash tomorrow is worth less than cash today. This method is used widely in investment finance, project appraisal and corporate financial management to calculate the value of future cashflows in today's money using a discount rate.

The discount rate used should be the cost of capital for the company (the weighted average cost of capital). This will vary from company to company and allows for the return expected by shareholders and debtholders. This is quite crucial as it means companies that are capable of producing steady cashflows and are stable (typically larger) companies will have a lower cost of capital. Whereas new companies, those with no cashflows to date, will have a higher cost of capital. This has the impact of making cashflows from riskier companies less valuable, and therefore stable companies often appear to be expensive in comparison when using measures like PE. This cost of capital changes over time and has a large impact on the final value assigned to the company, so it is worth keeping it under review.

The weighted average cost of capital (WACC) can be calculated using numbers from the annual report with the exception of the cost of equity (which relies on some external numbers).

$$\text{Weighted average cost of capital} = (\text{percentage of debt} \times \text{cost of debt}) + (\text{percentage of equity} \times \text{cost of equity})$$

The percentage of debt/equity can be calculated using the leverage ratio above, and the cost of debt figure can be obtained by calculating the interest payable on bank and other borrowings compared to the total debt figure. The cost of equity figure is more complex as this relies on three elements that are part of the capital asset pricing model.

$$\text{Cost of equity} = \text{the risk free rate} + (\text{the market risk premium} \times \text{the company's beta})$$

The risk free rate is the return you expect from very low-risk investments, like government bonds (currently 3.2%). The market risk premium can be calculated by comparing the return on shares versus the return on government bonds which is approximately 5.5% a year. The current beta of the London Stock Exchange is 1.46, and this number is on most financial websites. The typical weighted average cost of capital will be 8–14%.

For the London Stock Exchange, the WACC is

$$(31\%)(6.4\%) + (59\%)(3.2 + (5.5 \times 1.46)) = 8.6\%$$

The predicted free cashflow can now be turned into a present value of cashflow figure as shown above and using the equation below.

$$\text{Present value of cashflow in year N} = \text{CF at year N} \times (1/\text{WACC}^y)$$

where CF = cashflow, WACC = weighted average cost of capital, and y = number of years in the future.

The valuation

The London Stock Exchange cashflow over the next ten years is worth £1314m based on the assumptions around growth, operating profit and free cashflow. It is not feasible to project a company's future cash out to infinity, year by year. I have predicted over the course of ten years, but if you are unsure about the likely growth of the company, then you can choose to predict a lower number of years. The London Stock Exchange has produced revenues for over 200 years and will probably continue to generate profits for a long time. It is necessary to place a value – called a perpetuity value – upon these future cashflows.

$$\text{Perpetuity value} = (CF_y \times (1 + COE))/R - COE$$

where CF_y = cashflow in the last individual year estimated, g = long-term growth rate (typically the growth of the economy, 2.5%), COE = cost of equity.

A conservative approach to perpetuity value is best, even with the strongest of companies, as we are predicting far into the distant future. Growth rates are calculated using the average growth in GDP rather than based on the company itself, and instead of using the weighted cost of capital, use the cost of equity part of the formula. The less certain you are of predicting future cashflow, the more you should be using perpetuity value as a conservative approach to valuation. If a company is at extreme risk of not surviving, you should be wary of using perpetuity value. Hopefully those companies have already been excluded from carrying out research.

The London Stock Exchange perpetuity value is

$$(£265m \times (1 + 0.025))/(0.1123 - 0.03) = £3292m$$

This perpetuity value also needs to be discounted to the present value.

The London Stock Exchange Net Present Perpetuity Value is

$$3292m \times (1/1.123^{10}) = £1031m$$

The two cashflow numbers are added together to give a discounted cash-flow value for the company.

The London Stock Exchange discount cashflow value is

$$£1314m \text{ (years 1–10)} + £1031m \text{ (perpetuity)} = £2345m$$

By dividing this against the number of shares in issue (271m), we have a valuation for the company per share.

The London Stock Exchange discount cashflow value per share = £8.65 per share.

Final assessment

Predicting cashflows across time, making assumptions around the competitive position of the company and dealing with the vast amounts of information is no easy exercise. It is unlikely that events will happen the way that you expect. Significant changes will happen to the company and to the industry which may benefit or harm the company's prospects. With hindsight you will be able to see the flaws of your analysis – both the information you didn't consider and the information that at the time didn't exist.

The annual report tells a story in great detail. You will learn more than you ever knew about the company. By spending time working through the report, you will come to learn about the stock. As an investor you now have the information to decide how good your initial story was and to place a level of confidence in the analysis you have completed to support the idea of investing.

Key questions

You need to ask the following questions:

- How predictable are the sales?
- Will the company be able to maintain or improve the operating margins?
- Will the company be able to manage its level of debt?

■ What specific event in the future could radically change the company's value (up and down)?

■ How much confidence do you have in the assumptions you have made to support the discounted cashflow value per share?

Benjamin Graham and David Dodd came up with the concept of purchasing a share with a 'margin of safety' in their seminal 1934 book, *Security Analysis*. Graham maintained that for investors the margin of safety is always dependent on the price paid. It is of course beneficial to maximise the margin of safety for any investment but clearly the margin of safety required for a great company, in which we have high levels of confidence based on our research, needs to be lower than a company where the research has indicated concerns.

Typical levels of confidence and required margin of safety

High level of confidence – 20% discount to intrinsic value
Medium level of confidence – 30% discount to intrinsic value
Low level of confidence – 50% discount to intrinsic value
Very low level of confidence – 60%–80% discount to intrinsic value

Researching the annual report and building a discount cashflow formula is a complex way of valuing a company, but it allows an investor to include future assumptions around growth, profit margins and the risks faced by the company. The knowledge gained from completing the process is worth the effort. The rigour of the exercise will improve your investment decisions through a well considered and cautious approach built around the only thing investors can benefit from, free cashflow.

9

Shooting stars
John Mulligan

The challenge of hunting down decently priced, fast growing quality stocks is notoriously tricky as we discovered in our earlier chapter on GARP strategies. There are a great many different approaches to finding these elusive quality stocks and in our experience very few are either tested in real live portfolios or easy to copy if you're a private investor here in the UK. In my experience one approach stands out – it's called the STAR system and it's been developed by British economist and private investor John Mulligan. He's been running his system live for a number of difficult years now and as you'll discover in this chapter, so far, it's survived and prospered. In this chapter John spells out the thinking behind his strategy and looks at how it's worked over the past decade.

Background

The Share Tracking and Ranking (STAR) system of equity portfolio selection and management are focused on screening a large universe of quoted shares and selecting those that exhibit the potential for rapid earnings growth while also possessing a relatively low valuation.

The stimulus for creating and developing the STAR methods of screening shares for longer-term growth emanated from my own personal frustration with trying to create a logically constructed portfolio of leading UK shares as a private investor.

Prior to spending some 20 years as a development economist overseas I had worked for some ten years as an analyst and fund manager in the City of London in the late 1960s. At that time equity analysis and the production of detailed estimates regarding future sales, profits and earnings of companies whose shares were listed on the London Stock Exchange was really in its infancy. I think it is probably fair to say that at that time many of the investment decisions made by many investors were still based as much on rumour, hunch and indeed what is now generally termed inside information as on serious impartial analysis.

However, those working for the bigger investment institutions were able to tap into the growing database of both published and private research on larger companies. During the last decades of the 20th century the increasing importance of London as a global financial centre was greatly stimulated by its opening up as a result of the 'Big Bang' in the late 1980s. Sell-side analysis produced by the teams of highly paid analysts employed by the large brokerages and banks improved in quality and quantity and enabled professional institutional investment managers to improve their judgement relating to the selection of individual securities comprising their equity portfolios.

Despite the apparent improvement in data analysis available to the larger institutional investors it seemed to me that most private investors, in the 1980s, were poorly served in terms of access to information that would enable them to create and manage their own portfolios. Partly because of the paucity of quality share data and partly because I wished to manage my own investments in order to reduce management costs I decided to see if I could create a mechanical method that would enable me to manage my own share portfolio using an approach that would not be too time consuming, that would be objective and would not require me to make endless subjective decisions on specific shares.

Creating and testing the methodology

Intuitively I felt that I would create attractive long-term value by building up a portfolio of shares that were relatively lowly priced but whose growth potential seemed to be above average. As there was no way that I could personally analyse the earnings potential of all the 300 or so larger companies listed on the London Stock Exchange I had to find an external source for this information. In this I was lucky in that I was able to tap some of my old contacts and ask them to get hold of past copies of monthly equity research reports from three leading City of London brokers at that time.

Armed with piles of monthly dividend and earnings forecasts going back many years I then set about tabulating monthly prices and earnings estimates for some 300 of the largest quoted companies over a ten-year period in order to see if there was any correlation between forecasts and subsequent share price performance.

The results shown in the tables and charts in this chapter are based mainly on estimates sourced from brokers James Capel's (now HSBC) monthly Red Book but I also used forecasts from a number of other brokerage sources in order to test a range of methods of share selection for their longer-term effectiveness.

The basic idea was to evaluate a range of formulae in order to test their effectiveness in selecting share portfolios which exhibit some consistency in out performing the main market indices. More specifically the objective was to generate, over the longer term, greater capital growth and higher incomes than that produced by the UK equity market as a whole. In essence the work involved developing and testing simple methodologies which objectively ranked shares according to predetermined criteria. These were effectively quantitative analysis techniques which used dividend and earnings estimates derived from the sources already mentioned.

Between 1986 and 1994, up to 300 of the larger companies quoted on the London Stock Exchange, with a market capitalisation greater than £250m at start of each year, were ranked according to nine different sets of criteria. The results, in terms of annual price change, were divided into groups of 20 shares which, for ease of presentation, are referred to as deciles in the accompanying tables.

The analysis comprised two stages. The first involved the testing of a number of different combinations of equations in terms of their overall consistency in ranking shares according to their future price performance and income paying abilities. The second stage concentrated on testing actual share selections after introducing a number of additional share selection filters.

The alternative selection methods

The analysis undertaken some 15 years ago tested a number of equations that related current share prices to various combinations of reported and forecast dividends and earnings. No less than nine different permutations were rigorously analysed and the resultant rankings from each version compared with the subsequent annual share price performance in order to assess the correlation of each equation with average share price gains during the following year.

- Both **Versions A and B** involved ranking by share price multiples derived from dividends weighted according to forecast future growth in earnings.

- **Version C** produced a ranking relating price to unweighted existing and future dividends.

- **Version D** ranked shares according to the multiple obtained by dividing the current share price by the sum of all unweighted future dividends and earnings.

- **Version E** ordered shares by current unweighted dividend together with earnings weighted by projected growth over the next two years.

- **Version F** ranked according to projected earnings per share two years hence after weighting for growth in the intervening period.

- **Version G** produced a ranking list derived from the multiple of the current share price divided by the current earnings and also the current earnings weighted by estimated annual earnings growth over each of the next two years.

- **Versions H and J** were somewhat different in that future estimates of earnings growth were related to future price earnings and dividend ratios, effectively variations on price earnings growth (PEG) factors. They were intended as the first stage in a two-stage process aimed primarily at capital growth share selection whereas the objective of the other versions combined both income generation and capital growth. The procedure for Versions H and J was to rank all shares according to their projected average annual growth in earnings over the next two-years and then to select shares according to predetermined criteria in each of the next two years.

The analysis

Stage one: comparative results from testing the basic ranking procedures

The first stage in the analysis was to determine the most promising overall result from among the various methods of ranking tested. Results were considered not only in terms of the cumulative capital outperformance by the top deciles but also by constancy of slope as determined by least squares regression analysis. An associated objective was to reduce inter-year volatility, as measured by the percentage divergence from the mean index performance in each period. A further aim was a low level of dispersion in results by each decile group from the trend predicted by regression analysis.

The summarised results, shown in Table 9.1 cover the calendar years 1986 to 1994 inclusive. They show the average annual percentage increase, over the nine-year period, achieved by each decile group (normally comprising 20 shares). These results relate to each of the nine versions mentioned above.

The initial valuation work was undertaken in order to generate a methodology that would prove useful for providing larger institutional portfolio managers with a low cost tool for the management of larger investment portfolios. The essence of the search was for a tested methodology that could produce a broadly consistent annual outperformance over the top three or four decile groups, with an acceptably small number of underperforming years.

The main objective for smaller private portfolios was of course somewhat different. In this case the search was for the top decile performance with the most consistently promising results. These were obtained from Version A (the original version tested), Version B (the version that was subsequently used in the first monthly high-income bulletins produced by brokers Sharelink) as well as Versions E and F. The best cumulative results, over the whole period, for the top three and four decile groupings were generated by Versions B, E and F, as can be seen in Table 9.1 (overleaf).

The average annual out performance, against the FTA All Share Index, by grouping, indicated a similar result with the top four deciles selected by Version B producing an average annual index out performance of 3.2% in

table 9.1 Average annual decile performance for each version relative to total field: 1986 to 1994 (percentage performance relative to all shares analysed)

Version	Top decile	Top two deciles	Top three deciles	Top four deciles
A	7.4	2.1	1.7	1.5
B	6.2	3.7	3.4	2.9
C	2.1	0.2	0.5	0.8
D	2.4	1.3	2.5	2.6
E	5.3	5.0	4.5	3.7
F	8.4	5.2	4.0	3.2
G	1.1	1.9	3.1	3.3
H	−1.3	−0.1	0.2	0.7
J	−2.3	−0.2	0.4	0.3

the nine years from 1986. The results from Versions E (4.1%) and F (3.5%) were even more impressive especially given the relative consistency of the regression line through all the decile groups.

Volatility

There are of course a number of ways in which volatility can be measured. In the first instance the divergence of each version's decile grouping from its predicted position, in terms of annual capital growth, was assessed using regression analysis. The results of this work were analysed statistically and graphically. A further measure studied was the annual variance from the mean of each of the top four decile groupings selected by each version.

Stage two: comparative performance of small portfolio selections

This required the careful evaluation of the annual performance of portfolios selected from those versions with the most promising results. Table 9.2 and Figure 9.1 summarise the simulated results from ten share portfolios established at the start of each year and selected from the ranking lists derived from the relevant ranking versions described above.

| table 9.2 | Initial results from selected share ranking methods |

Indicative annual capital appreciation percentage – ten share portfolios

	1986	1987	1988	1989	1990	1991	1992	1993	1994	Cumulative value
FTA ASI	22	7	6	30	−16	17	15	23	−10	223
Version A	43	18	9	35	−20	24	27	28	−3	383
Version B	41	21	11	18	−23	25	12	79	1	444
Version H	60	22	11	32	−17	50	28	50	2	698

Notes: Dates for each year as per J Capel Red Book January issue. Versions A and B are unscreened.

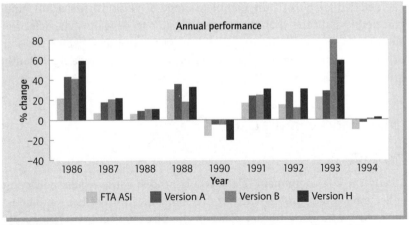

| figure 9.1 | Indicative annual capital appreciation: Versions A, B and H |

Conclusions derived from the initial testing phase

Share selection for smaller portfolios

Although Versions E and F appeared to give the closest overall correlation between ranking list order and annual capital appreciation the actual ten share portfolio selections derived from the ranking lists of Versions A, B and H have tended to provide the better final result – albeit with a possible increase in inter-year volatility. Version B, which is the current high income version in use, has the added advantage of attaching greater weight to existing income and is therefore more appropriate for the selection of income portfolios. As the capital performance figures do not include income the results from the income oriented ranking versions tend to understate their total out performance. The average yearly difference in gross running yield between Version B ten share selections and Version H capital growth ten share selections over the nine-year period was approximately 250 basis points – a not insignificant additional benefit.

The reason that the Version H ten share portfolio results, summarised in Table 9.2, are much better than would be expected from the first stage ranking data is that the second stage analysis adds an extremely effective filtering process which eliminates a large number of shares from the initial ranking.

Share selection for larger portfolios and institutional investors

The detailed analysis of the complete range of versions over a full nine-year period indicates that it has been possible to develop share selection methods, based on the recurrent analysis of forecast data, which are able to generate share selections that outperform the indices over a significantly wide field.

How STAR works in practice

Sourcing data

Clearly the key component of the whole process is the regular collection of accurate data regarding each of the companies whose shares are being analysed. In the early testing phase of the STAR project I was able to use the estimates supplied directly from the research departments of several leading brokers. At that stage, in the mid- to late-1980s and early-1990s, this proved to be a most efficient and cost effective way of sourcing data. However, as the project expanded this route became impractical and it was necessary to switch to published sources such as the Estimate Directory, now no longer published. More recently it has become possible to use the internet for updating the relevant metrics with Hemscott and Company (www.hemscott.com) being useful sources for UK company information and Reuters (www.reuters.co.uk) and Morningstar (www.morningstar.co.uk) helpful for both US and global corporate information.

Past performance in selecting and managing share portfolios

One of the problems with investment is that fashion, or perhaps more accurately emotion, plays such a big part in shaping the hopes and fears and
thus the actions of most investors. There are therefore bound to be periods
when an objective share selection and management approach is going to
be wrong-footed. It is partly for this reason that I believe the long-term
record of the STAR approach is so vital. As the STAR share screening process
is essentially based on value investing it obviously becomes less effective
in periods when this approach is out of favour. I believe that the 20-year
period over which I have been analysing the STAR growth selections gives
a fair impression of the usefulness of this basic methodology. Table 9.3
(overleaf) and Figure 9.2 record the yearly gains and losses achieved by the
nominal investment of £1000 in each of the ten shares selected for growth
in early January each year.

These selections were based on the middle market prices ruling as at the
close of business on the relevant day with a limited number of switches
signalled during most years. The aim of the exercise was to show how the
method compared with that of the wider market as represented by the FT
All Share index. Although dealing costs were excluded so were dividends.
The final column in the table therefore indicates the stock picking ability
of the STAR process rather than a total compounded return over the period.

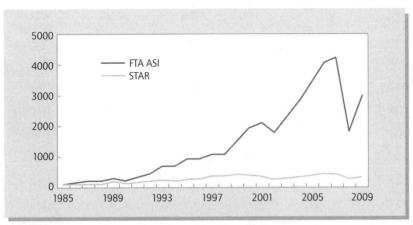

figure 9.2　STAR ten growth selections 1985–2009

table 9.3 STAR ten growth share results 1985–2009

Annual gains/losses (%)			Cumulative gains/losses (%)		
Year	FTA ASI	STAR	Year	FTA ASI	STAR
1985			1985	100	100
1986	22	60	1986	122	160
1987	7	22	1987	131	195
1988	6	11	1988	138	217
1989	30	32	1989	180	286
1990	−16	−17	1990	151	237
1991	17	50	1991	177	356
1992	15	28	1992	203	456
1993	23	50	1993	250	684
1994	−10	2	1994	225	697
1995	18	32	1995	266	918
1996	9	2	1996	291	936
1997	26	17	1997	365	1092
1998	5	−1	1998	383	1081
1999	12	42	1999	431	1532
2000	−4	27	2000	413	1941
2001	−14	9	2001	355	2108
2002	−25	−16	2002	266	1762
2003	15	31	2003	306	2310
2004	9	20	2004	333	2777
2005	20	25	2005	398	3463
2006	13	17	2006	449	4062
2007	−2	−1	2007	418	4239
2008	−33	−57	2008	280	1823
2009	11	63	2009	311	2971

Note: Results for 2009 are to mid-September 2009.

Where it can be used and where it can't

As the STAR screening methods work best when the earnings projections for each company covered are sourced from more than one independent analytical team, and preferably from at least half a dozen different unbiased sources, the methods work best in markets and sectors that are well covered by the top teams of stock and share analysts. Thus, the STAR screening methods, unsurprisingly, appear to deliver the best results in larger international equity markets when used to regularly rank the largest and best researched companies in the respective markets.

Strengths and weaknesses

Strengths

One of the main strengths of the STAR approach is its objectivity. The very act of setting out strict criteria by which shares are selected for purchase and sale removes one of the main obstacles to successful investing, namely the element of human emotion.

Another positive feature is the enforced spreading of risk, as a feature of this form of objective share selection is that no fewer than ten shares should be held in any given portfolio and no more than two shares in any ten share list should be in a single sector of the market.

A further factor in support of this approach is that the consensus estimates represent the collective knowledge of most of the leading analysts who cover each of the companies. In this context it is relevant to remember that it is not the analysts' buy and sell advice that is being employed but rather their estimates regarding the future sales, profits and earnings for each company covered. My original contention was that even though they frequently get their projections wrong they should on balance get it right more often than wrong.

This brings me to the results of a year's joint collaboration with the *Financial Times* undertaken in 2004 to 2005. This exercise, which was written up by Philip Coggan,[1] was designed to analyse the analysts over a period of a year. Briefly, I took a sample of the ten largest brokerages and listed their profits and earnings forecasts for approximately 100 leading companies as at January 2004. I also constructed portfolio selections of ten and 20 shares

---

[1] Coggan, P. (2003) 'A mechanical approach', *Financial Times*, 25 October.

derived from each broker's original forecasts and constructed a total of 18 lists. One broker was excluded because its initial company cover was not wide enough. By January 2005 every portfolio except one had beaten the market substantially and even the poorer performer had slightly exceeded the 9% gain on the FT All Share Index over the same period.

Weaknesses

Clearly this process doesn't always work. The element of objectivity that appeals to me in running my own portfolio will not appeal to those who have time for detailed company research and who enjoy selecting and monitoring their share investments. Equity investment is an activity that will repay time spent in careful research and analysis and successful individual investors should be able to beat STAR provided that they are able to maintain their interest and keep a close eye on every investment.

There are times, such as the recessionary period following the 2007 credit crunch when investment priorities switch to defence mode and at such times of risk aversion even growth at a reasonable price, the essence of the STAR approach, becomes too aggressive a strategy for many people.

It must be remembered that most of the estimates are derived from analysts working for the sales side of the stockbroking business and although there are supposed to be Chinese walls between the analysts and the sales teams there is always the danger of a sell side bias in estimates sourced from brokers.

A further element of weakness in using consensus estimates as a source of basic data is that there is often a time lag between production of the estimate and its publication. This delay can mean that shares have either moved up or down before the STAR signals can be put into action.

More information and background to the STAR screening methods may be found at www.whitechurch.co.uk/star.html.

10

The ShareMaestro system
Glenn Martin

In the next chapter we'll look at how you can use different systems
and software to help you select shares and run a screen. These
quantitative-based systems are essentially blind to actual strategies and
methodologies – they don't attempt to suggest a particular strategy
or prioritise a particular bunch of measures. For many investors that
absence of 'thought' so to speak is fine – they apply their own ideas to
the screening process. Yet in my experience some of the most interesting
systems are those that combine some empirically tested strategies
with actual screening systems – these products can actually tell you
precisely what to buy and when! One such system aimed at British
private investors is ShareMaestro developed by Glenn Martin. Like John
Mulligan's STAR system from the chapter before it's born out of personal
experience – even frustration – with the information and advice offered
to the private investor. It's a much more comprehensive system than
Mulligan's and in our experience incredibly useful in its predictive powers.
We've asked Glenn to explain the background to the system and how it
can be used in practice.

Introduction

Stock markets are inefficient. Prices are driven by supply and demand,
which in turn are driven by the human emotions of fear and greed. This is
what leads to the development of bubbles and to the subsequent bursting
of bubbles, when panic forces prices too low.

As markets are inefficient, it follows that most of the time share prices are either too expensive or too cheap. But how can you tell which is which? This is where ShareMaestro is an invaluable tool. The ShareMaestro software dispassionately calculates the real values of UK shares from the fundamental factors which determine these values.

The inefficiency of stockmarkets creates great profit opportunities for investors. If markets were efficient, share prices would always represent fair value and prices would only change in line with changes to the underlying fundamental value factors. In short, markets would be far less volatile and there would be less scope for making money.

The conception and birth of ShareMaestro

As a private investor, I became increasingly disillusioned with the simplistic market valuation approaches adopted by investment analysts. For example, a common method is to value equities by the prospective PE ratio (current price per share divided by the expected earnings per share for the current financial year). There are at least two fundamental errors in this approach:

1 The reciprocal of the PE ratio is the earnings yield (earnings per share divided by price per share). This is the return which the investor receives from holding the share. It comprises the dividend and the earnings retained in the company after paying the dividend. It is a major error to judge the prospective earnings yield in isolation from the economic environment. In the same way that you will expect a higher cash interest rate in times of high inflation, so you will expect a higher earnings yield in times of high inflation. So the concept of a universally good PE ratio is false.

2 A high earnings yield for the current financial year is of little value if it crashes in subsequent years. Markets always look forward beyond the current year.

Whilst I was Chief Operating Officer for a Swedish equity derivatives firm in 1994, I studied the Nobel prize winning Black-Scholes system. This system values equity options (options to buy or sell equities at a set price) from both the characteristics of the underlying equities and from the economic and market environment.

On return from Sweden, I developed my own system for valuing cash equities. Like Black-Scholes, this system calculates the value of cash equities from the characteristics of the equities *and* from economic and market factors. Having seen ShareMaestro valuations repeatedly proven reliable, often against the forecasts from the City pundits, I decided to launch the system for use by the serious private UK investor. This is a key point. The system was not retro-fitted to match historical data. It was developed from first principles and repeatedly found to work. So in 2007 ShareMaestro was born.

The financial press have given ShareMaestro a very positive reception. For example, in the business section of the *Daily Telegraph*, Tom Stevenson said that ShareMaestro 'ticks all the right boxes in my holy grail quest'.[1] Dominic Picarda of the *Investors Chronicle* described ShareMaestro as 'a system with a great record of correctly valuing the FTSE and its constituent shares'.[2]

ShareMaestro's track record

In order not to waste the reader's time assessing a system which does not work, this section provides clear evidence to show that it does work. This information is current at the time of writing (end August 2009). The up-to-date track record is available from www.sharemaestro.co.uk.

FTSE 100

ShareMaestro FTSE 100 valuations have been produced for every single trading day since the start of the index in 1984. A valuation of 100% represents fair value. Using the standard FTSE 100 valuation signals of 105% to buy and 95% to sell:

- A ShareMaestro buy signal has always delivered a profit on the subsequent sell signal.
- The FTSE 100 capital growth has been on average 23 times greater during ShareMaestro's signalled investment periods than at other times (16.6% p.a. vs. 0.7% p.a.).
- ShareMaestro correctly signalled both the huge bubble at the start of this century and the major buying opportunity when the FTSE 100 subsequently crashed to this century's low of 3287, on 12 March 2003 (see later for more detail).

---

[1] www.sharemaestro.co.uk
[2] www.sharemaestro.co.uk

Share selections

Since 2006, ShareMaestro has selected 13 best-value and worst-value share portfolios. Most of these selections have been published in the financial press (e.g. the *Investors Chronicle*). All can be independently verified.

In addition to using the ShareMaestro proprietary calculation engine, these selections use consensus broker forecasts for dividend and earnings growth. Each best-value portfolio has out performed the market and each worst-value portfolio has under-performed the market, often by substantial amounts. The probability of this 100% success rate occurring by chance is less than 1 in 8000 ($\frac{1}{2}^{13}$).

Fund management

Two model ShareMaestro funds have been developed. They use the standard ShareMaestro FTSE 100 buy/sell signals, together with basic risk controls, to switch between investment in cash and in the FTSE 100 or in FTSE 100 covered call warrants.

In the ten years to 30 June 2009:

- The ShareMaestro FTSE 100 Fund delivered a ten-year return of 6.0% p.a. compared with a negative return of –1.9% p.a. from a typical FTSE 100 tracker fund.

- The ShareMaestro FTSE 100 Covered Warrant Fund delivered a ten-year return of 17.1% p.a. compared with the upper quartile threshold of 5.9% p.a. (and a median return of just 0.5% p.a.) from all UK equity funds. Since 1984, this ShareMaestro fund has delivered a stellar return of 16.3% p.a. No comparative figures are available for other funds going back to 1984.

- Both ShareMaestro funds delivered consistent upper quartile performance over one, three, five and ten years. *Each fund achieved a higher average period return than all other UK equity funds.* The average return of these four periods was 4.7% p.a. for the ShareMaestro FTSE 100 Fund and 14.9% for the ShareMaestro FTSE 100 Covered Warrants Fund. By comparison, average return for these four periods was:

  - just 3% p.a. for the best-performing UK Equity fund (Schroder Recovery A)

  - –5.8% p.a. (i.e. negative) for the median UK Equity fund

  - –6.6% p.a. (i.e. negative) for the typical FTSE 100 Tracker fund.

The above ShareMaestro fund returns assume management fees of 1.5% p.a., which would not be payable by private investors who manage their own funds. It shows the immense power of ShareMaestro that a simple strategy of switching between cash and FTSE 100 investment, according to ShareMaestro's FTSE 100 investment signals, can produce a better consistent performance than the best stock-picking talent in the huge UK fund management industry.

How ShareMaestro works

When you invest in a share (or index) your return on investment will come from two sources:

- the price at which you sell
- the dividends which you receive while holding the share.

ShareMaestro uses a five-year investment period to allow sufficient time for growth companies to grow and for bubbles to burst. This period has proved consistently reliable for valuing UK equities.

Stockmarkets always look forwards rather than backwards. Shares are valued according to future prospects rather than on the basis of past performance; 'the stock market is a forward-looking discounting mechanism'.[3]

ShareMaestro calculates the current value of a share through applying logical calculations to the fundamental factors which determine that value. ShareMaestro:

- calculates the future price of the share (in five years' time)
- adds the accumulated value of post-tax reinvested dividends to this price to determine the future value of the investment
- discounts the future value of the investment by the risk premium, which compensates for the greater risk of holding equities instead of virtually risk-free gilts
- discounts the resulting risk-adjusted future value back to today's value using, as a discount rate, the current return on a five-year gilt (if held to redemption)
- compares the resulting current value of the share to the current market price to see if the price represents good or bad value.

[3] Thompson, S. (2008) *20 Hard and Fast Rules to Help You Beat the Stock Market*, Pearson Education Ltd.

ShareMaestro input values

The ShareMaestro input values are the fundamental factors which determine a share's value in relation to its current market price. There are two modules of ShareMaestro – one for the FTSE 100 and one for individual shares. A couple of extra input values are required to value an individual share. All the factual input values are freely available on the internet.

The input values, and their impact, *in isolation*, on the FTSE 100/share valuation are briefly described below. More detail is available from the User Manual, which is free to download from the ShareMaestro website.

Factual input values

FTSE 100/share price

An increase in the price will reduce the percentage valuation.

FTSE 100 net dividend yield percentage p.a.

An increase in the dividend yield will increase the percentage valuation. For share valuations, the share net dividend yield percent p.a. is also required. An increase in this yield will also increase the percentage valuation.

Inflation factors 1 and 2

The Bank of England publishes daily a report which shows the average-period and end-period UK inflation rates implied by the market prices for a range of instruments. The periods extend up to 25 years. The five-year period is used for ShareMaestro, as the system uses a five-year investment period.

The input values for factors 1 and 2 produce, in the results field, the average-period and end-period inflation rates. An increase in inflation will reduce the percentage valuation.

Inflation factors 3 and 4 are reserved for possible future use.

Redemption yield percentage p.a. five-year gilts

This is the yield available from virtually risk-free UK government-backed gilts. An increase in the gilt yield will reduce the percentage valuation, as it becomes comparatively more attractive to hold gilts rather than shares. The yield on a five-year gilt is used, as ShareMaestro uses a five-year investment period.

Judgement-based input values

Risk premium percentage

For the FTSE 100, the default value is 10%, which is the long-term average. For individual shares, the default valuation method calculates the risk premium from the historic volatility of the share price to the market. However companies face other risks which could affect their value (e.g. competitive or political risks) and users are encouraged to adjust the risk premium accordingly.

An increase in the risk premium will reduce the percentage valuation.

Real dividend growth rate percentage p.a.

This is the most powerful factor in the valuation of the FTSE 100 share. It shows the sustainable rate of dividend growth over the five-year investment period. As well as heavily influencing the future FTSE 100 share price, dividends are a major component of long-term investment value. The ShareMaestro prediction of investment value at the end of five years includes the value of reinvested dividends.

The normal assumption for the real dividend growth rate of the FTSE 100 is 2% p.a. This is the long-term average. However, after the advent of the credit crunch and the collapse of several major banks, the FTSE 100 dividend fell by more than it had ever done since the inception of the index in 1984. It is not currently (August 2009) appropriate to use 2% for this input value. Current assessments of this key FTSE 100 input value are given in the User Manual and on the website.

As regards the real dividend growth rate for companies, the default valuation method uses consensus broker forecasts and other relevant data to derive this input value. Users can adjust this value on the basis of their own research and judgement.

Net dividend yield percentage for sector (for share valuations only)

Companies are grouped according to industrial sectors (e.g. banking, mining etc.) and dividend yields are published for each sector. The yields differ significantly from sector to sector.

The default share valuation method adjusts the sector yield for a company by reference to the relative strength of its prospective dividend cover (earnings per share divided by dividend per share). Users can also adjust this default value on the basis of their own research and judgement.

Getting results

Once you have keyed in the input values, you just click on the calculate button and the results immediately appear in the results fields (right-hand column).

ShareMaestro FTSE 100 valuation results

The ShareMaestro valuation of the FTSE 100 at its highest ever price is shown in Figure 10.1.

ShareMaestro correctly identified the size of the dotcom bubble which had formed at the end of 1999. The bottom two figures in the right-hand column show the ShareMaestro valuation as 3942, just 57% of the price. The FTSE 100 price subsequently crashed, as predicted by ShareMaestro, and plunged to a low of 3287.

From the 'Projected End-Period FTSE 100 Value' results field, you can see that the projected price of the FTSE 100 at the end of the five-year period (30 December 2004) was 5042.6. The actual price proved to be 4820.1, just

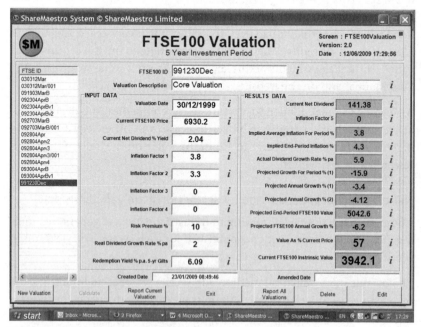

figure 10.1 Valuation of the FTSE 100 at its highest ever price

4% different. Many analysts fail to forecast the FTSE 100 price in a year's time to within 15% of the outcome, let alone five years hence.

Other key investment information is given in the results fields:

▨ **Projected Growth For Period % (1) and Projected Annual Growth % (1)** These are the projected investment returns after UK basic rate tax, including reinvested dividends but excluding the risk premium adjustment. In this example the projected returns are negative because ShareMaestro has correctly calculated the current FTSE 100 price as being very expensive.

▨ **Projected Annual Growth % (2)** The projected annual return after UK higher rate tax.

For comparison, the ShareMaestro valuation of the FTSE 100 at its lowest price this century is shown in Figure 10.2.

The bottom two figures in the right-hand column show the ShareMaestro valuation as 4957, 151% of the current price. The FTSE 100 price subsequently increased sharply, as predicted by ShareMaestro, and exceeded the ShareMaestro valuation within two years.

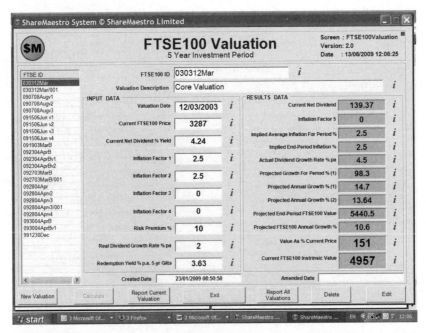

figure 10.2   Valuation of the FTSE 100 at its lowest price this century

Note that the projected price of the FTSE 100 at the end of the five-year period (12 March 2008) was 5440.5. The actual price proved to be 5776.4, just 6% different.

The annual return, post basic rate tax, is projected to be a very healthy 14.7% p.a. This high projected return results from the correct ShareMaestro calculation that the FTSE 100 price on 12 March 2003 was very cheap. Panic had taken hold following the bursting of the dotcom bubble and prices had fallen too far. The FTSE 100 price subsequently soared, increasing by 81% in three years.

ShareMaestro share valuation results

Figure 10.3 shows the valuation of Kazakhmys on 7 January 2009. This shows the share as a strong buy, and it was included in the ten ShareMaestro best-value FTSE 100 shares published in the January 2009 edition of *What Really Profits* magazine.

The sector yield shown was the yield for the mining sector, adjusted for the strong prospective dividend cover of Kazakhmys. The real dividend growth

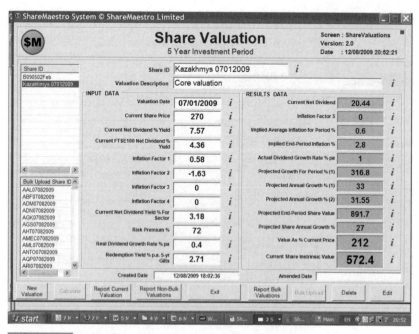

figure 10.3 Valuation of Kazakhmys (7 January 2009)

rate was derived from consensus broker forecasts and other relevant data. The risk premium is high, influenced by the high relative historic volatility of the share price. All the other data inputs are factual.

By 7 August 2009, the share price has powered ahead to 930, an increase of 244% on the 7 January 2009 price.

ShareMaestro now has a bulk share valuation feature. This enables you to value all the shares in your chosen index or sector automatically, using the default assumptions for the judgement-based input values. Each share valuation is stored in a separate file so that you can easily edit and review the valuation (see next section).

You can also export bulk share valuation results to an Excel spreadsheet, so that you can take advantage of Excel features such a data sorting (e.g. ranking shares in order of value as a percentage of current price) and printing.

Editing and reviewing valuation results

ShareMaestro has a unique scenario testing feature. When you have seen the results of your initial valuation, you can, via the edit button, change any of the input values, either in isolation or in combination. By simply clicking again on the calculate button, you can instantly see the impact on the valuation of these changes.

Say, for example, you think that interest rates and inflation are going to rise more sharply than the markets expect. You would simply click on the edit button and enter your chosen values in the following fields: Inflation Factors 1 and 2 and Redemption Yield % p.a. 5-yr Gilts. Then click the calculate button and the revised valuation will appear.

Using this valuable feature you can see that there were no realistic assumptions which could justify the extremely high price of the FTSE 100 at the start of this century, even though some analysts predicted that the market would power ahead beyond 8000. The bubble was bound to burst: in short a one-way bet. This valuable information would have allowed painful losses to be avoided and, for short-sellers, great profits to be made.

Similarly, if you are reviewing a share valuation from a bulk valuation run, you can easily see the impact of replacing the default values for the judgement-based input values with your own assumptions, if you believe these to be more appropriate.

When to buy and sell

In my experience the more extreme the ShareMaestro valuation, the more likely it is that the price of the FTSE 100 or share will revert in due course to fair value. However, if you only buy the FTSE 100 when the valuation is at least, say, 140%, and only sell when the valuation is at least, say, 60%, you will not make many trades. You will miss out on the profits to be made from using narrower buy/sell valuation spreads.

For the FTSE 100, a buy/sell valuation spread of 105%/95% strikes a fair balance between risk and reward. This has worked very well for the Share-Maestro FTSE 100 funds (see 'ShareMaestro's track record' section above), subject to the risk control measures mentioned below. Using this spread, there have been just 13 buy/sell signals since 1984 (as at August 2009). So you do not incur large dealing costs in following this strategy. Your investment horizon in following this strategy should be medium-term. It may take several months or, in some cases, over a year, before the FTSE 100 price moves towards the fair-value price indicated by the ShareMaestro FTSE 100 valuation. But patience is generally rewarded.

A wider buy/sell spread is more appropriate for individual shares because:

- There is far more risk in holding individual shares than the FTSE 100. The value of a share can totally evaporate whereas the value of the FTSE 100 would only evaporate in the unlikely scenario that all the constituent companies were nationalised without compensation to shareholders.
- There is far more scope for error in valuing an individual share than an index.
- There is a much greater range of percentage valuations for individual shares than for the index.

For these reasons, it is wiser to use a valuation of at least 115% before buying a share, but still use the 95% valuation as a trigger to sell. The User Manual also describes a number of safety checks which you should undertake on share valuations to ensure that they are as accurate as possible.

In terms of relative performance against the index, the investment horizon for share investment using ShareMaestro can be a lot shorter than for the index itself – often a matter of weeks rather than months. And there will always be shares which have much more extreme valuations than that of the index to which they belong. In other words you can make much greater profit from selecting the right shares than in trading an index.

ShareMaestro does not aim or claim to identify the precise tops and bottoms of the market. As explained in the introduction, share prices can be driven to extremes by human emotions. The principle of ShareMaestro, which is confirmed by its excellent track record, is that, if you buy the index/share when the price is cheap and sell when the price is expensive, you are far more likely to make a profit than by either:

- buy and selling randomly, or
- remaining permanently invested in the market (as fund managers, in their own interests, often recommend).

Chartists and a new breed of analysts called 'financial behaviourists' claim to be able to pinpoint peak and trough prices. However they never offer any systematic long-term proof that their systems work.

Risk control

Whilst the correct and careful use of ShareMaestro stacks the odds in your favour, there is no guarantee that prices will move in the direction indicated by the valuation. The fundamental input values could change sharply, which will change the valuations significantly, or human emotions could drive prices to irrational extremes.

It is therefore wise to employ some basic risk control measures in addition to using ShareMaestro valuations.

FTSE 100

Very occasionally the FTSE 100 price will go into freefall. This has happened just twice since the start of the FTSE 100 in 1984. In this situation, you should exit the market irrespective of the ShareMaestro FTSE 100 valuation.

Under this risk control measure, the signal to exit the market occurs when:

- the moving average (MA) of the last 145 days' FTSE 100 closing prices has fallen below the moving average of the last 242 days' FTSE 100 closing prices (used as a sell signal by some chartists) *and*
- the FTSE 100 price has fallen a further 10% below the closing price when the above crossover has occurred.

Several share data services (e.g. ShareScope, www.ShareScope.co.uk) will calculate moving averages for you. Alternatively you can download to a spreadsheet FTSE 100 prices from Yahoo Finance (www.yahoo.co.uk), for example, and calculate the moving averages yourself.

These rare freefall conditions are likely to arise in one of two circumstances (or possibly a combination of both):

1 The bursting of a bubble

This was the case on the first occurrence, when ShareMaestro had been indicating the FTSE 100 as massively over-valued for some time, as a result of the creation of the dotcom bubble. On 6 July 2001 the FTSE 100 price fell to 5483, 10% below the 145-day/242-day MA crossover price of 6093 on 19 February 2001. Therefore, on this occasion, it was not necessary to exit the market as the ShareMaestro valuation had already given a market exit signal when the valuation fell below 95%.

2 A dramatic and sudden deterioration in the prospects for dividends and earnings growth

This was the case in 2008 when the collapse of banks, the credit crunch and the looming recession suddenly slashed the real dividend growth prospects from the long-term average of 2% p.a. to deeply negative. Very rapidly, for example, many bank dividends, which formed a key element of the FTSE 100 dividend yield, just disappeared. So the default value of 2% p.a. for real dividend growth was not appropriate in these conditions. Dividends were going to fall sharply but it was not clear by how much and for how long. This sell signal occurred on 17 March 2008, when the FTSE 100 price had fallen to 5513, 10% below the MA crossover price of 6215.7 on 14 January 2008.

Having exited the FTSE 100 under this risk control measure, when do you reinvest? Using this risk control method, the signal to reinvest in the FTSE 100 occurs when the 145-day moving average rises above the 242-day moving average *and* the ShareMaestro FTSE 100 valuation is at least 105%.

Shares

However well you research the value of a company, the earnings prospects and/or market sentiment can change very rapidly. A common mistake made by private investors is to watch the price of a share continue to fall in the mistaken belief that the price will recover to the price which they paid. Psychologically it is far harder to realise a loss than to realise a profit. It is essential, therefore, to have a disciplined, systematic approach to minimise losses and to realise paper profits before they evaporate as a result of a plunging share price.

An effective risk-control measure is to put a trailing stop loss on new investments.This ensures that you lock in any gains and limit any losses. The stop loss can be for a set amount (say 25p) or a set percentage of the highest price achieved since you bought the share. So, for example, if you buy a share for £1.00 and you put a trailing stop loss of 25p on the share, the share will be sold if it falls more than 25p below the highest price achieved since you bought it. If, therefore, the price increases to a peak of £2.00, it will be sold, if it subsequently falls below £1.75 so that you lock in a 75% profit. If, however, the share falls steadily as soon as you have bought it, it will be sold as soon as the price falls below 75p. Several brokers (e.g. Barclays Stockbrokers) offer trailing stop losses as an automated facility. You should also consider selling a share if the ShareMaestro valuation falls below 95%.

Managing your own funds with ShareMaestro

A prime reason for launching ShareMaestro was to enable private investors to manage their own funds, especially with the advent of SIPPs (self-invested personal pension schemes).

When you invest in a managed investment fund (e.g. unit trust or OEIC), you do not know how the investments in the fund are going to perform. In fact most funds under-perform their benchmark index. Some funds sparkle for a few years (which are highlighted in their selective advertising) but they then fizzle out. Hardly any deliver consistent, long-term, market-beating performance.

What is certain, however, is that the costs and charges levied by the fund will substantially erode your long-term savings. Most active funds have annual fees of at least 1.5% p.a. in addition to entrance charges of around 5%. This means that, even assuming identical investment performance, after 25 years your own fund, free of charges, will be over 50% bigger than a managed investment fund. However, as shown in the section 'ShareMaestro's track record', the ShareMaestro model FTSE 100 funds have a much better track record than most UK equity funds and the best record for consistently high performance over both the long and short term. So you can make even bigger gains by managing your own funds.

FTSE 100 funds

A simple way to run your own FTSE 100 fund is to switch investment between the FTSE 100 and interest-bearing cash according to ShareMaestro's FTSE 100 valuations. You can use the 105%/95% buy/sell spread and employ the risk control measures described in the 'Risk control' section above. Investment in the FTSE 100 can be via a FTSE 100 ETF (exchange-traded fund) such as iShares. These funds aim to replicate the performance of the FTSE 100, and have low management charges of around 0.4% p.a. They also do not attract stamp duty for UK investors, have low buy/sell spreads and, unlike unit trusts, you always know the exact price at which you are trading.

A high-octane ShareMaestro FTSE 100 fund is the FTSE 100 Covered Warrant fund. Instead of investing in the FTSE 100, you invest in FTSE 100 covered call warrants, according to the ShareMaestro FTSE 100 valuations. This fund bears much higher risk, because warrants are effectively options to buy the FTSE 100 at a set price. The warrants can quickly become worthless if the FTSE 100 price falls sharply. It is therefore essential to use effective risk controls measures in running this fund. This model fund has delivered very high returns over the past 25 years but is only suitable for experienced investors who understand the risks involved and have taken appropriate professional advice. You must be prepared to monitor you positions daily and, in fast markets, intra-daily. You must also be ready to take swift action to realise profits or minimise losses. Details are available to ShareMaestro subscribers.

Funds of individual shares

Through using the ShareMaestro bulk valuation facility, you can buy a portfolio of at least ten shares, at roughly equal cost, each according to your choice of criteria. To control the risk you should:

- Invest only when the FTSE 100 valuation is above 105%.
- Invest only in shares which are valued at least 115% of the market price.
- Validate the valuations as far as possible, as described in the User Manual. This process will eliminate quite a few candidate shares.
- Choose shares from several different sectors.

- Put a trailing stop loss of, say, 25% of the original purchase price, on any shares purchased.
- Monitor the portfolio regularly and sell any shares for which the trailing stop loss value has been triggered or whose ShareMaestro valuation falls below 95%.
- Replace any sold shares with new shares which meet the original valuation criteria.
- Consider selling the whole portfolio if the FTSE 100 value falls below 95%. If the FTSE 100 falls significantly most UK shares will follow suit.

Further information on ShareMaestro

Further information on ShareMaestro is available at www.sharemaestro. co.uk, from where the free User Manual can be downloaded.

11

Using ShareScope and Investor Ease

In this chapter we're going to roll our sleeves up and start looking at some of the most useful computer-based 'screening' systems which can be used to implement various strategies – either offline through software applications or online via a website.

As we spin through the various offers a number of issues will be immediately apparent.

The key one is cost – as with so many things in modern life, you pay for what you get! A top of the range software-based system such as CDREFS (a software-based version of the paper-based CompanyREFS) is hugely expensive at many hundreds of pounds but it is nevertheless a class act and probably worth every penny! It boasts a comprehensive range of features, masses of tools and very sound data sources. But it's not the only top of the range system on the market as the system that works. Investors should also look at a software package from Ionic called ShareScope – it is also hugely powerful but crucially it's much less expensive.

The web-based screening services are, with a few exceptions, all free (all the offline software packages are paid-for) but the range of features, tools, measures and quality of data is far more limited. These web-based platforms are great for beginners and an outstanding deal especially when you consider that they're free – but don't expect premium features such as detailed measures or the ability to export shortlists on to Excel worksheets.

Introduction

Quality of data sources is hugely important and cost is a major determinant of the quality of data that sits inside a screening system. With the exception perhaps of the FT.com online screener, I regard the quality of fundamental data in many web-based applications as low. Many inaccuracies begin to creep in if the data isn't updated regularly and some key measures such as the quick ratio or the current ratio aren't included on some websites.

The range of additional features besides just stock screening is also important – good packages like ShareScope are much more than just screening systems. ShareScope – like another software system called Investor Ease – allows its users to run technical analysis and monitor portfolios as well as dig into a company's regulatory news service (RSN) announcements. This last feature is absolutely critical – using stock screens to run a strategy is only one part of careful stock selection. Quantitative-based analysis simply shortlists suitable companies – investors then need to run their own 'due diligence' process where they look at the company's newsflow, watching out for any potential problems. Therefore any system that integrates RNS news coverage with powerful stock screening tools is bound to have an advantage over a simple online screener.

Another big issue is ease of use. By and large the web-based services offered by the likes of the FT.com are easy to use with functionality built in via a Java platform or similar. Beginners will probably take quickly to these web-based services whereas the offline services using software packages are much more complex and require an awful lot of concentration and focus. As we'll discover in this chapter, getting to grips with a package like Share-Scope will probably take a couple of hours of careful experimentation and a good memory! But in our view that extra effort will pay off – the expensive offline software packages are, indisputably, more powerful and will provide better information to the end user.

In this chapter we're going to start with these more powerful offline software-based systems and then step through the market. We've deliberately not set out to conduct an exhaustive search of the market – all the packages and sites mentioned in this chapter have their individual virtues and downsides. In summary we'll look at the following:

▪ ShareScope. This is an offline software-based package which we use on a regular basis. It combines a powerful monitoring front end that lets you watch your portfolio or watchlist and then drill down using data mining tools that are easy to use but enormously complex. We'd hesitate to recommend this software for absolute beginners though – they may be better off using the FT.com online screener or Investor Ease.

■ CDREFS. Chris Coles from Capital Ideas, the firm behind this software package, will illustrate how to run a simple screen using its CD-based software (there's also an online version available with almost exactly the same features). This package is more expensive than ShareScope but is probably slightly easier to use. It doesn't have quite the same extensive range of technical analysis features present in ShareScope but the quality of its data and its range of fundamental measures, plus simplicity of presentation, are unmatched. Many institutions make use of both ShareScope and CDREFS.

■ Investor Ease. This is a much cheaper system than either ShareScope or CDREFS and combines many of the same features present in its peers but is packaged in a much simpler front end that makes the software a joy to use for beginner investors. Its stock screening tools are useful while not on a par with either ShareScope or CDREFS, but it does boast a wonderful feature that allows users to daily check on newsflow from companies on an investor's watchlist. Cheap, cheerful, moderately powerful and great for beginners.

■ The FT.com stock screening tool. This is by far the best UK-based screening tool online with great data from ThomsonReuters and a wonderful software engine that is a joy to use. Its range of measures is a bit limited but it is free and a great place to start for beginners. The FT screener tool faces tough competition from another online screener courtesy of www.advfn.co.uk – its Power X tool is overly-complicated but free and surprisingly effective.

■ DigitalLook. This also offers a paid-for stock screening tool through its Research Plus service which boasts a wide range of features but it is, truth be told, relatively expensive (compared to the FT's which is free!) and we're not convinced by the quality of all the underlying data.

Running a strategy using ShareScope

We'll start with ShareScope primarily because I use it and it probably has the best balance of cost and range of features available on the market. It's not the most comprehensive software – that accolade probably belongs to

CompanyREFS CDREFS – but we think it's absolutely worth the £16 per month subscription. ShareScope is available at Ionic's website at http://www.ShareScope.co.uk/.

ShareScope has a number of great advantages, chief amongst them:

- a wonderful data mining screening system with reliable data and lots of measures
- fantastic market monitoring tools that include intra-day pricing for the more expensive Plus and Pro packages
- great technical analysis of share prices (ShareScope is widely used by investors with a strong charts-based bias and its range of TA tools is excellent)
- barely a month goes by without some form of upgrade. (That continuous process of innovation has recently produced a set of features that allows investors instantly to call up the Regulatory News Service's comments on a particular company simply by hitting Control+N.)

But ShareScope isn't perfect – perhaps its greatest flaw is the sheer quantity of information on display. The software allows the user to set up their own windows and adapt the front page to their own requirements but many investors will simply be overwhelmed by the layout and feature set. Simpler, more basic packages such as Investor Ease arguably do a better job of 'corralling' the deafening tide of newsflow and price information into a simple, easy to read summary page. Nevertheless although ShareScope needs an investment of time by the user we think it's an investment that will pay off handsomely!

Basics

Your first step is to download the software – in our case Gold package (a large download it has to be said although it can also be sent to you as a CD) and then install the program which is itself a fairly lengthy process. Once your installation is up and running you can start using the system in earnest.

The main page should look like Figure 11.1 (overleaf) – it's full of boxes (you can add more if you wish!) which gives investors a wide range of tools and features. This section (like all the other explanatory sections) isn't a guide to all ShareScope's main market monitoring functions but it's worth pointing out some of the main windows in Figure 11.1. You'll see that we've put reference numbers on the figure to help and these correspond to the following:

1 The main window. This contains your main portfolio or watchlist
– there's a list of shares that you're tracking and you can add
different columns with different measures including intra-day price
information. This is the window that will later be transformed into
our main screening window when you hit a button indicated above
the arrow – the data mining tool represented by the picks and shovels.
Clicking this button turns this portfolio/watchlist monitoring into the
main screening page.

2 The main historical price graph. This plots the share price over the
maximum data set and also allows you to run technical analysis as
well as comparisons with other shares or indices. In the figure we're
monitoring African conglomerate Lonrho and comparing its price to
the FTSE 100 index.

3 The bottom row starts on the left with broker forecasts, which include
estimated earnings per share and dividends per share, organised by the
brokerage issuing the forecast – with a separate column for the date of
issue of the forecast. This is an invaluable feature as it allows you to
see how the ranges of brokers' estimates are changing over time.

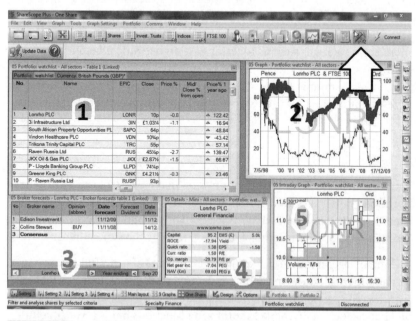

figure 11.1 The main page

4   The middle box on the lower level is called Details and in this case contains a snapshot of all the main measures including market cap, PE ratio and even operating margin.

5   The last box on the lower level is the intra-day graph which shows the progress of the share price of the day's trading.

You can of course change any or all of these windows – make them bigger, make them smaller, change the measure or tool and change the list. There's huge flexibility on offer here – all you have to do is right-click on a window/box at which point you'll be presented with a range of choices.

From now on though we're going to focus on the data mining features of this program – that means we're going to click the Picks and Shovels button indicated by the arrow in Figure 11.1. This tool set allows you to filter through either your own list of shares or the complete UK market (you can monitor US shares as well but data mining isn't enabled for foreign shares).

Once you've clicked on that picks and shovels button your main box (Figure 11.1) changes into the one shown in Figure 11.2. For clarity we've enlarged the box to cover the whole screen – this can be done by simply placing your cursor over a corner on the window and dragging the box to the size required.

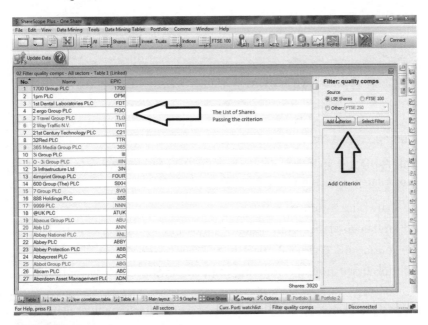

figure 11.2   List of shares passing a criterion

This front page for the data mining tool shows you on the left-hand side the long list of all companies – in our figure ordered alphabetically – and on the right-hand side a section headed Filter with Source below and two buttons called Add Criterion and Select Filter. The list on the right is currently the full UK market – we haven't selected any criterion (measures). To select a measure simply click on that Add Criterion button (see Figure 11.3).

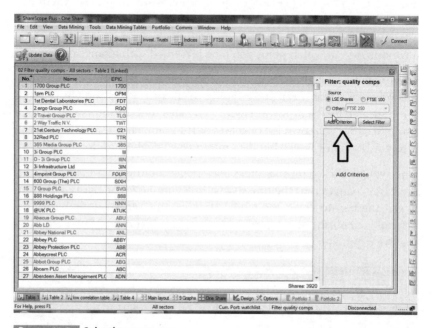

figure 11.3 Selecting a measure

Once you've clicked on the Add Criterion button you'll be presented with a new box – see Figure 11.4.

This is the first step of the all important Data Mining Wizard – it lists the broad categories on offer including:

- share price information
- fundamental measures (headline ratios and advanced results)
- Volume and Technical Analysis
- tools based around comparing companies within their sector (Rank in Sector)
- basic measures in the Other Criteria section which includes market cap.

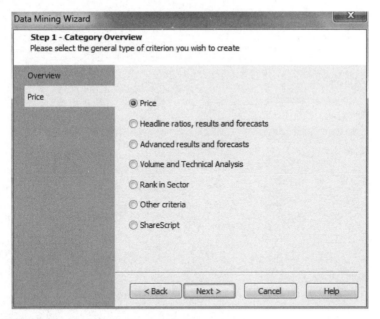

figure 11.4 First step of the Data Mining Wizard

Lastly you'll also see an option called ShareScript – this loads up a series of preconfigured technical measures. This is especially useful for those with a strong charting focus but it's unlikely to interest more fundamentals-based investors.

We're going to start our screen or data mine by clicking on the first button marked Price. This window changes to the one shown in Figure 11.5 (overleaf) which offers a wide range of share price-based measures – these include last share price, change in price between certain dates and price lows and highs.

If we then hit the button marked Back we return to the Category Overview page again. We now click the next button Headline ratios, results and forecasts – this contains a very useful quick list of key fundamental measures used by most analysts including the PE, the PEG, and key profit and sales figures (see Figure 11.6, overleaf).

The seven main groups of measures listed are just a small subset of the wider list of fundamental measures that are built into ShareScope – the box on page 343 details the full list.

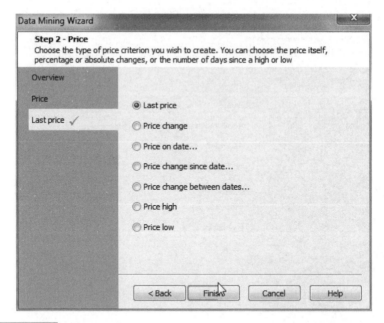

figure 11.5 Second step: Price

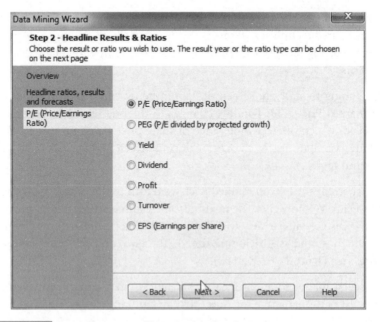

figure 11.6 Second step: Headline Results & Ratios

Full list of measures used in data mining in ShareScope

All the following measures can be accessed in Data Mining under Advanced Results.

- Normalised pre-tax profit
- FRS3 pre-tax profit
- FRS3 post-tax profit
- Turnover
- Dividend
- Tax
- Book value (or NAV)
- Tangible book value (NTAV)
- Cash
- Cashflow
- Capex
- R&D
- Depreciation
- Date

- ROCE
- ROE
- Quick ratio
- Current ratio
- Operating margin
- Interest cover
- Interest paid
- Net borrowing
- Net current assets
- Net gearing
- Cash %
- Gross gearing
- Gross gearing (<5 years)
- Gross gearing (<1 year)

Most of the detailed measures listed in the box above can be found in another of the options accessible from the initial Category Overview page – in a section called Advanced results and forecasts. Click on this button and you'll see the result in Figure 11.7 (overleaf)... we'll come back to some of these measures in greater detail later in this chapter.

The Category Overview page also contains a Volume and Technical Analysis option which provides very detailed share price and volume-based tools that include volume trends, moving averages, relative strength plus a cornucopia of stochastic tools and candlestick patterns – see Figure 11.8 (overleaf). We've not covered technical analysis in this book but if you do want to learn more about the principles behind these TA tools it's worth reading Alistair Blair's excellent guide.[1]

---

[1] Blair, A. (2002) *Investor's Guide to Charting: an analysis for the intelligent investor*, FT Prentice Hall.

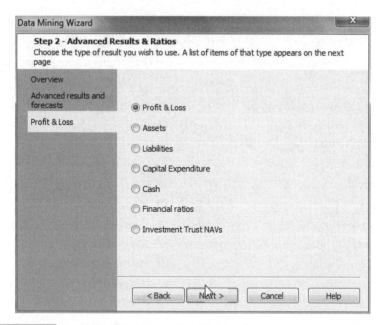

figure 11.7 Second step: Advanced Results & Ratios

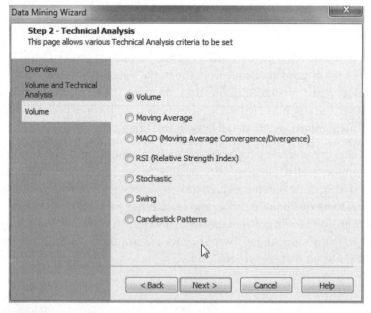

figure 11.8 Second step: Technical Analysis

The last major option from the Category Overview page is called Other criteria. This features a motley collection of tools that focus on the market size of most trades, share price volatility, correlation to a major index plus market cap (see Figure 11.9). This last measure is extremely useful as virtually every major strategy – and screen – tends to ignore stocks with a market cap of below £10m. Tiny micro-caps are notoriously difficult to analyse and rarely feature on most analysts' radar. Many are also penny stocks and are hugely volatile.

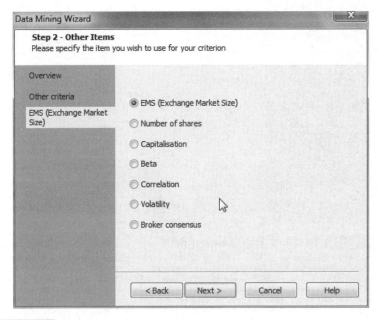

figure 11.9 Second step: Other Items

Drilling down

Now that we've looked at the major options accessible through the Category Overview page, it's time to drill down into more detail, using a series of simple to understand fundamental measures. If we start at Overview and then select Headline ratios, results and forecasts we can see a list of key measures – we'll choose the Price to Earnings Ratio or PE. Once this is selected we'll see another page – giving you a range of different PE ratios including the past or historical PE (using publicly declared earnings numbers) plus Rolling 1, Projected and Rolling 2 (see Figure 11.10, overleaf). The projected

PE ratio is based on analysts' estimates for future year EPS while the Rolling 1 and 2 measures are defined in the note below the picture. They're a mix of the other measures on a rolling basis.

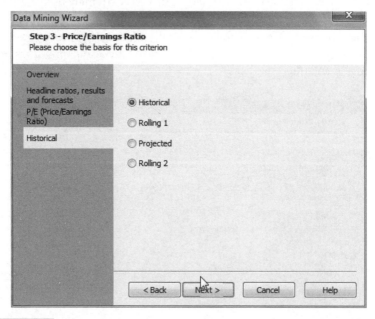

figure 11.10 Third step: Price/Earnings Ratio

NOTE – According to ShareScope Rolling 1 PE is a measure that 'includes some of the historical results and some of the projected (forecast) results for the following year. At the start of the financial year it is made up entirely of the historical figure; as the year progresses it includes more of the forecast figure. It 'rolls' between historical and projected – this figure is only available for those companies with both historical and forecast results. ROLLING 2 includes some of the next year's forecast results and some of the second year's forecast results. At the start of the financial year it is entirely the first year forecast; as the year progresses it includes more of the second year forecast. It 'rolls' forward from *projected* (forecast) – This figure is only available for companies with 2 years' forecast results.'

Once we've selected one of these PE-based measures we're presented with another choice – do we simply use the actual PE figure/number or do we want to rank the shortlisted companies based on the sector (see Figure 11.11)? Most of the time you'd opt for the first measure although the ability to compare a company against its peers is invaluable. Finally, it's time to hit the Finish button.

We've now selected one, single criterion – the Historical PE ratio. The Filter Results Page (see Figure 11.12) has three key elements:

■ a long list of all the companies boasting a PE ratio

■ below that you'll see a graph which shows the distribution of PE ratios over all the companies in that list

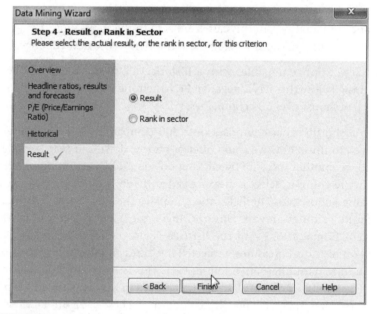

figure 11.11 Fourth step: Results or Rank in Sector

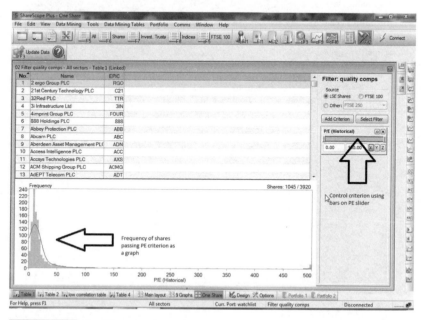

figure 11.12 The Filter Results Page

■ a box on the right under Filter which has a drag bar indicating the range of PE ratios – in this case from zero to the thousands. (Using your cursor you can now drag these two bars to the desired range.)

If we select only companies with a historical PE in the range between 0 (anything below this has a negative PE which indicates a loss) and 15 we end up with just over 500 companies.

Sadly, a shortlist that comprises over 500 companies isn't much use, so we need to think how we could filter or narrow down our search. Time to introduce another measure by clicking on the Add Criterion button. This time we're going to select a measure called the PEG ratio accessed via the Headline Ratios step. The PEG ratio compares the PE ratio with estimates for future earnings growth. Unsurprisingly, there are in fact a number of different forms of PEG – in the list (see Figure 11.13) you can see PEGs based on historical measures, projected measures and the rolling basis plus the all important alternative rolling PEG. This is based on a definition of the PEG developed by Jim Slater and pioneered in his company REF service – featured later in this chapter. In the note at the base of Figure 11.13 we've defined the Alternative PEG.

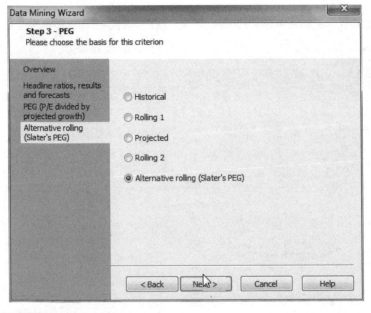

figure 11.13 Step 3 – PEG

NOTE – ShareScope defines the Alternative Rolling PEG as one that 'looks more at the forecast values and calculates the forecast PEG on a rolling basis'. The calculation is as follows: Price Earnings Ratio (PER) / expected future growth rate or (Price / Rolling EPS 2) / ((Rolling EPS 2 – Rolling EPS 1) / Rolling EPS 1)

Once we've selected this Alternative PEG we hit Finish and move to the results page (see Figure 11.14). We can narrow down the criteria used – in this case we're only going to investigate companies with an alternative PEG of between 0 and 1, which in total comprises 190 companies in all (they all boast a historic PE of between 0 and 15 as well).

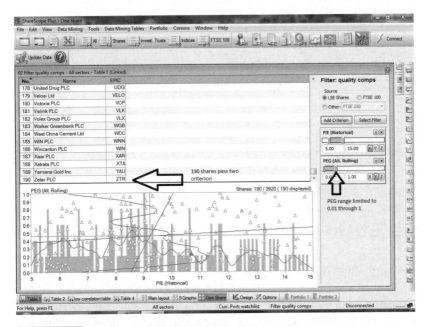

Results of an Alternative PEG 0–1

Our shortlist is definitely getting shorter now but it's nowhere near short enough. Any private investor is going to spend days searching through 190 companies in detail. We need to add some more fundamental measures to narrow down our universe of shares. We're first going to add companies with a projected dividend yield of more than 4% and less than 10%. Any company paying more than 4% is probably above average in most markets while most companies paying out more than 10% in dividend will struggle to cover that payout with enough cash profits. Our shortlist is now down to 61 companies in the list to the left – see Figure 11.15 (overleaf).

We're now going to add one last fundamental measure – the relationship between the assets backing the company and its share price. Using a measure called tangible book value per share or PTBV we only focus on those companies that pass all the other criteria plus a PTBV of more than 0 (there are actually positive net assets per share), and less than 1, meaning that

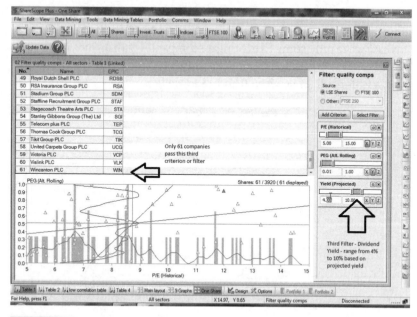

figure 11.15 A reduced shortlist

there are more assets per share than the actual share price (i.e. for every £1 paid in shares you're getting more than £1 in actual tangible assets). Our shortlist is now down to just five companies – see Figure 11.16. At the end of our first very simple data mining screen we've discovered just five companies which have:

■ an historical PE of between 5 and 15

■ an alternative rolling PEG of between 0.01 and 1

■ a projected or forecast yield of more than 4% and less than 10%

■ a PTBV of more than 0 and less than 1.

Ideally we'd like a few more details on the companies shortlisted – that means it's time to add some additional columns to the right of the five companies on the list. These additional columns can give you more information on the companies highlighted and it's incredibly easy to add columns (vertical lines of information) by right-clicking on the grey line immediately above the list of companies – see Figure 11.17. You'll now see a number of choices that let you add columns based on fundamental (found in either the General Column or advanced Column) or technical data (add price Column).

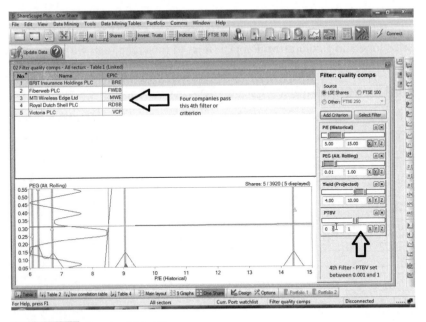

figure 11.16 Our shortlist of five

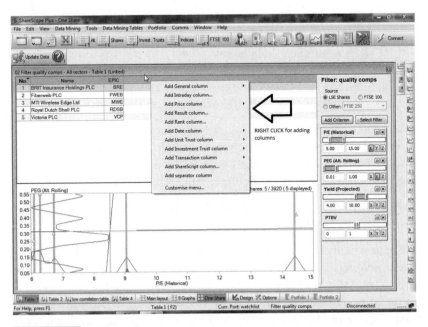

figure 11.17 Adding columns

If you choose Add General column you've now got a full range of choices including market cap and some of the headline numbers and measures. Select one and a column will appear next to the companies with that data listed – see Figure 11.18.

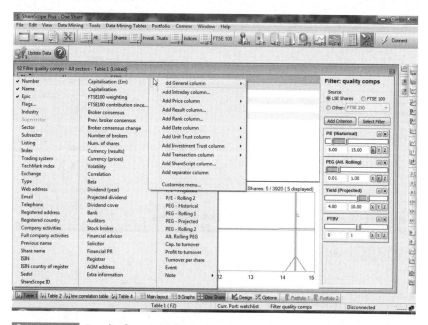

figure 11.18 Results from Add General

Highlighting the Add Price column gives you an equally large number of choices – the full range of technical analysis tools shown in Figure 11.19.

If you add a column using the Add Result column you're given the choice of either adding some Headline results (ranging from three years in the future based on estimates to eight years in the past) – see Figure 11.20 – or you can add some Advanced results & ratios – see Figure 11.21 (overleaf).

In Figure 11.22 (overleaf) we've added four columns in total detailing information on the PE, the PEG, Projected Yield and most recent PTBV.

We're now ready to save our screen based on PE, PEG, Yield and Book Value – and investigate the five shortlisted companies in greater detail. To save this 'screen' simply click on the Data Mining Tab at the top left-hand side of the page, choose Select filter, then choose a name for the 'filter' and hit Save – see Figure 11.23 (overleaf). You can now come back to this filter or screen later and run the same set of four filters.

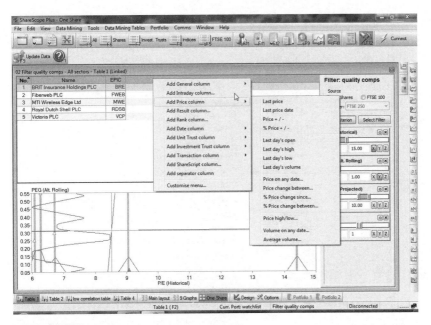

figure 11.19 Results from Add Price column

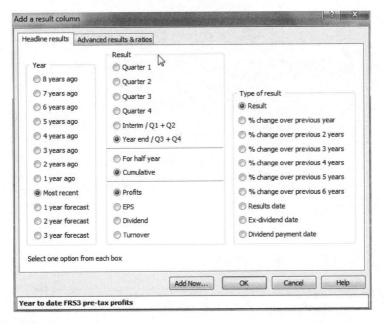

figure 11.20 Headline results

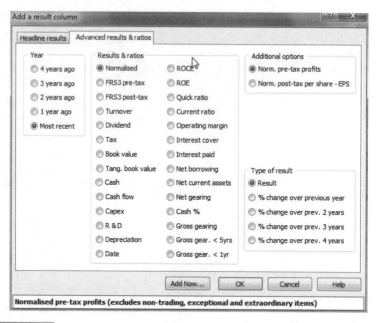

figure 11.21 Advanced Results & Ratios

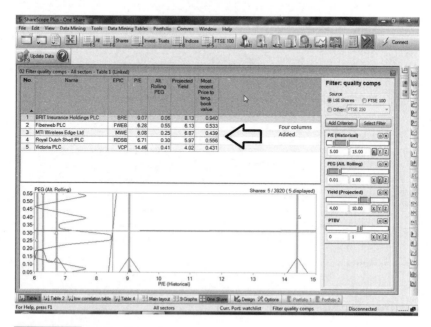

figure 11.22 Adding four columns

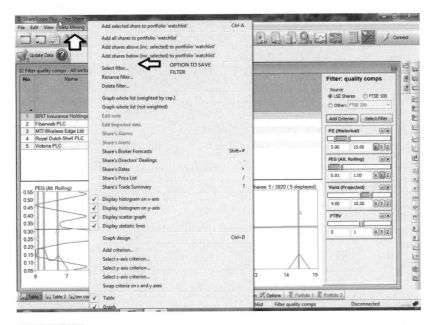

figure 11.23 Saving a filter

One of the most useful features of ShareScope is that you can also export this list of five companies, with corresponding columns, to an Excel worksheet that can then be easily manipulated and presented in a document. To do this use the same tabs on the top left-hand corner and select File, and then Export list table – see Figure 11.24 (overleaf).

In this book we've constantly emphasised the need to use these quantitative filters and screens as just one part of a strategy for selecting shares. However, investors also need to spend some time looking in detail at the shortlisted companies and that means checking the newsflow, looking at share price weakness or strength, and then examining the accounts and cashflow statements in great detail. In ShareScope much of the key information about the company is summarised on a company Details page. This can be accessed by looking at the buttons on the top bar and clicking the one with a magnifying glass symbol called Show details – see Figure 11.25 (overleaf). You'll then see a very comprehensive summary of the company and all the key financials. News on the company can be accessed by right-clicking the cursor and then scrolling down a long list of options to the one that says Shares news archive. You can get to this through a shortcut (Control+N). You'll now see a long list of all recent company news stories.

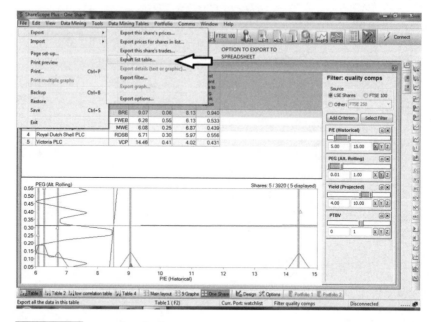

Figure 11.24 Exporting the list

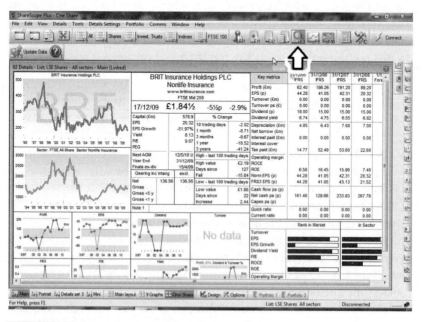

figure 11.25 Accessing the Details page

CompanyREFS and CDREFS

Chris Cole of CompanyREFS

REFS is a highly effective stock selection tool, available on subscription and used by thousands of UK investment professionals and private investors to find UK listed companies of interest to them.

The product was first released to the market in November 1994, the outcome of over two years' development and meticulous refinement. It was devised by the noted UK private investor Jim Slater, who wanted to slice through mountains of company information and summarise the essence of each investment story into just one page. At the same time he needed an effective tool to sift the most crucial performance indicators for all UK equities together, so that potential winners would clearly stand out from the crowd. These indicators were developed over many months of intensive debate and research to become the Really Essential Financial Statistics that give CompanyREFS its name.

It's important to note that CompanyREFS has been specially designed to accommodate the needs of all stockmarket investors. As such, it is unlike other investment products. Investors can follow their own choice of investment styles: including 'top-down' and 'bottom-up, 'value' or 'growth' stocks, and technical analysis.

In essence, REFS consists of three parts:

1. a bespoke database of company information that's specifically designed with the needs of stockmarket investors in mind, updated daily at the close of London Stock Exchange markets

2. a screening tool that lets you search the database for stocks that match any combination of 'filters' you choose, and

3. a detailed summary for each company that condenses financial performance and prospects into a single, easy-to-read REFS page. The distinctive REFS 'moons' give an instant fix on growth and value potential; you get two years of forecasts and five years' history in detail; and there's enough newsflow, outlook, price performance and dealings information to put the full picture at your fingertips.

Typically, REFS users build a search by running the full population of 1500+ stocks through a series of 'sieves' that filter fewer and fewer companies from the total. You quickly reach a manageable shortlist of interesting companies that merit further, individual research.

In this way REFS users hope to uncover value in the stock market that has been overlooked by most investors.

Undertaking a search

Let's take a typical look at how REFS users might undertake a search. By way of example we will use REFS Online to look for stocks that demonstrate 'growth at a reasonable price', or GARP.

When devising REFS Jim Slater incorporated two unique features:

1 In REFS the price-earnings ratio (PER), earnings per share (EPS) and price-earnings growth factor (PEG) are all calculated on a forward-rolling basis for the 12 months ahead. This enables direct comparison of companies with differing financial year ends, a feature unique to REFS, allowing you to analyse prospective performance on a like-for-like basis.

2 Although many financial journalists quote PEG factors, these often refer simply to the current financial year. Slater decided that a company should qualify for a PEG rating only if it generates continuous EPS growth for the latest four years, including forecasts.

The award of a PEG rating in REFS is therefore a major achievement, and out of the entire REFS universe of 1510 companies only 90, or 6%, qualified when this search was undertaken on 4 February 2010 at the previous day's close. Other considerations being equal, lower PEGs are more attractive and just 43 companies, less than half, had a PEG of less than 1.

Our starting point was the entire Company REFS universe of 1510 companies. This comprises all UK-registered companies having UK-listed equity shares, apart from investment trusts and non-UK companies which are excluded so that REFS statistics can be compared like-for-like.

If you'd like to learn more about share selection using PEGs as well as other criteria, Jim Slater's book *Beyond the Zulu Principle* explains in detail how to use the REFS system. Remember that the data in REFS is dynamic because the entire database is completely refreshed and overwritten at the end of each trading day. Therefore a search like this can produce different results over time, including even the following day.

Here are our five chosen filters for this search:

Filter			Results
Market Cap	>	15	920
PER	<	20	795
Cashflow/EPS	>	1	387
1yr Rel strength	>	0	248
PEG	<	0.8	11

Our first filter is a minimum market capitalisation of £15m, because this increases the likelihood of reasonable liquidity in the shares. This reduces the population to 920 companies. It is wise to be aware of the normal market size traded (NMS) before dealing.

Next we demand a PER of less than 20 on a forward-rolling basis to ensure the shares are not too highly valued. We are now down to 795 stocks.

Then we want cashflow to exceed earnings. All companies must demonstrate they were good generators of cash in the last financial year. This step reduces the population by more than half to 387.

Fourth, we look for positive 12-month relative strength to ensure the shares have behaved well in the market over the past year. Only 248 companies remain.

Finally, we look for a PEG rating of 0.8 or less. This ensures the company satisfies the minimum standard of EPS growth demanded by REFS to qualify for a PEG, yet shows attractive value at the same time. This has a big impact, reducing the final list to just 11 companies, less than 1% of the entire REFS universe.

Figure 11.26 (overleaf) shows how these search parameters are entered into REFS – it's easy to pick the columns and listing order you want. Table 11.1 (overleaf) shows the search results in detail.

Drilling down

Now, let's take a closer look at one of these companies by turning to its full-page profile in Company REFS at close-of-business on 3 February 2010.

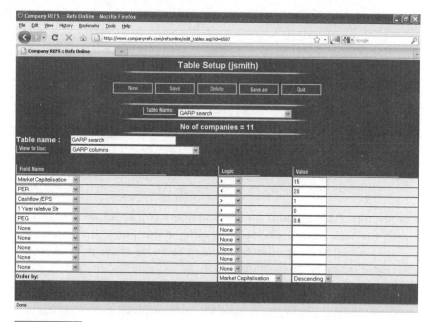

figure 11.26 Entering the search parameters

Group NBT (AIM listed – EPIC code: NBT) is engaged in the provision of domain name management and web-hosting services. Domain name management and internet brand protection is a growth industry and Group NBT appears to be a major player in this field.

The REFS page (see Figure 11.27, overleaf) shows a strong array of black 'moons' in the growth section – the blacker they are, the more attractive they look against the market (the 'm' column) and against their own sector ('s' column). Turnover grew threefold from £13.8m in 2006 to £41.5m in 2009.

Operating margin has stayed up in the mid-teens and cashflow consistently exceeds earnings. At the June 2009 year-end there was £5.2m in cash, equivalent to 28.3p per share. Institutions own 51.7% of the shares, and directors own 12%.

At 320p on 3 February 2010 the share's prospective PER was 13.4 and a prospective EPS growth rate of 18.8% gave a PEG of 0.72. Occupying a valuable space in a rapidly growing industry, Group NBT appeared to offer good value in view of its bright growth prospects.

table 11.1 The search results

Company name	Market cap £m	Current price (p)	12-month high (p)	12-month low (p)	12-month rel str (%)	Prosp DY (%)	PER	PEG	EPS gth rate (%)	Cashflow/ EPS
Petrofac	3,405	986	10.6	409	86.2	2.85	12.1	0.38	31.6	1.82
Hargreaves Lansdown	1,394	294	312	167	33.5	3.35	18.5	0.66	27.9	1.13
Chemring Group	1,151	32.60	32.80	18.20	9.16	1.66	12.6	0.57	22.1	1.45
Micro Focus International	1,039	508	523	264	30.2	2.31	13.1	0.69	19.0	1.08
ASOS	319	437	505	272	24.0	0.04	19.7	0.68	29.1	1.36
Healthcare Locums	272	259	287	114	44.1	3.08	9.56	0.39	24.6	1.21
Immunodiagnostic Systems Holdings	192	691	728	132	281	0.31	16.7	0.32	51.8	1.25
Games Workshop Group	121	388	403	169	46.3	0.35	11.9	0.69	17.2	2.21
Group NBT	82.8	320	336	190	18.2	1.28	13.4	0.72	18.8	1.52
Education Development Intl	80.1	139	162	50.8	111	1.35	10.5	0.60	17.4	1.39
Brooks MacDonald Group	56.4	555	579	245	73.8	1.31	16.9	0.67	25.3	1.69

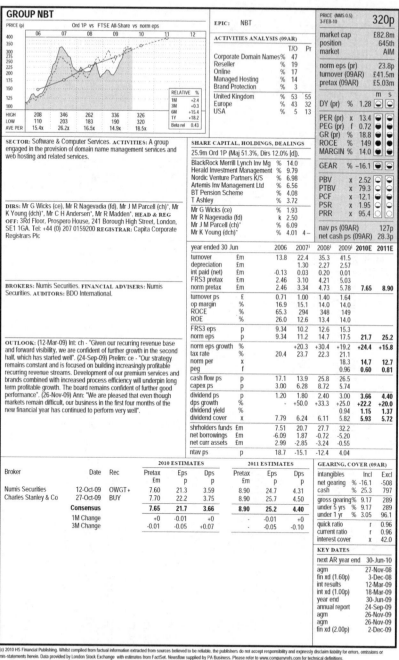

GROUP NBT

PRICE (p) Ord 1P vs FTSE All-Share vs norm eps

	06	07	08	09	10	11	12

RELATIVE %
1M	+2.4
3M	+0.3
6M	+15.4
1Y	+18.2
Beta rel	0.43

HIGH	208	346	262	336	326
LOW	110	203	183	190	320
AVE PER	15.4x	26.2x	16.5x	14.9x	18.5x

EPIC:	NBT	

	PRICE (NMS 0.5) 3-FEB-10	320p
market cap		£82.8m
position		645th
market		AIM

ACTIVITIES ANALYSIS (09AR)

		T/O	Pr
Corporate Domain Names	%	47	
Reseller	%	19	
Online	%	17	
Managed Hosting	%	14	
Brand Protection	%	3	
United Kingdom	%	53	55
Europe	%	43	32
USA	%	5	13

			m	s
norm eps (pr)		23.8p		
turnover (09AR)		£41.5m		
pretax (09AR)		£5.03m		
DY (pr)	%	1.28	⊖	⊖
PER (pr)	x	13.4	●	⊖
PEG (pr)	f	0.72	●	⊖
GR (pr)	%	18.8	●	
ROCE	%	149	●	
MARGIN	%	14.0	●	
GEAR	%	-16.1	⊖	⊖
PBV	x	2.52	⊖	⊖
PTBV	x	79.3	⊖	⊖
PCF	x	12.1	●	⊖
PSR	x	1.95	⊖	⊖
PRR	x	95.4	○	⊖
nav ps (09AR)		127p		
net cash ps (09AR)		28.3p		

SECTOR: Software & Computer Services. **ACTIVITIES:** A group engaged in the provision of domain name management services and web hosting and related services.

DIRS: Mr G Wicks (ce), Mr R Nagevadia (fd), Mr J M Parcell (ch)*, Mr K Young (dch)*, Mr C H Andersen*, Mr R Madden*. **HEAD & REG OFF:** 3Rd Floor, Prospero House, 241 Borough High Street, London, SE1 1GA. Tel: +44 (0) 207 0159200 **REGISTRAR:** Capita Corporate Registrars Plc

BROKERS: Numis Securities. **FINANCIAL ADVISERS:** Numis Securities. **AUDITORS:** BDO International.

OUTLOOK: (12-Mar-09) Int: ch - "Given our recurring revenue base and forward visibility, we are confident of further growth in the second half, which has started well". (24-Sep-09) Prelim: ce - "Our strategy remains constant and is focused on building increasingly profitable recurring revenue streams. Development of our premium services and brands combined with increased process efficiency will underpin long term profitable growth. The board remains confident of further good performance". (26-Nov-09) Ann: "We are pleased that even though markets remain difficult, our business in the first four months of the new financial year has continued to perform very well".

SHARE CAPITAL, HOLDINGS, DEALINGS

25.9m Ord 1P (Maj 51.3%, Dirs 12.0% [d]).

BlackRock Merrill Lynch Inv Mg	%	14.0
Herald Investment Management	%	9.79
Nordic Venture Partners K/S	%	6.98
Artemis Inv Management Ltd	%	6.56
BT Pension Scheme	%	4.08
T Ashley	%	3.72
Mr G Wicks (ce)	%	1.93
Mr R Nagevadia (fd)	k	2.50
Mr J M Parcell (ch)*	%	6.09
Mr K Young (dch)*	%	4.01 4−

year ended 30 Jun		2006	2007i	2008i	2009i	2010E	2011E
turnover	£m	13.8	22.4	35.3	41.5		
depreciation	£m		1.30	2.27	2.57		
int paid (net)	£m	-0.13	0.03	0.20	0.01		
FRS3 pretax	£m	2.46	3.10	4.21	5.03		
norm pretax	£m	2.46	3.34	4.73	5.78	7.65	8.90
turnover ps	£	0.71	1.00	1.40	1.64		
op margin	%	16.9	15.1	14.0	14.0		
ROCE	%	65.3	294	348	149		
ROE	%	26.0	12.6	13.4	14.0		
FRS3 eps	p	9.34	10.2	12.6	15.3		
norm eps	p	9.34	11.2	14.7	17.5	21.7	25.2
norm eps growth	%		+20.3	+30.4	+19.2	+24.4	+15.8
tax rate	%	20.4	23.7	22.3	21.1		
norm per	x				18.3	14.7	12.7
peg	f				0.96	0.60	0.81
cash flow ps	p	17.1	13.9	25.8	26.5		
capex ps	p	3.00	6.28	8.72	5.74		
dividend ps	p	1.20	2.40	3.00	3.00	3.66	4.40
dps growth	%	-	+50.0	+33.3	+25.0	+22.2	+20.0
dividend yield	%				0.94	1.15	1.37
dividend cover	x	7.79	6.24	6.11	5.82	5.93	5.72
shrholders funds	£m	7.51	20.7	27.7	32.2		
net borrowings	£m	-6.09	1.87	-0.72	-5.20		
net curr assets	£m	2.99	-2.85	-3.24	-0.55		
ntav ps	p	18.7	-15.1	-12.4	4.04		

Broker	Date	Rec	2010 ESTIMATES			2011 ESTIMATES		
			Pretax £m	Eps p	Dps p	Pretax £m	Eps p	Dps p
Numis Securities	12-Oct-09	OWGT+	7.60	21.3	3.59	8.90	24.7	4.31
Charles Stanley & Co	27-Oct-09	BUY	7.70	22.2	3.75	8.90	25.7	4.50
Consensus			**7.65**	**21.7**	**3.66**	**8.90**	**25.2**	**4.40**
1M Change			+0	-0.01	+0	-	-0.01	+0
3M Change			-0.01	-0.05	+0.07	-	-0.05	-0.10

GEARING, COVER (09AR)

		Incl	Excl
intangibles			
net gearing	%	-16.1	-508
cash	%	25.3	797
gross gearing	%	9.17	289
under 5 yrs	%	9.17	289
under 1 yr	%	3.05	96.1
quick ratio	r		0.96
current ratio	r		0.96
interest cover	x		42.0

KEY DATES

next AR year end	30-Jun-10
agm	27-Nov-08
fin xd (1.60p)	3-Dec-08
int results	12-Mar-09
int xd (1.00p)	18-Mar-09
year end	30-Jun-09
annual report	24-Sep-09
agm	26-Nov-09
agm	26-Nov-09
fin xd (2.00p)	2-Dec-09

figure 11.27 The REFS page for Group NBT

Pricing details

CompanyREFS is available in a range of formats, designed to meet the varying needs of investors. City fund managers and other professional investors invariably favour the 24/7 online version, or the monthly-updated CD. Private investors who deal less frequently, or may be new to stock market investment, often start with the quarterly hardcopy directory, the quarterly CD-ROM or the REFS Online Plus service, and then upgrade when they require more regular access to the latest company information.

The hardcopy version of CompanyREFS is bound in four large volumes, delivered either monthly or quarterly, with three dedicated to the 1500+ REFS pages and a Tables volume summarising directors' dealings, results, forecast changes and a full range of performance rankings. The convenience that page-turning brings must be balanced against portability and storage requirements as back issues accumulate.

To enable investors unfamiliar with CompanyREFS to appreciate for themselves what REFS can do for them, the service is currently available on a 10-day, no obligation free trial basis at www.companyrefs.com.

The full range of CompanyREFS products and services is as follows:

CompanyREFS hardcopy	Monthly	£930 p.a.
	Quarterly	£335 p.a.
CDREFS	Monthly	£775 p.a.
	Quarterly	£335 p.a.
REFS Online	Professional (always-on, 24/7 access)	£796 p.a. or £67 p.m.
	Premium (non-trading hours access)	£39 p.m.
	Plus (weekends-only access)	£17 p.m.

Investor Ease

This software-based application is the least specified of all its peers, but it boasts the lowest price and the simplest presentational layout. It also offers a very easy to access way of monitoring a portfolio and has a wonderful end of the day news summary which is on its own worth the £9.75 a month plus VAT charge. On the downside the software has limited stock screening tools and the data is not quite as reliable as we'd want. Nevertheless this is a great piece of software for a beginner.

Once you've downloaded the software from the company website at http://www.investorease.com and then installed it (like ShareScope this can be a time consuming process as Investor Ease installs lots of add-ons) you're presented with the welcome or front page (see Figure 11.28).

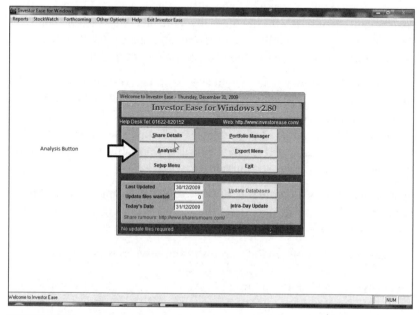

figure 11.28 Welcome page for Investor Ease

Each of these white on grey buttons controls the main tools:

- Share Details brings on a single company summary.
- Analysis contains the stock screener.
- Portfolio Manager is self explanatory!
- Setup Menu allows the user to control the main settings while Export Menu allows shortlists and graphs to be exported to other programs.
- The Update Databases and Intra-Day Update buttons launch programs on the internet, giving up to the minute price data.

To run a screen based on a set of fundamental measures, click the Analysis button – this will take you to a simple page with the following options (see Figure 11.29):

- Share Analysis – the main fundamentals-based tool.
- Price Performance – this allows you to screen for companies based on the behaviour of the share price.

⬛ Sector Analysis and Industry Analysis – these two options allow you to focus on returns from key sectors.

⬛ Forecast Analysis – this is an especially useful tool and lets you screen for companies based on earnings estimates and their change over time. In the concluding chapter we'll highlight the critical importance of accelerating earnings estimates in spotting growth stocks.

figure 11.29 Which type of Analysis? page

We'll focus in this section just on the share analysis tool, which is this program's main stock screener. Selecting this tool brings you to the first level of the screen (see Figure 11.30, overleaf) where you can specify how wide you cast your net. You can, for instance, focus on particular sectors or industries or just certain types of shares (warrants) in different parts of the market (say only FTSE 250).

Once you've narrowed down your 'universe' of stocks, you can then select particular filters or measures. First you Select Criteria, then you specify a range of values (e.g. a PE between 5 and 15), and finally hit Generate to produce a shortlist of companies that meet this criteria – see Figure 11.31 (overleaf).

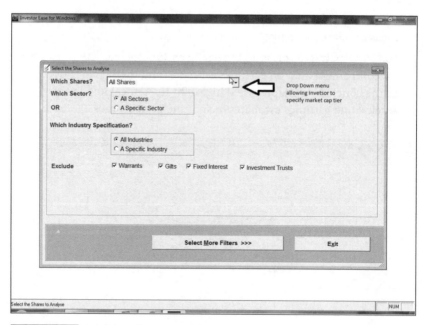

figure 11.30 Selecting shares to analyse

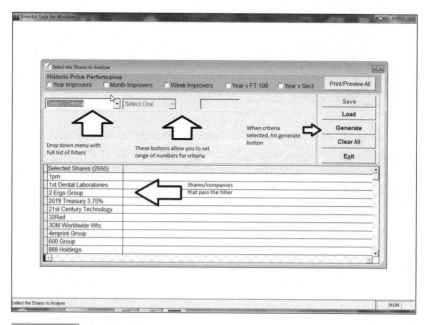

figure 11.31 The shortlist

Like ShareScope and CDREFS you can add multiple criteria, generating ever shorter lists of companies to investigate – see Figure 11.32.

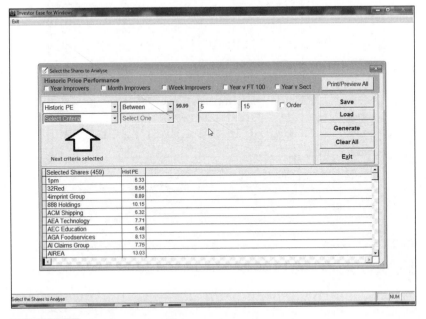

figure 11.32 The shorter shortlist

Once you've narrowed down your list you can then look in detail at the list of shares generated. The companies are listed to the left (see Figure 11.33, overleaf) with different columns featuring different measures. You can view even more columns by clicking the Toggle button – this shuffles the columns along increasing the numbers of measures you can see at any one time.

If you want to look in detail at any one particular company on your short-list simply click the Go to Share Details button. This summary page lists everything from price history through to key measures such as the PE ratio and yield – see Figure 11.34 (overleaf). The range of measures is nowhere near as definitive as CDREFS or even ShareScope but it should suffice for most beginner investors.

Once you're happy with your measures you can then save the resulting shares and measures, allowing you to run the screen at a later date (see Figure 11.35, overleaf).

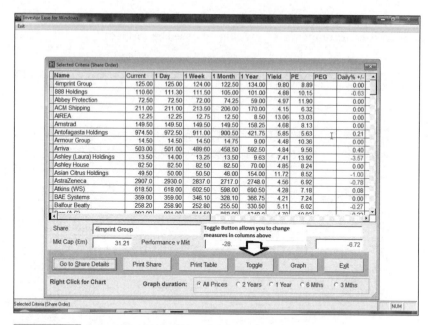

figure 11.33 Increasing the number of measures in view

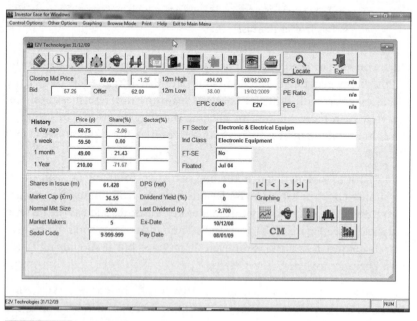

figure 11.34 The summary page

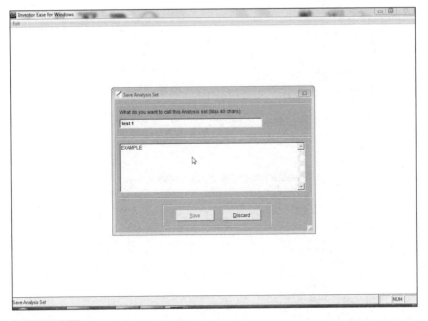

figure 11.35 Saving the results for later

Investor Ease's greatest strength isn't really its stock screening tool as the range of measures used is fairly limited. The software does feature a fantastic way of monitoring your portfolio or watchlist accessed through the main menu. Obviously you need to set up these lists first by clicking on the StockWatch tab on the top line (see Figure 11.36, overleaf), and creating a watchlist that looks something like that in Figure 11.37 (overleaf).

Armed with your shortlist of shares on the StockWatch you can now update the news and price data via Investor Ease's Update options – either at the end of the day after 7pm or on a regular intra-day basis (the program doesn't offer real time data). Once you've updated this internet data feed you'll then be presented with an end of day update statistics page – see Figure 11.38 (overleaf). This wonderful summary page tells you how many companies announced results or informed the markets of major news stories, as well as information on directors' dealing. You can then either check your StockWatch or Portfolio shares and look to see if there were any comments for the companies you've highlighted.

This summary of all news stories relating to your shortlist of monitored shares is concisely presented (see Figure 11.39, overleaf). An investor with

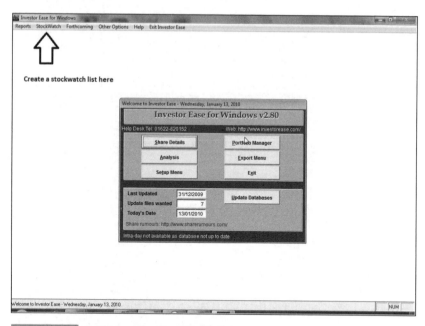

figure 11.36 Setting up the StockWatch lists

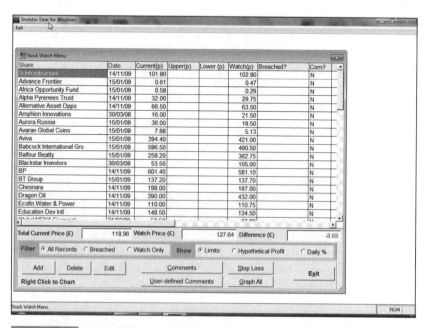

figure 11.37 The resulting matchlist

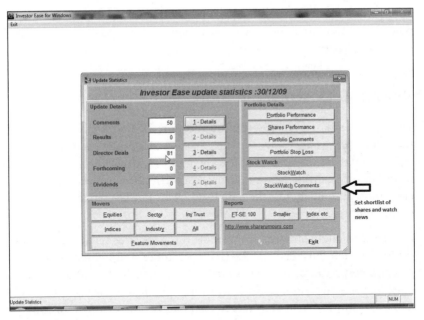

figure 11.38 End of day Update Statistics page

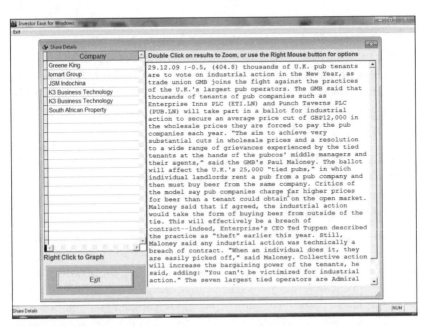

figure 11.39 Summary news stories

a shortlist of a dozen or so shares can probably skim through all the major news and comment stories within just a few minutes. Neither ShareScope or CDREFS has this summary tool.

Web-based stock screening tools

The best web-based stock screening tool for UK investors is offered by the *Financial Times*. Go to http://markets.ft.com/screener/customScreen. asp?ftauth=1263407795050 to access the tool, though you will be required to register to use this feature (at no cost). The FT screener is incredibly easy to use, the quality of the data is excellent but the range of measures is fairly limited.

UK investors might also want to consider the stock screener at Digital Look, via its Research Plus service. This is a much more comprehensive tool but it is also very expensive: access starts at £20 a month or £240 per annum. I also like the free Filter X stock screening tool at www.advfn.co.uk. This is fairly complicated to use but it is free and fairly well specified for features and measures. The Filter X tool also features some ready-made strategies and screens.

The FT screener

We'll start with the *Financial Time*'s free screening tool. The home page for this tool is wonderfully simple and very clean (see Figure 11.40) – none of the clutter which spoils the Filter X tool from ADVFN. Very quickly this Java-based application lets you choose whether you want to set up your own custom screen or choose one of the predefined screens – based on strategies devised by Warren Buffett, Ben Graham, Jim Slater and Joseph Piotroski. If you do decide to choose the custom screen you can quickly focus on a particular country, different sectors, and then specify key equity attributes (these fundamental measures are the equivalent of criteria in other screeners such as ShareScope).

You can select a large number of these equity attributes and specify exactly the numerical range of these measures. In Figure 11.39 above we've specified a market cap between £22m and £24bn by moving the little toggle bars on either side. Once you've selected a range of equity attributes – in Figure 11.41 we have chosen five, with 31 matching companies – you can then view all the matches by clicking the blue button in the bottom right-hand corner of the page.

figure 11.40 The ft.com home page   Source: http://markets.ft.com, The Financial Times Ltd.

figure 11.41 Five equity attributes   Source: http://markets.ft.com, The Financial Times Ltd.

Adding extra attributes is also very easy – just click on the Add additional criteria which will then produce another small window with a long list of measures and filters (see Figure 11.42).

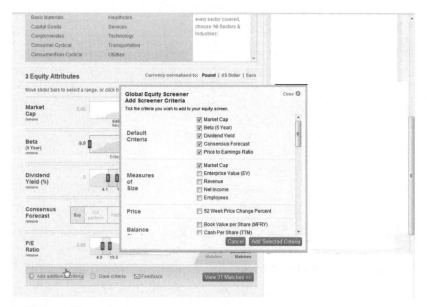

In Figure 11.43 you can see that we've gone from a shortlist of 31 shares down to just seven companies – these are then listed in Figure 11.44. One quick observation – always choose the widescreen option as this gives you greater detail to examine your shortlist.

If you want to see more detail for a particular shortlisted company, simply hover your cursor over the company and an additional box will appear giving you intra-day pricing details – see Figure 11.45 (overleaf).

You can also save your screen by selecting the Save Criteria tab towards the top of the page – see Figure 11.46 (overleaf).

Digital Look

The Digital Look stockscreening service is run by options and spreadbetting company CMC and is arguably the most powerful online screener in the UK. It's very well specified, with lots of different measures, and it offers the ability to test out a screen using past data. This last feature is a unique sell-

Figure 11.43 Reducing from 31 to seven   Source: http://markets.ft.com, The Financial Times Ltd.

figure 11.44 The shortlisted seven   Source: http://markets.ft.com, The Financial Times Ltd.

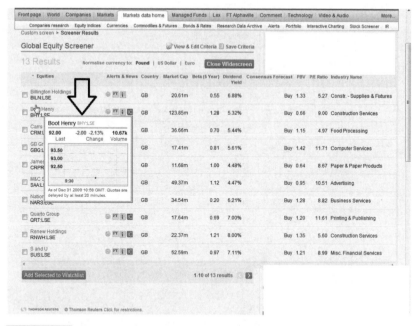

figure 11.45 Intra-day pricing details

Source: http://markets.ft.com, The Financial Times Ltd.

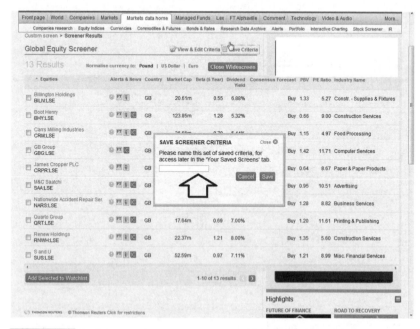

figure 11.46 Saving your screen

Source: http://markets.ft.com, The Financial Times Ltd.

ing point as no other screening system in the UK offers this feature – you can test out your strategy over the past seven years. The downside is that all this functionality is very expensive, costing a minimum of £20 a month.

To find the service head over to the Research plus part of the main Digital Look website at http://www.digitallook.com/research_plus. On the left-hand bar you'll see the tools menu and Screening Tools – see Figure 11.47. You'll now be taken to the main UK Stock Screener page and be given the choice of Getting Started with a simple, ready made screen or, for experienced users, the chance to Build your own screen.

The first option for beginners takes you to a simplified Screening Wizard page (see Figure 11.48) which highlights a small (5) number of key measures – you simply select one of the three options and then hit the submit question.

If you decide to build your own screens, you'll be taken to the My Saved Screens page (see Figure 11.49) where your screens plus a number of detailed pre-selected Premium and Popular strategies are highlighted. By clicking on the range of buttons you can immediately run that screen in real time or even select Test Strategy which will show you the returns over previous years versus a benchmark index.

figure 11.47 Selecting or building a screen

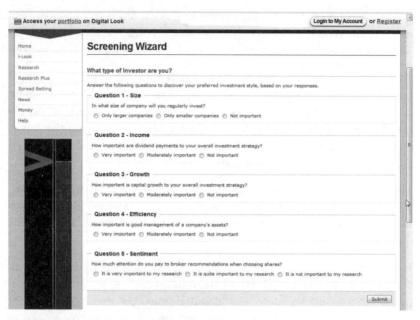

figure 11.48 The Screening Wizard

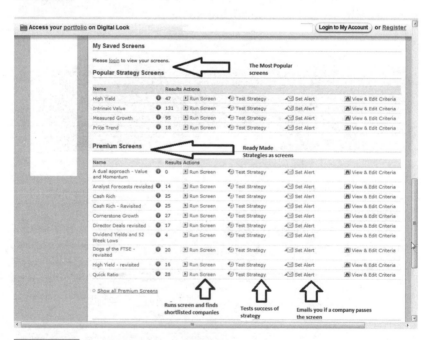

figure 11.49 The My Saved Screens page

Comparing the options

Table 11.2 provides a summary of what the various options we have discussed have to offer.

table 11.2 Comparison of the stock screening options

Product	Cost	Web-based or software	Advantages	Disadvantages	Reliability of data	Range of fundamental measures	Layout and simplicity/ease of use	Overall rating
ShareScope	Gold £16 a month	Software	Great technical and price analysis tools	Can be difficult to understand	★★★★	★★★★	★★★	★★★★
	Pro £32 a month (real time data)		Very comprehensive range of tools	Not cheap!				On balance the best value for experienced users
			Wide range of measures					
			Easy to export to spreadsheet					
			Fantastic charting tools					
CDREFS	Online from £17 a month	Software and web	Brilliant company summary pages	Can't be exported to spreadsheets	★★★★★	★★★★★	★★★★	★★★★
	Quarterly CD REFS £335 p.a.		Fantastic overview of markets	Expensive				The premium offer to experienced users
			Very reliable company data	Online service looks old fashioned				

(continues)

	Price	Type	Pros	Cons					Comment
Investor Ease	£11.45 per month inc. VAT	Software	Great update summary / Excellent portfolio/ watchlist monitoring / Easy to export	Limited range of measures / Old fashioned interface	***	***	****	***	Excellent software for beginner investors
FT.com screener	Free but need to register first	Web	Simple, clean layout / Global range of companies / Very easy to use	Limited range of measures / Can't be exported to spreadsheets	****	***	****	****	Great free web-based screener. Very easy to use
Digital Look	From £20 per month	Web	Extensive range of measures / Great tools and pre-selected screens / Tests the strategy	Underlying data can be unreliable / Not cheap!	***	****	****	***	Premium online screener but expensive
Filter X from ADVFN	Free	Web	Extensive range of measures / Great tools and pre-selected screens / Easy to export to spreadsheet	Messy website	****	***	**	***	Not as powerful as Digital Look but free!

The new fundamental indexing revolution
Rob Davies

A vocal and hugely sophisticated group of analysts and fund managers have coalesced around a simple idea – they contend that the traditional index is flawed in its design and that it needs to be rethought and linked back to ideas built around value investing. Fund manager Rob Davies, from Fundamental Tracker Investment Management (based in Glasgow), is one of these 'new' indexers trying to combine the best of 'value' investing with the transparency and efficiency of index fund investing. He's in the front line of a new movement of 'fundamentalists' who think that simply following a traditional index like the S&P 500 or the FTSE 100 is a deeply flawed exercise. In the first part of this chapter he explores these ideas and demonstrates how he's developed a fund strategy focused on the all-important dividend cheque!

At the end of Rob's overview we also feature an interview with the doyen of fundamental indexers, Rob Arnott of Research Affiliates and RAFI. In this wide ranging discussion we look at everything from whether equities are a good idea compared to bonds through to how Arnott constructs a fundamental index.

What's wrong with conventional indexing?

Accepting the logic of index investing is a big step but it's only the first one! The next step is to understand what you're actually tracking in an index. For most people that will amount to a choice between segments of the market usually based on size, such as the FTSE 100, the FTSE 250 or an all encompassing single index such as the FTSE All Share, which captures nearly all the UK listed market. All these popular indices use a similar methodology and, until just a few years ago, there was no choice as every index was based on capitalisation. That meant the weight of each stock in the fund was determined by its market capitalisation, with its total value determined by multiplying the share price by the number of shares outstanding.

For many academics this methodology for constructing an index simply reflects the underlying ideas of the efficient markets hypothesis (EMH) namely that the share price of a company captures everything that is known about the business. That includes its balance sheet, business prospects and the quality of the management. The theory is that modern capital markets are so efficient that it is impossible for any individual to secure a sustainable, legal, information advantage over their competitors. The fact that 80% of the market is still managed on an active basis by people who don't believe markets are efficient does not compromise the theory in the eyes of its academic adherents.

An equally important reason for using capitalisation as the mechanism for constructing a fund is that most, but not all, major stock exchange indices are based on the sum total of the value of the constituents. Basing a fund on the same principle as the index is a neat way of ensuring that the performance of the fund will never deviate too far from that of the index. There are exceptions however. Both the Dow Jones Industrial Average and the S&P 500 are determined by a committee and can best be viewed as 'active' indices in contrast to the rules-based indices like the FTSE and the Russell. The old FT30 used a similar, committee-based, subjective approach.

Whatever the process, both rules-based and subjective indexes have a growth bias. At first pass, this looks illogical: why does a market cap based index have a growth bias? The reason for this comes back to the issue of market capitalisation. Any company on the threshold of accession to the FTSE 100 will, by definition, be doing better than its peers. That means its valuation will be at a premium to its near neighbours, in other words valued as a growth share. In contrast the company that is about to be ejected will have fallen on hard times and its value will be discounted relative to its comparable companies. So companies joining an index will always be expensive and those leaving will always be cheap. The largest 100 companies in the FTSE All Share will not necessarily be the largest 100 by profits, book value, dividends or revenue; just price.

A real life example of how this works in practice can be found in the March 2009 changes for the FTSE 100. Out went Tate and Lyle with a price to book value of 1.37 and a PE ratio of 7.4. It was replaced by Fresnillo trading at a price to book ratio of 5.1 and a PE ratio of 25. The fact that the Tate share price has slid from 400p to 250p while Fresnillo had soared to from 100p to 434p in the few months prior to these changes confirms the view that indexes overpay for growth.

But there is a problem with using just share prices to create a portfolio – they don't have a direct correlation to the value of the underlying asset, namely the company that the market is valuing. Instead they represent the opinions and views of all the market participants and that means they are subject to all the manias and fashions that dominate financial affairs. In the past few decades those fashions have included technology, commodities, property and biotechnology. In previous centuries they have included railways, tulip bulbs and South Sea bubbles. Conversely, at the same time as one sector is fashionable another one is out of favour. At some point or other these have included commodities, utilities and banks. What this means is that an investor buying into a conventional index fund will always have a larger position in sectors that are popular and a smaller position in unpopular sectors, irrespective of the relative valuation of those sectors. In practical terms this means that any capitalisation weighted index will always overweight expensive share and underweight cheap shares, as this little exercise will demonstrate.

Assume the components of a stock index have aggregate earnings of £100m and the whole market is valued on a PE ratio of 10. Therefore the total market is valued at £1000m. Assume also that half the stocks have an above average valuation of 11 so the other half must be valued at 9× earnings. It follows therefore that the expensive half of the market is valued at £550m and the cheap half at £450m. Consequently any index tracker fund will have 55% of its assets in the expensive stocks and only 45% in the cheap stocks. We might not know which of the stocks are cheap and which are expensive. But we do know that cheap stocks outperform expensive stocks over time, yet the index fund is underweight in them. However, the situation is worse than that. Because the fund is overweight with expensive shares it has a higher PE ratio than the market. In our example it actually has a PE ratio of 10.1, i.e. 1% more than the index itself. You might be buying £100m worth of earnings, but doing it this way you are paying 1% more than the average. That is not good for long-term returns. The situation is even less attractive if there is a bigger discrepancy between the high and low valuations. If the market values the most expensive shares at 15× earnings and the cheapest at 5×, the average PE for the index fund becomes 12.5.

If that seems counter-intuitive this analogy might help. Imagine going shopping for apples and oranges. The apples are priced at 5p a pound and the oranges 15p. A buyer, using the logic of a tracker, wanting equal amounts of the different fruits would buy one pound of apples for 5p and three pounds of oranges for 45p. He buys three times as many oranges because they are three times as valuable. So the shopper has spent 50p for four pounds of fruit at an average cost of 12.5p a pound. A more rational shopper would buy a pound of each for an average cost of 10p a pound.

Of course no-one really knows which shares are expensive and which are cheap at any given time. However, we do know two things.

1   The market always overpays for growth. That is why value stocks out perform.

2   Valuations always revert to the mean. Expensive earnings, like those of Vodafone in 2000, eventually become earnings that are priced in line with the market. That erodes returns for the investor.

Over time the actual index components will change as the popularity of a stock or sector waxes and wanes, yet starting a portfolio with an over-weight position in an expensive sector and an underweight position in a cheap one is almost inevitably going to have a negative impact on returns in the long run. One of the oldest, and best, clichés in the money manage-ment business is that in the short term markets are voting machines; in the long run they are weighing machines. Conventional index funds are great at capturing the voting element of the stockmarket yet what is actually needed is a way of weighing the market.

Is there a better way to index?

It is clear from this discussion that there's a potentially fundamental flaw in creating a portfolio based solely on capitalisation, i.e. share price alone. After all, in what other walk of life do we make purchase decisions solely on the basis of price? We don't for instance choose our mix of vegetables at the supermarket by buying most of whichever is the highest price on that day. Indeed, we do the opposite. Any special offers are snapped up redu-cing our average cost per pound of vegetable. Cars are purchased on the basis of their size, reliability and performance, not just on price. Indeed, in every other avenue of commercial life we prefer to pay less for more. Supermarkets don't make buy-one-get-one-free offers without knowing what the reaction of shoppers is likely to be. Normally, when we spend our money we want some measure of what we are buying other than price. It might be the weight of a cauliflower, the top speed of a car or the number of springs in a bed. Why should we not do something similar when we buy shares? What we need is some fundamental measure of the value of a company.

A far sighted investment manager called Robert Jones at Goldman Sachs is credited as being the first to ponder these issues in 1990. He designed and ran a fund based around earnings, but the fund was closed down after it failed to beat the in-house enhanced index fund. Since then the main proponents have been Rob Arnott at Research Affiliates (who's interviewed at the end of this chapter), and Jeremy Siegel of Wisdom Tree. The main issue these two American-based analysts have had to address is which measure, or measures, should they use as well as working out more mundane issues such as the frequency of rebalancing and whether to use historic or forecast data.

The attraction of a tracker fund is that it buys all the shares in a particular index. That reduces risks by ensuring that the fund holds all shares that might do well. Equally, it will hold ones that might do badly thus dragging down the whole portfolio. So if we are going to design a mechanism that can be used across all stocks in the market we have to use some measure that is appropriate to a wide variety of companies and industries. Fortunately, there is no shortage of measures that can be used, and ways in which they can be applied, though each has advantages and disadvantages.

One point to note is that all fundamental funds are blind to the data they use. This is in sharp contrast to active fund managers who categorise companies by the sector they are in. Each sector will have its own valuation range to reflect the underlying nature of the business. That is why, for example, yields from utilities are always expected to be higher than yields from tech companies. The market is saying that dividends from tech companies are worth more than dividends from water or power companies. Fundamental funds say all dividends, book values, revenues and profits are equal. All index funds treat data in this agnostic way. But which measures should we focus on?

Book value

One traditional measure of value is the book value of the company, also sometimes known as net asset value. This is a pure accounting measure of the capital subscribed to create the company, the initial equity, less any debt but including the profits it has retained over its life and minus the dividends paid out. This narrow definition can work for some industries such as those that develop a product or service over time and sell those profitably, but there are a number of necessary caveats. The financial accounts can become quite distorted where companies have made a lot of acquisitions as goodwill and write-offs became significant. Periods of high inflation also have an impact by eroding the real value of debt and increasing the nominal value of tangible assets such as property or inventory. Companies working in natural resources that have made large discoveries of oil or other commodities are not able to include that additional value in the books. All they can do is record the cost of finding the deposits. Equally, a pharmaceutical company that develops a new drug can only charge the cost of discovery and development to its profit and loss account. As far as its book value is concerned inventing a drug is just research and development expenditure. Other companies may have established important brand names but it is hard to quantify their value and even harder to find a way to give that a value in the accounts. Without advertising many brand names fall by the wayside. Finally, markets and tastes change so that what was valuable several years ago may be worthless now. Records and cassettes, for example, are no longer so much in demand when music can be digitally downloaded. Book value then has some merits as a measure, but it also has many drawbacks. Book value is usually seen as a key factor in selecting value stocks so it is no surprise that it figures strongly in the approach used by a leading American fund management firm Dimensional (DFA). Research Affiliates also uses it as one of its four measures.

Profit and loss

The profit and loss (P&L) account is the traditional source of data for determining value. Starting at the top of the P&L statement many are attracted to the idea of using revenue as a measure because there is less scope for distortion. After all, it makes sense to assess a business on how much it sells. There is a problem with that though, and it is summed up in this little ditty:

Revenue is vanity

Profit is reality

Cash is sanity.

Quite often companies will chase business and then fail to make any money from it because the margins are too low. Unprofitable business has no value and giving it a weighting will lead to an index with a bias that does not reflect the real source of profits. In some industries even defining revenue can be tricky – the banks spring to mind as an example! Other businesses are agency businesses, such as advertising where the scope for gaming the numbers can be considerable – they can move booked sales back and forth between accounting periods, especially if the contract is over a long period of time. It is also fair to say that some industries, such as retailing, will always have large revenue numbers relative to the size of the business in comparison to say a drug company. Commodity companies such as miners and the oil majors are particularly susceptible to wild gyrations in their top line as prices change. Finally, currency volatility can make a big impact on sales. Depending on whether the costs that are associated with those sales are in the same currency can make a huge difference to whether that volatility is beneficial or not. Notwithstanding these concerns revenue is one of the four measures used by Research Affiliates as it is a very simple measure of a company's economic footprint.

Profits are a logical measure to base an index on – they could be the operating profit, profit before tax or net profit. The problem is that whichever level is chosen there is a high degree of subjectivity as to what items are included and which are excluded. A particular problem is the issue of exceptional items that can affect one year but reflect the accumulation of many years of business success, or problems. In essence the uncertainty here is that a great deal of the profit and loss statement has a large discretionary element to it and that makes comparisons between companies difficult. The last decade has seen an unusually large number of seemingly profitable companies suddenly collapse either through fraud or dramatic changes in their business conditions. In sum, profits have not always been what they seemed.

Many would argue that the cashflow statement is a better basis for comparison but again the issue of different standards is a key problem – what one company counts as capital expenditure another might include as operating costs. On top of that there are great differences in the nature of the cashflow between industries. A retailer, for example, will have a very different structure to its cashflow than, say, an oil company. Cashflow from a retailer might vary hugely over the course of the year as seasons change but an oil company might be faced with years of exploration before it receives any cash. Moreover, cashflows for financial companies such as banks and insurance companies have a completely different nature to what might be called 'conventional' companies. Using their data would distort any index based around them to a significant extent.

Dividends

There is though one measure that can be used across companies and has the great virtue of being independently verifiable. Dividends are the cash paid out by a company to its owners – the shareholders. That means this is a real transaction and can be confirmed by the recipients. Moreover, a dividend cheque from an oil company is just the same as a dividend cheque from a retailer, although usually larger! There are though cultural differences to the way companies view dividends. These are mostly between countries and usually derive from their tax treatment. Until quite recently the tax treatment of dividends in the US was quite adverse compared to stock options so it therefore suited companies to issue fresh stock rather than cash, especially as issuing new stock diluted shareholders but did not impact the cash in the company. That was one reason why many US companies did not pay dividends. The other was a rather machismo reasoning that only mature companies paid them. It was argued that true growth companies reinvested cash to build the business. The tech bubble showed the fallacy of that argument.

The most important point about dividends is that in reality they account for virtually all the returns from equity investing. Active investors desperately seek capital gains but study after study by the likes of Barclays, Credit Suisse and Société Générale on both sides of the Atlantic show the importance of reinvested dividend income and the growth of the dividend. Even over a short period of five years Société Générale showed that these two factors accounted for 80% of the return. Jeremy Siegel of Wisdom Tree has calculated that the figure rises to 96% for US stocks over the 80 years from 1926 to 2006. You ignore dividends at your peril. For these reasons all three fundamental fund processes use dividends either on their own or as part of a blend of measures.

A key argument of Rob Arnott at indexing firm RAFI is that he aims to measure the economic footprint of a company rather than its financial one – that means that looking at key indicators such as number of employees, square footage of factory or retail space are all valid because they give an assessment of how significant a company is to the community. The problem is that comparing people on the sandwich production line at Compass with advertising executives at WPP will necessarily give a distorted comparison.

Single measure or blended, historic or forecast data

With all these different measures the would-be fundamental tracker or index builder now has to make two decisions:

■ Should you use a single measure in isolation or blend several of them?
■ Is historic data the best to use or should you rely on future estimates or forecast data?

Using one fundamental measure like profits or earnings per share is obviously simpler, and easier to comprehend, yet that measure might be unfavourable for some companies, or even exclude whole sub-sectors of the market? If, by contrast, a blend of measures is chosen what proportion of each valuation metric for instance should be used? Would equal weighting be valid? Blending has the obvious advantage of not giving preference to any one particular measure that might favour, or disadvantage, one particular company or sector but it doesn't avoid that second, equally daunting challenge, namely whether a series of blended measures are backward looking or forward facing in their use of data.

This second challenge – whether to use forward or backward looking data – is based on the reality that companies report full accounts twice a year, usually two or three months after the period end. That is the most accurate picture we are ever going to get of a company. Sadly even when the companies report we'll be faced with the challenge of working out what some of those numbers actually mean. Terry Smith in his famous book *Accounting for Growth*[1] pinpointed the many ways that companies can flatter the way they present themselves to the investing public. Remember too that com-

---

[1] Smith, T. (1996) *Accounting for Growth: Stripping the Camouflage from Company Accounts*, Century Business.

panies have a habit of restating figures when it suits them, so we should not treat everything in the accounts as gospel. Nevertheless, published accounts are the best we have to go on. But accounts published in, say, February, tell us what happened to the company as far back as the January of the previous year. In stockmarket terms that is ancient history. This historic data is obviously going to be the most accurate but, in a rapidly changing world, how much value is there in knowing the precise amounts for a company from as much as 14 months ago. To get the hard data we really need we have to, in effect, wait for a whole 12 months, with an update every six months. That suggests the data in the index could be quite stale!

Would the fund not be better off using forward looking estimated data rather than accurate, but historic, data? Is it better to be roughly right about the future than precisely wrong about the past? Markets change and what was a market leading product last year might be obsolete today. Having a factory geared up to produce CDs isn't much use if everyone is downloading music from the internet. That plant might have cost £10m to build, but it might not be worth that to a buyer today. Forecast data though is not without its problems, the key one being there isn't much of it. Analysts tend to focus only on a few key measures like earnings and dividends. Not all will have reliable estimates for book value, or maybe even revenue. There is also the small matter of the reliability of those forecasts. That said, forecasts of fundamental measures do have the unique benefit of being able to incorporate expectations of the future on a real time basis. Steadfastly holding to the historic book value of a company as a fundamental measure when its credit rating has changed from AAA to junk is clearly not satisfactory.

There are obvious attractions in using a blend of measures, namely that it smoothes out the numbers. Equally, there are some significant drawbacks too. The most important being which ones do you use and how do you weight each parameter? The more subjectivity that is added by decisions such as these the further the process moves away from being strictly fundamental. Research Affiliates is the only one to use a blended approach while Wisdom Tree and Fundamental Tracker use single measures. My fund management company, Fundamental Tracker, is the only one to use forecast data.

Having set out some of the issues related to data, we now need to consider the different research-based approaches to fundamental indexing offered by the big asset management firms.

The runners and riders

One of the first advocates of fundamental indices was Rob Arnott, head of a California-based firm Research Affiliates. He and his team use a blend of historic data to construct their indices. On the east coast of America the boffins at Wisdom Tree, by contrast, have opted to use two measures; dividends and earnings, but not in the same funds. In the UK there is only one fund using the fundamental tracker concept, the Munro Fund, and it uses forecast gross cash dividends. This approach uses dividend payouts, weighted by volume not price as they would in a conventional index yield fund like the FTSE Dividend Plus.

Table 12.1 details the unique approaches of the key fundamental tracker/index managers – although they all use different measures and processes not one of them has any use for the traditional share price way of constructing an index.

table 12.1 Three individual approaches

	Wisdom Tree	RAFI	FTIM
Measures	Cash Dividends Earnings	Blend of revenue, earnings, dividends and book value	Gross cash Dividends
Time	Current annualised	Five-year historic smoothed	One year ahead
Rebalancing frequency	Annually	Annually	Monthly
Vehicle	Exchange traded funds	Exchange traded funds	Open ended investment companies

A proper analysis of these different approaches is a long and detailed exercise and is beyond the scope of this chapter, but probably the most important factor to be considered is the benchmark the funds are compared with. Exchange traded funds (ETFs) are typically compared to the indices that were created for them so they can appear to be less risky, as measured by tracking error, than they are when measured against more familiar indices. A fund might appear to be doing very well against its own benchmark, but when compared to a traditional index it might appear as having a higher risk and a lower return. Ultimately, the test of any investment process must be whether it delivers better returns at lower risk than a conventional passive tracker.

Analysis of the data is also complicated somewhat by the profusion of funds that many of the fund providers have created, making it hard to choose one fund that is truly representative of each process. In the next section we take a brief look at each of the different index construction processes.

Dimensional Fund Advisors

One fund manager that doesn't quite fit into any conventional definition of fundamental indexing but is worth considering first is US firm Dimensional Fund Advisors (DFA). It doesn't describe itself as either a passive or active fund manager. Like some of the fundamental fund managers it has a clear and strong investment process but, unlike most of them, it has an overlay of subjectivity that makes it more akin to an active fund. Its aim is to outperform the index it is benchmarked against by taking positions that are biased to small cap and value stocks. Its logic is based on the ground breaking work by economists Eugene Fama and Kenneth French (discussed in Chapter 3) that small cap and value stocks have an historic record of out performance. DFA applies its process on a continuous basis so is not subject to the tyranny of being tied to only rebalancing a fund once a year. As we saw earlier, even when an index is rules-based, such as the FTSE 100, it still has an inherent growth bias, so any process that promotes value will have a built in advantage over an index that has an inherent growth bias.

DFA's unique approach is very different from that of the three main fundamental indexing outfits.

Wisdom Tree

Wisdom Tree builds indices based on earnings and dividends using the latest trailing 12-month data while rebalancing is run on an annual basis, on 30 November. That passive approach can have its flaws as Chief Investment Officer Jeremy Schwarz admits. In 2008, for instance, Wisdom Tree was hostage to stale and out of date data centred on rapidly changing dividend payouts and suffered dreadfully, as all value biased funds did, when formerly reliable dividend payers cut payouts in response to extreme market conditions. Wisdom Tree is the brainchild of Jonathan Steinberg and started out as an indexing as opposed to fund management company.

He kicked off with the concept of creating a blended index using market capitalisation and dividends and approached Professor Jeremy Siegel of Wharton to validate the exercise. Siegel, like many others, had realised the inherent flaws of cap weighted indices during the dotcom bubble at the turn of the millennium. His regular surveys of long-term returns demonstrated the problems caused by cap weighting and in his 1994 publication reviewing capital market returns he acknowledged that other measures might be preferable. That started him on the road towards the concept of using dividends to create an index. The triangle was closed when hedge fund manager Michael Steinberg joined and provided the financial backing to enable Wisdom Tree to launch its range of funds in June 2006.

Wisdom Tree creates indices for a very wide range of markets and sub-sectors. Some are based totally on dividends while some are based on earnings – in both cases annualised data is used. Its main funds are benchmarked against the S&P 500 index which, oddly, is a subjective index. This does present a slight inequality if only because a rules-based portfolio (Wisdom Tree's) is being measured against a subjective index like the S&P 500 whose composition is determined by a committee. In total Wisdom Tree runs 42 separate funds on fundamental indexing principles to track a variety of indices in and outside the US. All its funds are ETFs and in March 2009 it managed about $3.6bn. Like many value orientated strategies it suffered in the 2008 bear market relative to the main indices but the lags were not large. To address the issue of a value bias Wisdom Tree has launched an earnings weighted fund based on NASDAQ stocks which uses a more complex blend of measures.

Research Affiliates

Rob Arnott of Research Affiliates (also known as RAFI) is probably the most high profile advocate of fundamental indexing and his seminal 2005 paper simply called 'Fundamental Indexation'[2] co-authored with Jason Hsu and Philip Moore sets the arguments out very clearly. He uses an equally weighted blend of four measures to create the index. These measures are the trailing five-year smoothed data for revenue, book value, earnings and dividends. As with DFA and Wisdom Tree the danger here is that the data

---

[2] Arnott, R., Hsu, J. and Moore, P. (2005) 'Fundamental Indexation', *Financial Analysts Journal*, Vol. 61, No. 2.

can become very stale as the annual rebalancing approaches. Like many observers he watched the turn of the millennium tech bubble with alarm and resolved to find a better way to construct an index. He assembled a vast array of data stretching back to 1957 when the S&P 500 index was created. From this mass of data he and his team deduced that the most efficient construction – the process that gave the best return for the lowest risk – was an equally weighted blend of the revenue, profits, book value and dividends. His back tested time series starts in 1962, the first year on which five-year trailing data (data from the previous five years) can be assembled. This huge back test showed clearly that Arnott's version of an index generated better returns than the S&P 500 index with lower risk – although part of the reason for this relative success has, in my opinion, more to do with the construction of the S&P 500 index, which is subjective, than his fundamental index.

Arnott delves into even greater detail in his book, entitled *The Fundamental Index: a better way to invest*[3] co-written with Jason Hsu and John West. In it he explores in the growth bias of traditional market capitalisation weighted indices and details the extensive back testing work he and his team have done to prove that their fundamental indexation produces better returns with lower levels of risk. He also argues that the efficient markets hypothesis is still a hugely important concept, but one that doesn't actually work in the real world anymore. An interview with Rob Arnott follows at the end of the chapter.

Fundamental Tracker Investment Management

My own company is Fundamental Tracker Investment Management (FTIM) – the only UK-based firm to offer a fund-based fundamental indexing approach through its Munro Fund, which uses forecast gross cash dividends to create a portfolio benchmarked to the FTSE 350 index. It differs from the Wisdom Tree and RAFI approach in that it was forecast data, not historic data, on the basis that it is better to be roughly right than precisely wrong. We use the consensus forecasts from all the analysts sourced by Bloomberg for the financial year beyond the current one and then adjust for share buybacks. Like our two US peers, FTIM uses the gross dividend the company will distribute, not the more commonly used per share figure. We weight

---

[3] Arnott, R., Hsu, J. and West, J. (2008) *The Fundamental Index: a better way to invest*, Wiley.

dividends by volume not price as a conventional yield-based index fund would do. By rebalancing the model portfolio every month we are also able continually to adjust to the small changes that are made by analysts on an almost daily basis. Last but by no means least we assume our key measures (the dividends) are all equal – in other words the pound of dividend from an oil company is worth the same as a pound of dividend from a retailer. In conventional active management this is not the case.

Our Munro Fund OEIC was launched in September 2007, just at the start of one of the worst bear markets in recent years and in absolute terms the initial performance was poor as the stock market collapsed under the weight of the credit crunch. In relative terms – and that is what really counts for an index fund – it has delivered on its promise, namely better returns in its asset class relative to conventional index tracking funds.

The Munro Fund investment process, in detail

As this fund is run by this writer it might be fruitful to describe the mechanics of the process in detail. Each month we run the following process:

- The consensus forecast dividends per share, for one year ahead, for all the companies in the FTSE 350 are downloaded together with the issued share capital.
- Adjustments are made where appropriate for changes in share capital for such things as rights issues or share buybacks.
- The forecast dividend for each company is then multiplied by the expected number of shares to calculate the forecast gross cash payment, converted to sterling if needed. For a company such as Vodafone this can be as much as £4.5bn while Marks and Spencer might only be £213m. Individual contributions are then aggregated to get a total for the FTSE 350. In March 2009 this figure was £63bn.
- Finally, each company's contribution to the total is calculated as a percentage. So in one month, for instance, Vodafone's weight in the model portfolio might be 6.8% while Marks and Spencer's is 0.33%. These new weights are then applied to the portfolio. Normally this is done by using uninvested cash to top up underweight holdings to keep trading to a minimum.
- Occasionally, where positions have become substantially overweight, the holding is trimmed back to bring it in line with the model. In essence the process keeps the fund aligned to the largest flows of cash, from dividends, into the market.

Wegelin & Co

Finally, it is worth mentioning one last fund manager that boasts its own very unique process – it's not a pure fundamental index provider or tracker fund manager although it does follow a strict rules-based procedure for its investment process. Swiss private bank Wegelin & Co operates what it calls an 'active indexing' process to manage its SFR3bn portfolio of pension and private money.

Wegelin & Co has based its approach to markets around the simple concept that markets eventually revert to mean over the long term, especially at the national level. It doesn't buy individual stocks but looks to invest in national markets that represent good value. Central to this approach is that it has no exposure to markets viewed as expensive – the secret ingredient in its process is its proprietary process for determining the value of stocks relative to cash that underlies the methodology. This calculation uses a variety of measures such as leading indicators, risk premiums, credit spreads and investment behaviour that are blended (with equal weights) to give a measure relative to the global market. Once it has determined which national markets have good prospects, and which don't, it aligns its portfolio accordingly, with the overall universe of stocks (the potential markets to invest in) based on the MSCI World index which contains 22 different countries including Japan, the USA and the UK. This wide 'opportunity set' doesn't mean it will have a position in every nation – if the measure or indicator is negative it might have no position or even go short.

One of the authors of the process is Dr Magne Orgland and he says one of the great virtues of the process is that they no longer have interminable investment committee meetings: they simply rely on their process as they have found it throws up better results than the consensus of experts. This simple statement is actually one of the most important aspects of any rules or fundamentals-based investment process – if done properly fundamentals-based investing saves an enormous amount of time in decision making with investment committees suddenly redundant because of the quantitative-based processes. While that may be disturbing to those who enjoy the cut and thrust of debating business models, valuation metrics, demographics and money supply there is a great deal of evidence that decisions made by such groups are rarely consistently good. Anyone with experience of investment clubs will quickly realise that democracy and investing are not compatible.

As with many rules-based investment processes much of the value derives from rebalancing to bring the actual portfolio back into line with the model. Wegelin rebalances its funds every month, which it claims is a major reason for its low tracking error.

Why fundamental funds?

So, to conclude, the advantages of fundamental tracking/indexing over mainstream actively managed funds are numerous and easy to understand and include:

- a defined process that eliminates subjectivity and human emotion
- that elimination of subjectivity reduces manpower, reducing costs and time to action changes
- lower management fees improve returns to investors
- the defined process improves transparency for investors
- most fundamental processes focus on dividends, the largest source of wealth creation in equity investing
- the process won't change even if the fund manager does – active fund managers suffer from high turnover so you never know who will be managing your money in five or ten years' time.

Fundamental funds also offer some substantial advantages over conventional index-based funds as well:

- They remove the growth bias – eliminating price from the construction process provides a better way of tracking the underlying earnings because it eliminates the popularity measure inherent in share prices.
- Fundamental index funds generally offer higher yields.
- Some fundamental fund managers offer more frequent rebalancing.

No-one should expect any index fund to shoot the lights out. These funds are designed to give the returns of the index they are benchmarked to, but because they are process driven they are (hopefully) cheap to run and boast lower management fees. Reducing costs has the same effect on the investor as higher returns, but without the risk. Most importantly with index funds you are only paying for what's called beta – the returns of the market. With active funds you pay more for the pursuit of alpha (the ability of a manager or process to deliver more than the returns of the market) but often fail to even get that beta. Conventional index funds will never beat the index, indeed many lag the index by a considerable amount because of fees and the factors mentioned above. The advantage that fundamental funds offer is the ability to close the gap between the return of the fund and the return of the index.

Interview

Rob Arnott, Research Affiliates

When it comes to fundamental indexing, the real pioneer in this space is Rob Arnott, founder of research firm Research Affiliates, also known as RAFI. He's one of the most articulate exponents of fundamentals-based indexing – and one of the most brilliant analysts of stockmarkets in the US. In the summer of 2009 we met up with Arnott in London and asked him to map out his views on various stock selection strategies in volatile markets. In particular, did he still hold to the view that shares were a great long-term investment, regardless of whether they were value stocks or growth stocks? We also talked to him about the importance of value investing and explored how he constructed his own fundamental RAFI indices.

Interviewer: In the beginning of 2009 you published a very interesting paper in the *Journal of Indexes*, suggesting that bonds have actually out performed equities over the last decade.... actually over the last couple of decades.

Arnott: Over the last 40 years!

Interviewer: Now that raises an interesting question, which is that most people's windows of opportunity, in terms of investing both in bonds and equities is probably a 20 or 30 year time span, over which they can accumulate a pot of money. Your analysis suggests that actually shares – equities – haven't been a very good idea for most investors over the last 10 to 20 to 30 years, which is not exactly the conventional wisdom!

Arnott: What's going on is something very simple. Basically we have an industry which has developed a cult of equities. A notion that if you buy stocks you will win, if you're patient. And patience is defined as five or ten years, that starts to march to new highs, interrupted by occasional inconveniences known as bear markets. The reality is something very different. And that is that stocks do win over the very long run, and indeed they should because they're a secondary claim on company resources relative to bonds. But they win over spans measured in generations, not measured in years. And they win in fits and starts. The stocks for the long-run thesis, promoted by Jeremy Siegel, has been embraced by the investment banking and brokerage community, the financial advisor community, and has been morphed into something more than it is. It's been morphed into the notion that it doesn't matter what you pay for stocks as long as you're patient. And that's wrong. Anything you invest in, if you buy it cheap, you'll likely to be pleased fairly quickly. If you pay too much, you're likely to have to wait a long, long time to be happy – if ever.

Interviewer: Don't you think therefore that that raises a difficult problem for investors? What do they invest in? If equities are not a good idea over their window of opportunity what should they do?

Arnott: [Very few] investors look at an array of investment choices and pose the question – out of this rostra of choices, which of these has done really badly over the last one, three and five years? And is it a bargain now? People don't do that. What people do is look through a range of choices and say, 'What's done well?' As if buying something that's done well allows you to participate in that past success – which is rubbish.

Most investors look for what's done well and the better it's done, the more willing they are to pursue it. Imagine back in 2002, looking at emerging markets stocks, which had had a negative return for ten years. And imagine thinking gosh, this is now really cheap. I ought to buy this. These economies are growing faster than ours. How wonderful is that? People don't think that way. And so, one of the core messages, is a very simple one and that is the markets don't reward comfort. The markets reward discomfort. If you invest in something that is popular, you are likely to be disappointed.

And in 2000, and again in 2007, stocks were very popular. There were those promoting the notion that stocks were safer than bonds – based on the fact that, over very long periods of time, there are very few 20-year spans where stocks underperform bonds. Well that's true. But if the view that stocks are safer, and that leads them to a valuation level that is quite extraordinary, they may indeed underperform bonds for 20 years. And in fact, that's exactly what happened over the 40-year span that ended early this year. Those who bought stocks in early 1969, that's a long time ago, would have been better off in long treasury bonds. Pretty startling.

And it's because 40 years ago, stocks were yielding 2½%, bonds were yielding 6%. Bonds were out of favour, they became more out of favour in the early 1970s, they did very badly, so did stocks. But with some see-sawing back and forth, eventually stocks became extravagantly expensive, and crashed. And at the end of that crash, they had managed to under-perform bonds not for ten years, or 20 years, but for 40 years.

Interviewer: Professors Elroy Dimson and Paul Marsh [at the London Business School] have also observed the momentum effect, and they have suggested picking shares with the greatest momentum. Can this generate extra return?

Arnott: Momentum works in the short run; it doesn't work in the long run. And also momentum works until it doesn't work. When it doesn't work, it bites you very hard. The problem with momentum is it doesn't work at market turns. So, if something has performed brilliantly, yes, momentum may carry it higher. But there's no harm in trimming it. And continuing to trim it, and continuing to trim it. Because eventually it will turn. Momentum works in spans measured in months, and anti-momentum works in spans measured in years. What has performed brilliantly over the last five years, for instance, is highly unlikely to be brilliant the next five years. Highly unlikely. While momentum is powerful, it is a short-term phenomenon.

Interviewer: So should we therefore all be racing out buying bonds? Should we be stuffing our portfolios full of bonds and get rid of those equities?

Arnott: Absolutely not. We should not replace a 'cult of equities' with a 'cult of bonds'. Our point is that the price we pay for an asset matters tremendously. If we buy an asset when it's cheap, we'll likely to be pleased very soon. If we buy it when it's expensive and popular and trendy and everyone loves it, we're likely to have to wait a long time.

Interviewer: So are you suggesting we should treat bonds like we treat equities, which is to buy them cheap? Buy them when they yield a very substantial margin? Buy them when they just strike you as a bargain – they're cheap?

Arnott: Yes! The best asset allocation opportunities are not always choosing between stocks and bonds, but choosing within the bond market and within the stock market, specifically [when the spread] between growth and value stocks [is] almost without precedent. [At the beginning of 2009 that] spread in valuation multiples, in yields and price to sales ratios, was almost without precedent. It was a wonderful time to buy deep value. By the same token, within the bond market the gap between the very low 3% treasury yields at that same time, and the extraordinary 20% yields in junk bonds and in convertible bonds, was the widest spread ever seen. The spread was wider than it ever reached in the Great Depression, so the best opportunities in bonds in early 2009 were not in treasuries. They were in what is generally seen as the riskier parts of the bond market.

The best way to invest often is to contra-trade against what has done best and is most popular, and into what is done worst and is most loathed. That's very hard to do. It means buying junk bonds when everyone knows they are all going bust. It means buying the deep value stocks, the autos, the banks, the industrials when everyone knows that there's a new economy and these are all going bust.

It may be uncomfortable, but it works because the most powerful mechanism in the market is mean reversion. It's like a pendulum. When the pendulum swings too far, it's going to swing back. We can't know how far it's going to swing back, we can't know when it's going to swing back, we can't see the pendulum with enough accuracy to pick the top of the swing and catch it just before it goes the other way. But if we're getting more and more invested in the asset during an upswing, before it swings back, the reversal will clobber us.

Interviewer: Are you suggesting therefore, that endlessly tinkering around with finding the perfect index fund and also trying to get it right in terms of perfect balance of assets... is slightly beside the point? That what you should actually be doing is, as you say, buying low, selling high! The current kind of thinking about portfolios which suggest the perfect mix − should it be 31.6% UK equities, versus 42.3% foreign − is slightly missing the point?

Arnott: I think it makes a lot of sense to diversify; I do not think it makes sense to put all of our eggs in one basket. If we were to choose the single most out of favour, loathed market in the world and constantly revisit that portfolio and make sure we're always in it, chances are very good that we would do beautifully. In the long run. Chances are also reasonably good that one or another of those investments deserves to be loathed and hurts us badly. I think diversification has a lot of merit. Sometimes it doesn't work. [At the end of 2008] diversification failed miserably. Everything was cratering, everything.

So efforts to diversify hurt us in 2008, they didn't help. But they helped us − with a lag, because after mid-November [2008], the safe havens that people use for diversification recovered handily. So I think we all need a diversified portfolio. I think the notion of arguing over 31% UK equities versus 33%, is a complete waste of time. Unless we're just doing rebalancing as our sole means of adding value. If we're broadly diversified, the key question is, what half dozen assets are seriously out of favour and seriously cheap?

Interviewer: Now this raises a very interesting question. Warren Buffett maintains that maybe we diversify too much? Actually Warren Buffett's on record as saying he's always made his biggest profits from the smallest number of big bets.

Arnott: Oh yes. That's absolutely right. The notion of diversifying happens with three or four significant positions in seriously cheap assets. And if we go beyond ten, we're diluting the opportunity set. We're reducing our ability to add value. So, it's a tradeoff. [Warren Buffett] is very well diversified. His largest positions tend to be maybe 20% of his assets. And if we have 20% of our money in something that goes bust, how bad is that? It's very unpleasant but it's not lethal. For example, if we have 20 assets, 5% in each, it sharply mitigates the pain if something goes bust, but if something quadruples, we've just made 20%. Now, if we've got 20% in each of five bets, and one quadruples, we've just made $60 profit on the one winning bet. So...

Interviewer: What about hunting down growth stocks? People like stock picking and they like going out there and picking companies that are growing. Do you think that's a fool's game for most people?

Arnott: I think the market does a beautiful job of identifying where the growth opportunities are. And it then overpays for them. We have some new work based on a concept that we call 'clairvoyant value'. Wouldn't it be nice if we could get a copy of the *Financial Times* with share prices listed, and next to them the true fair value – what the companies will actually deliver – the present value of all future cashflows. If we had that, it would be very valuable. We obviously don't have that, but we can create a 1980 copy of the FT with the prices and the fair value over the subsequent 29 years. That's easy. If we do that, we find a very interesting pattern. Companies commanding premium multiples mostly do better as a business than companies commanding lower valuation multiples – the correlation between the valuation multiples that they have and that they ought to have is 50–60%; it's huge. But, here's the problem. The companies that deserve a higher multiple, on average, deserve about a 50% premium to the ones that deserve a lower multiple, but they command an average premium of 100%. The market overpays for the growth that it correctly perceives.

Interviewer: So that's fascinating isn't it, because what you're suggesting is that trying to spot growth stocks in advance is a mug's game! You're never going to spot them until after they've already caused a sensation!

Arnott: That's not true. As an example let's take Bank of America vs. Google. The market pays a very large premium multiple for Google and a very deep discount for Bank of America. I think there's an extremely high likelihood that Google will grow far more than Bank of America over the next ten years. Even over the next 20 years. I also think there's a very high likelihood that Google's shares will underperform Bank of America's shares, over the next ten to 20 years. The market tends to pick the right companies and pay approximately twice as much premium for them as it should.

Interviewer: Is it even worth trying to get ahead of the crowd then when it comes to spotting growth stocks?

Arnott: The challenge is that so many people are doing it now – [that's] the key hurdle. And if you think you're there before the crowd, look at the valuation multiples. Is it trading at a substantial premium? If so, someone else is there with you. The other challenge is to take those beloved, wonderful companies and sell them when they become too expensive. Even if they're still wonderful companies and they still have glowing prospects, they become overpriced.

Interviewer: Let's return now to value – value hasn't done terribly well recently has it [2009]?

Arnott: That's the time to buy value. Mean reversion.

Interviewer: Yes, let me interrogate that for one minute though. Don't value enthusiasts always say that it's time to buy, when value hasn't worked?

Arnott: And they'll often be right, whenever value hasn't worked.

Interviewer: Value has been an observed phenomenon. If you buy cheap stocks, you go against the market, it's done well. But that doesn't necessarily mean it'll do well in the future. The past is not necessarily the guide to the future, is it?

Arnott: Correct.

Interviewer: What happens if the markets have recently fundamentally changed and that the weight of money out chasing value has swamped the value effect or anomaly? What happens if the market has changed so much that that risk premium or inefficiency or whatever you call it has been arbitraged away. It won't exist in the future because the minute anything becomes cheap it'll be pounced on and then the market price of a share will reflect it. So therefore, value has gone?

Arnott: The easiest test for this idea is to pose the question: has the spread between growth and value become very narrow? If the spread in valuation multiples is very narrow, as it was in mid-2007, value can do rather badly; the phenomenon you're talking about was perhaps an important part of what happened two years ago. When the spread becomes very narrow it can then widen again; as growth becomes more expensive and value becomes less expensive.

Now in March [of 2009], the spread between growth and value measured on price to book or price to sales, was the widest it's ever been in history with the sole exception of the peak of the technology bubble in 2000. What happened after that 2000 tech bubble peak, when people said value was dead? Value out performs for seven consecutive years.

I'm not saying that value [strategies and shares] will out perform for seven consecutive years from the wide valuation spreads of early 2009. I'm saying that value is very cheap. The spread between growth and value historically averages a two to one ratio. As value has underperformed, it's become a two and a half to one ratio. At the peak of the technology bubble, it was three to one. The spread never got there before or since. Two and a half to one is a big spread. That two and a half to one ratio means that the spread is likely to contract which helps value to win even more than it normally does. So I think we're looking at an extraordinary opportunity to buy deep value. The most loathed companies!

Interviewer: So should we all be racing out and buying banking stocks?

Arnott: That could be one of your five buckets of deeply loathed assets in a diversified portfolio. I would not put most of my money in banking stocks... but I would be very comfortable with a meaningful allocation, sure.

Interviewer: How do you actually build a growth strategy then? You could look at dividends for instance. Dividends are extremely powerful... But then other people say no, no, no, the dividends aren't important because actually people have been cancelling dividends right, left and centre. And therefore if you get stuck with the high dividend yield in portfolio, you'll be in trouble. So actually what you should do is focus on things like book value? Which measures and strategies should you use? Should you focus in on the balance sheet or the dividend?

Arnott: They both point in the same direction.

Interviewer: But what about the cashflow generated by the business? Or the tangible book assets?

Arnott: They all work. And they all point in slightly different directions. You've put your finger on exactly the reason that we decided not to use a single measure of a company's fundamental scale in developing the Fundamental Index® concept; we rely on four measures to mitigate this effect. We rely on company sales, which are the root source of all profits and dividends. We rely on book value, which are the net assets that companies use to operate and to fund future developments. We rely on profits, but we use cashflow not reported earnings. And we rely on dividends. For each of these, the Fundamental Index (methodology) doesn't pay any attention to price. It weights companies according to how big they are, based on sales, profits, book value and then dividends.

By using a blend of several measures, we smooth the rough edges of each of the four. They all have rough edges. A dividend approach focuses us on mature companies late in their evolution, with high dividend yields and slow growth. It shuns growth companies. A sales-based approach focuses on companies with vast sales and thin margins. A book value approach focuses attention on companies with aggressive accounting. Enron looked great on a book value basis. And a cash-flow basis will focus on cyclical companies at cyclical peaks and earnings. None of them is without its warts and bits of awkwardness, so using a blend gives us a much more comfortable ride.

Interviewer: And you've put these ideas into practice through your fundamental indices – the RAFI indices – haven't you? The index has a value bias doesn't it?

Arnott: It has a value tilt, measured relative to the stock market, but it has a very special kind of value tilt. But, let's not forget that the market has a growth tilt relative to the economy. Most of the stock market's value is in stocks which are popular, with lofty growth expectations. A Fundamental Index portfolio is a mirror image of the market's willingness to pay a premium for growth. So if the market's willing to pay a huge premium for growth, as it is now, the Fundamental Index portfolios look [by contrast] like they've got a deep value tilt. In mid-2007, when the market wasn't paying much of a premium for the growth stocks, the Fundamental Index portfolios looked like a market portfolio with a slight value bias.

Compared to the market, where the size of a company in the index is constantly changing, often by a wide margin, our mix of assets is more stable over time. Because cap weighting is going to chase every fad, every bubble, every change in expectations in the market, the sector and company weights are constantly changing. So, most of the value added from the Fundamental Index concept doesn't come from its value tilt; it comes from contra-trading against the market's constantly changing whims.

And that's worth something. I found it really interesting in the last 12 months: 2008 was a miserable year for value, all over the world. The Fundamental Index strategy globally underperformed the MSCI All Country World Index, for the first time since 1999. It underperformed by a lofty three-tenths of a per cent – a tiny shortfall, but it was a shortfall. Clients weren't thrilled because normally a Fundamental Index strategy will mitigate down markets and here was a big down market, and we underperformed it very slightly. But clients weren't that alarmed, given the slight size of the underperformance. What alarmed them was the pending rebalance. Coming into the new year, we got lots of calls from clients saying, 'You're about to rebalance into financials, autos, industrials, consumer discretionary. These areas are going to be savaged in the forthcoming depression.' And my reaction was, 'That's what the Fundamental Index methodology does: It rebalances into the most loathed companies and out of the most trendy, popular and comfortable holdings, because that's what works.'

Interviewer: If you are effectively engaging in a contrarian strategy where you are deliberately picking the most unloved stocks, is it not better to go with the disciplined active manager, who will instead of picking 100 of the FTSE 100, will pick say ten?

Arnott: The challenge is that active fund managers can only win by having a loser on the other side of their trades. On average, therefore, they have no skill; on average they add no value. If you can identify the one out of 20 that has solid skill, and is not managing so much money that he isn't eliminating his profits because of the costs of the trades, more power to you. Because that should win by even more than the Fundamental Index concept. But the Fundamental Index methodology is a really nice simply way to get the benefits of the insightful contrarian active manager, without the headaches of wondering whether he still has the fire in his belly, whether he still has the insights that allow him to divine what is really out of favour and poised to turn.

This latter bit is the piece that the Fundamental Index concept misses. It indiscriminately dives into the unloved; some of those stocks will rebound quickly, some of those will rebound after a long delay, and some of those will crater. Some of them will even go to zero. And some will go up five- or ten-fold. So the Fundamental Index approach winds up being a really interesting disciplined way to get contrarian investment decisions into your portfolio.

part

three

Putting it all together

13

An action plan

This book has made a determined attempt to remind investors that they need to be guided by sound theory, observation of past trends and rigorous-based analysis of the evidence. That journey from knee jerk, tips-fuelled investing based on rumour and tittle tattle has encountered a great many fine minds and even finer investors, but it has probably left many of you in something of a quandary. The evidence suggests that a wide range of ideas and strategies appear to work some of the time, but the choice is great! Many readers are probably wondering what they should do next – which strategy or screen should they use? In this concluding chapter we'll try and cut through all the analysis and academic study and look at what actually works, examine which are the preferred strategies and explore how you might actually implement these ideas within a portfolio.

Introduction

A number of key themes will run through this chapter. The first and perhaps most important is that there is no one solution, no one magic screen or strategy that works all the time. At the end is an interview with one of the best quantitative analysts in finance – Andrew Lapthorne of SG. Over this long and detailed conversation, Andrew discusses why he thinks investors have to be thorough, check with the evidence and be contrarian where necessary. But his concluding thought is perhaps the most powerful and certainly one that I wholeheartedly agree with: 'The idea that only one thing works at any one point in time, or there's only one way to invest, or one way to make money, seems ridiculous. Various types of things might work.' I'd go further and say that various types of strategy do work at varying times and in varying stockmarkets.

Smart investors have to pay attention to the direction of volatile markets and at the very least have to question whether they think *now* is a good time to be investing in shares. With the answer to this firmly in mind, investors need to realise that in many volatile, downward moving markets, some hugely successful strategies falter and fail – for extended periods of time in fact. At this point investors need to examine alternative ideas. But even in steadily rising, low volatility markets investors should think about running a number of strategies at once, maybe with one or two in the core and a 'satellite' strategy for risky opportunities. Later in this chapter are some favourite strategies, a repeat of the screens and suggestions as to how and when you might match these strategies within your portfolio.

Another key observation is that *markets evolve and change*. MIT-based economist Andrew Lo has made a very convincing case for a theory that suggests that markets adapt and change radically over time as market participants observe behaviour and analyse different returns from different assets. His theory of adaptive market efficiency suggests a number of powerful conclusions: that the relationship between risk and reward is unlikely to be stable over time as different market participants change their view of the markets; that classical arbitrage opportunities exist and persist in spite of markets being largely efficient, and that new opportunities are 'also continually being created'; lastly Lo suggests that investing strategies will 'also wax and wane, performing well in certain environments and performing badly in other environments'.[1] I suggest that Lo is right and that any one of the seemingly successful strategies identified in this book could stop working simply because the market has evolved.

If you accept Lo's logic the inevitable solution is that investors need to continually experiment with new – and old – ideas and strategies. If markets are exhibiting strong momentum-based trends, why not experiment with a relative strength strategy on paper even if you're deep down a value-based investor: use a computer-based system to analyse progress of your experiment rather than actually putting money on the strategy.

---

[1] Lo, A. (2010) 'The Adaptive Markets Hypothesis: Market Efficiency from an Evolutionary Perspective', *Journal of Portfolio Management*, available at http://ssrn.com/abstract=602222.

But as you experiment you must also realise that much of the quantitative analysis discussed in this book is only the beginning of a process that ends with a stock purchase and along the way you need a proper due diligence process! Many private investors are dazzled by the power of modern quantitative-based systems and accept that the data is always vetted and checked (it isn't) and that numbers are a substitute for a proper due diligence process. I'd simply remind these investors of the consensus view of most (though not all) academic economists – that active stock selection is difficult and *risky* and that most of the time most prices are probably about right. Blindness to numbers opens investors up to those extra risks of stock picking – if you are going to defy the efficient markets theorists, do it from strength and go beyond the numbers to investigate the business franchise, and remember Warren Buffett and Ben Graham's injunction that you're buying into a business not just the shares. Is it really growing fast? Is its business franchise really that strong? Is the dividend well supported? Can you really believe the balance sheet? If we had a mantra for smarter investing it would be 'good theory tested, against the evidence, and investigated at the company level'.

In this book are the outlines of a number of great theories about good, smart investing including value-based investing, the hunt for quality companies and the power of momentum. In this chapter we'll zero in on a number of strategies I really like.

But first we're going to look at what the evidence tells us at an overall, aggregate level of the UK stockmarket: we're going to dive into the vast database of quantitative fundamental-based data maintained by Andrew Lapthorne's team at SG. His analysts have been crunching the numbers and relating them back to a number of different *factors* (measures) and *styles* (strategies and themes) for the UK market over the past 20 plus years. It's a massive comprehensive source of market data and its conclusions are compelling – and they'll help inform our nine-point survival plan for modern, volatile, adaptive markets!

The evidence from SG's style counselling

Throughout this book we've bombarded you with academic studies and quantitative analysis but in this concluding chapter we're going to try and keep it simple and to the point, starting with the top line results from an analysis of the SG database. Before we dip into the detail of the results it's worth detailing some of the context to this analysis:

■ It's a global database based on developed world markets such as the UK and the US.

■ Most of the core data comes from 1993 through to 2009. Some data goes back even earlier but most of the results are based on a 16-year time frame which is significant but far from being conclusive or definitive.

■ The SG team looked at both *factors* – certain key measures – and *styles* – investing strategies and investing styles.

■ Most of the SG data relates only to larger companies – in the UK all of the analysis that follows is based on the largest 350 companies on the London market.

■ Wherever possible the SG team have operated both a *long* version of their strategy and a *short* version, i.e. if a stock scores highly on the Piotroski test, for instance, they buy the shares or go long. If it scores spectacularly badly, they sell the shares or go short.

■ In all the analysis, the SG team has identified either a *top decile* or *top quartile* of stocks that relate to the relevant factor or style.

With these provisos in mind, we'll start with Table 13.1. This looks at a number of contrasting *styles* and how they've performed globally since 1993, with a starting index level of 100. The first big conclusion that emerges is that the success of different styles varies globally. In the UK the least successful strategy has been one based on chasing companies experiencing high forward looking earnings per share growth (High versus low year 1 EPS growth) and fastest growing companies based on earnings growth in the past. The best performing style has been one based on companies experiencing strong EPS momentum based on analysts' estimates. In the US, by contrast, this style has been very unsuccessful with price to book stocks a better idea. It's also worth noting that in the US the worst idea has been to chase high yielding stocks!

Table 13.2 (overleaf) tells us a very different story – it focuses in on the UK but looks at the years between 1993 and 2009. Again we look at various different styles and it's clear that traditional value-based styles such as price to book and picking stocks with a low PE relative to the market did very well in the years between 2000 and 2002 but then failed miserably after. This should remind us that different styles of ideas of investing vary in success over different years.

table 13.1 Contrasting styles and their performance (1 January 1993 to 30 November 2009)

Style	Area					
	Japan	UK	Eurozone	Europe	US	Global
High versus low dividend yield	161	158	176	148	45	90
Low versus high PE ratios	282	144	234	184	105	154
Low versus high price to book	466	172	210	181	148	210
High versus low Year 1 EPS growth	60	110	113	87	114	98
High versus low historical EPS growth	96	113	64	82	122	104
High versus low EPS momentum	153	307	191	134	82	119
High versus low relative price momentum (3months)	151	156	186	114	96	125

Source: SocGen Analysis.

Tables 13.3 and 13.4 (overleaf) consider a slightly different time span – from 1990 through to 2009 – and a different set of variables, notably individual measures or *factors*. For simplicity's sake we've looked at the *top quartiles* for all shares in the sample based on the following – share price relative to the dividend (the yield), share price relative to earnings momentum, cashflow, price to book and price to sales. Over this 19-year period high dividend stocks have done well as has cashflow as a key measure, but the winner has to be earnings momentum again (the benchmark was the FTSE 350 excluding investment trusts). The bottom line – focus on stocks showing strong earnings momentum, decent yields and strong cashflow.

table 13.2 UK analysis by year (1999–2009)

Year	Annual returns						
	Low vs. high price to book	High vs. low dividend yield	Low vs. high PE ratio	High vs. low year 1 forecast EPS growth	High vs low year 2 forecast EPS growth	High vs. low long-term forecast EPS growth	High vs. low historical EPS growth
				Investigate 0s			
1993	25	8	−1	1	10	−7	3
1994	2	−1	3	−5	−7	9	10
1995	−4	−6	−2	2	−1	3	7
1996	−4	−8	−7	4	7	−1	4
1997	3	1	−2	4	−2	−2	4
1998	−10	−7	−17	5	−2	6	7
1999	−14	−24	−18	16	23	0	10
2000	17	42	24	0	−20	0	−13
2001	28	47	50	−7	−25	0	−5
2002	26	29	48	3	−29	0	−17
2003	9	4	0	−5	4	0	−3
2004	9	7	8	−3	−8	0	3
2005	1	−6	6	5	1	0	1
2006	3	−2	3	1	−3	0	−3
2007	−15	−9	−13	7	-4	0	6
2008	−19	−6	−23	3	0	0	−2
2009	13	0	4	−19	−5	0	5
Average	4	4	4	1	−4	1	1
Standard deviation	14.5	18.7	20.4	7.3	12.5	3.4	
Total return	72	58	44	10	−54	8	13

Source: SocGen Analysis.

table 13.3 Summary

	Benchmark (equal weighted FTSE 350 ex IT)	Dividend	Earnings	Cashflow	Book	Sales
30/11/1990	100	100	100	100	100	100
30/09/2009	404	600	1258	1038	387	540

Source: SocGen Analysis.

In Table 13.4 we've broken these returns down by decade – returns for the years 1991 through to 1999 and from 2000 through to 2009. Earnings momentum was a pretty consistent star throughout both decades whereas higher dividend payers came into their own in the second half of the period.

table 13.4 Decade returns (% cumulative)

	Benchmark (equal weighted FTSE 350 ex IT)	Dividend	Earnings	Cashflow	Book	Sales
1991 to 1999	162	94	214	142	103	94
2000 to 2009	54	209	300	328	90	78

Source: SocGen Analysis.

Figure 13.1 (overleaf) shows all the returns from each of the factors over the full period with earnings momentum out on top challenged only by firms with a strong cashflow relative to their share price, especially in the last five to six years. Table 13.5 (overleaf) puts this graph into hard numbers, spelling out returns between 1990 and 2009. Each of these measures is stripped out and we can see which ones have produced the greatest returns with earnings momentum and price to cash measure way out in front, followed by the all important dividend measure.

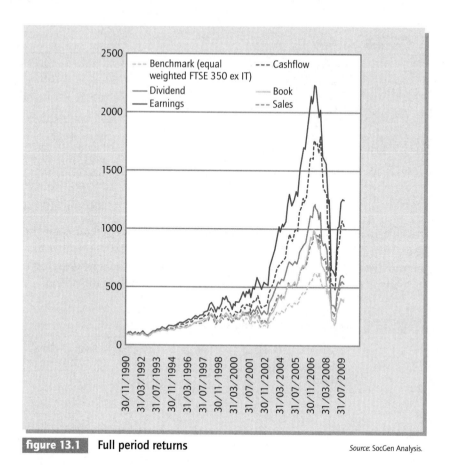

figure 13.1 **Full period returns**

Source: SocGen Analysis.

table 13.5 **Decade analysis**

	Benchmark (equal weighted FTSE 350 ex IT)	Dividend	Earnings	Cashflow	Book	Sales
30/11/1990	100	100	100	100	100	100
30/09/2009	404	600	1258	1038	387	540

Source: SocGen Analysis.

Armed with this data and analysis consider a number of simple ideas:

- Earnings momentum is a strong force especially if forecast data and its revision is built into the measure – remember that the City loves positive surprises!
- Dividends are important.
- Cashflow is equally important.
- Sales to share price and the book value of a company relative to its share price are less important in stock selection terms.
- What works for the UK absolutely might not work in the US.

With these very simple, early conclusions in mind you might want to focus in on our nine-point survival plan for modern, volatile markets.

The nine-point survival plan

1 Dividends matter

In Chapter 4 we looked in detail at the evidence of why dividends matter. Just to remind you, we concluded that dividends matter simply because:

- they are a form of hard cash paid to the investor as income
- the dividend cheque grows over time progressively for many companies
- the real power of dividends comes through their constant reinvestment back into the company (i.e. what really matters is how that dividend accrues or compounds over time and is then reinvested back into the underlying ordinary shares)
- over the short term, investors respect those constant dividend cheques, especially if they're progressively increasing, and reward those companies with a higher share price.

We'd add a number of important caveats to these observations. The first and perhaps most important is that dividends don't appear to be a strong predictor of long-term price movements, i.e. just because a stock pays a high dividend don't assume that the market will always automatically re-ward the shares over the very long term with a higher rating. Columbia academics Angy and Bekaertz looked at the predictability of share price returns over time and in particular dividends, and found that: 'At long horizons, excess return predictability by the dividend yield is not sta-tistically significant, not robust across countries, and not robust across different sample periods... results suggest that predictability is mainly a short-horizon, not a long-horizon, phenomenon.'[2]

By contrast, we do contend that dividends are especially useful as you dive down into detailed company analysis, i.e. they're useful in giving you some clues as to whether you're looking at a decent, high quality, solid company. Academic Kent Baker looked at 309 dividend paying firms that made certain that they distributed most of their available free cashflow as a dividend. Amongst those virtuous companies he discovered that they were 'more profitable, more liquid, and less highly levered'.[3] They also tended to stick with their dividend policy through thick and thin and 'be unconcerned about the cost of raising external funds'.[4] In sum, this and other research suggests to us that well financially secure, cash rich, divided paying firms with a progressive policy of increasing the payout every year are more likely to be high quality, solid companies with a decent business franchise.

Overall, we'd suggest that if you want to prioritise income as your core strategy, consider using the Progressive (Dividend Hero) Strategy and accompanying screen.

The Progressive (Dividend) Hero Screen

- We looked at the more recent past – the past eight years for instance – and excluded any company which hasn't increased its dividend year on year over those eight years.

- Crucially we looked at forward projections of dividend growth by analysts and only included those where dividends are set to increase. Bear in mind though that this is only an estimate and that analysts could have got it wrong!

- We've also only included companies where there is a stated dividend policy. This will usually consist of a simple commitment to growing real sterling dividends (Pennon for instance is committed to growing it at 3% per annum), or a commitment to paying a fixed percentage of earnings.

- Only companies with a proper dividend reinvestment plan have been included.

---

[2] Angy, A. and Bekaertz, G. (2001) 'Stock Return Predictability: Is it There?' 4 March, AFA Atlanta Meetings, http://ssrn.com/abstract=262315
[3] Baker, H.K. (2006) 'In Search of a Residual Dividend Policy', *Review of Financial Economics*, Vol. 15, No. 1, pp. 1–18.
[4] Ibid.

We'd also suggest that investors carefully scrutinise a range of wider issues including:

■ The potential FX risk – examine how much of the business is conducted outside the UK. If a large portion of turnover is derived in dollars and euros this opens the company up to some risk if the exchange risk goes against them (the opposite has been happening in the past six months).

■ We've also included a measure for cashflow per share in the most recent accounts. This shows you how much the dividend per share is covered by operating cash inflows. As long as it's above 1 the company can afford the payment and anything above 2 is pretty safe.

■ We've also noted any pensions scheme liability, where disclosed.

■ Last but by no means least we've also included the level of gearing – this could be an indicator of future trouble.

Interview

Graham Secker on value-based stock screens

Morgan Stanley's Graham Secker is a quantitatively-focused strategist who, like Andrew Lapthorne at SG, makes extensive use of different strategies and screens. He combines an interest in value-based strategies with a penchant for reasonably priced growth stocks especially in the FSTE 350. In August of 2009 Graham was interviewed for the *Investors Chronicle*. In this short version he outlines his own preference for value-based strategies.

Interviewer: You constantly use screens to focus your strategy? It's fair to say that you're a fan of what could be called *quality* dividend orientated stocks?

Graham: Absolutely. We've done studies in the past that show that some of the best performers – one of the best performing styles – are companies that produce top quarter dividend growth. That means companies that are growing their dividends strongly – good dividend growth is always a sign of management confidence about the company. History will suggest that the best, the top dividend growers out perform market quite significantly.

Interviewer: What about strategy based around value measures such as a Piotroski screen for instance?

Graham: Yes. I think that we are at heart big value investors – valuation is our creed if you like, when it comes to long-term investing. And we've got many valuation strategies that are doing very well. I don't think value strategies will work quite as well over the next two to three years, as they have done over the last six months [through to Autumn 2009], but we're always believers that buying cheap companies and watching them appreciate in value, is a rewarding experience.

Interviewer: Looking at specific measures within your screens – what would you use?

Graham: Personally we use a combination of measures. We like to use free cashflow yield. We like to use price to book or ideally, enterprise value to fixed assets. And we like dividend yield. I would always keep an eye on the balance sheet – interest cover or gearing. These factors are more than enough. But you just need to keep an eye on lots of things. It isn't a question of just picking the price to sales, or the PE ratio, and that's all you focus on. I think it's important to use a number of different ratios in your analysis.

Interviewer: You mentioned free cashflow yield then. What would be your target for this measure?

Graham: I think you'd be looking at high single digit (7 to 9%), that's the kind of area that I think would be particularly appealing.

Interviewer: In the dividend space what would you look for in terms of measures?

Graham: You have to look at dividend cover. You should also look at whether the company has a specific dividend policy [such as a progressive dividend policy]. Also look at the health of the balance sheet in general – everyone's using tangible book value. It's safer to stick with [PTBV]. We sometimes use enterprise value (equity and long-term debt) to fixed assets which is even more secure! If you can buy stuff with an EV to fixed asset ratio of close to 1, or under 1, then theoretically, you could just close the company down, sell off all the bits and pieces, and make a nice profit that way. Overall though we would prefer to focus on tangible book.

Interviewer: Any view on what constitutes a reasonable price to tangible book value measure?

Graham: Previously there have been a lot of companies below 1. There aren't that many companies below 1 now, but I'd say 1 to 1.5 is OK.

Interviewer: What about growth stocks and measures that identify these companies?

Graham: I'd rather be buying contrary and value ideas that'll take a bit longer to come to fruition probably but also try to keep your trading costs down. If you pick the right ideas, have conviction in them – that way you can make a lot of money. We always think value strategies will out perform growth strategies significantly in the long run.

Interviewer: What would be your warning to investors looking to use screens to spot shares?

> **Graham**: I personally think it is very, very hard to consistently add value – and do it consistently well. You have to have good sources of data. I think people should stick to their core competences and if you can find an investment manager whose core competence in this area is very high, then I suggest you use them!
>
> **Interviewer**: Last but by no means least – looking to the long term, what do you think investors should expect from equities generally? What's the sustainable or long-term rate of return now?
>
> **Graham**: I would be reasonably happy to clip 6, 7% per annum, consistently year in, year out.
>
> **Interviewer**: Which would equate to an equity premium of about 3.5% pa?
>
> **Graham**: We normally use the dividend yield as a proxy for the equity premium, so yes, 4% is about right!

2 Balance sheets also matter!

Balance sheets are hugely important in a number of different ways but that observation is frequently warped by value investors into a view that they should only chase companies where the balance sheet strength is not reflected in the share price rating. This view tends to result in a focus on measures such as the relationship between the share price and the tangible book or net asset value (PTBV). Some investors also focus on the relationship between gearing and the share price (net gearing) and the share price and net cash held in the firm.

This view finds an echo in the work of Ben Graham and subsequent value investors such as Tweedy Browne but a focus on just static balance sheet measures can be dangerous. As the SG analysis above suggests, price to book value (PBV, or PTBV where intangibles are excluded) hasn't been an enormously successful factor or single measure in stock selection. Part of the reason for this is that a singular focus on, say, PTBV leads investors to pick deep value stocks where the market has convinced itself that the underlying business franchise is unsound and incapable of generating above cash interest rates of return, i.e. that the business has decent assets but its management can't produce a sufficiently generous enough cash profit. At some point in the future that intrinsic value in the shares may be realised, say by a private equity buyout, but investors may be left waiting an awful long time for value realisation of those hard assets. Many strategies built around Graham's Net Net ideas fall foul of this, plus there's also the more obvious problem that there aren't many suitable candidates in the first place as modern markets consistently award high multiples to company shares.

We'd suggest that the balance sheet is absolutely useful but only as part of a wider set of measures that combine both a static snapshot of the assets and liabilities *plus* a dynamic look at the operational efficiency of the firm, and the manner in which it generates cash. It's worth repeating two key words from the last sentence – *efficiency* and *cash*. A business franchise full of hard, potentially valuable assets is only valuable in the future if the company is capable of generating future profits (otherwise the business may as well be liquidated) and those profits can only come about if the business is efficient enough to generate a decent margin and repay the capital invested. Additionally profits are only useful in our view if they're not accounting chimera but real hard cash earnings, which are preferably growing over time.

The most compelling strategy for capturing this kind of company – lots of decent, under-valued assets producing strong cash earnings through efficient use of capital – is to use the Piotroski screen as your *core* screen, especially if you're more of a value investor. We think it captures the essence of a quality stock for any value investor – and the evidence from study after study shows that Piotroski-style stocks tend to be a great long-term investment. In the following box the main nine-point Piotroski F Score system used by many analysts is repeated. You should start to investigate any company with a score of 5 or above, but focus your attention on those with a score of 7 or above. Also rigorously examine any company in your portfolio with a low score of 2 to 3 or less. You need to satisfy yourself that you're owning the right share as any low scoring stock should be automatically excluded from any value-based investor's portfolio.

The Piotroski screen

Points are as follows:

- One point for a positive return on assets – this is defined as net profits before exceptional items divided by the total assets of the firm.
- One point for a positive cashflow.
- One point for an improvement on return on assets over the past year.

- One point for a company where cashflow from operations exceed net income. This should be the case as depreciation and non-cash expenses normally reduce the net profits but have no impact on cashflow.
- One point if the measure of financial leverage, ratio of total debt to total assets, declined in the past year.
- One point also given if the current ratio (working assets or current assets divided by current liabilities) increased over the year.
- One point comes with companies that have not issued any new shares in the current financial year – firms that issue too much debt might be struggling to manage liquidity and be running short of funds.
- One point for an increase in gross margin.
- One point if asset turnover (total sales divided by total assets at the start of the financial year) has increased during the year.

3 Hunt down quality stocks

Many readers will be slightly concerned by the suspicion of growth inherent in many value-based analyses of the market – after all, modern markets are increasingly built around the idea of growth equity. This suggests that boring, barely growing sectors or slow growth companies are better off under private control or even private equity ownership, rather than in the public markets.

I suspect that many investors think that if they want income they'll invest in bonds rather than boring dividend paying equities – and suspect this introduces an overall style bias in modern markets that is certainly reflected amongst fund managers who mostly like growth and GARP stocks. In these circumstances, even value influenced investors need to develop some strategies and ideas about selecting growing, successful firms at a reasonable price. This could lead one into the world of growth at a reasonable price or GARP investing but average private investors can't possibly match the market power and analytical insight of people like Warren Buffett who operate in this space. The resources needed to research whether a company really has a solid franchise, is generating cash and is really growing as fast as it says to the markets, is formidable and probably beyond most investors. Researching GARP stocks will take an awful lot of due diligence and investigation. In these circumstances, the idea of using simpler ideas that focus on capital efficiency is preferable. Earnings growth is great but it's only useful to private investors if it is translated into cash profits which could eventually turn into cash dividends. The simplest way of finding these stocks is, in my view, to use Joel Greenblatt's ideas for selecting stocks – detailed again in the box below.

A Greenblatt-style strategy for the UK

In the UK we'd suggest using either the RBS Greenblatt Magic Index – or products that track the index – or our own version of Greenblatt's strategy, using the following screen:

- Screen for companies in the top quartile for return on capital employed. Most of the time that's above 25%.

- To screen for the earnings yield, reverse it, and use the PE ratio – we prefer using the forward PE ratio but you could use the historic one instead. Again look for the lowest quartile which usually translates to under 15, or even 13. We'd also apply a lower cut off of 5 or below. Most companies with abnormally low PE ratios are statistical freaks that are usually in deep trouble.

- Exclude foreign stocks and banks and utilities.

- Award a rank for the PE ratio – the lowest one gets 1 and so on. Then award a rank for the ROCE. If you can export screens as spreadsheets this is easy to do – simply apply a filter or sort by the measure. Add the two ranks up.

- With your final long list, only select the top 25 or 20 shares.

---

4 Earnings acceleration is powerful

Be cautious when it comes to focusing on companies that are growing earnings fast. Before you build a portfolio that attempts to capture only earnings stars such as ASOS (or even Netflix) where profits are growing consistently fast, remember the fate of what Andrew Lapthorne calls 20% Rentokil. As he notes in the interview at the end of this chapter: 'Historically it had grown its earnings at 20% p.a., it traded on a PE of 20 and everyone forecast it to grow at 20%. And you got people using things like the PEG ratio and saying, "Hey look, it's trading at a PE of 20, PEG ratio of 1." But the trouble is that it went ex-growth and the share price collapsed. No one forecast it and it pretty much happened in a very short period of time.'

Any strategy focused on capturing fast growing stocks needs to be alert to a number of dangers. The first and most obvious is that, like Rentokil, growth businesses can very suddenly go ex-growth, i.e. they can stop growing fast very quickly. This frequently happens because other investors realise that the sector the company operates in is indeed hugely profitable and they start up new competitors. These rival businesses may not be able to entirely overcome what many call the 'wide moat of competitive advantage' but what they do is to start a price war. These rivals may not be as efficient and profitable as the dominant player but they can undercut it, pushing ROE down with the inevitable impact on first, earnings, and then the price to earnings multiple the market is willing to attach to the share price.

Another key risk is the difference between operating and pro forma earnings, especially in the US. The gap between these two items can be huge and has been growing over time, making the task of any growth investor incredibly difficult in establishing what the actual trend in organic, normalised earnings is!

Last but by no means least, consistency in the growth of earnings is important but beware those companies showing a simple straight line upwards. Any company that constantly keeps growing at, say, 5% every quarter without fail is likely to end up as another Rentokil sooner or later. What's preferable is Graham Secker's methodology which looks at the *standard deviation* or variability of earnings per share results. In this he's trying to weed out companies that shock the market with abnormally different EPS results, i.e. he wants to exclude companies that regularly miss analysts' estimates for EPS growth. As we'll discover a little later, the one stock you absolutely want to avoid is the company that keeps putting out profits warnings.

The kind of company that you do want to focus your research on, by contrast, is the one that pleasantly surprises the analysts with earnings growth. A company that produces an earnings surprise is a potent force in stockmarkets and the subject of many growth orientated strategies. You also need to be alert to another powerful force in modern stockmarkets, namely post-earnings drift – this refers to companies producing good EPS figures which then find their shares drifting back as the market fails to fully comprehend the good news from those results. Some evidence for this effect comes in a paper called 'Post Earnings Drift in the UK'.[5] Liu, Strong and Xu looked at non-US markets and found 'evidence of significant post-earnings-announcement drift', robustly

---

[5] Liu, W., Strong, N.C. and Xu, X. 'Post Earnings Drift in the UK' (2000), LUMS Working Paper No. 2000/010, July.

across most markets and segments. In particular they noted 'cumulative abnormal returns for stocks announcing extreme positive unexpected earnings drift upwards for an extended period after the announcement'. They go on to add that 'the price-based measure of earnings surprise gives the strongest drift... Our conclusion is that the UK stock market is inefficient with respect to publicly available corporate earnings information'.[6]

These authors suggest – as do other analysts – that investors do not process earnings information efficiently, especially in the way that they consume regular public information on earnings. Therein lays the opportunity for more growth orientated investors – trying to spot growing companies where the market hasn't really cottoned on to full implications of the positive story on profits. But one last element needs to be added: you do need some measures that focus your attention back on *quality*. You should check that margin is indeed strong and growing and that sales are actually growing – crucially you also need to be sure that you're not paying too much in terms of the share price. A high PE multiple or rating may have already been attached to the shares by the largely efficient market, denying the investor of any real opportunity moving forward. In these circumstances, the simplest way of spotting these stocks is to use our version of the Martin Zweig screen, detailed in Chapter 6 and reprinted below. We think this should be the core screen for growth investors with a value bias.

Our version of a Martin Zweig Screen

Zweig's main emphasis is on quarterly earnings growth which can be a little tricky for British investors as most companies only report twice a year. One modification for the UK market might be to focus EPS growth for a six-monthly and yearly basis. Other than this, we'd recommend screening for the following:

- EPS growth in current year is at least 20%.
- EPS growth over past three years is at least 15%.
- EPS growth over past five years is at least 10%. (With all these three figures put them side by side and look for evidence of earnings acceleration, i.e. the current EPS growth rate is more than the three-year and preferably more than the five-year rate.)

---

[6] Ibid.

■ Sales per share should be up at least 10% if not 20%. Also look at the last two sets of annual sales and check that sales growth has been accelerating.

■ One additional thought, suggested by the investment writer Peter Temple, is that the margin trend should actually be negative. His thinking is that if sales are supposed to be growing faster than earnings, a slip in the margin trend is obvious and probably a good thing.

■ The PE ratio is between 5 and 43. Most Zweig enthusiasts would probably reduce that top PE figure down to 25 for the UK.

■ Screen out firms whose relative share price strength over past month, three months and six months is negative.

Investors should consider applying a number of important thresholds suggested by Zweig to miss out poorly traded firms, small caps with no real analysts coverage and companies with poor balance sheets:

■ Exclude firms where the shares are illiquid, i.e. low trading volumes.

■ Compare the company's debt position with that of its industry peers. Try and concentrate on companies where the 'relative debt levels' are low.

■ Look for insider selling of shares. Exclude companies where there's been director selling in the past three months. If there have been three insider buys in the past six months then that constitutes a strong buy signal.

5 Use momentum with care

Most academics reckon that the momentum effect is still the strongest of all the 'anomalies' that supposedly fly in the face of those efficient markets. Not one academic interviewed by this author denies its existence and most think it's the premier anomaly. It's also relatively easy to capture according to commentators such as Professor Elroy Dimson and Professor Paul Marsh at the LBS. As discussed in Chapter 7, they've looked at the following simple rules-based strategy:

Pure momentum strategies involve ranking stocks into winners and losers based on past returns over a ranking period. One then buys the winners and short-sells the losers, over a holding period. To ensure implementability, there is usually a wait period before investing. Strategies are thus described as 'r/w/h'. For example, a 12/1/1 strategy ranks returns over the past 12 months, waits 1 month, and then holds for 1 month until rebalancing.[7]

---

[7] Dimson, E. and Marsh, P. (2008) *Global Investment Returns Yearbook 2008*, ABN Amro.

According to the LBS academics this strategy has produced stunning results.

It's also worth reminding ourselves of the *Investors Chronicle*'s Algy Hall and his simple momentum strategy to go long on the best 10 performing FTSE 100 stocks of the previous three months and short on the 10 worst performing stocks.

Some hedge funds use another alternative, which looks at a measure called relative strength as a measure. You can find this technical-based measure in virtually any screening or technical analysis system. A common application of this principle suggests that every six or three months you should look for companies where the key relative strength measure on a one- three- and six-month basis versus the market is positive and then pick the ten strongest shares. Hold for six months and then sell!

But all these simple ideas face two big issues – the first and perhaps most obvious is that trading costs can rapidly eat into your returns! The bigger issue is that momentum only works some of the time. Here's analyst Rob Arnott again on momentum investing:

Momentum works in the short run, it doesn't work in the long run. And also Momentum works until it doesn't work. When it doesn't work, it bites you very hard. The problem with Momentum is it doesn't work at market turns. So if something has performed brilliantly, yes, momentum may carry it higher. But there's no harm in trimming it. And continuing to trim it, and continuing to trim it. Because eventually it will turn. Momentum works in spans measured in months, and anti-momentum works in spans measured in years. What has performed brilliantly over the past five years, for instance, is highly unlikely to be brilliant the next five years. Highly unlikely. While momentum is powerful, it is a short-term phenomenon.

Perhaps the best bit of advice on momentum investing comes from those analysts who suggest momentum investing fails when volatility shoots up and the markets suddenly turn from a bull phase into a bear phase. At that point momentum collapses, triggering huge losses. A simple word of advice – turn off momentum in volatile months!

One last bit of advice on momentum – there's some evidence to suggest that momentum works best in bull markets and especially with smaller to medium cap stocks. Professional investors tend to stay focused on big 'beta' plays – big stocks that let you easily capture big trends on a 1:1 (beta) basis. That means they don't always put the research into spotting those fast growing smaller and mid-cap stocks which are beating all those earnings expectations we discussed above. As these shooting stars, like ASOS, climb ever higher, fund managers finally wake up and realise that they might have to hold these stocks, especially if they find their way into a major index like the FTSE 250. At this point the herd piles into the stock, giving the shares extra momentum upwards. If an investor is able to spot these stocks before the pack moves in, they could make a very robust profit from picking fast growing smaller caps early. It's not an easy task but it could be made easier if you use our version of the Motley Fool Small Cap 8 strategy, repeated in the box below.

A UK version of the Motley Small Cap strategy

Our version of the Foolish 8 features eight measures in the first screen but all of them are slightly different in emphasis and tone. It's very much our 'own label' version of a Foolish 8 strategy. The measures used include:

- Relative Strength (RS) of the shares versus the market return in the past three months is in the top quartile for the market. This is a tough yardstick and shows clearly that the firm's shares are motoring ahead.
- The net profit margin must also be in the top quartile for the market. In practice this means well above the 7% suggested by Motley Fool and tends to be in the 10–15% range.
- A share price that is more than 10p. This is designed to avoid the difficult to trade and highly volatile penny stocks of old (daily trading volumes can also be very low).
- Market cap should be in the £10m to £100m range.
- The price to cashflow measure should be at least positive. This helps to narrow down our shortlist to those that will have positive operating cashflow.
- Earnings per share over the last three years should be in the top quartile for the market and earnings for the current year should be growing by at least 25% over the year.
- Our last measure is a bit unorthodox and is not mentioned by Motley Fool but it's ROCE. This is designed to answer Motley Fool's own observation that one of the shortcomings of small caps is their frequent inability to keep up with large caps when it comes to key measures like return on equity or ROCE. We've picked ROCE because if our small cap is going to grow bigger – along with the share price – analysts will need to know that the company is sweating its capital base efficiently. In reality it's not an overly demanding target as most fast growing small cap companies boast very high ROCE rates. We've set this filter at 15%.

> The second screen is much more qualitative and looks at more company specific issues. These are:
>
> ■ Sales growth at the top line should be at least 25% in the past year.
>
> ■ There should be strong evidence of 'insider ownership' – management – with a suggested minimum of 10% of the entire equity.
>
> ■ ROCE of 15% should be present for at least the past two years.
>
> ■ A sales maximum of £500m. In practice this could easily be set lower – at around £200m.
>
> ■ Make sure that the cashflow at the operating level can easily pay for capex and dividends.
>
> ■ Run the screen and like CAN SLIM you won't find yourself overwhelmed with maybe 12 shares to 20 shares shortlisted, all of which will need further investigation.

6 Think about combining all the elements in one screen

In our next section (point 7) we'll look at how you might combine all of these different strategies into one portfolio but first it's worth examining one alternative idea – that you use only one screen that borrows on all of the big strategies. This classic best of all worlds proposition has been tried a number of times and seems to be pretty successful if you have the analytical fire power and access to comprehensive data sources. We encountered one stab at this in Chapter 6 where we looked at the work of the Goldman Sachs quant team who identified six key factors that seemed to be positive factors for future share price growth:

1 Valuation – is the share price reflecting the intrinsic value? 'All being equal, cheaper stocks are more attractive than stocks selling at high multiples.'

2 Profitability. Are the returns on capital sufficient? 'The stocks of companies that earn higher margins and use their assets more efficiently outperform the stocks of their lower margin, less efficient industry counterparts.'

3 Earnings quality. The 'cash component of earnings... is highly persistent' while the remorseless build up of EPS figures, year on year, is more 'transitory'.

4 Management impact. 'Well managed companies don't waste assets on unprofitable investment opportunities or on empire building, but instead return excess capital to shareholders.'

5 Momentum. Stocks with some momentum in their share price tend to out perform as investors slowly wake up to the potential for the firm.

6 Analyst sentiment. Analysts who are slow to change their estimates create 'trading opportunities for investors who buy on upward revisions... as stocks prices later adjust to reflect the information conveyed by the consensus signal'.

You might want to look at another, successful attempt at a synthesis, this time from SG, courtesy of its WISE strategy. As with the Goldman's version this tries to combine elements of value, growth and momentum, all in one strategy. Key factors identified by the quant team at SG include:

1 Investors like cheap stocks. 'Although every stock is unique, there are several common measures that are frequently used by many investors to determine relative cheapness of stocks.' These include:

■ price/earnings ratio relative to sector (P/E)

■ price/book ratio relative to sector (P/B)

■ price/sales ratio relative to sector (P/S)

■ price/cashflow ratio relative to sector (P/CF).

2 Investors like popular stocks. 'We believe the past performance, while not always indicative of the future returns, is a good measure of investor confidence in a particular stock.' Key measures for momentum include:

■ stock price changes over the past 12 months (R12)

■ stock price changes over the past six months (R6).

3 The smart money strategy. 'We believe a dramatic rise or fall in short interest (the measure that is used to show how much stock is held by investors intending to short a stock) contains information that can be materialised. By selecting stocks based on changes in short interest, we are following the path more sophisticated investors such as hedge funds take with usually a one-month lag, since short interest figures are only published once a month.'

■ Short interest as a percentage of total shares outstanding (SIR).

■ Change in short interest over the past six months (SIC).

4 Last but by no means least, investors like 'profitable stocks'. The two factors chosen for this strategy are:

■ return on common equity relative to sector (ROE)

■ change in return on common equity quarter over quarter (REC).

The SG team also add a number of other additional features including the mysterious and elusive SG Alpha which appears to include a 'technical factor measuring relative affordability of stock' and a 'proprietary price volatility metric'. Using these bundles of measures the team then go away and analyse a major index such as the FTSE 100 or the S&P 500 and rank each company based on 12 factors. Crucially the strategists admit that they 'overweight the valuation strategy as we believe that its factors are more stable and consistent, therefore this helps maintain volatility and turnover of the overall strategy at a low level'.

7 Different strategies work in different markets

Investors could combine the individual strategies mentioned above into one overall single portfolio, i.e. they shouldn't focus their entire portfolio on just one strategy but use a combination of screens and strategies. Most investors split into two groups, alongside two smaller, adventurous specialist profiles. The two main groups – and the suggested strategies – are as follows:

■ **Cautious, value orientated investors** should focus on the Piotroski screen for most of their portfolio with a large cap Progressive (Dividend) Hero lesser or satellite strategy (possibly as much as 25% of the portfolio) alongside a Zweig strategy in bullish markets (again no more than 25% of the portfolio).

■ **Risk friendly growth orientated investors** willing to look for growth should go for a three-way split between a Piotroski screen, a Progressive (Dividend) Hero screen and a Zweig screen, with the first two perhaps comprising 30% each of the portfolio weighting and the Zweig screen 40%.

Not every investor will be happy with these combinations – two groups of adventurous investors probably stand out as exceptions. The first are what I'd call the out and out **contrarians** who are willing to take extra risk by stalking deep value stocks. For this group a three-way combination of the 1. Piotroski strategy, 2. the Progressive (Dividend) Hero strategy and 3. a Tweedy Browne or Graham Net Net deep value strategy is suggested.

Some *adventurous types* might prefer an exclusive **growth** tilt or bias towards their portfolio, especially if markets are buoyant. In this case, another three-way combination involving 1. our version of the Zweig screen, 2. a strategy that is based on Joel Greenblatts's Magic Number and 3. our version of a Foolish Small Cap portfolio, is probably best.

Both of the last two adventurous portfolio strategies come with a big proviso – beware market conditions! In particular look at three key issues, starting first with an examination of the market cycle. Many deep value stocks are concentrated in either cyclical sectors such as engineering or in defensive sectors such as utilities. The stockmarket tends to move back and forth between a cyclical bias and a defensive bias as investors respond to changes in the business cycle. Some professional investors such as Tim Russell at Cazenove run very successful hedge funds and unit trusts based largely on the switch back and forth between cyclicals and defensives based on the business cycle, and adventurous investors need to be aware of where their main strategies sit on this divide.

We'd also suggest that investors think long and hard about overall market valuations – and what aggregate market valuations tell you about the attractiveness of equities in general. In Appendix 1, we look at various aggregate market-based valuation metrics and how they help give signals to investors to buy or sell. Extreme caution needs to be applied to any market timing-based system especially if investors don't have access to solid data academic.

Study after academic study suggests that most market timing systems fail! But it's also true that adventurous contrarian-based types will struggle in stockmarkets where valuation multiples are stretched – in bubble markets there aren't many deep value opportunities. In fact in peak bull markets there aren't that many conventional Piotroski style candidates either and this makes constructing a portfolio for value investors very tricky indeed. Some value investors, especially deeply contrarian ones, tend to end up defaulting back into extensive cash holdings in these circumstances – a sensible step if markets are about to fall dramatically but potentially wealth destroying if markets keep on rising. There is no right or wrong answer as to whether strategic market timing and a willingness to hold lots of cash is a good or bad thing – although most academic economists suggest that it's dangerous and destroys returns.

Investors also need to look carefully at volatility and how it impacts different styles. Andrew Lapthorne of SG notes how 'dividend yield styles typically exhibit lower beta properties [i.e. they don't do as well as the main

figure 13.2 Rolling betas of low price to book, high dividend yield and low PE strategies

Source: SG Quantitative Strategy Research.

market] compared to strategies such as low PE, and subsequently tend to do well during periods of equity market weakness. [Figure 13.2 shows] rolling 36-month betas of long-short portfolios based on price to book, price to earnings and dividend yield. Price to book and P/E have been exhibiting higher betas recently, whilst dividend yield consistently stayed a low beta strategy through the ten-year period'. Be aware that in highly volatile, bearish markets strategies built around some deep value investing ideas can and do fail as investors flee risk!

8 Think about using strategies to short the market

This book has been targeted mainly at long only investors – that is investors who want to focus their energies on buying shares for the long term for their portfolio. But many of these strategies can also be used to short shares. If you are an adventurous type and a contrarian you might for instance use a strategy such as Piotroski to identify shares and companies that you think are poor quality and bad value, i.e. look for stocks with low scores. In fact our core Piotroski and Zweig screens could be explicitly used in an inverse fashion, i.e. to identify poor value, poor quality stocks that are likely to go down in price. But be aware that shorting comes with a series of risks.

The first and most obvious is that your strategy may end up focusing on smaller to mid-cap stocks where the supply of shares available to short is limited. In these circumstances you could end up paying a lot of money for the privilege of shorting stock or you may not even be able to borrow the stock at all. Adventurous types who short might also want to consider the dangers of being caught in a short squeeze – over the long term you might be right that a stock is poor quality and appallingly over-valued but none of that matters in the short term. If for whatever bizarre reason the share ticks up sharply you might be forced by your broker to liquidate the position as the shares move up and away. That forced sale could happen at the same time as a number of forced sales, triggering a short squeeze, as shorters are all forced to unwind their position. Market veterans will tell you that quantitative analysts frequently make the mistake of assuming that the inverse of your longs are your shorts. As one analyst puts it, we also know that 'companies like Google, can be extremely expensive, but can have a fair amount of momentum in their growth story, still to go'.

Look for the warning signs

The last suggestion for surviving in difficult, perhaps even volatile markets, tells you that some key measures act as a warning to all investors. These are *warning signs* to all investors – companies flagged using any of these warning signals should at the very least be the subject of thorough investigation or, preferably, be avoided at all costs! Below are highlighted two *major* warning signals followed by four *to watch* measures.

The biggest major risk is that you may have invested in a company that's issued a *profits warning*. A number of academics have looked at this area and virtually all have concluded that a company that issues an open profit warning to the market is likely to suffer subsequent share price disappointment. Jennifer Tucker, an academic at the University of Florida, looked at the existing research to see whether a profit warning company management was likely to be penalised for its openness – her conclusion was a hearty affirmative!

Tucker quotes one study (from Kasznik and Lev, 1995) that suggested that 'warning firms experience larger price declines than non-warning firms in the window that covers both the warning and the subsequent earnings announcement'.[8] This research also found that 'warning firms' returns are significantly lower than the returns of those that likely anticipate an earn-

---

[8] Tucker, J.W. (2006) 'Is Openness Penalized? Stock Returns around Earnings Warnings', December. AAA 2007 Financial Accounting & Reporting Section (FARS) Meeting Papers, http://ssrn.com/abstract=744706

ings shortfall but do not warn ('non-warning firms'). This finding has been interpreted as a market penalty for openness... Surprisingly, the number of warnings increased in the past decade.'[9] She also cites research from Xu (2003) who 'collects 151 warnings about large earnings shortfalls during 1991–1994. She finds that warning firms have larger downward analyst revisions and lower operating income than non-warning firms in the year after the event quarter... in the short-term return test, she finds that warning firms have weakly significantly lower returns than non-warning firms'.[10]

James Montier, formerly of SG and now GMO has also looked at this subject. In one of his *Mind Matters* reports from 2008, he suggests that:

When they [profits warnings] occur we find ourselves making excuses for the company. Perhaps calling the management in, who unsurprisingly reassure us that it was only inventory build or unexpected margin pressure but that everything will be alright next quarter. We walk away satisfied right up to the next profit warning! Procrastination at its very best... Bulkley et. al. examined some 455 UK profit warnings between 1997 and 1999. On the day the warning was announced the average stock dropped nearly 17%. However, notice thereafter that it continues to drift away. This argues in favour of an automatic rule of selling on profit warnings.[11]

Intriguingly Montier does add a very important coda to his sensible warning – if you wait to buy, profit warners might prove an interesting investment proposition for true contrarians:

After a very poor 12 months of performance and the disappointment of a profit warning, few investors will be tempted to buy. However, the gains from doing so are obvious from the above. So forcing yourself to buy 12 months after a profit warning could be a useful tool.[12]

We'd add yet another coda to James's coda – in our experience profit warners tend to come like buses, in threes! Once managers get into the routine of warning the market they get caught in what can be a death spiral for their companies, and their management careers – sentiment moves against them, trading partners become suspicious, investors desert the shares and another profits warning comes along!

---

[9] Ibid.

[10] Ibid.

[11] Montier, J. (2008) 'Maximum pessimism, profit warnings and the heat of the moment', *Mind Matters*, 22 September, www.sgcib.com/

[12] Ibid.

Investors also need to tread very carefully around companies that *cut dividends* or even stop dividends. The reaction to this management announcement can be equally drastic as evidenced by the behavioural economist Richard Thaler's team's analysis. This research concludes that:

Consistent with the prior literature we find that short run price reactions to omissions [dividend terminations] are greater than for initiations (–7.0% vs. +3.4% three day return)... In the 12 months after the announcement there is a significant positive market-adjusted return for firms initiating dividends of +7.5% and a significant negative market-adjusted return for firms omitting dividends of –11.0%... A trading rule employing both samples (long in initiation stocks and short in omission stocks) earns positive returns in 22 out of 25 years.[13]

What can investors do to be on the lookout for either of these dramatic occurrences? Profits warnings are usually triggered by abnormal trading conditions but there's also a strong overlay of cynicism about earnings manipulation. You need to be especially alert to companies where EPS has been increasing over a number of years at a suspiciously consistent rate! Look for sudden changes in the cashflow or top line sales growth. For dividends, make a very careful analysis of the cashflow at the operating level and look at dividend cover – is the trend in cash profits strong enough to sustain the regular dividend payment?

Beyond profit warners and dividend cutters investors should be alert for our '**to watch**' measures – in no particular order of priority, look at:

- **Heavy debts**. Many companies, especially in heavily regulated industries such as utilities, can sustain very high net gearing. Our example of SSE in Chapter 2 showed a successful company with very high debt levels but a generous dividend policy funded by a truckload of cash earnings. But if that company is not in such a fortunate position and is experiencing an increase in net borrowing you should pay attention. In my experience anything above 100% net gearing is of real concern and anything above 50% requires some investigation. Also look carefully at the interest cover – if it's declining, pay particular attention – and at the maturity of the debt.

---

[13] Michaely, R., Thaler, R.H. and Womack, K.L. (1995) 'Price Reactions to Dividend Initiations and Omissions: Overreaction or Drift?', *Journal of Finance*, Vol. 50, No. 2, June.

- **Worsening current ratio.** We discussed this measure in Chapter 2 – it's only a useful indicator not a core measure but if the current ratio keeps falling year after year you should start to investigate the company in greater detail.

- **Directors selling.** There are a great many perfectly sensible reasons why a director might choose to sell their shares, especially if the number sold is small. You should be very worried if more than one director starts selling and sells a large quantity of shares in quick succession – a very bad signal in our view.

- **Investigate strong short-term negative momentum.** Contrarian investors might like shares that are constantly falling in price but even these adventurous souls must realise that there's usually always a better price at which you can buy in! Look at short-term price momentum and if a share is constantly falling watch for some form of bottoming out and possibly wait for the day-to-day share price to move back above its 200-day moving average before timing a purchase.

Interview

Andrew Lapthorne, Chief Quantative Strategist, SG

Throughout this book we've encountered the work of Andrew Lapthorne, Chief Quantitative Strategist at French investment bank SG. He's one of the most articulate proponents of quant analysis and a voracious user of different strategies and screens. We're going to finish off this concluding chapter with a long interview with Andrew from the summer of 2009. It's a fascinating journey through value and quality investing, and a clear statement of what Andrew thinks works in markets. More to the point, what follows is based on many years of evidence-based analysis but built around a fundamentally contrarian investment philosophy. We started the interview by looking at the work of professional academic economists who maintain that constructing strategies that attempt to beat the market is a pointless exercise, if only because markets are basically efficient. If these equally data driven academics are right, surely any strategy or screen to find, say, cheap stocks or growth stocks is doomed from the start!

Interviewer: Do you think that markets are generally efficient and that therefore it's quite difficult to adopt a strategy which makes you money consistently?

Andrew: No – I totally counter the efficient markets theory. Some of the theories from efficient market hypothesis have proved to be empirically wrong. The route most investors have taken is a combination of modelling-based empirical analysis of what's going on, as well as behavioural orientated models. And there is plenty of evidence that certain models, over time, can systematically make money.

Interviewer: Many academics would accept that certain 'anomalies' exist that investors have exploited in the past. But aren't these just extra rewards for taking extra risk and don't get in the way of the argument that markets are efficient?

Andrew: They just continually introduce new risk factors into their excuses. I mean, let's face it, Eugene Fama and Ken French [leading academics who've helped develop the efficient markets hypothesis] were very late into analysing value investing. It was almost 20 to 30 years after people had recognised the value factor that they decided to come in and admit it existed.

Interviewer: But what about the failure of all those value orientated fund managers to beat that index tracking fund over time?

Andrew: I think the quote from Warren Buffett is that how come all the guys who beat the index happen to live in roughly the same place [value and GARP strategies]. That's a lot of random coin flipping. There is evidence that if you can apply systematic ways of investing, that as long as you adhere to them, you will beat the market. It's a question of whether human frailties in investing allow us to systematically pursue a model.

Interviewer: OK, so strategies in your opinion can beat these supposedly perfect markets? Before we look at some in detail are there any insights from say the world of behavioural finance that we need to think about first?

Andrew: I'd start with the importance of the strategy and how you build it in the first place. Because if you build one based solely on back testing and the model starts going wrong, all that you've got to cling onto is the back testing.

I'd also say that if you're confident in your analysis, then you have to stick by what the model is throwing out. And that will make you do uncomfortable things. For example James Montier [Lapthorne's former colleague at SG and now at GMO] in 2008 was saying, 'Hey look, Japanese small cap.' But [this sector] is a god awful group of companies yet it's cheap... and very nasty but it's also one of the best performing indices, over the past 12 months!

Interviewer: So what you're saying is we need consistency, we need analytical rigour and not an exclusive reliance on data. But are you also suggesting actually, that you need to be a contrarian?

Andrew: All my models have a central value tenor in them. Even if it's quality or momentum or deep value, you do not want to buy anything which is expensive. To get a thing to look cheap you've got to have the majority not liking it. So by that definition, yes, you have to be contrarian. I mean, you need to be able to say,

'Hey look, France Telecom's yielding 9%, and then be hit with a torrent of abuse saying that's because it's got problems X,Y and Z.' That just reassures me – I'm getting it cheap.

Interviewer: OK, so we've run into the first of the risk factors or anomalies that even the efficient markets academics accept, namely cheap stocks, or value investing – we'll discuss that a little later. But there are other risk factors, aren't there? Momentum which we'll talk about later as well as small cap companies out performing large caps?

Andrew: I don't agree that there is a small cap phenomenon. I don't necessarily agree that momentum exists. They exist in the historical data. So again it's the efficient market guys doing some kind of physical, science activity to analyse what is a human and economic system. It's not physics – it's full of human participants!

Interviewer: OK – so it's clear that you think that the sensible use of strategies can make money. Let's start with one of your favourite ideas, quality stocks.

Andrew: I think this is where a lot of the institutions are now based. They say well actually we're in the equity investment game seeking out high-quality companies, which are trading at a good price. So that for me fits very nicely with this concept of quality and income, or even quality and value. That last one [quality and value] is an area that a lot of the quant people have difficulty with. Because when you read academic papers, they easily identify value, they easily identify things like momentum. But there aren't papers which recognise that there is a long-term alpha [superior return] from being over-weight quality stocks.

Interviewer: Isn't there a problem here though – a great many investors are trying to track down these high quality companies but the risk is that they all end up over-paying for them? Don't all those growth at a reasonable price stocks end up becoming highly priced, quality stocks?

Andrew: I think there is confusion between growth and quality. The trouble with growth at a reasonable price is that we have no idea what the future growth is going to be, and we have no idea if the historical growth is at all relevant. I mean some of the assets with the strongest and most stable growth profiles, up until 2007, were the banks. They'd been growing dividends at double-digit rates – they'd also been growing their earnings at double-digit rates. So sitting in the middle of 2007 how do you recognise that a bank is going to go ex growth [growth slows or stops] or not? Growth at a reasonable price depends heavily on what your estimates of growth are. The classic stock for that in the 1990s was Mr 20% Rentokil. Historically it had grown its earnings at 20% pa, it traded on a PE of 20 and everyone forecast it to grow at 20%. And you got people using things like the PEG ratio and saying, 'Hey look, it's trading at a PE of 20, PEG ratio of 1.'

But the trouble is that it went ex-growth and the share price collapsed. No-one forecast it and it pretty much happened in a very short period of time.

What you're trying to do with quality is that you're trying to recognise attributes of the business, which means that over time it will not need to come back to you and ask for more money. Will its balance sheet be strong, so therefore it's capable of paying out a sustained dividend? Is it operationally efficient, so therefore it can take advantage of new growth opportunities if they were to come along?

That's why we like the Piotroski screen – [this strategy] is based on the idea that you are trying to identify companies which are profitable, operationally efficient and self-financing. Once you have that in groups of stocks – you price it. So then you bring in your valuation metrics. And because you've identified a quality asset, it brings fundamental risk control into your portfolio, which for me is far more meaningful.

Quality is for me about being cheap. But it really depends (1) on how you measure your quality and (2) how you value it. For example, higher quality stocks, typically have a better dividend yield than lower quality stocks, because as we've seen over the last 12 months [summer 2008 to summer 2009], the lower quality companies can't sustain that dividend stream. Now if you're a long-term investor, and believe, as I do, that yield is a big generator of your returns from equities, then finding assets that have a good yield and can sustain that yield over the medium and long term, will deliver good returns.

Interviewer: So what you're talking about really is classic equity income investing isn't it, as practised by fund managers like Neil Woodford at Invesco Perpetual?

Andrew: Yes, I think so. And I think people get confused between strategies that focus on the dividend yield and what I call income investing. Income investing is about recognising companies which are at a stage in their life cycle where they're starting to kick off some fairly sustainable cashflows and are of sufficient quality that actually they could also exploit other opportunities as they come along.

Interviewer: So your idea of a quality is simple then, in summary?

Andrew: You're looking maybe for a dominant sector position. You're looking for a strong balance sheet: which one can defend its growth franchise and has money to develop new growth franchises, if additional threats come along? So Google is a case in point.

Interviewer: What about big, quality companies that also pay a steady, well backed dividend – maybe even one that keeps growing year on year?

Andrew: Yes, certainly. I think that's a good long-term investment philosophy anyway. Certainly, you'll miss out on the huge upswings you've seen in the last three to four months. But you would have lost far less money during 2008, anyway. So you have more money in the game to enjoy the upswing, anyway.

Interviewer: If you are going to adopt a progressive dividend policy maybe you should just focus on certain sectors like utilities and big drug companies?

Andrew: Yes – some are good, some are bad. Some have nice strong monopolistic type cashflows. They have good progressive dividend policies and they're doing OK. I've never been a fan of sector investment though. I've always preferred to look at factors to define where my investments should go. Remember that none of us can name a famous sector investor. We know there are good [individual] stock investors, we know there are good macro investors, but I have never come across anybody who has made a fortune doing sector investment.

Interviewer: Moving on... this overall focus on quality brings us to another dangerous trap doesn't it – earnings? A lot of these companies' reputations are being built on constantly increasing earnings. But let's be honest here. Management loves to manipulate earnings, especially around the peak earnings reporting season, don't they? They love to generate a surprise? They also love to manipulate the process leading up to that quarterly announcement, don't they?

Andrew: I think companies are logical in what they do in a sense – if you come to the market using quarterly reporting, and report a miss, the share price reaction is drastic. So therefore, even if you know that your next quarterly target is unachievable, what you need to do is bring the number down before you report. So you just drip the detail into the market to get the number down [if analysts' expectations are too high]. And then once you've got that number low enough, then you proceed to beat it. Yes, it's ridiculously time consuming I imagine, and totally pointless really. But the way the market reacts to profit warnings, which is net bad, you can see the logic in them doing it.

Interviewer: So – in this interview you've made it very clear that you like quality companies and even progressive dividend stars. You've also mentioned that you make extensive use of the Piotroski screen, don't you?

Andrew: The idea is simple. It's relatively easy to build, doesn't require a vast quantity of mathematics, so it's accessible. It's just a tick sheet, so you know, if you pass all tests you get nine, and if you don't pass any you get zero. You could also check the measures relatively easily, so you could go to the report and accounts. It's also one of the more obvious ways to recognise quality, which has been proven. But it doesn't work in Japan though! I think that's come about from having a lacklustre economy for 20 years where you're just so used to disappointment that you're not willing to participate in any story which is not dirt cheap.

Interviewer: So let's just leave this notion of quality behind now. Let's move on back to value. The great modes and strategies in value investing have usually been built around Ben Graham's work... but the problem surely is that it's very difficult to find these really cheap, deep value socks on modern, expensive markets.

Andrew: To be a deep value stock, you typically have to have a share price fall that falls a lot and if you're a multi-billion fund, you can't get enough of those kind of shares. Warren Buffett came across the same problem – he originally started doing deep value Ben Graham type processes, but he started hitting against capacity problems, because of his size and his reputation.

Interviewer: Warren Buffett doesn't buy these Graham Net Net deep value stocks anymore does he? He looks for quality companies now, doesn't he?

Andrew: Yes certainly. I think, I mean I would still want to have exposure to deep value assets. Over the long term you're never going to shoot the lights out with the value approach and you will suffer under-performance assets which have become extremely cheap. And, therefore, I would have say 80% of my assets in a value quality type approach and maybe 20% of my assets monitoring deep value type screens, to see who pops up.

Interviewer: Are there any other deep value screens that you think have some validity and power?

Andrew: Well I mean, when you look at combinations of say value metrics, you tend to find combinations of simple things like share price to the cash and share to book value. Price sales and price cash – work.

Interviewer: What about those fund managers that focus on a business's free cashflow?

Andrew: These strategies have worked extremely well in Japan over the past 20 years, just avoiding people who are boosting artificially, earnings, and look for those who are generating better cashflow.

Interviewer: But could you, construct just a pure free cashflow model? Could you just go in the market and just go, 'that's it – my core measure is freecash flow and I'm going to build everything back from there?'

Andrew: No – the problem is that the ideal time to buy, say, some of the deeper value stocks, is when cashflow has collapsed! Often companies will have negative free cashflow and that's why you need another measure like book or sales. Deep value approach is all about trying to recognise assets which may not be operationally efficient at the moment, but which are mis-priced.

Interviewer: And what about focusing exclusively just on dividends?

Andrew: I think it becomes a huge regional problem. I mean take, for example, Japan where the absolute level of dividend yield is just shocking. So you're immediately limiting the number of companies that you could purchase, and the one's that you can purchase aren't particularly good quality anyway. Then you've got the US market, where dividend yield is very much treated just as a defensive play, and there is no evidence that dividend yield as a factor delivers much out performance.

Interviewer: What about price of sales?

Andrew: I'm cynical on price of sales. The classic quote is that you could sell dollars at 90 cents. Your sales would be through the roof, hopefully. But you won't make any money. I think it's more useful in the deep value area, because the deep value investor is looking for businesses which are operationally inefficient, where maybe their margins are depressed versus their peers. Where you can come in, try to buy a fairly large stake in it, and then maybe petition for change. So price to sales as a measure for deep value is good. In the more quantitative, systematic models, you need to combine it with other elements on its own. That said a price to book or a price to sales type strategy, in Japan, has been very successful.

Interviewer: Just before we finish with value measure in general – one last detailed question. Do you operate a market cap cut off to avoid really tiny companies? Do you say, no stocks under say £10m in market cap?

Andrew: Not really – ironically one of the biggest uses of Piotroski screen is in the mid-cap to small cap area. I know various fund managers who use it extensively in the US mid-caps space. One of the difficulties if you're a small cap or a mid-cap company is access to funding. You either get to be a small cap company by your business being destroyed, or you're a potentially big company which is going to grow. Now if you're not profitable, not self-financing and not operationally efficient, the chances are, you are a big company who's become small. But if you're a small or mid-cap stock, who ticks all the boxes in terms of Piotroski quality, then these are areas where you can find good returns.

Interviewer: So far in this interview we've focused on value and quality-based strategies. There's one set of strategies we haven't mentioned at all yet – strategies built around finding great growth stocks.

Andrew: I always ask investors to name me five growth stocks in Europe. You can list a whole raft of them in the US – like Google or eBay. But name me five mega cap growth stocks, or even large cap growth stocks in Europe.

Interviewer: I'm sure I could name loads!

Andrew: Good because if you know more than one, can you tell me.

Interviewer: But these growth-based strategies are hugely popular in the US aren't they and they seem to work?

Andrew: I think it's all trading orientated – not an investor orientated strategy. Most of the growth investors I've met in the US tend to have a quite short-term trading focus, they're focused on the near term data. Also earnings momentum-based strategies don't work in the US and that's because, as we mentioned earlier, there's such manipulation of the market [through earnings]. But saying that, you do get good reaction to positive earnings surprises so perhaps it's worth creating some kind of earning surprise model, but a lot of the models I've seen are not hugely successful. Price momentum strategies work in the US but they're far less strong in fragmented markets like Europe. You could argue that's because they've been [data] mined out [by quantitative strategists].

Interviewer: Talk to a lot of academics and they suggest that a pure momentum strategy does, in fact, work.

Andrew: It has worked very well in places like the US, and Europe and the UK. I haven't made up my mind at the moment – is it just a function of what's happened before us? And if you think about it, buying a stock which has been one of the best performers for the last six months, means at some point you're going to get caught out, because it must be getting more expensive? And there's lots of evidence from places like Japan, where momentum strategies have not worked.

Interviewer: Does it work in the UK?

Andrew: It does work in the UK, it's been very strong in the UK [but] it's very difficult to execute, so a lot of the momentum is driven by the smaller and the mid-caps part of the market. When you look at the mega caps in the UK you don't see it so much....

Interviewer: So what you're saying is that if you did operate a momentum strategy, but only focused on the most liquid large cap, mega cap stocks, it would be as strong?

Andrew: Yes, exactly.

Interviewer: What about GARP investing, as a middle course between growth and value – what about growth at a reasonable price as a strategy? Doesn't that mean using measures such as the PEG factor?

Andrew: With growth at a reasonable price I worry about the assumptions – particularly the word reasonable, as well as its over dependence on forecasting and on historical growth patterns. Rentokil, was a classic! Certainly I think ridiculous measures like the PEG ratio are dangerous in the extreme, because if you've got a forecast of growth which is solid, but the market decides that is unreasonable, then the PE's going to go lower, and all it's saying is, we don't believe the growth... if you're using a PEG ratio you're doubling up on risk.

Interviewer: Jim Slater uses PEGs doesn't he? You'd say that was a bankrupt strategy?

Andrew: It could kill you! I mean it's one of those things which just falls out of bed extremely quickly. In the UK market, I mean I used to monitor it fairly regularly, but just gave up.

Interviewer: On a concluding thought, there is a key theme emerging from this conversation – it's that investors shouldn't stick religiously to one strategy or screen. Combine screens, combine quality with value or core, quality and growth! Look at the data and experiment!

Andrew: Yes – it's diversification. The idea that only one thing works at any one point in time, or there's only one way to invest, or one way to make money, seems ridiculous. Various types of things might work – maybe a core, value quality strategy, plus maybe a deep value satellite strategy. Also a focused short portfolio. Maybe you do want exposure to momentum because you might see an emerging trend and that could be just a risk control.

Appendices

Valuing markets – Market timing systems

Introduction

Many strategy-based stock pickers maintain that investors need to carefully time their entry and exit points, not necessarily on a day-to-day basis but on a more strategic basis using simple ideas about the relative aggregate value of a market such as the FTSE 100. Some systems such as Share Maestro explicitly incorporate this 'strategic market timing' into their stock selection while other analysts such as James Montier at GMO maintain that investors need to keep a wary eye on key measures we'll encounter in this chapter, such as the cyclically adjusted price to earnings ratio of something like the S&P 500. These behaviourally influenced value investors maintain that if the market overall looks expensive, investors would be well served to cut back on stock selection and wait for the euphoria of market bubbles to fade away after the inevitable market collapse. This appendix focuses on a number of key, widely used aggregate market timing measures – it's based on an *Investors Chronicle* article from May 2009[1] when markets were just beginning to recover from record lows.

---

[1] Stevenson, D. (2009) 'The right time to buy: dynamic measures', *Investors Chronicle*, 8 May.

Markets are volatile

This constant flux of optimism (and despair) is a distinguishing feature of markets and in any secular bear market investors should prepare themselves for violent mood swings based on the prevailing market psychology, although there'll always be a bias towards growth. Many analysts choose to adopt a more rigorous approach to judging whether markets are worth buying or not, with most basing their judgement on 'fundamental' measures as a way of establishing aggregate fair value, although a small minority also supplement this with technical analysis of market pricing.

In essence this approach asks investors to look on the stock market as a whole, in aggregate terms, and then ask whether the market is cheap or not. What constitutes 'cheap' is, as you'd expect, subject of much debate but a small number of key measures or metrics tend to crop up frequently. Most of these measures are simple snapshot tools, i.e. they take a snapshot of relative value in time and fail to account for the flux of modern economies and their effect on profits and dividends growth. Some analysts eschew these snapshot measures and prefer to focus on more dynamic, trending measures focusing in particular on PE growth.

Regardless of which measure you use – a snapshot measure or a more dynamic approach – the reason for using a valuation-based approach is that it's a strong indicator of future returns, i.e. if markets are relatively cheap they tend to produce better long-term returns afterwards. The evidence for this has come from study after study. Table A1.1 for instance is from economist Andrew Smithers. His analysis suggests that those periods displaying the biggest under pricing – relative cheapness – produced the highest long-term returns.

table A1.1 Past examples of world market under pricing

	Per cent p.a.	Percentage under-priced
Average return for all years	5.44	
Average 1 to 30 years from 1920	12.07	−54
Average 1 to 30 years from 1932	11.35	−58
Average 1 to 30 years from 1948	14.22	−71
Average 1 to 30 years from 1957	10.22	−50.99

Source: Andrew Smithers.

Smithers' analysis is backed up by another study by Ed Easterling from Crestmont Research who's looked at returns from the S&P 500 US market over the period 1919 to 2008. He breaks stockmarket returns down into 90 different 20-year periods and then looks at the average PE ratio (we'll look at this measure below) at the start of the 20-year period. His conclusion? The biggest annualised returns over different 20-year periods came when the PE ratio was at its lowest. Easterling then breaks the returns down into deciles (10% groups) and his research demonstrates that when the PE ratio started a 20-year period at 10 the average net total returns were between 12% and 15% p.a. – see Table A1.2.

table A1.2   20-year periods ending 1919 to 2008 (90 periods)

Decile	Net total returns		S&P 500 decile	Average beginning PE	Average end PE
	From	To	(average)		
1	1.2%	4.5%	3.2%	19	9
2	4.5%	5.2%	4.9%	18	9
⋮					
9	11.5%	11.9%	11.7%	12	22
10	12.1%	15%	13.4%	10	29

Source: Crestmont Research, www.crestmontresearch.com

There's one crucial caveat to add to this approach of valuing markets – although nearly all major academic studies suggest that lower valuations tend to lead to higher long-term valuations, this is a long way from indicating a short-term buy signal. As Andrew Smithers, an independent economist from Smithers and Co admits, 'value' is a fairly poor short-term indicator but nevertheless an excellent long-term indicator. If you're looking for short-term indicators, many economists concede that technical analysis is a better place to start with most suggesting short-term price momentum as the best indicator. Nevertheless understanding the 'value' in markets is still vital for investors if only because, as Smithers says: '(i) It provides a sound way of assessing the probable returns over the medium-term; (ii) it provides information about the current risks of stockmarket investment; and (iii) it enables investors to avoid nonsense claims about value!'[2]

---

[2] Quoted in an interview with the author.

US markets lead the way

Whether we like it or not, the best market for judging the relative value of global stockmarkets is the US – only with indices such as the S&P 500 and Dow Jones Industrial Average do we have long enough statistical series to make any meaningful analysis. Economist Andrew Smithers bases most of his analysis of the affordability of developed markets on the US markets and for measures like CAPE (cyclically adjusted price earnings ratio) he only uses the US market: 'Frankly the data's not there for other markets – for Europe for instance the only data sets available are from the 1980s onwards which isn't enough.'

This scepticism is based on fairly solid reasoning – 20- or even 30-year data sets aren't very statistically significant. Many critics of the Fed Model, featured later in this appendix, suggest that its great weakness is that it's only really partially true for the period since 1980. US investor John Hussman makes this criticism of the model and notes that there's strong evidence that even during the successful years for the model (successful as defined by its predictive power), it was only plausible because earnings (profits) had been routinely over-estimated. This focus on the US markets shouldn't trouble British investors greatly though – statistical correlation between the US and UK markets is actually fairly high, i.e. the UK markets tend to move broadly in line with the US markets. Figure A1.1 shows the price data for the S&P 500 and the FTSE 100 with the lower section of the graph showing correlation. For much of the time the correlation between the two indices is between 0.4 and 0.8, and in times of market distress that correlation can increase to over 0.70 – indicating very high levels of correlation.

This statistical relationship also makes common sense – the US market is by far the biggest market in the world and it will come as no surprise that major movements in the US market are likely to have a major influence on the rest of the world.

But investors need to understand that although this relationship is generally true it's *not always* true – many analysts suggest that the UK and European markets are currently very cheap compared to the US market which is only regarded as fair value based on some measures. Japan by contrast is regarded as inordinately cheap on most valuation metrics but therein lays the problem – Japan has been regarded as cheap for years and yet the local stockmarkets have continued to grind lower. Just because shares are cheap doesn't necessarily mean that shares will move up in price in the short term, although by and large mean reversion is reliable, i.e. prices do tend to revert to average levels over the very long term. Also even if you accept that Japan is a great buy now, it may amount to nothing unless the US markets recover their poise, i.e. the direction of the next

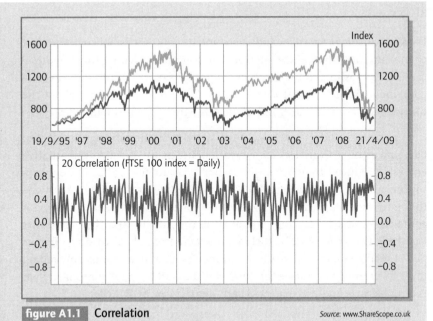

figure A1.1   Correlation   *Source*: www.ShareScope.co.uk

global market move may be determined by the US markets regardless of other markets' relative valuation. The correlation between major markets is shown in Table A1.3.

table A1.3   Correlation between major markets (2000–2010)

	France	Germany	Japan	UK	US
France	1.00	0.94	0.61	0.89	0.85
Germany	0.94	1.00	0.55	0.84	0.84
Japan	0.61	0.55	1.00	0.61	0.61
UK	0.89	0.84	0.61	1.00	0.86
US	0.85	0.84	0.61	0.86	1.00

Source: Smithers and Co.

Earnings

Look in the *Financial Times* and you can fairly quickly establish a snapshot of the current 'value' of the market, but don't be fooled by these figures – these are snapshots in time and they refer to actual earnings and the data contained within it is historical. They tell you next to nothing about the likely direction of earnings and dividends which are both falling fast.

If you want to understand why these stated, current earnings are viewed by some as next to useless it's worth looking at the detailed quantitative analysis produced by most of the major investment banks. Andrew Lapthorne and his weekly *Global Equity Market Arithmetic* is a bible for anyone trying to understand if the markets truly represent 'good value'. Table A1.4 contains summary data from SG's analysis for March 2009. The data shows that back then the world's stockmarkets were not valued in single figures (for PE) but at a rather high 13.9× current estimates of earnings only falling to 11.2× earnings estimates for 2010. But that fall in the PE ratio next year is only because analysts expected earnings to grow by 24.6%.

table A1.4 SG data on current global markets (2009): all figures in percentages

	World			Europe		
	2008	2009e	2010e	2008	2009e	2010e
PE current	12.3	13.9	11.2	9.8	11.0	9.4
Regional earnings growth	−27.0	−11.5	24.6	−29.0	−11.5	17.7

	2009 estimate			2010 estimate		
	PE	EPS growth	Div. yield	PE	EPS growth	Div. yield
US	14.7	−11	2.6	11.8	24.7	2.7
Japan	39.6	−5.2	2	18.8	not meaningful	2.1
UK	10.6	−29.7	5	9.3	14.5	5.3
France	10.9	−15.1	4.8	9.2	18.7	5.2
Germany	12.1	11.3	4.1	9.5	26.8	4.5

The sad reality, according to many analysts and quants, is that no-one in March 2009 has any idea of what the earnings bit of the PE ratio for 2009 will really be. Table A1.5 spells out this confusion in horrific detail – it's from US commentator John Mauldin and it looks at the combined estimates for the EPS produced by the 500 companies in the S&P 500. This is usually expressed as a single bundle of dollar profits. At the beginning of 2007 for instance analysts estimated that the S&P 500 would produce $92 worth of earnings yet by April 2009 the figure was down to a frankly jaw dropping $14.

table A1.5 Falling earnings estimates for the S&P 500 in 2008 and 2009

Date	Earnings ($)
For 2008	
March 2007	92
December 2007	84
February 2008	71
June 2008	68
July 2008	72
September 2008	60
October 2008	54
February 2009	26
10 April 2009	14.88
For 2009	
March 2008	81
April 2008	72
June 2008	70
August 2008	64
September 2008	58
October 2008	48
February 2009	42
End of February 2009	32
10 April 2009	28

Source: Maudlin's www.frontlinethoughts.com

Many analysts have completely given up using the current PE ratio – they prefer to use an alternative measure for the PE called the cyclically adjusted price/earnings ratio (or CAPE). You might also see it termed the Graham and Dodd cyclically adjusted earnings measure after the investor Ben Graham who first developed the tool. In recent years a variant on the same approach has been publicised by Yale economist Robert Shiller. His version of CAPE compares the current share price with average earnings during the past decade, rather than to the most recent year's earnings – see Figure A1.2. The idea behind this alternative look at the all important PE ratio is to even out the ups and downs in the ratio over a long-term (ten-year) profit cycle. Because profit margins are mean-reverting, in boom times, companies will probably boast high margins and big earnings. In busts, profit margins collapse and companies have small earnings. According to one enthusiast of this approach: 'Taking a single-year PE ratio can therefore provide a misleading picture of value: in booms, with high profit margins, stocks look cheaper than they really are. In busts, with low margins, stocks look more expensive than they are.'[3]

The graph from SG (Figure A1.3) shows the Dodd and Graham version of CAPE for the US, the UK and continental Europe since the 1980s. Most

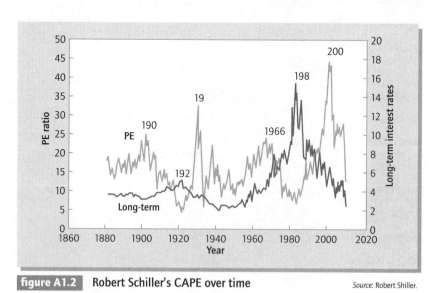

figure A1.2   **Robert Schiller's CAPE over time**   *Source:* Robert Shiller.

---

[3] Posted on http://finance.yahoo.com/tech-ticker/article/190252/

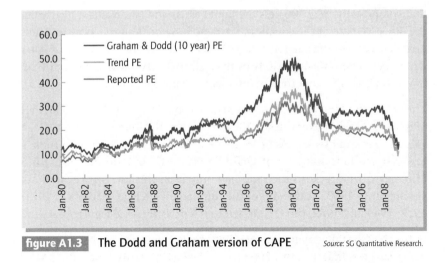

analysts would expect any CAPE of less than 12 to be cheap, between 12 and 18 to be fair value and anything over 20 to be expensive.

The big question though is whether or not this measure has any predictive power. According to the FT's investment editor John Authors, the CAPE measure has proved to be a great market timing tool as 'highs and lows for this metric have overlapped almost perfectly with highs and lows for the market'.

The Q ratio

This is also known as Tobin's Q ratio and is extensively used by analysts including Andrew Smithers from Smithers and Co in London. The ratio was originally devised by Yale economist James Tobin and suggests that the combined market value of all the companies on a stockmarket should roughly equal their replacement cost or asset replacement value:

Q ratio = Total market value of a firm/total asset value

If the stockmarket produces a value of less than 1, according to this measure, the cost to replace firms' assets is greater than the market ascribes to the value of its shares, which suggests that the company/market is undervalued, i.e. it's cheaper to buy the assets than to start the business from the beginning. Calculating the numerator (the first value) for the Q ratio is relatively straightforward, as it equals the market value of the equity and debt of the companies that comprise the S&P 500, less net liquid assets and land value. Calculating the other element of the equation, the denominator, is a little more difficult. That data comes from a report called *Flow of Funds Accounts of the United States Z1*,[4] which is published quarterly by the Federal Reserve, with data from 1952 onwards although other sources offer data as far back as 1900.

The Q ratio for US equities has moved between 0.29 (1921, 1932, 1949, and 1982) and 3 (1999) over the last 130 years – over the long term, the average value of q is around 0.63. As of 15 March 2009 it's 0.43 according to Tobin's research assistant and current guardian of the US Q ratio measure, John Mihaljevic, who reckons the ratio had only been this low on six other occasions since 1900. At the end of the four largest US bear markets in 1921, 1932, 1949 and 1982, the Q ratio fell to 0.3 or lower – see Figure A1.4.

But is the Q ratio actually any good at predicting future returns? The evidence suggests that it is. In a 2003 paper[5] Duke University Researchers Matthew Harney and Edward Tower looked at all the value-based ways of mea-

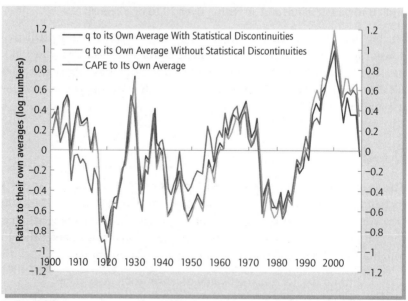

figure A1.4   US stockmarket values at end 2008 according to q and CAPE

Source: Smithers and Co.

---

[4] www.federalreserve.gov/releases/zl/

[5] Harney, M. and Tower, T. (2003) 'Rational Pessimism: Predicting Equity Returns Using Tobin's q and Price/Earnings Ratios', *Journal of Investing*.

suring the market. In particular they tested the Q ratio against the CAPE measure – and virtually in every time frame the Q ratio proved successful with the use of a 30-year CAPE coming in second in terms of predictive power. Mihaljevic himself has looked at which measure works. He found that the best strategy was to buy when the Q ratio was below 0.40 and sell when it was above 1.00. Over the past several decades, this strategy would have produced a compounded annual rate of return of several percentage points higher than the S&P 500 index.

But there are some big caveats that are worth bearing in mind when using the Q ratio. The first is that the measure may be beginning to lose its predictive value because of profound changes in the US economy as more and more business moves to the service-based knowledge economy – the Q ratio does not consider the replacement cost of intangible assets. Also like many of the measures used discussed here Mihaljevic doesn't think the Q ratio should be used as a short-term market timing tool. He's particularly insistent that investors look at the trend in the Q ratio, not just at its current level. On this score he's said that he's 'confident' that Q will actually reach extreme levels of closer to 0.3! One last note – the Q ratio is only ever used by most analysts to describe the US markets. According to Andrew Smithers q data for 'countries other than the US is either non-existent, or too short-term, or of poor quality, to be used to value the markets'.[6] Q ratios also can't be used for individual companies.

The Fed model

This is perhaps the most controversial way of judging how cheap the markets really are: it compares the stockmarket's forward earnings yield (EP) to the yield on long-term government bonds. Its logic is that stocks should yield (in dividends) less and cost more when bond yields are low, as stocks and bonds are competing assets.

The earnings yield is simply the inverse of the forward PE ratio – it measures the aggregate forward PE ratio of the market, currently about 14 for the US markets – and then turns this into a percentage. So for each $1 of the aggregate value of the US markets, 7cents of earnings are currently being declared, which equates to an earnings yield of 7%. The yield on long-term Treasury Bills (20 years or more) was, at March 2009, around 4.75%, which

---

[6] www.smithers.co.uk/faqs.php

suggests a positive gap of just over 2% – a very positive sign. The problem is that very few strategists bother with this model anymore – they believe it's a fatally flawed model as a predictor of what might happen in the future. One of the most powerful rebuttals of the Fed model came in a paper called 'Fight the Fed Model: The Relationship Between Stock Market Yields, Bond Market Yields, and Future Returns' by Clifford S. Asness of AQR Capital Management. Asness points out the key conceptual flaw – the 'reasoning compares a real number to a nominal number (earnings), ignoring the fact that over the long-term, companies' nominal earnings should, and generally do, move in tandem with inflation. The crucible for testing a valuation indicator is how well it forecasts long-term returns, and the Fed Model fails this test – long-term expected real stock returns are low when starting PEs are high and vice versa, regardless of starting nominal interest rates'.[7]

Legendary US investor John P. Hussman has also attacked the theory:

There is, in fact, no stable relationship between earnings yields and interest rates. The relationship is actually negative in data since 1929, is marginally positive (but statistically insignificant) in data since 1950, and is only strongly positive in data from 1980 through 2000 as a statistical artifact of the disinflationary period from 1980 to 2000.[8]

Andrew Smithers is equally not impressed by the Fed model:

We've showed that the observed positive correlation between dividend and earnings yields on shares and the yield on bonds applied only in the US from 1977 to 1997. It has not applied since. Furthermore, there was a marginally stronger negative correlation from 1948 to 1968 and no long-term relationship whatever. The bond yield myth is thus an egregious example of data mining.[9]

Bearish commentators like Albert Edwards at SG and economist Roger Nightingale suggests a rather different way of looking at this relationship – we should expect the earnings yield and dividends to remain well above the bond yield. Edwards points to data from the bear market in Japan that shows that both the earnings yield and the dividend yield has remained consistently above bond yields for nearly 20 years while Nightingale reminds us that in the 1930s investors 'bought bonds for their capital gains

---

[7] Asness, C.S. (2002) 'Fight the Fed Model: The Relationship Between Stock Market Yields, Bond Market Yields, and Future Returns', December, http://ssrn.com/abstract=381480.

[8] 'How Much Do Interest Rates Affect the Fair Value of Stocks?' www.hussmanfunds.com/wmc070521.htm, 21 May 2007.

[9] www.smithers.co.uk/faqs.php.

(i.e. they increased in value, pushing the yield ever lower) and stocks for their yield (as valuations dropped, the earnings yield increased alongside the dividend yield)'.[10]

Dynamic measures – profits growth or decline

Not all measures used by economists and strategists rely on static snapshots in time – some use more dynamic measures centred on the direction of key measures such as profits growth (or decline). Andrew Lapthorne at SG tracks actual earnings momentum alongside the change in estimates for future growth provided by market analysts, i.e. the forecasts.

Back in the spring of 2009 the future looked bleak using these measures. To give just one example, earnings for the S&P 500 have dropped, in aggregate terms, for six straight quarters through to December 2008 with the stretch of declines the longest since the Great Depression. Figure A1.5 tells you everything you need to know about analysts' estimates. It looks at reported earnings growth forecasts (just the forecasts!) and shows analysts are slashing their estimates of future earnings at a truly alarming rate!

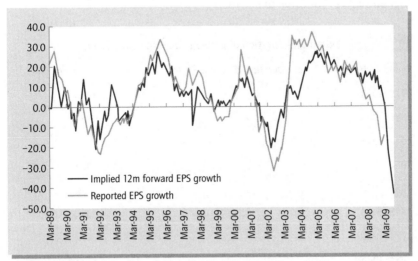

figure A1.5   **Global reported earnings growth forecasts to hit −40% within the next six months**   *Source:* I/B, E/S and MSCI. Andrew Lapthorne, SG, Spring 2009.

---

[10] Roger Nightingale in interview with the author.

According to Lapthorne, analysts are in panic. Table A1.6 shows earnings revisions in the first three months of 2009 with over 7% taken off total global earnings estimates in the four weeks of March alone!

table A1.6 Monthly earnings revision by region

	Europe (exc. UK)		UK		US		Japan	
Market	−7.9	−6.5	−11.6	−10.6	−4.1	−4.6	−23.1	−9.5
Market exc. oils	−7.7	−6.4	−11.5	−11	−3.2	−3.8	−23.3	−9.9
Market exc. financials	−6.9	−5.2	−5.1	−5.4	−4.7	−4.4	−26.1	−11.1
Market oil and financials	−6.4	−4.9	−3.1	−4.3	−3.8	−3.4	−26.4	−11.7

Source: www.sgcib.com

Andrew Smithers also looks at the dynamic trend in earnings growth – and operating margins. His core view is that profits growth can only ever be a function of economic growth and that as the global economy keeps on falling, profits will continue to decline.

table A1.7 Extent and duration of previous margin contractions

Period of decline	Duration of decline – years	Extent of decline (%)
1929–1933	4	−34.02
1936–1938	2	−8.62
1942–1946	4	−23.39
1950–1953	3	−11.18
1955–1958	3	−8.87
1965–1970	5	−16.10
1977–1980	3	−6.84
1984–1986	2	−4.86
1988–1992	4	−4.19
1997–2001	4	−10.14
2006–2008	4	−3.6

Source: Smithers and Co.

Table A1.7 is especially compelling. It suggests that when a recession or depression strikes, operating margins and thus profits tumble heavily. In the table Smithers looked at previous economic downturns and then examined what happened with operating margins.

Fund flows

One dynamic indicator favoured by many economists is to look at fund flows, i.e. who's actually buying shares and the flow of purchases – see Figure A1.6. According to Andrew Smithers if corporations themselves are buying shares (much of the time their own shares) then that is usually associated with positive future returns.

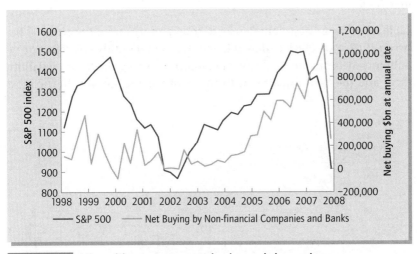

figure A1.6 US equities: net corporate buying and share prices

Volatility

The concept of volatility doesn't quite fit into any normal discussion of relative value or cheapness – volatility isn't concerned with trying to establish whether something has fair value. Most analyses of volatility are only concerned with a relative rate at which a share or bond moves up or down in price compared with a key measure for volatility such as an index like the VIX from the Chicago Board Options Exchange. The VIX index actually measures the market's estimate of future volatility, based on something called the weighted average of implied vols over a wide range of strike dates and, in general, bear market falls are associated very high VIX readings. Figure A1.7 shows that even at the low levels experienced in spring 2009, VIX levels were still close to all time highs.

This long series data though needs to be treated with some caution: many technical analysts think that using a snapshot of the VIX is a dangerous exercise. As with the PE ratio it's a dynamically changing index and some maintain that the best way of using VIX as an indicator is to compare its current level (36.09 in March 2009) with its simple ten-day moving average.

Many fundamentals-based analysts accept that volatility is a useful measure although few use it as a leading indicator. Nearly every leading analyst and economist accepts the basic idea that high volatility usually involves massive losses.

Table A1.8, from Crestmont Research, shows returns from the S&P 500 between 1962 and 2008 based on different levels of monthly volatility. We've only included the quartile with the months boasting the lowest volatility (first) and the fourth quartile with the most volatile months. In the most

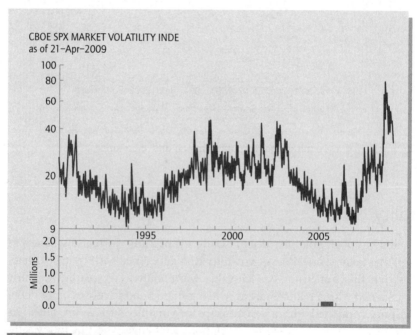

figure A1.7 VIX levels

Source: http://finance.yahoo.com

volatile quartile, 57% of the months showed losses with the average loss of 4.7% during that month. The first quartile, by contrast, was more likely to produce a gain (68% of months) with the average gain of 2.8% – all with the lowest relative volatility.

table A1.8 Returns from the S&P 500 between 1962 and 2008 based on different levels of monthly volatility

Quartile	Volatility range (%)	% chance up month	% chance down month	If up month average gain	If down month average loss	Expected gain or loss
First	0% to 1%	68%	32%	2.8%	−1.9%	1.3%
Fourth	1% to 6.6%	43%	57%	5%	−4.9%	−0.7%

Source: Crestmont Research, www.crestmontresearch.com

Andrew Smithers has taken this analysis one step further and tried to see if heightened volatility is a lead indicator of future returns. 'It is widely recognised that volatility is persistent' declares Smithers from a paper entitled 'Market Volatility' in 2002, echoing the view of most economists that high volatility levels tend to last over distinct periods of time. 'High volatility', Smithers concludes 'is... associated with poor returns...'. But he also concludes that: 'research indicates that current levels of vol tell you next to nothing about future market direction'.[11] Smithers' conclusion – don't bother using vol as a measure to time the markets!

---

[11] www.smithers.co.uk/faqs.php

The tools of the trade

Measures in detail

Earnings

This is fairly easily worked out by dividing the PBT (with or without exceptionals) by the number of shares in issue. You might also notice an additional EPS figure quoted called fully diluted EPS which simply refers to the pre-tax profit per share with all shares and convertibles and warrants included. This slightly different figure is relevant for some companies because they issue lots of non-ordinary shares that could be converted into stock. The diluted figures simply refer to the total numbers of shares in issue if these various classes of stock were redeemed and converted into stock.

EBIT or EBITDA

EBIT stands for earnings before interest and tax while EBITDA stands for earnings before interest, tax, depreciation and amortisation. EBITDA started off as a key measure used by telecoms companies in the 1990s. They were faced by a number of obstacles to financial reporting – notably their huge expenditure on capital equipment, buying licences and other networks through takeovers, all of which conspired to depress reported profits because of the vast interest bill and depreciation allowance. To build their networks they had to spend huge quantities of money – cash – that required depreciation, frequently at a quite rapid rate as technology changed.

Reporting a simple profit figure became next to impossible so they started systematically reporting EBITDA figures with their huge depreciation figures excluded. The amortisation component also matters – amortisation refers to the gradual elimination of say a mortgage or, crucially, the writing off of an intangible asset such as goodwill accumulated after buying another company or network. EBITDA was considered to be a better gauge of the company's performance than net earnings or profit which was obviously heavily weighed down by those large debt payments, depreciation and amortisation.

But EBITDA spread way beyond telecoms during the dotcom boom and scores of technology companies started quoting the figure. Some refined it by quoting the EBIT figure which conveniently excluded hefty interest payments on debt, but the overall effect was the same – earnings looked like they were taking off.

Some perfectly respectable analysts have been using EBITDA in a completely different way – as a way of measuring adjusted cashflow. Because EBITDA strips out so many non-cash items (amortisation, goodwill and depreciation) they found it useful as a way of expressing the cash available to a new owner if they had to pay for the purchase of a business. But EBITDA was in reality largely being abused as a headline grabbing measure of profitability not cashflow and with implosion in the dotcom boom in the past few years its use has steadily receded.

But there's an added complication even with mainstream EBIT numbers – the use of the word 'normalised'. This term matters enormously and it's one that most private investors gloss over with reckless indifference. Normal profits describe the underlying operating business stripped of all exceptionals such as redundancy costs associated with closing a bit of a business, or restructuring costs or, in fact, any one-off item the management chooses not to include in the core operating costs.

tip

Wherever possible try and strip out exceptionals as they make comparison, especially important in screening systems, next to impossible. Try to use the 'normalised' figures wherever possible.

Exceptionals

Managements love exceptionals! In the US there are companies that spend their entire corporate life producing quarter after quarter of exceptionals, defying the very meaning of the word exceptional. It may seem a tad cynical to say this but exceptionals are supposed to be one-off items. Note the word again – one-off.

Many analysts and investors prefer using normalised profits by contrast because they tell us something very important – what economists define as the rate of minimum profit which a firm must earn in order to survive in the market in which it operates. That means normalised earnings tell us if the original business plan – why the firm was set up – is working or not. You'll also see another term widely reported namely the FR3 earnings. These initials stand for a set of regulations imposed by the Financial Reporting Council (part of the Accounting Standards Board (ASB)). This guidance issued in 1993 laid out exactly how companies must treat their exceptionals and other one-off items to arrive at an alternative definition of profits – the FR3 earnings. It's worth quoting these definitions in some detail as the regulation requires all companies to report their earnings in a number of layers, all of which give investors valuable clues about financial performance. They are:

- results of continuing operations (including acquisitions)
- results of discontinued operations
- profits and losses on the sale or termination of an operation, costs of a fundamental reorganisation or restructuring and profits or losses on the disposal of fixed assets, and
- extraordinary items.

To quote the ASB:

The effect of this standard has been to effectively outlaw extraordinary items. If any were to arise, the standard requires them to be included in the earnings figure used to calculate earnings per share. The standard also requires a statement of total recognised gains and losses to be shown. This is a primary financial statement that includes the profit or loss for the period together with all movements in reserves reflecting recognised gains and losses attributable to shareholders.[1]

---

[1] www.frc.org.uk/asb

Which to use – normalised or FR3? Many analysts prefer the normalised figures because they make comparisons much easier. Normal figures are also easier to use when comparing companies with each other. Some businesses might be constantly restructuring and taking on exceptionals which will hit the FR3 bottom line. By contrast FR3 figures have honesty on their side – they properly detail the bottom line to investors. Exceptionals are, after all, real costs, and have to be accounted for. They also impact on the final profits retained by the business which it can use to grow over the future. FR3 is a great way of drawing a big red line at the bottom of the profit and loss account, indicating what profit is left for the shareholders before tax is paid.

tip

Most screening systems tend to use FR3 earnings. If at all possible do use normalised earnings.

The PE ratio

In equation form this ratio is:

Price/earnings or PE ratio = current market share price/earnings per share

This ratio is for many investors the best, quick snapshot of underlying share value. They look down at a PE ratio of say 60 and tut tut, sagely noting that this is a 'bit high', while suggesting that a single figure PE ratio is reasonable value, all things being equal. Put bluntly, a PE ratio much above 20 is regarded pricey in the UK while 15 is closer to the long-term average, and 10 could be said to be reasonable value in most sectors.

The earnings yield

This is simply the PE ratio expressed as a percentage:

$$\text{Earnings yield} = \frac{1}{\text{PE ratio}} \times 100$$

If a company like SSE is trading at 10× earnings – the PE ratio is 10 – then the earnings yield is 10%. If the PE ratio had been closer to 20 that earnings yield would have dropped to 5% – about what you'd get from a savings account. At this point you might start to ask yourself if an earnings yield of

5% is good value. If you can get 5% risk free for holding cash, why take on the extra risk of holding equities? If the company is growing fast that risk might be worth taking, but most companies are actually only managing to push earnings forward by a point or two every year, and the risks of failure or exceptional costs are great.

The PEG factor

The PE ratio we mentioned earlier in this section is a blunt instrument. As we've defined it, it's essentially a static snapshot of value at one point in time. The crucial point is that it expresses historic values and not future expectations. Many analysts, including some screening systems like CompanyREFS, get over this by quoting a different type of PE ratio, namely the future or prospective PE ratio. This is exactly the same as the historic PE ratio except that the EPS figure being used is based on forthcoming or next financial year.

The point is that the PE ratio is not a very dynamic measure and doesn't really tell us very much about the earnings/profits growth. Many investors choose instead to use a related but different measure called PEG or price earnings growth factor:

$$= PE\ ratio/EPS\ growth\ rate$$

Investors who like growth stocks but don't want to overpay for them seek a PEG ratio no higher than 1. Anything much below 1 is good, below 0.5 is great and anything below 0.3 is hugely impressive. In sum – the lower the ratio, the faster the company is expected to grow.

There are some huge caveats at this point. The big caution is that these figures use estimates of future growth – usually based on an average of estimates called a consensus – and that these are hugely speculative. Investors also need to bear in mind that the smaller the number of analysts covering the stock, the greater the chance of a big mistake with these forward looking estimates.

PEGs also tend to work mainly with growth stocks – that is companies steadily growing over the long term. The PEG ratio by contrast tends to break down in the highly volatile world of the cyclical stock (there's not much consistency there) and is not of much use to analyse recovery situations or asset rich companies with poor trading prospects.

As Jim Slater in his guide to using the CompanyREFS database points out in his discussion of the PEG factor:

*it works best with companies which have earnings growth at 15 to 25% per annum
with PE ratios within five points either way of the average. Based on the average
PER of 15 (it's now closer to 180), the best and safest results would be obtained with
growth stocks with PE ratios in the 12 to 20 bracket.*[2]

Dividends

Defining dividends is easy – they're the cheques sent out by companies to
their investors on a yearly or twice-yearly basis (the interim and final payment). When this payout is compared back to the share price we can easily
work out the yield – it's simply the total dividend payout relative to the
share price as a percentage.

Moving beyond these simple measures we soon encounter a key measure
called the dividend cover. This uses the estimated full earnings per share
number divided by the gross dividend per share number. If a company produces an EPS of 50p and pays out 12.5p a share in dividends, its dividend
cover is 4. This is, in historical terms, seen as a very acceptable number as
it means the dividend payout is covered more than 4× by profits. Cover
of much below 2× is seen by most income investors as a little suspicious
and anything below 1 is viewed as highly dangerous as the firm is likely to
struggle to make its dividend payments from current profits.

---

tip

A dividend yield of more than 3% is generous but a dividend yield above 10% is
usually (though not always) unsustainable. A dividend cover of above 2× is generally
regarded as safe.

The PSR or price to sales ratio

This is defined as:

$$PSR = \text{market cap/sales}$$

Investors like Ken Fischer and James O'Shaughnessy think that earnings
can easily be manipulated by cynical managers and so should be treated with some caution. They're also a bit cynical about income investors'
obsession with the dividend as they believe it obscures the fact that

---

[2] Guide to CompanyREFS (only available to service users), www.companyrefs.com

investments in a firm should be seen as a way of buying into a steady cash flow indicated by the sales or turnover figure. Theirs is a hard headed assessment that if all else goes wrong and profits growth falters, potentially jeopardising the dividend payout in the future, a smart, ruthless management can always take an axe to costs, chop out expenses, boost cash flowing into the business and improve shareholder returns. A big boost in cash inflow and potent future earnings should eventually feed through into a better share price after the initial setback.

tip

A PSR below 1 is low, although most retailers and food producers do boast a PSR below 1. A PSR above 10 is expensive for most stocks except technology firms and especially biotech outfits.

Cashflow

By now it'll be obvious that a great many analysts and investors alike share a deep and lasting suspicion of earnings statements. As John Bogle, founder and former CEO of the hugely successful Vanguard fund management group says:

Today we live in a world of managed earnings... like it or not corporate strategy and financial accounting focus on meeting the earnings expectations of the 'The Street' quarter after quarter. The desideratum is steady earnings growth – manage it to at least the 12% level.[3]

Many earnings cynics – Warren Buffett and many value stalwarts included – prefer to increasingly focus on the cashflow statement. Managements don't tend to highlight cashflow figures in their glowing presentations and so they're much less likely to be the subject of manipulation. Also most analysts tend not to set targets based on cashflow per share, so there's no great pressure to meet those targets by playing with the numbers.

Perhaps most importantly cashflow figures give you a clear insight into the lifeblood of an enterprise, hard cash. Earnings figures can all too regularly include plenty of non cash items obscuring true underlying performance. But try and run a business with consistently negative cashflows, i.e. with

---

[3] Quoted in the foreword to Heiserman, H. (2005) *It's Earnings that Count: Finding Stocks with Earnings Power for Long-Term Profits*, McGraw-Hill.

cash constantly leaving the business overall, and you'll soon be knocking on bankruptcy's door.

Net cashflow

Most of the time you'll encounter a specific term called the net cashflow, expressed typically as a ratio called PCF or price to cashflow. This is worked out as follows:

Price to cash flow = market cap/net cashflow

tip

By and large a low ratio is less than 5, while much above 10 is seen as a bit pricey. But as a figure it really shouldn't be used on its own too much. The business could, for instance, be making losses at the operating level because of huge depreciation, and goodwill charges but still be churning out cash. So, be aware of its limitations.

Net cashflow is incredibly useful in a number of key respects. First off it tells us a lot about a business's ability to service its dividend payment. If at the net cash level, it's struggling to cover its dividends and resorting to borrowings to fund the payment, alarm bells should be ringing. This is clearly an unsustainable dividend payment and a sudden cut in the dividend payment caused by a cashflow crisis inevitably leads to a sudden drop in the share price.

Cashflow figures can also indicate some worrying trends at the trading level. A firm might be boasting about increasing earnings yet cash inflows might be decreasing, indicating what accountants call 'over-trading'. That means the firm might be trading beyond its means and its customers are not paying up on time, leading to a worrying increase in debtors – debtors who might default on their payments at some later stage.

Book or net asset value

For a great many investors the P&L statement and the cashflow statement are just too dynamic: there are too many items and too much room for manipulation. For many investors the only true source of knowledge is the balance sheet. This statement contains a summary of all the key assets and liabilities. For many deep value investors this is the best guide to the underlying or intrinsic value of the firm. If all else failed, and the trading business faded away, you'd still have core assets (less liabilities) left to sell and return to investors.

The key measure for deep value investors is the net asset value per share. This is easily obtained (and frequently stated on the balance sheet) by:

- deducting all short- and long-term liabilities from the assets
- what remains is either called the equity of a firm (and shareholders reserve), the net asset value (NAV) or, more traditionally, the book value
- this is then divided by the number of shares in issue to derive the NTAV per share.

Most screening systems you'll use turn this NAV or book value on its head and use something called PBV or price to book value.

PBV = book value (or net asset value)/market capitalisation

Ben Graham, the doyen of deep value investors, generally believed that it was unwise to buy a share much above its book value. He preferred to buy shares which were valued at less than two thirds of the current NAV or book value. In this day and age, most companies trade at well above their book value, in some cases at 20 or 30 times NAV.

PBV has also been steadily undermined as a measure by the definition of what constitutes an asset. As Jim Slater says in his REFS guide 'copyright, patents and brand names… can be worth little or nothing or many times their book value'.[4] Others problems arise when different companies account for the use of such intangibles, as 'some companies revalue them in their balance sheets, [while] others write them off completely'.[5]

Intangibles

These are a notoriously tricky area of accounting – they are necessarily arbitrary and subjective. More than a few PLCs currently trading have asset bases that consist of more than 80% intangibles. Ignore these intangibles completely and technically the firm would be insolvent with no equity.

Some analysts and more than a few screening systems – like Slater's own CompanyREFS system – use an alternative measure called tangible book

---

[4] CompanyREFS guide, www.companyrefs.com/Jimslater/slater.htm
[5] Ibid.

value or PTBV. This is exactly the same as PBV except that it excludes all intangibles, making comparison between firms easy and consistent.

But fixed assets or tangible assets are not without their own problems. As Slater again points out, 'more tangible assets such as plant and machinery... can also have dubious [real] value'.[6] If they had to be sold in an emergency firesale at auction they may be worth a fraction of their stated book value.

tip

A PTBV below 1 is usually regarded by 'value' investors as cheap. Also wherever possible try and use tangible book values, or PTBV, as this makes comparison so much easier. But don't completely ignore companies with a lot of intangible value in brands or intellectual property.

earing

By and large, for most value orientated investors it's probably true to say that cash held in the bank account is regarded as a good thing and debts a potential area for concern. This is not to deny that a well-run business necessarily has loads of cash on its balance sheet nor that all debts are bad. Some companies, and especially utility firms like SSE with regulated charging structures, can easily borrow at low rates and then charge much more for the goods and services produced.

In fact gearing can be very positive if the economy is booming, demand is rising and the company is very efficient in using its asset base.

The net gearing ratio is defined as:

Net gearing = total borrowings less cash/equity (net asset value)

Some analysts use equity less intangibles as a variant in this definition while a negative gearing figure indicates a company that is sitting on no net debts and has excess cash on the balance sheet.

It's also important to realise that not all debts are created equal. Short-term bank overdrafts might have to be repaid very quickly, prompting a liquidity crisis at a company. Also short-term overdrafts tend to have higher

---

[6] Ibid.

interest rates than long-term debts and bonds. A company with net gearing of 100% with all its debts held in long-term bonds is likely to be on a stronger financial footing than a company with say 60% net gearing where all its debts are short-term in the form of an overdraft. As a general rule, net gearing of much more than 50% warrants further investigation. Bear in mind also that a company with lots of debts is much more likely to be vulnerable to sudden changes in interest rates or the wider economy. A sudden downturn could deliver a double whammy – declining cash earnings and rising interest charges.

The quick ratio

This tells us what would happen if the company had to suddenly pay off all its current liabilities. In effect it's an indicator of a company's financial strength (or weakness). It is calculated by taking current assets less inventories, divided by current liabilities, and provides the investor with information regarding the firm's liquidity and ability to meet its obligations.

Current ratio

This measures a company's liquidity, or its ability to pay its short-term debts. It is calculated by dividing current assets by current liabilities. As a general rule a high ratio of more than 2 is a sign of financial strength while a ratio of below 1 is generally seen as a sign of financial weakness.

Interest cover

This is another much used accounting ratio that measures the level of a company's profits relative to its interest charge in the profit and loss account. It is usually defined as profits before interest and tax divided by interest charges, but the precise definition will vary depending on the circumstances. Generally the higher the ratio, the less 'gearing' a company has.

Index